For Charlie, Oliver and Pip

Dark Matter
A thinking fan's guide to Philip Pullman

Tony Watkins

Thinking Fan's Guide series editor: Steve Couch

DAMARIS
www.damarispublishing.com

First edition published in 2004 by
Damaris Publishing
PO Box 200, Southampton, Hampshire, SO17 2DL
www.damarispublishing.com

ISBN 1-904753-03-5

A catalogue record for this book is available from the British Library
Designed and typeset in 11pt Century ITC Book by AD Publishing
Services Limited
Printed and bound in Malta by Gutenberg Press
Cover design by Gerald Rodgers

Contents

Preface

His Dark Materials is one of the most engaging stories
I've ever read – it instantly drew me into its magical
world and I quickly came to love its cast of vividly
drawn characters. I found the gripping plot almost
unrelenting in its demand that I keep on reading. The
power and scope are quite simply breathtaking, and it
seemed inevitable to me that *His Dark Materials*
would become a huge influence in popular culture. But
with such depth in the issues with which it grapples,
and with such a range of sources from which Pullman
drew inspiration, it was also clear that it would not simply become a bestseller but would also stimulate end
less discussion. And it combines so many of the subjects
I love – literature, physics, philosophy and theology –
that I could not sit back and let other people contribute
to the growing discourse without pitching in myself.
There are already two very helpful books on Philip
Pullman and *His Dark Materials* – by Nicholas Tucker[1]
and Claire Squires[2] – but I am coming at Pullman's work
from a distinctively different perspective from them. I
am unashamedly a fan, but I also take issue with
Pullman on the question of his attack on God and
Christianity.

In the chapters that follow I want to help you to
understand and appreciate Pullman's work more fully,
and also to analyse his underlying ideas and worldview.
I do not assume or expect that you share my own
Christian perspectives, but I do believe that it's helpful
for all fans of Pullman's work – Christian or otherwise

– to *understand* a Christian perspective on it. That does not mean there is an obviously Christian angle right through this book, nor that it is consistently negative. And I am not presenting this book as the definitive way in which to read Pullman's work so I don't expect you to agree with everything. As Pullman himself says:

> The last thing I want to say is you've got it wrong. Because then you enter a kind of fundamentalist mode where you're saying you've got to understand it this way, not that way . . . that's dreadful. People are at perfect liberty to find in my story whatever they want to find and I wouldn't dream of saying to someone they've got it wrong. I'm just very flattered and happy that lots of people are reading my books.[3]

In Part One, I look at some of the background to Philip's writing: the things that have shaped Pullman himself; his career as a storyteller, including a brief look at his other work; and the major influences not just on *His Dark Materials* but on his wider thinking. In Part Two, I look in more detail at the narrative world of *Northern Lights*, *The Subtle Knife*, *The Amber Spyglass* and *Lyra's Oxford*, to try and tease out some of the key strands of the story. In Part Three, I look at some of the big themes and issues that play a prominent part in the story: dæmons and the whole business of growing up; the nature of Dust and its connection with 'original sin', the Fall and consciousness; truth and integrity; and finally the Church, God and the republic of heaven. There's also an appendix on two aspects of the science that Pullman weaves into the story – my background as a physicist couldn't let that opportunity pass by. There are many omissions: themes I don't develop, wonderful passages from *His Dark Materials* which I don't even mention, perspectives I apparently ignore, great quotes from Pullman or others which are left behind, added to which I have given Pullman's other work only a fraction of the attention it deserves and that I intended to give it. Restriction on space is a hard taskmaster and it makes a writer necessarily ruthless. You will find some additional material including a transcript of my interview with Philip Pullman, articles, and study guides on some of his books at www.damaris.org/pullman.

I owe my sincere thanks to many people for their help while I was writing this book, not least Philip Pullman himself. He has been gracious in giving time to both talk with me and correspond by email, and in allowing me to quote extensively from his work. I'm also grateful for his practical assistance in giving me a lift back to my mother-in-law's stranded car after it had suffered a puncture on my way to visit him. I'm sure contending with Oxford's rush hour traffic was the last thing Philip wanted at the end of a busy day, but he was quick to volunteer and saved me a major headache.

I am grateful for the opportunity to engage with many groups and individuals on the subject of Pullman's books. Particular thanks to Wade Bradshaw for the first invitation to lecture on *His Dark Materials* at L'Abri in Hampshire, and to Alex Aldous for inviting me to sharpen my ideas with an audience of young fans at Oakham School. The CultureWatch Group (Damaris Study Group) in Southampton; Above Bar Church, Southampton; and various other groups around the country have also stimulated, challenged and shaped my thinking over the last two years. Thanks also to the enthusiasts who maintain various *His Dark Materials* websites – they have been an invaluable source of information. I must make particular mention of Merlyn and the rest of the team at Bridgetothestars.net, which was my first port of call on the Internet on many of my writing days. Specific snippets of information came from many sources – my thanks to the many others who have not been mentioned here and my apologies for not mentioning you by name. Having valued David Wilkinson's books on science and faith over several years, I am particularly grateful for his time in bringing me back up to speed on cosmology. Thanks also to Gillian Hansford for information on South American shamans; David and Pippa Trollope, and Ruth Armstrong for transcribing my interview with Philip; and to Roger Eldridge and Richard Stuckey for photographs on the book cover.

Very special thanks must go to the team at Damaris for bearing with me in the months of working from home rather than in the office. Peter Williams and Caroline Puntis both made valuable comments on various sections of the manuscript of this book, and both have taken up some of the slack while I have devoted my energies to writing, as have others in the team. Caroline in particular has taken on the role of assistant CultureWatch editor in the last four months, which has been an enormous help. Of all the Damaris team, it is Steve Couch who earns most gratitude and admiration for editorially steering me to completion with his gentle chivvying rather than beating me with a stick, and with metaphorical – though still edible – carrots (Turkish Delight, Stilton, good wine . . . time to start the next book!) to spur me on from stage to stage. He has been a model of encouragement, patience and (almost) impeccable pedantry. Pullman's editor David Fickling has three golden rules for editors: first, the author isn't always right; second, the book is the author's, not the editor's; third, neither rule works all the time. Steve has obeyed these rules to the letter and with great spirit.

And finally, more thanks than I can express to my dearest friend – my wife, Jane, and to my three boys, Charlie, Oliver and Pip, who have endured my absorption in this project over months.

Tony Watkins
July 2004

Throughout this book, references to *Northern Lights*, *The Subtle Knife*, *The Amber Spyglass* and *Lyra's Oxford* are given as abbreviations. All page numbers refer to the paperback editions published by Scholastic under their Point imprint in 1998 (*Northern Lights* and *The Subtle Knife*) and 2001 (*The Amber Spyglass*), except for *Lyra's Oxford*, which is the first edition published by David Fickling Books in 2003. All URLs for articles on the Internet, which are referenced in the notes, were accessible in July 2004.

[1] Tucker, Nicholas, *Darkness Visible: Inside the world of Philip Pullman* (Wizard Books, 2003).

[2] Squires, Claire, *Philip Pullman's His Dark Materials Trilogy* (Continuum, 2003).

[3] Brunton, Michael, 'You Don't Know How Famous You Are Until Complete Strangers Stop You In The Street To Talk', *Time* (www.time.com/time/europe/arts/article/0,13716,579063,00.html).

PART ONE
The Storyteller

CHAPTER I

The Once Upon a Time Business

'Pullman is a brilliant writer,' wrote Nicholas Tucker, adding that he is 'capable of lighting up the dullest day or greyest spirit with the incandescence of his imagination.'[1] The *Observer* asked 'Is he the best storyteller ever?'[2] *The Sunday Times* called him 'inexhaustibly versatile' and a 'prodigiously gifted author'.[3]

But according to Peter Hitchens, Phillip Pullman is 'the most dangerous author in Britain'.[4] The *Catholic Herald* is often quoted as saying that Pullman's books are 'far more worthy of the bonfire than Harry Potter . . . and a million times more sinister'. It is a reputation in which Pullman revels. He even stuck Hitchens' article on his study wall saying, 'It's a great compliment to me, isn't it?'[5] and, 'Of course, I sent him a warm card of appreciation and thanks.'[6] Controversy is good for a book's profile – and sales. But he enjoys comments like this for another reason. He openly admits, 'I'm trying to undermine the basis of Christian belief.'[7] Hitchens recognizes this and it distresses him. Leonie Caldecott, the *Catholic Herald* writer, recognizes it too, but her tongue was firmly in her cheek when she wrote the now infamous comment about bonfires. She was not actually saying that *any* books are worthy of the bonfire, but rather that the heated opposition to Harry Potter in some Christian circles in America was directed at a fairly insignificant target compared to what Pullman was writing.[8]

Why does Pullman's work excite people to such strong feelings? Most obvious is the sheer quality of his writing with its enchanting inventiveness, rich use of language, striking and well-honed phrases, vivid characterization, and pacy, exhilarating plots. *Publishers Weekly* praised Pullman for being 'a master at combining impeccable characterisations and seamless plotting, maintaining a crackling pace to create scene upon scene of almost unbearable tension',[9] while Robert McCrum wrote in the *Observer*, 'As well as giving his readers stories that tick with the precision, accuracy and grace of an eighteenth-century clock, he also writes like an angel.'[10] According to Andrew Marr, the trilogy is destined to become a classic:

> *His Dark Materials* will be being bought, and
> pulled dog-eared from family bookshelves, in
> 100 years' time. That is so because of a quality
> of writing that makes one think in turn of Milton
> . . . but also of Dickens and Tolkien.[11]

Pullman is constantly compared with Tolkien, and also with C. S. Lewis. For many people *The Lord of the Rings* and the *Narnia Chronicles* are the greatest British fantasy stories of the twentieth century. Pullman cannot bear either of them, but to be considered at the same level shows how highly people think of him.

Paradise retold

Philip had already found success and acclaim as a children's author before anyone had heard of *His Dark Materials*. Fifteen of his books and two plays had been published before *Northern Lights* hit the shelves in 1995. Since then, he's written six more books,[12] besides *His Dark Materials* and *Lyra's Oxford*. He's become a major force in the literary world and in 2004 was awarded a CBE[13] for his services to literature. Two years previously he won the Eleanor Farjeon Award for his 'crusading advocacy' of the children's book world.[14] Pullman said:

> I'm delighted by this prize because it's unlike other awards – it's not for a single book, but for something more long-term than that; and I'm honoured to be following in some highly distinguished footsteps. It's nice to get an award that doesn't always go to a writer, too – a general children's book world recognition.[15]

But in 1993, Philip had a conversation with his editor, David Fickling, then with Scholastic Publishing, which would eventually lead to Pullman's life being transformed. When he told Fickling that he wanted to do Milton's *Paradise Lost* for teenagers, his editor immediately encouraged him to develop the idea. Pullman says:

> Off the top of my head I improvised a kind of fantasia on themes from Book 2 of *Paradise Lost*. And [Fickling] got quite excited because he loves *Paradise Lost* as well. By this time I knew the kind of thing I wanted to do – I knew the length, I knew it was going to be in three volumes and I knew it was going to be big and ambitious and enable me to say things I'd never been able to say in any other form.[16]

He began work on the first volume, *Northern Lights*, and many ideas came together easily. But something about it was still not working as he redrafted the first chapter again and again, until 'one day I found myself writing the words "Lyra and her dæmon" and that was the key'.[17] The first part of the story was published in 1995 as *Northern Lights* in the UK and as *The Golden Compass* in the USA.[18]

It was a huge success with readers and critics alike, attracting readers of all ages and in many countries. The *Guardian* describes it as 'an eye-widening fantasy, a scorching thriller and a thought-provoking reflection on the human condition'. Pullman was already hard at work on the second volume, *The Subtle Knife*, which followed two years later. By this time many fans were desperate to get their hands on the third volume of the trilogy,[19] *The Amber Spyglass*. Eventually one of them sent Pullman an anonymous letter with a picture of a squirrel and a note saying:

> I enclose a picture of a very cute squirrel.
> Please admire it.
> Now that you have admired it, I want you to remember your book, which the world has spent eons waiting for.
> Please admire the squirrel again.
> Cute squirrel, isn't it?
> Now, release your book or the squirrel dies.

Pullman finished the first draft of *The Amber Spyglass* in 1999, and it was published the following year. During a promotional tour following publication, Philip often told audiences about the letter. Several people approached him claiming to be the author of the note, or to be the author's friend. He didn't believe any of them until a teenager named Sophie spoke to him and asked why he had misquoted her letter – he had substituted the words 'so long' for 'eons' as he thought the word might not mean much to younger members of the audience. She presented him with a plastic squirrel with a knife through it, which he keeps on a shelf in his study.[20]

This shows the level of devotion that some people feel to Pullman, and especially to *His Dark Materials*. There is a global army of loyal fans – adults as well as teenagers – and a number of Internet fan sites delivering news, background information, discussion boards, fan art and more.[21] Then there are *His Dark Materials*-related role-playing games[22] and fansites in other languages (French, German, Portuguese and Russian at least).

Thanks to *His Dark Materials*, Pullman has become one of the most significant writers in the English-speaking world – a far cry from the obscurity of being a teacher in Oxford. He has sold more than seven million copies in 37 languages as well as in audio books. BBC Radio 4 broadcast a major dramatization to considerable acclaim in 2003, and London's National Theatre staged an extraordinary two-part adaptation in late 2003 and 2004,[23] which the Archbishop of Canterbury called 'a near-miraculous triumph'.[24] In the BBC's 2003 poll of Britain's favourite book, *The Big Read*, *His Dark Materials* came in at third place – the highest position for any living author.[25] *Northern Lights* won the *Guardian* Children's Fiction Award and the Carnegie Medal.[26] *The Amber Spyglass* won the Children's Book of the Year,[27] and the Whitbread Prize for 2001 – the first time that a children's author had won this major literary award. Jon Snow, chair of the Whitbread judges' panel said:

> The wind was against Pullman, possibly because you feel that a literary prize is going to be for something exceptional, and you don't necessarily think of the children's genre as doing that.[28]

But it only took the judges two minutes to unanimously agree that *The Amber Spyglass* deserved to win the overall prize. Boyd Tonkin, literary editor of the *Independent,* said that 'Those two minutes will resonate in British publishing and literature for many decades.'[29]

All encompassing

A key element in the appeal of *His Dark Materials* is the dazzling breadth of Pullman's story and its complexity. He weaves into the narrative powerful themes and big philosophical issues which engage any active mind: growing up, wisdom, separation, misuse of authority, freedom, responsibility, consciousness, God, the meaning of life, and more besides. Millicent Lenz says:

> *His Dark Materials* interweaves an engrossing, breath-taking adventure story with a deeply felt examination of existential questions, such as Mrs Coulter's anguished plea to know whether God is, as Nietzsche asserted, 'dead', or why, if he still lives, he has grown mute. In his bold willingness to take on this and other 'big' questions . . . Pullman differs from more timid contemporary writers.[30]

It has often been suggested that what marks out a literary novel is ambiguity – not tying everything up in a neat plot resolution; having grey areas as well as black and white. *His Dark Materials* delivers ambiguity in abundance. Think for instance of Lord Asriel's character, or even of Mrs Coulter's in *The Amber Spyglass*; think of the veil Pullman draws over the grove where Lyra and Will express their love for each other; the mystery still surrounding Dust; or the questions about dæmons that persist even at the very end of the trilogy. For older readers there is plenty to reflect upon with these and many other issues.

The less satisfying elements are when Pullman leaves no ambiguity. The example most frequently commented on is his portrayal of the Church as unremittingly awful. In *The Sunday Times*, Nick Thorpe drew attention to 'the almost pantomime evil of his churchmen, who are conspicuously lacking in . . . redeeming features'.[31] Related to this, several critics have complained that *The Amber Spyglass* gets bogged down in the philosophical issues, and crosses the line from storytelling into propaganda for Pullman's atheistic worldview. Peter Hitchens commented that after the first two 'captivating and clever' books, *The Amber Spyglass* is 'a disappointing clunker . . . too loaded down with propaganda to leave enough room for the story'.[32] Sarah Johnson called *His Dark Materials* 'the most savage attack on organised religion I have ever seen'.[33] Minette Marin sides with Pullman in calling herself a 'godless scientific materialist', but laments that:

> This third book is frostbitten in parts by the freezing fingers of didacticism; overt didacticism is death to art; the magic of stories is too elusive for moralising.[34]

Mixed messages

Pullman denies that he is trying to communicate a moral or philosophical message:

> It's a story, not a treatise, not a sermon or a work of philosophy . . . I'm showing various characters whom I've invented saying things and

doing things and acting out beliefs which they have, and not necessarily which I have. The tendency of the whole thing might be this or it might be that, but what I'm doing is telling a story, not preaching a sermon.[35]

On his own website, Philip writes:

As a passionate believer in the democracy of reading, I don't think it's the task of the author of a book to tell the reader what it means. The meaning of a story emerges in the meeting between the words on the page and the thoughts in the reader's mind. So when people ask me what I meant by this story, or what was the message I was trying to convey in that one, I have to explain that I'm not going to explain. Anyway, I'm not in the message business; I'm in the 'Once upon a time' business.[36]

But he does admit that he is attempting to explore the big issues:

In the hearts of many, many people there is a longing for significance, for meaning, for answers to the question, 'Why? What's it all about? Why are we here? What have we got to do?' and so on. 'What happens when we die?' and so on.

In writing [*His Dark Materials*], I was not trying to give answers to these questions, but to give expression to the questions . . . Clearly this resonates with a lot of people.[37]

These protests highlight a tension in Pullman's comments on his work. On the one hand he denies having a message; on the other, his uncompromising anti-religious stance is far more explicit in *His Dark Materials* than in any of his previous books.

I think the resolution of this tension is probably to be found in the fact that writers always communicate their worldviews whether they intend to or not (unless, perhaps, they make a deliberate attempt to write from the perspective of another worldview). So Pullman, having decided to explore some of the great themes that were important to him from *Paradise Lost*, William Blake, and other sources, wrote a story about a little girl who grows up *in the context of* a cosmic struggle against the idea of God. As the plot progresses, this becomes less of a background feature and more part of the plot itself. It is almost inevitable that Pullman would express some of his own animosity towards religion through the mouthpiece of his characters. He may not have *intended* to do so in such a blatant fashion, but he has nevertheless ended up with a story that expresses his worldview very clearly.

The man who killed God

But who is the man behind the stories? Philip is tall, balding and middle aged and still has the look of a teacher about him with his spectacles, sports jackets and penchant for vividly coloured socks, shirts and ties. He and his wife Jude, a former teacher turned hypnotherapist, have been married for over thirty years. They have two grown-up sons – Jamie, a professional viola player, and Tom, currently doing postgraduate studies in linguistics at Cambridge – and a grandson, Freddie. Philip is an unassuming, mild-mannered and genial man with a sharp mind and a lively curiosity about all kinds of things. It is partly this breadth of interest which makes his books so enjoyable. His enthusiasm is infectious when talking about something which particularly fascinates him.

When I talked with him we disagreed about a number of subjects but he gave the impression of relishing the intellectual cut and thrust of our discussion. His deep antipathy towards Christianity does not seem to have come about as a result of a negative personal experience of the church. In childhood, at least, it was quite the reverse. Philip considers his grandfather, a Church of England rector, to be the most important influence on his life. In childhood he accepted everything his grandfather believed. But in time Philip lost any confidence he had in this:

> As I grew up and began to look around and see
> how other people thought about things, and read
> books and so on, naturally I began to question
> this, as people do. And I eventually came – after
> a lot of swinging this way and that, and trying
> things out – to the position I hold now.[38]

Pullman acknowledges that God may be out there somewhere, but insists that he has seen no evidence for his existence:

> I'm caught between the words 'atheistic' and
> 'agnostic'. I've got no evidence whatever for
> believing in a God. But I know that all the things
> I do know are very small compared with the
> things that I don't know. So maybe there is a
> God out there. All I know is that if there is, he
> hasn't shown himself on earth.
>
> But going further than that, I would say that
> those people who claim that they do know that
> there is a God have found this claim of theirs the
> most wonderful excuse for behaving extremely

badly. So belief in a God does not seem to me to result automatically in behaving very well.[39]

This conviction that God is at best irrelevant to life, and that religious people have used their beliefs to justify intolerance and cruelty, drives much of the plot of *His Dark Materials* as well as at least part of Philip's real life – he is a supporter of the British Humanist Association and the National Secular Society. To say that Philip's naturalist worldview[40] 'drives much of the plot' suggests that I *do* see this as one of the central messages that come through *His Dark Materials*, despite Pullman's protests. His comment quoted above that he is 'trying to undermine the basis of Christian belief' would tend to confirm this, as would his statement that, 'My books are about killing God.'[41]

This is important in our reading, not just of *His Dark Materials* but of Pullman's other works too, because it helps us as readers to see how Pullman expresses *himself*.[42] But it is equally important not to focus on this issue to the exclusion of others. I have already listed several themes which will be addressed in this book, and it is vital to let Pullman speak for himself on these issues rather than simply force them into the grid of his 'anti-Christian agenda'. It is important that we allow Pullman's values to be seen – many of them, it turns out, are quite consistent with a Christian worldview. Philip says:

> We must be cheerful and not go round with a face like a mourner at a funeral. It's difficult sometimes, but good will is not a luxury: it's an absolute necessity. It's a moral imperative.[43]

Here he shows that unlike many contemporary writers, Pullman is not a moral relativist. The centrality of values like these makes *His Dark Materials* a very life-affirming story in many ways. Another moral imperative for Pullman is to be hopeful. His optimism about people shines through:

> When you look at the news sometimes, you despair. But then you look at the achievements of the human race and you feel optimistic again . . . I think I'm 51 per cent optimistic. I think I have to be . . . It's a moral duty, isn't it, to be optimistic?[44]

[1] Tucker, Nicholas, 'Paradise lost and freedom won', *Independent*, 28 October 2000.

[2] Quoted on the back cover of *The Amber Spyglass* (Point, 2001 edition).

[3] Kemp, Peter, 'Master of his universe', *The Sunday Times*, 19 October 1997.

[4] Hitchens, Peter, 'This is the most dangerous author in Britain', *Mail on Sunday*, 27 January 2002.

[5] Weinberg, Anna, 'Are you there, God? It's me, Philip Pullman', *Book*, November/December 2002 (www.bookmagazine.com/issue25/inthemargins.shtml).

[6] Ross, Deborah, 'Philip Pullman: Soap and the serious writer', *Independent*, 4 February 2002.

[7] Wartofsky, Alona, 'The Last Word', *Washington Post*, 19 February 2001.

[8] Harry Potter had stirred up strong opposition from the Christian Right in America – wrongly, in her view. Since it was close to Guy Fawkes Night, she 'joked in a regular column . . . for the Catholic Herald that any book-burners out there could find many other stories far more "worthy of the bonfire" than Harry Potter. I went on to use Pullman's books as an example of something that was far more likely to harm a child's capacity for faith . . . I pointed out that, in these books, everything we normally associate with safety and security – parents, priests, and even God himself – is evil, is indeed "the stuff of nightmares".' Since this was before *The Amber Spyglass* was published, Leonie Caldecott also speculated that Pullman might turn it all around in the final instalment (Caldecott, Leonie, 'Paradise Denied: Philip Pullman and the uses and abuses of enchantment', *Touchstone*, 2003; www.touchstonemag.com/docs/issues/16.8docs/16-8pg42.html).

[9] *Publishers Weekly* (www.reviews.publishersweekly.com/searchDetail. aspx?id=0679879242).

[10] McCrum, Robert, 'Not for children', *Observer*, 22 October 2000.

[11] Marr, Andrew, 'Pullman does for atheism what C. S. Lewis did for God', *Daily Telegraph*, 24 January 2002.

[12] This includes *The Scarecrow and the Servant*, which is due to be published in November 2004, shortly after the publication of this book.

[13] Commander of the Order of the British Empire.

[14] Eleanor Farjeon Award, Book Trust website (www.booktrusted.co.uk/ prizes/prizes.php4?action=2&przid=128).

[15] Eccleshare, Julia, 'Letter from London', *Publishers Weekly*, 2 December 2002.

[16] Pullman, Philip, 'An introduction to . . . Philip Pullman' in James Carter (ed.), *Talking Books: Children's authors talk about the craft, creativity and process of writing* (Routledge, 1999), p.187–188.

[17] Pullman, 'An introduction to . . . Philip Pullman', p.190.

[18] The change in name came about because Pullman provisionally entitled the trilogy, *The Golden Compasses* (from Book VII of *Paradise Lost* where it refers to compasses for drawing circles with). Someone at the American publishers, Knopf, mistakenly thought this referred to the alethiometer and that became their working title for the first volume. When Philip informed them that he had changed the trilogy's title to *His Dark Materials*, Knopf refused to change the title of the first volume. Pullman says, 'Their obduracy in this matter was accompanied by such generosity in the matter of royalty advances, flattery, promises of publicity, etc, that I thought it would be churlish to deny them this small pleasure' (www.bridgetothestars.net/index.php?p=FAQ#4).

[19] Pullman says, 'It's a mistake really to call it a trilogy as it's one story, one book in three volumes. It has to be published in three volumes for various financial, physical and marketing reasons' ('An introduction to . . . Philip Pullman', p.192). Since the *Cambridge Advanced Learners Dictionary* defines a trilogy as 'a series of three books or plays written about the same situation or characters, forming a continuous story', this seems a rather curious protest to be making.

[20] Sophie recounts the story herself at www.darkmaterials.com/archive/ 0005.htm.

[21] Some of the best sites are www.bridgetothestars.net; www.hisdarkmaterials.org; www.darkmaterials.com; and www.geocities.com/darkadamant.

[22] For example, 'Tell Them Stories' at www.inkypot.com/tts.

[23] A revival is scheduled from 20 November 2004 until 2 April 2005 – see www.nationaltheatre.org.uk.

[24] Williams, Rowan, 'A near-miraculous triumph', *Guardian*, 10 March 2004.

[25] In first and second place were J. R. R. Tolkien's *The Lord of the Rings* and Jane Austen's *Pride and Prejudice*, which consistently came top of other polls – even before the films of *The Lord of the Rings* came out.

[26] The Carnegie Medal is the United Kingdom's highest honour specifically for children's literature.

[27] At the 2001 British Book Awards.

[28] Lister, David, 'Children's book wins Whitbread top prize', *Independent*, 23 January 2002.

[29] Tonkin, Boyd, 'Whitbread Award: An inevitable victory for a dark and complex fable', *Independent*, 23 January 2002.

[30] Lenz, Millicent, 'Philip Pullman' in Hunt, Peter and Lenz, Millicent, *Alternative Worlds in Fantasy Fiction* (Continuum, 2001), p.122–123.

[31] Thorpe, Nick, 'The anti-Christian fundamentalist', *The Sunday Times*, 4 August 2002.

[32] Hitchens, 'This is the most dangerous author in Britain'. A copy of the article is online at pers-www.wlv.ac.uk/~bu1895/hitchens.htm.

[33] Johnson, Sarah, 'On the Dark Edge of Imagination', *The Times*, 18 October 2000.

[34] Marin, Minette, 'What happens to the Kingdom of Heaven when God is killed?', *Daily Telegraph*, 21 October 2000.

[35] Roberts, Susan, 'A dark agenda?' (www.surefish.co.uk/culture/features/pullman_interview.htm).

[36] Pullman, Philip, 'About the books' (www.philip-pullman.com/about_the_books.asp).

[37] Quoted in Mooney, Bel, *Devout Sceptics – Conversations on faith and doubt* (Hodder and Stoughton, 2003), p.123.

[38] Roberts, 'A dark agenda?'.

[39] Roberts, 'A dark agenda?'.

[40] Naturalism as a worldview is the belief that everything has purely natural causes; it is a denial of the supernatural.

[41] Meacham, Steve, 'The shed where God died', *Sidney Morning Herald*, 13 December 2003 (www.smh.com.au/articles/2003/12/12/1071125644900.html?from=storyrhs).

[42] James W. Sire, in his book *How to Read Slowly* (second edition, IVP, 1988), argues that to read well means being alert for, and taking account of, the worldview that is being communicated through the writing.

[43] Pullman, Philip, 'The Republic of Heaven', *Horn Book Magazine*, November/December 2001, p.667.

[44] Quoted in Mooney, *Devout Sceptics – Conversations on faith and doubt*, p.132.

CHAPTER 2

Philip Pullman: Places and People

Philip Nicholas Outram[1] Pullman was born on 19 October 1946, in Norwich, England, the son of an RAF fighter pilot, Alfred Pullman, and his wife Audrey. Although in many ways his childhood was very unsettled, he looks back on it with great warmth. He recalls vividly some of the experiences and places of his childhood. On his website he describes a moment of joy as a young child – an incident which he later worked into *The Broken Bridge*:

> My mother was hanging out some washing on a sunny day, and singing, as happy as a lark. The wind was chasing fat white clouds through the blue sky, and the sheets on the line billowed like the clouds, big fresh-smelling moist clouds that swelled and flapped and swung up high. The song my mother was singing filled the sheets and the clouds and the immense blue beaming sky, and I felt so light that I too might swing up and be blown along in the wild blue splendour; and she took me and swung me up, high up among the snowy-white sheets and the billowing clouds and the wind and the song and the endless dazzling sky, and I shouted and sang for joy.[2]

Voyages of discovery

When Alfred Pullman was posted to Southern Rhodesia (now Zimbabwe), the family, including Philip's younger brother Francis, went too and some new experiences were lodged deep inside Philip's mind:

> Sometimes my father would take us to the compound, where the Africans lived, to see a boxing match . . . In the evening the most beautiful smell in the world, roasting mealies (corn on the cob), would drift out from the compound into the place where the white people lived. I loved that smell so much that when years and years later I happened to smell it unexpectedly in a street market in London, where someone was roasting mealies to sell, I found tears springing to my eyes.

Alfred Pullman died when Philip was just seven. His mother remarried two years later to another RAF officer and the family moved to Australia for eighteen months. This travelling gave him some great experiences:

> I'm very thankful that I lived at a time before universal air travel meant that I didn't have a chance to realize how big the world is . . . When you go by sea, you know how far it is, because it's taken you a long time to get there. And the weather changes on the way as you go over the Equator. It gets calmer, it gets hotter, the sea gets stiller, and you go down towards the Cape of Good Hope and the sea changes colour and it becomes green and blue and the waves change shape. There'll be much longer waves [so] that the ship plunges up and down as well as rocking from side to side . . . If you have felt in your body the difference between the Southern Hemisphere and the Northern Hemisphere, you

really have experienced it. And so a lot of my childhood was spent doing that.[3]

He recalls,

> . . . nothing was more exciting than making a landfall. After days of steadily beating through the sea, the ship would alter its motion; the ever-present creak would quieten; even the light would change; there'd be a different smell in the wind: trees, vegetation, swamp. We would all crowd to the rail and watch the line of land come closer and turn into a mountain, a city, a port – a foreign land! With foreign faces on the quayside, and a strange language in the air, and advertisements for unheard-of drinks and cigarettes on the hoardings. They even rowed their boats around the harbours differently – short choppy strokes in this place, long graceful sweeps in another. We would go ashore and spend strange money on souvenirs of sewn leather or carved wood, or ride in a taxi with open windows through which boys threw flowers as they ran along beside us.[4]

Love of the landscape

Returning to Britain meant new school experiences for Philip: first a prep school in London, and then, when the family moved to Llanbedr in North Wales, a school in Harlech. Ysgol Ardudwy is close to the beach and almost opposite the imposing thirteenth-century Harlech Castle – a fantastic location to be at school. It was not easy being a new boy at school – he was rather rootless after the various upheavals of his early childhood, and he got into a fight on his first day because of his English accent. But he soon settled in and looks back with great fondness for those carefree days:

My friends and I seemed to be free in those days to wander where we liked: the woods, the wide hills, the miles of beach were open to us, and the edge of our playground was the horizon. We roamed the hills and broke into a derelict house where the last occupant had left a Welsh Bible and a set of false teeth on the kitchen table. We made go-carts, or trucks as we called them, and hauled them up slopes (there were plenty of those) and hurtled down recklessly. We dared each other to walk past the Hanging Tree in the clearing in the woods at night. We swam in the sea; we swam in the river; we invented a new sport, waterfall climbing. We put pennies on the railway line and retrieved them, flat and distorted and shiny, after the train had gone over them. We hung about the bus shelters in the local town on Saturday night, spying on the lovers. We went to the tiny cinema in the next village and came back on the last bus, running down to the bus stop clutching bags of chips from the fish-and-chip shop, losing our footing, skidding along on the gravel with the chips held triumphantly to our chests. We held spitting contests out the window of the school train. We held grass-bomb fights at night: a handful of grass and a careful tug, and you had a very satisfactory clump of earth to hurl through the air at the dimly seen enemy across the field. We teased the short-tempered pig in the farmyard by the river. We put fireworks on the roof of the

ladies' toilets. We howled like banshees in the
garden of cross old Mr Pugh till he came out and
chased us away . . .

I drew obsessively, the landscape, mainly: the
massive rounded hills, the wide pearly estuary,
the tumbled sand dunes, the dry stone walls, the
ancient church half-buried in the sand. I learned
that landscape by drawing it, and I came to care
for it with a lover's devotion. Later in *The Broken
Bridge* I wrote about a girl making the same
discoveries, loving and drawing the same landscape. Many other strands went into the making
of that book, but what lay at its heart was love; it's
a love letter to a landscape.[5]

Philip's Oxford

After leaving school in 1965, Philip studied English at
Exeter College, Oxford. It was the obvious thing to do
after enjoying English at school and having such a flair
for it. But he didn't enjoy studying English at Oxford at
all. He says he never mastered the 'coherent, focused,
disciplined sort of reading which I imagine you need to
do if you want an academic career . . . I couldn't do it
then, and I don't do it now.'[6] In fact, discipline in studying doesn't seem to have been a strong point then at all,
although he is an extremely disciplined writer now.

Although the academic side of university life was not
a great success (he finished with a third class degree),
the experience of being a student in Oxford made a
huge impact on him. Writing about his time at Exeter
College Pullman says: 'I had a group of idle friends who
occupied their time and mine betting on horses, getting
drunk, and sprawling about telling creepy tales.'[7] Some

aspects of his time there were later incorporated into *His Dark Materials*, and Lyra's origins in Oxford are an important part of her sense of identity. Exeter College formed the basis for the fictional Jordan College, although Pullman made Jordan the biggest, best and grandest of colleges. Lyra's rooftop escapades were based on real incidents, as Pullman recalls:

> In my second year I occupied the rooms at the top of staircase 8, next to the lodge tower, and one of the friends I mentioned, Jim Taylor, discovered that you could get out of the window and crawl along a very useful gutter behind the parapet. From there you could climb in through another window further along. I gave Lyra a better head for heights than I have, but I did the gutter crawl a number of times, usually when there was a party on the next staircase.[8]

Shed master

The day after Philip Pullman graduated, he started work on his first novel. It was harder than he'd expected so he moved to London and worked for a time in the gents' outfitters, Moss Bros, which was, he says, 'an extraordinary experience'. Each lunchtime he would cross the road to write poetry in the churchyard of St Paul's Church. After eighteen months he took a new job at Charing Cross Library, but to progress as a librarian would mean taking a postgraduate diploma. By this time, Philip had met and married Jude (Judith) Speller, and their first son, Jamie, was born the following year. Since Jude was a teacher, Philip began to think for the first time about going into teaching himself. It seemed to offer 'quite a nice life with long holidays' and scope for progressing with his writing. He chose to do his teacher training in Weymouth simply because he liked the place, then returned to Oxford where he taught in two middle schools (ages 9 to 13) until 1986. After twelve years in the classroom, Philip Pullman became a part-time senior lecturer in English at Westminster College, Oxford, and was involved in training a new generation of teachers for eight years. Eventually he was able to give himself entirely to the business of writing.

For years, Philip wrote in a shed at the bottom of his garden – he claims it was to escape the noise of his son playing the violin. The shed seemed to be becoming famous almost in its own right. Pullman described its contents.

> . . . manuscripts, drawings, apple cores, spiders' webs, dust, books in tottering heaps all over the floor and on every horizontal surface, about a thousand jiffy bags . . . which I'm also too mean to throw away, a six-foot-long stuffed rat . . . a saxophone, a guitar, dozens of masks of one sort or another . . . an old armchair filled to capacity with yet more books, a filing cabinet that I haven't managed to open for eighteen months because of all the jiffy bags and books which have fallen in front of it in a sort of landslide . . . bits of chewed carpet from when my young pug Hogarth comes to visit . . . It is a filthy abominable tip.[9]

By the time I visited Philip to interview him in the autumn of 2002, the shed was history – at least for him. He and Jude moved out of north Oxford to a nearby village – a move made desirable by the increasing numbers of people turning up on his doorstep, and made possible by the extraordinary sales of *His Dark*

Materials. But although a roomy study within the new – and quiet – house made the shed redundant, Philip couldn't bear to just leave it behind. Instead, he gave it to his friend, the writer/illustrator Ted Dewan on condition that it was passed on to another writer or artist at the end of its service to Ted.[10] Ted removed one of the windows to use as a frame for a montage of bits and pieces from the shed, including a scrap of curtain and some of the legions of Post-It notes. Philip's study was tidier than I'd expected after reading several accounts of the shed. The six-foot rat was nowhere in sight but the walls were lined with books, and around the room were all kinds of odds and ends, mementos and things that might stimulate another story one day. I suspect it may not always stay as tidy because, since I visited, Philip has apparently also moved some of his woodworking tools in. Working with wood is his passion – he has made a rocking horse for his young grandson. He loves drawing too and is delighted to be learning more and more about how to do it well. He was competent enough to draw the little illustrations at the start of the chapters in *Northern Lights* and *The Subtle Knife*.[11] He's also musical, playing the guitar and the piano, and is a great fan of the music of Nicholai Medtner.[12] He writes three pages in longhand every morning, and then the first sentence of the page for the following day, just to get him started.

A 'half-orphan'

It's not just places that have made a huge impact on Philip Pullman of course, but many people too. Philip recalls the birth of his baby brother as being a rather surprising event:

One day when I was a little boy I went out for a
walk with my grandmother. There was a big pile
of dark brown earthenware pipes by the side of
the road for the workmen to put underground,
and Granny let me clamber about over them for
a while and crawl inside and out the other end.
But she was anxious to go back home, and I
couldn't persuade her to stay, so I went with her,
reluctantly; and when we got home, who could
believe it? I had a new brother. A little crying
baby, of all things. Where had he come from?[13]

When his father's tour of duty in Rhodesia ended, his
mother Audrey and the two boys went to stay with her
parents in Drayton, just outside Norwich in Norfolk. But
while they were there in 1953, they received a telegram
informing them that his father had been killed in an air
crash while fighting Mau Mau terrorists in Kenya. They
presumed that he had been shot down. Philip was just
seven years old.

It's hard to imagine the impact this could have on a
young boy, but Pullman claims that it hardly affected
him at all. In interviews he maintains that he didn't see
a great deal of his father anyway, so didn't miss him
much. On his website he writes,

I suppose that my brother and I cried, though I
didn't really feel sad. The fact was that we hadn't
seen my father for a long time, and apart from
the glamour surrounding him, he was a figure
who hadn't played much part in our lives. So my
brother and I went back out to the sunny wall,
where we'd been picking off the moss and
throwing it at each other, and carried on.[14]

He told Sue Lawley something very similar on BBC

Radio 4's *Desert Island Discs*:

> It was a drama but it was offstage . . . So we felt
> that something rather grand and important had
> happened to us, that we were almost orphaned!
> . . . I don't think it was dispassionate, but maybe
> part of me was already thinking 'Ah, so this is
> what it feels like to be half an orphan. That's
> interesting, I'll make a note of that.'[15]

But at other times, Philip has acknowledged that his
father's death did have consequences for him. In an
interview on Amazon.com, he says,

> Peter Dickinson and I were talking one day and
> this subject came up and we agreed how strange
> it was that so many children's authors had lost
> one or both parents in their childhood. My father
> died in a plane crash when I was seven, and
> naturally I was preoccupied for a long time by
> the mystery of what he must have been like.[16]

Here Pullman hints at the possibility that losing a par-
ent can be a factor in someone becoming a children's
author. Does writing about children provide an opportunity to re-examine the feelings and questions from all
those years ago? Does it help a writer to feel that something positive has finally come about through the experience of losing one or both parents? Or does it simply
give them a sensitivity to the joys and pains of childhood that many others would not have? These are spec-
ulations but it is interesting that several of Pullman's
protagonists have also lost one or both parents. In *His
Dark Materials*, Lyra believes her parents were killed
in an accident; Will's father is missing presumed dead.
Outside the trilogy, Sally Lockhart has just become an
orphan at the start of *The Ruby in the Smoke*; the main

character, Roger, in *I Was A Rat* knows nothing about his parents; *Count Karlstein* has two orphan girls at the centre; *The Firework-maker's Daughter* has lost her mother, as has Ginny in *The Broken Bridge*.

Heroic father

At the very least, Pullman concedes that a substantial period of time was spent thinking about the father he feels he never knew. His father was a mystery – one that he could not let go of for some time. That doesn't seem to quite fit with saying that his father's death barely affected him. Although his father may have been away for long periods of time, at least he was *somewhere*, and would come back to the family at intervals. One imagines it would have been exciting to have a fighter pilot as a father, and family times, although rare, would be very special to a seven-year-old. Not missing his presence in the home isn't the same as not grieving. Philip could easily have lamented the fact that he hardly knew his father before the crash, as well as the impossibility of now ever getting to know him. He *knew of him* as a glamorous hero (he was posthumously awarded the Distinguished Flying Cross) but could never *know him* intimately as a father. In one interview he said that, 'It is a traumatic thing, but also kind of a gift, because it enables you to imagine that the father who is missing is better than the one you end up with.'[17]

Nearly 40 years later, after his mother had died, Philip discovered some surprising facts about his father that shattered the impressions he had always had of him:

> He hadn't been shot down in battle; he had been drinking, and he'd crashed while practising for

an air display. That was the first thing I found out, and the second was even more of a shock: I learned that it was generally known among his friends that he'd crashed his plane on purpose. He'd committed suicide. That had been covered up so that he could be awarded the medal and so that my mother could receive a widow's pension. Apparently he had been in all kinds of trouble: he'd borrowed money without being able to repay it, his affairs with other women were beginning to get out of his control, and he had had to agree to a separation from my mother. I knew none of this while my mother was alive; I've found it all out in the past few years since she died. So all my life I've had the idea that my father was a hero cut down in his prime, a warrior, a man of shining glamour, and none of it was true. Sometimes I think he's really still alive somewhere, in hiding, with a different name. I'd love to meet him.[18]

In *The Subtle Knife*, Will is also preoccupied with the heroic father he had never known. Could something of Philip Pullman's own deep – even subconscious – longings be expressing themselves in Will's search for his father?

Glamorous mother

Both his parents were very glamorous in Philip's eyes:

There were two kinds of glamour: my mother's, which consisted of a scent called Blue Grass by Elizabeth Arden, and my father's, which was more complicated. There were cigarettes in it, and beer, and leather armchairs. The smell of my

> father's glamour was very strong in the Club,
> which we children were sometimes allowed in,
> but not to run around.

But after Alfred Pullman's death, it was Philip's grandparents (along with his great aunt who lived with them) who provided the stability and emotional support needed by the two young boys: Philip and his brother lived with them while their mother went to work in London. Audrey's life there was remote from them in many ways, not simply in terms of geography but in terms of lifestyle too. Compared to their life in rural Norfolk in the mid-1950s, they perceived her life as very sophisticated:

> She worked at the BBC and lived in a flat in
> Chelsea, and once or twice we went to stay with
> her and saw another dimension of glamour. She
> had lots of friends, and they were all young and
> pretty or handsome; the women wore hats and
> gloves to go to work, their dresses were long
> and flowery, and the men drove sports cars and
> smoked pipes, and there was always laughter,
> and the sun shone every day.[19]

Something feels a little Mrs Coulterish in this comment from Pullman; was his mother's glamour part of what lies behind this extraordinary character? When Audrey remarried, it was to a pilot from the same squadron as his father (Pullman suspects they had been having an affair before his father's death). Although it took a while to adjust to the new situation, Philip warmed to his stepfather. He says, 'I was very fond of him. He was a difficult man, but there was not one moment during my childhood when he made me think that I wasn't his son.'[20]

Beloved Grandpa

The time spent living with his grandparents had a major impact on Philip because his grandfather, Sidney Merrifield, came to be the most significant figure in Philip's childhood. He was the father figure Philip needed so much:

> Both Granny and Auntie, and my brother and I, and everyone else for that matter, regarded Grandpa as the centre of the world. There was no one stronger than he was, or wiser, or kinder. People were always calling to see him, for a parish priest was an important man, after all. He led the church services in his cassock and white surplice; he took weddings and funerals and christenings; and he was the chaplain of Norwich Prison[21] (though I didn't find out about the prison until much later, when I was old enough). When I was young he was the sun at the centre of my life.[22]

Living with his grandfather meant that church played a big part in Philip's childhood:

> [It] involved, of course, going to church and going to Sunday School and listening to Bible stories and all the rest of it. He was a very good, old-fashioned country clergyman and a wonderful storyteller, too. He knew all the stories that one should know from the Bible. So it was a very familiar part of my background and it was something that one didn't question. Grandpa was the rector, Grandpa preached a sermon and of course God existed – one didn't even thinking of questioning it.[23]

Later Pullman came to reject the faith that his grandfather stood for. He insists that his rejection of Christianity had nothing to do with the kind of man his grandfather was – it was not a reaction against him: 'that would be preposterous. I've got nothing but love and affection for his memory.'[24] He says, 'He was the centre of my life. He was the sun around whom my emotional life revolved as a boy.'[25]

Inspirational teacher

One other influence on Philip must be mentioned – the teacher who had more impact than any other on the course of his life: his English teacher, Enid Jones. She introduced him to the Metaphysical Poets of the seventeenth century (John Donne, George Herbert, Andrew Marvell and others), to Wordsworth, and especially to John Milton's epic poem, *Paradise Lost*. She encouraged him in his writing too and, in the acknowledgements at the end of *The Amber Spyglass*, Pullman writes that he owes to Enid Jones 'the best that education can give, the notion that responsibility and delight can co-exist' (*AS*, p.550).

[1] Philip Pullman says, 'I was told that there was some family connection with the General Sir James Outram of the Indian Mutiny, but it turns out that we're not related . . . it's just that my great-grandfather was Outram's godson' (personal email to the author, 13 May 2004).

[2] Pullman, Philip, 'I have a feeling all this belongs to me' (www.philip-pullman.com/pages/content/index.asp?PageID=84).

[3] Odean, Kathleen, 'The story master', *School Library Journal*, 1 October 2000 (www.schoollibraryjournal.com/article/ca153054).

[4] Pullman, 'I have a feeling all this belongs to me'.

[5] Pullman, 'I have a feeling all this belongs to me'.

[6] Pullman, Philip, 'From Exeter to Jordan', *Register* (Exeter College Association, 2001), p.18. This article is available online at www.oxfordtoday.ox.ac.uk/archive/0102/14_3/03.shtml.

[7] Pullman, 'From Exeter to Jordan'.

[8] Pullman, 'From Exeter to Jordan'.

[9] 'Achuka Interview' (www.achuka.co.uk/archive/interviews/ppint.php).

[10] Dewan, Ted, 'Lots more about Ted' (www.wormworks.com/tedpages/tdbioex.htm).

[11] These are all reproduced on Philip Pullman's website with a little explanation about each one (www.philip-pullman.com/pages/content/index.asp?PageID=90).

[12] Pullman, Philip, 'Medtner', *Granta*, No. 76, 9 January 2002 (www.granta.com/extracts/1469).

[13] Pullman, 'I have a feeling all this belongs to me'.

[14] Pullman, 'I have a feeling all this belongs to me'.

[15] First broadcast 6 October 2002.

[16] Fried, Kerry, 'Darkness Visible: An Interview with Philip Pullman' (www.amazon.com/exec/obidos/tg/feature/-/94589/103-2179560-1236619).

[17] Curtis, Nick, *Evening Standard*, 2 January 2003.

[18] Pullman, 'I have a feeling all this belongs to me'.

[19] Pullman, 'I have a feeling all this belongs to me'.

[20] Billen, Andrew, 'A senile God? Who would Adam and Eve it?', *The Times*, 21 January 2003.

[21] As chaplain of the prison, one of his roles was to accompany condemned prisoners to their execution – a role that he found very difficult.

[22] Pullman, 'I have a feeling all this belongs to me'.

[23] Roberts, Susan, 'A dark agenda?' (www.surefish.co.uk/culture/features/pullman_interview.htm).

[24] Billen, 'A senile God?'.

[25] Odean, 'The story master'.

CHAPTER 3

Storytelling and Other Stories

Philip Pullman says he's a storyteller more than a writer:

> For me the story is paramount and the actual literary texture is secondary. That's not to say that I think the literary features are not important, because I do take great care to use words properly and have a certain grace and rhythmic propulsion. But it would be flattering, for example, to think that I had made up a story which other people could tell in different words and which would still have whatever effect it has now. I'm aiming high, but Hans Christian Andersen's tales are just as effective, just as powerful, when told by other storytellers.[1]

He enjoys the process of writing and crafting his prose, but he's desperate to tell his story to anyone who'll listen, and he's not afraid of telling his stories very straightforwardly. When he wrote in a shed, Philip had a warning stuck over his desk: 'Don't be afraid of the obvious.' He despairs of writers (usually of adult fiction) who feel they have to write in such a clever way that the story itself is an emaciated thing with hardly any life in it. Pullman describes them as 'picking up their stories with a pair of tongs', and says: 'We shouldn't be afraid of the obvious, because stories are about life, and life is full of obvious things like food and sleep and love and courage which you don't stop needing just because you're a good reader.'[2] It is one of the secrets of Pullman's enormous success – he gets on with the job of telling a great yarn, and people respond to it because we love stories. No, it's more than that – we *need* stories:

> Stories are vital. Stories never fail us because, as Isaac Bashevis Singer says, 'events never grow stale'. There's more wisdom in a story than in volumes of philosophy . . . We need stories so much that we're even willing to read bad books to get them, if the good books won't supply them. We all need stories, but children are more frank about it; cultured adults, on the other hand, those limp and jaded creatures who think it more important to seem sophisticated than to admit to simplicity, find it harder both to write and to read novels that don't come with a prophylactic garnish of irony.[3]

Luck

Storytellers, in common with all artists and craftsmen, need three ingredients for success: 'talent, hard work and luck',[4] and Pullman has had a good measure of all of them. By 'luck' he means the things that happened *to* him, rather than things within him (talent) or that he brought about (through his effort). For example, he frequently points back to the influence of his childhood on his future career, particularly the impact of living with his grandfather. Sidney Merrifield had an ability to tell stories that brought to life the places around their home near Norwich. His stories engaged the young Philip's mind so well that they have stayed with him:

He took the simplest little event and made a story out of it. When he was a young man in Devonshire before the First World War he'd had a friend called Fred Austin, a fine horseman, a big strong man with a fierce moustache, and he and Grandpa had joined the army together to fight in France. When Fred came home to his farm after the end of the war, the baby he'd left behind was now a little girl who didn't know him and was frightened by this big dark laughing man who knelt and held out his enormous hands for her. She ran away and hid her face, but Fred was a wise man and didn't hurry. Little by little over the next days he coaxed her and was kind and gentle, and finally she came to him trustfully. When Grandpa told that story he said that God would appear to us like that; at first we'd be alarmed and frightened by him, but eventually we'd come to trust in his love.

Well, many years later, when Grandpa and Fred Austin were both long dead, I used to tell the story of *The Iliad* to the children I taught; and there's a part of that story where the great Prince Hector goes up on the walls of Troy to watch the battle below and finds his little son Astyanax in the arms of his nurse. He reaches for the boy, but Astyanax is frightened by the great nodding plumes on his father's battle helmet and hides his face in the nurse's shoulder until Hector, laughing, takes off the helmet and reassures the little child. Whenever I told that story, I used to think of Grandpa's story about Fred Austin. Between my childhood and now,

> I've lost sight of God; but Hector the Trojan
> prince and Fred Austin the Devonshire soldier
> are still brightly alive to me; and so is Grandpa.[5]

Philip was also fortunate in spending eighteen months in Australia as a young boy – it introduced him to new and exciting ways of encountering stories. At that point television had not made much impact on Australia, but the gangster and cowboy serials on the radio held him spellbound, as did *Superman*. He then discovered *Superman* comics imported from the USA, and *Batman*, which was even better. He says:

> Comic books changed my life because I saw for
> the first time an entirely new way of telling
> stories. The combination of words and pictures,
> of effortlessly vivid storytelling, made me want
> to tell stories more than anything else.[6]

As well as stories being *accompanied* by illustrations (he remembers with special fondness Tove Janssen's *Moomin* books, *The Magic Pudding* by Norman Lindsey, and *Emil and the Detectives* by Erich Kästner), he was discovering that they could be told *through* pictures. He felt the urge to tell stories himself, so each night, after lights out, he made up tales for his younger brother:

> I don't know whether he enjoyed it, or whether
> he even listened, but it wasn't for his benefit; it
> was for mine. I remember vividly the sense of
> diving into the dark as I began the story, with no
> idea at all what was going to happen or whether
> the story would 'come out' as I called it, by
> which I meant make sense or come to a neat
> end. I remember the exhilaration of the risk:
> Would I find something to say? Would I dry up?

And I remember the thrill, the bliss, when, a
minute ahead of getting there, I saw a twist I
could give to the end, a clever way of bringing
back that character who'd come into it earlier
and vanished inconclusively, a neat phrase to tie
it all up with.[7]

Talent

Later, back in Britain, Philip's English teacher, Enid
Jones, saw his talent and began to nurture it. He developed his skills through writing poetry, and though he
later decided that his 'real goal was not writing poetry
but storytelling',[8] it gave him solid foundations for
being a first-class writer. Through writing poetry he
developed discipline in writing, a feel for rhythm, and a
feel for the importance of word sounds. Philip sees his
time studying English at Oxford University as a wrong
move ('I should have gone to art college'). But, confident of his talent, his grand plan was to start a novel the
day after his final exams and finish it within a couple of
months. He thought it would be published quickly and
make him a milllionaire when the film rights were sold.

So I bought a big book to write in: three
hundred pages of beautiful smooth lined paper
in a stout binding, like a family Bible; and I sat
down on the first morning of my life-after-
education and began to write. And before I'd got
to the end of the first paragraph, I'd come up
slap bang against a fundamental problem that
still troubles me today whenever I begin a story,
and it's this: where am I telling it from? Imagine
the storytelling voice as being like a camera. A
film director has to decide where to put the

camera and what it's going to look at, and it's the same with the storytelling voice . . .

I was like the centipede who was asked which foot he put down first. I couldn't move. There were so many possibilities, and nothing to tell me which was the right one. What a shock! I had passed through the entire British education system studying literature, culminating in three years of reading English at Oxford, and they'd never told me about something as basic as the importance of point of view in fiction! Well, no doubt it was my fault that I got a poor degree; but I do think someone might have pointed it out. Perhaps it had been covered in one of those lectures I hadn't found my way to.

What I couldn't help noticing was that I learned more about the novel in a morning by trying to write a page of one than I'd learned in seven years or so of trying to write criticism. From that moment on, my respect for novelists, even the humblest, has been considerably greater than my respect for critics, even the most distinguished.[9]

Effort

Once Philip had begun working at Moss Bros, his writing was confined to the evenings and he began to learn the importance of serious, disciplined effort. It was at this time that he developed his practice of writing three pages every day. He eventually gave up on that first novel, but his second, *The Haunted Storm*, won joint first prize in a competition run by the publishers, New English Library. It was published in 1972 when Philip was just 25 – he was very pleased with it:

> I thought winning would change my life, but of
> course it didn't. Nothing happened. The book
> came out and it was completely ignored because
> it was terrible. I've kept quiet about it ever
> since.[10]

Claire Squires describes *The Haunted Storm* as 'a
weird narrative concerning murder and incest, and features a Gnostic cleric and a 23-year-old ridden by exis-
tential angst'.[11] Pullman says he wrote it 'out of a sense
of duty, rather than conviction', and felt 'glum and
resentful'[12] about it. A second novel for adults, *Galatea*
('a picaresque, magic realist tale . . . populated by a
profusion of characters including zombies, automata
and "Electric Whores"'),[13] followed in 1978, by which
time Pullman was a teacher.

Developing his craft

Teaching gave Philip the opportunity to develop the
craft of storytelling, as well as familiarity with children's
language, and insight into their emotional development.
He realizes how fortunate he was to be teaching at a
time when he was free to teach as he thought best without the constraints of the National Curriculum, targets
and testing.[14] 'I was able to tell and learn and get to
know dozens of myths and folk tales. It was the making
of me as a storyteller.'[15]

> I would tell them *The Iliad* and *The Odyssey*, all
> the way through. Whatever the children were
> getting out of it, I was getting several valuable
> things. Not least the thing that writers don't
> always have in a technical sense, which is a set
> of exercises – like a musical exercise . . . There's

no real equivalent in the literary arts. But I found one, and it's telling stories – the same stories, over and over, but not from the same words, always fresh, always speaking them – without a book or any props . . .

With storytelling you can learn so much about timing and also the kind of writer you are. You can find out what you're good at and what you're not. I'm not good, as I discovered, painfully, at telling funny stories that make people laugh – not aloud, that is. What I can do is evoke an atmosphere, I can paint a picture in the mind's eye. I can make it exciting, so that people will want to know what happened next . . . That was the most valuable thing I ever got out of my years of teaching.[16]

One of his former pupils is poet Greta Stoddart, who recalls that: 'He had an extraordinary energy. And he didn't need books. He would come in and just launch into some story. He had this great mane of long, wavy hair that he would scrape back with his long fingernails – he kept them long to play the guitar. And he had that very direct stare that stays just a little longer than you'd expect. All of us girls were a bit in love with him.'[17] On one Pullman family holiday, they ate in a restaurant each day. Each evening, as they waited for their meals to arrive, Philip told his second son Tom, the story of *The Odyssey*. On the final evening Tom was so excited that he bit a chunk out of the glass he had been gripping, startling the poor waitress so much she dropped the food she was bringing to their table.

Teaching also gave Philip the chance to take his storytelling skills in a new direction – by writing plays for the pupils to perform. It was vital to him that they should entertain both children and parents; his ability to write for a wide audience is a large part of his appeal now. The first play was *Spring-Heeled Jack*, 'a sort of melodrama, with an outrageous villain and larger-than life heroes and comic policeman and that sort of thing'.[18] He was beginning to find his groove as a writer: 'I thought "I am really enjoying this! I like this way of telling a story. It's grotesque, absurd and not realistic, but it is really good fun!" . . . This was where my imagination was active instead of sullen and glum.'[19]

A little later Pullman realized that he could rework some of the plays into books – he was making his transition from being a writer of adult fiction to a children's writer, though he insists that he tells stories for everyone:

> My ideal . . . is the old notion of sitting in a
> marketplace, where all kinds of other
> transactions are going on around me. People
> are buying food and selling food, and somebody
> doing tricks over there in the corner, and the
> pickpocket over there, and there's a public
> hanging over in the corner, all sorts of stuff.
> And there I am on a bit of carpet with a hat in
> front of me, telling a story. And whoever wants
> to stop and listen is welcome to do so. I do not
> put up a sign saying 'this story is only for
> twelve-year-olds' or 'no children welcome here'
> or 'only women need be interested in this story'
> or anything like that. I don't want to exclude
> anyone, because as soon as you say 'this story is
> for such and such a group', what you're actually
> saying as well is 'this story is not for anybody

else'. I don't want to do that. I would like to tell
the sort of story which brings children from play
and old men from the chimney corners, as
somebody used to say. I'd like to tell a story
which is entertaining and interesting, in
necessarily different ways, but nevertheless to all
kinds of people and all different age groups.[20]

Brought to book

The first play to become a book was *Count Karlstein
or the Ride of the Demon Huntsman* (1982). It was
followed by *The Ruby in the Smoke* (1985)[21] – a
reworking for older readers of a play called *The Curse
of the Indian Rubies*. It was with this book that he 'first
found the voice that I now tell stories in',[22] and he
enjoyed the characters so much it became the first of
the Sally Lockhart Quartet.[23] His first play, *Spring-
Heeled Jack*, was published four years later in 1989,
and by that time a second story about Sally Lockhart
had been published – *The Shadow in the North*
(1986).

Pullman has a deep fascination with the nineteenth
century as these books show. He jumped at the opportunity of a part-time lectureship at Westminster
College, Oxford where he taught a course on Victorian
novels. He is particularly drawn to the Victorian East
End of London. It was a seedy area, which Pullman
brings vividly to life – and you can't help feeling that he
enjoys himself enormously as he does so. It forms the
background for the Sally Lockhart stories, *Spring-
Heeled Jack*, the two *New Cut Gang* books[24] and *I
Was A Rat . . . or The Scarlet Slippers* (1999).
'Wapping and Limehouse and so on are attractive

because of their long-standing associations with crime, foreign sailors, sinister opium dens, etc.'[25] The ominous-sounding (but apparently invented) location of Hangman's Wharf in Wapping appears in at least three unrelated books[26] because it nicely captures the combination of crime and commerce.

However, Philip's love of the nineteenth century is not confined to London's more violent neighbourhoods. He is also drawn to German Romanticism, and this combines with both his love of folk tales and his enthusiasm for stories with pictures (two other courses he taught at Westminster) in *Count Karlstein* and *Clockwork or All Wound Up* (1996).[27] He refers to both of these as 'fairy tales', though they are darker than the three classic fairy tales that he has retold for a new generation (*Aladdin and the Enchanted Lamp* (1995), *Mossycoat* (1998) and *Puss in Boots* (2001)). Pullman believes fairy tales (and myths) are vital because of what, and how, they teach us:

> . . . fairy tales . . . are ways of telling us true
> things without labouring the point. They begin in
> delight, and they end in wisdom. But if you start
> with what you think is wisdom, you'll seldom
> end up with delight – it doesn't work that way
> round. You have to begin with fun.[28]

Pullman considers *Clockwork* to be the best of his short books.[29] The inspiration came from an old clock in London's Science Museum:

> I thought it would be fun to try and write a story
> in which one part turning this way connected to
> another part and made it turn that way, like the
> cogwheels of a clock. And when it was all fitted
> closely together, I could wind it up and set it

> going . . . Of course, it had to be spooky too,
> because old clocks are, somehow.

The tale features a writer who abandons telling his story part way through, and an apprentice clockmaker who has been too lazy to produce the traditional final work of the apprenticeship – a new mechanical figure for the town clock. The writer's story and the reality of the apprentice's situation interlock in a very clever and creepy way. Pullman draws parallels between clocks and stories to talk about the business of storytelling,[30] and about 'the inexorable nature of responsibility'.[31] *Clockwork* touches on talent and luck as helping towards success, but stresses the effort involved:

> Here's the truth: if you want something, you *can*
> have it, but only if you want everything that goes
> with it, including all the hard work and the
> despair, and only if you're willing to risk
> failure.[32]

Another of his fairy tales, *The Firework-maker's Daughter* (1995), winner of the 1996 Smarties Book Prize Gold Award, also addresses these themes.[33] Like *Count Karlstein*, it started as a play.[34] Pullman always wanted to incorporate new theatrical tricks into his school plays, and one year decided he wanted fireworks (he's very enthusiastic about fireworks – in 2002 he had his stepfather's ashes scattered by launching them in forty rockets). Inspired by some stage designs he had seen in a library for a play called *The Elephant of Siam, or The Fire-Fiend* by nineteenth-century dramatist William Moncrieff, Philip constructed a story which gave him 'bright lights and blazing rockets and loud bangs . . . gamelan music! Gongs and xylophones and lots of dancing – and masks – and an elephant!'[35] Later he revised the story and turned it into a book, and in doing so 'realised the real meaning of the story . . . I realised I was telling a story about the making of art.'[36] The Firework-maker says, 'You need talent and dedication and the favour of the gods before you can become a Firework-maker.'[37]

Tell them stories

It is clear that Philip's passion for stories is not merely *why* he writes, but is also one of the key strands of *what* he writes. Like *Clockwork, I was a Rat . . . or The Scarlet Slippers*[38] is a story *about* stories, spinning off from the story of *Cinderella* and satirizing the media's sensationalist storytelling. *Spring-Heeled Jack*, the two *New Cut Gang* books, and the Sally Lockhart quartet are all inspired by the stories in Victorian 'penny dreadfuls'. They also feature *in* the Sally Lockhart books – one of the central characters, Jim Taylor,[39] is a great fan of them. *The Ruby in the Smoke* is the story of Sally Lockhart trying to piece together the story of her father's death, but in the process discovering shocking new stories about her own life. *The Shadow in the North* contrasts 'spin' (public stories) with the real, behind-the-scenes stories of arms production and poverty. *The Tiger in the Well* sees Sally apparently defenceless against a maliciously untrue story, which results in her daughter being taken from her. *The Tiger in the Well* also has much to say about the political stories told about refugees, and one of the major characters, Daniel Goldberg, is a Jewish journalist. *The Tin Princess* revolves around the secret untold stories and the official cover-ups of a small central European principality.

Pullman's two books of teen fiction set in the contemporary world are also largely about stories. The plot of *The Butterfly Tattoo*[40] turns on the stories that the key characters tell each other – as well as the stories they don't. And the way that stories shape our lives is explored with great pathos in *The Broken Bridge*.[41] The central character, Ginny, has to re-examine her sense of who she is as a result of discovering that some of the stories of her early life are untrue. The stories that other people relate affect her deeply, and she fashions a story of her own to try to make sense of all she is discovering. But it is Pullman's most ambitious work, *His Dark Materials*,[42] which explores the importance of stories and storytelling most fully. Lyra is herself a consummate storyteller, and it is something very close to her heart. As she tells a story in the suburbs of the world of the dead, 'part of her felt a little stream of pleasure rising upwards in her breast like the bubbles in champagne' (*AS*, p.276). Whether or not Pullman feels this sensation, he relishes stories and storytelling. And he understands how vital they are to us. One of the messages of *The Amber Spyglass* is that we should live so that we have true and exciting stories to tell at life's end.

Pullman says, 'Stories are the most important thing in the world. Without stories, we wouldn't be human beings at all.'[43] Stories are how we construct our internal models of the world around us, whether they be creation myths[44] or scientific theories. Stories are how we make sense of who we are as people. Stories help us work out how to live:

All stories teach, whether the storyteller intends them to or not. They teach the world we create.

They teach the morality we live by. They teach it much more effectively than moral precepts and instructions . . . We don't need lists of rights and wrongs, tables of do's and don'ts: we need books, time, and silence. 'Thou shalt not' is soon forgotten, but 'Once upon a time' lasts forever.[45]

[1] Fried, Kerry, 'Darkness Visible: An Interview with Philip Pullman' (www.amazon.com/exec/obidos/tg/feature/-/94589/103-2179560-1236619).

[2] Pullman, Philip, 'Let's Write it in Red: The Patrick Hardy Lecture', *Signal 85*, January 1998, p.44–62.

[3] Pullman, Philip, 'Carnegie Medal acceptance speech' (www.randomhouse.com/features/pullman/philippullman/speech.html).

[4] Pullman, Philip, 'An introduction to . . , Philip Pullman' in James Carter (ed.) *Talking Books, Children's authors talk about the craft, creativity and process of writing* (Routledge, 1999), p.185.

[5] Pullman, Philip, 'I have a feeling all this belongs to me' (www.philip-pullman.com/pages/content/index.asp?PageID=84).

[6] Pullman, Philip, interview on Kidsreads.com, 12 December 2001 (www.kidsreads.com/authors/au-pullman-philip.asp).

[7] Pullman, 'I have a feeling all this belongs to me'.

[8] Pullman, 'I have a feeling all this belongs to me'.

[9] Pullman, 'I have a feeling all this belongs to me'.

[10] Pullman, in James Carter (ed.) *Talking Books*, p.182.

[11] Squires, Claire, *Philip Pullman's His Dark Materials Trilogy: A reader's guide* (Continuum, 2003), p.13.

[12] Mitchison, Amanda, 'The art of darkness', *Daily Telegraph*, 3 November 2003.

[13] Squires, *Philip Pullman's His Dark Materials Trilogy: A reader's guide*, p.13.

[14] Having been out of teaching for some years, Pullman says, 'I have maintained a passionate interest in education, which leads me occasionally to make foolish and ill-considered remarks alleging that not everything is well in our schools. My main concern is that an over-emphasis on testing and league tables has led to a lack of time and freedom for a true, imaginative and humane engagement with literature' (www.philip-pullman.com/about_the_author.asp). This strangling of the enjoyment of literature would stop him from considering teaching as a career if he was starting all

over again. He writes: 'I would sooner go out in the wind and rain and dig trenches with my bare hands than go into English teaching now! It's under the control of bureaucrats who are determined to impose a peculiar, depressing view of English on the nation. The words they use to describe it are "reinforce, apply, identify, record, categorise . . ." with no mention of "enjoyment". I had a lot of fun with a teacher recently who was reading one of my books with her class. She complained that she couldn't stop them jumping ahead to find out what was happening next. I thought this was fantastic, but she was dismayed because it wasn't on the tick-list of what they had to do!' (doctorjob.com/features/template. asp?ID=365).

[15] Pullman, 'Let's Write it in Red: The Patrick Hardy Lecture'.

[16] Pullman, in James Carter (ed.) *Talking Books*, p.182–183.

[17] Mitchison, 'The art of darkness'.

[18] Mitchison, 'The art of darkness'.

[19] Mitchison, 'The art of darkness'.

[20] Brown, Charles N., 'An interview with Philip Pullman' (www.avnet.co.uk/amaranth/Critic/ivpullman.htm).

[21] See Watkins, Tony, 'A study guide for The Ruby in the Smoke' (www.damaris.org/content/content.php?type=1&id=197).

[22] Pullman, in James Carter (ed.) *Talking Books*, p.182.

[23] *The Ruby in the Smoke* (Oxford University Press, 1986), *The Shadow in the North* (as *The Shadow in the Plate*, Oxford University Press, 1986), *The Tiger in the Well* (Penguin, 1991), and *The Tin Princess* (Penguin, 1994).

[24] *The New Cut Gang: Thunderbolt's Waxwork* (Viking, 1994) and *The New Cut Gang: The Gas Fitters' Ball* (Viking, 1995). Note that these are set in Lambeth rather than the East End – the atmosphere feels much less dangerous.

[25] Pullman, Philip, personal email to the author, May 2004.

[26] Most prominently, Hangman's Wharf is the location of the ghastly Mrs Holland's lodging house in *The Ruby in the Smoke*, but it is also mentioned in *Spring-Heeled Jack*. It returns much later in *Northern Lights* where it has moved from Wapping to Limehouse (*NL*, p.43).

[27] In *Clockwork* (illustrated by Peter Bailey), the pictures are used as a 'counterpoint' to the text – adding to the appreciation of the story without being quite part of it. In *Count Karlstein* (illustrated by Patrice Aggs), the pictures are mostly used to tell parts of the story in place of the text.

[28] Pullman, Philip, 'The Firework-maker's Daughter, and how she became a play, and then a book, and then another play' (www.sheffieldtheatres.co.uk/education/productions/fireworkmaker/pullman.shtml).

[29] *Clockwork* was the Smarties Book Prize Silver Award winner in 1997, and was also turned into an opera by composer Stephen McNeff and librettist David Wood for the Unicorn Theatre at the Royal Opera House, London. For more information on the making of this production, see info.royaloperahouse.org/ROHtoo/Index.cfm?ccs=553&cs=1322.

[30] See Watkins, Tony, 'Stories run like clockwork' (www.damaris.org/content/content.php?type=5&id=351).

[31] Pullman, 'Let's Write it in Red: The Patrick Hardy Lecture'.

[32] Pullman, Philip, *Clockwork or All Wound Up* (Corgi Yearling, 1997), p.36.

[00] See Watkins, Tony, 'Firework-makers and fairy tales' (www.damaris.org/content/content.php?type=5&id=346).

[34] *The Firework-maker's Daughter* became a play again at Sheffield's Crucible Theatre (adapted by Stephen Russell and directed by Paul Hunter and Hayley Carmichael) in March 2003, and Anthony Minghella is producing a film version.

[35] Pullman, 'The Firework-maker's Daughter, and how she became a play, and then a book, and then another play'.

[36] Pullman, 'The Firework-maker's Daughter, and how she became a play, and then a book, and then another play'.

[37] Pullman, Philip, *The Firework-maker's Daughter* (Corgi Yearling, 1996), p.10.

[38] *I Was a Rat* was televised by the BBC in 2001, and in spring 2004 was turned into a stage play by Oxford Youth Theatre.

[39] Jim seems to have been named after Pullman's friend in Exeter College who discovered the 'gutter crawl' (see page 34).

[40] See Watkins, Tony, 'A study guide for The Butterfly Tattoo' (www.damaris.org/content/content.php?type=1&id=183).

[41] See Watkins, Tony, 'A study guide for The Broken Bridge' (www.damaris.org/content/content.php?type=1&id=186).

[42] See Tilley, Steve, 'A study guide for His Dark Materials' (www.damaris.org/content/content.php?type=1&id=142); Watkins, Tony, 'A study guide for Northern Lights' (www.damaris.org/content/content.php?type=1&id=198), 'A study guide for The Subtle Knife' (www.damaris.org/content/content.php?type=1&id=199), and 'A study guide for The Amber Spyglass' (www.damaris.org/content/content.php?type=1&id=200).

[43] Pullman, Philip, 'About the author' (www.randomhouse.com/features/pullman/philippullman/index.html).

[44] 'Myth' is used here in its technical sense of a story that explains origins – whether or not the story is true is not relevant to its designation as a myth in this sense.

[45] Pullman, Philip, 'Carnegie Medal Acceptance Speech'.

CHAPTER 4

His Raw Materials

Philip Pullman's approach to writing is to 'read like a butterfly, write like a bee'.[1] He draws on many influences both consciously and unconsciously since all kinds of images and ideas lodge in a writer's mind to resurface years later. He gathers source material from all kinds of places, ranging from ancient esoteric beliefs to popular science; from Greek mythology to *Neighbours*.

The esoteric beliefs have strongly influenced Pullman's portrayal of God and the angels. These are mainly Gnostic ideas (some shared with the Jewish Kabbalah), especially as they have come to us through the western esoteric tradition.[2] In contrast, the science is right up to date – dark matter, many worlds, the problem of consciousness, superstring theory, quantum entanglement, and more[3] – forming an important part of the background throughout *His Dark Materials*. Greek myths show up particularly in the world of the dead with the boatman[4] and the harpies.[5] It's impossible to identify any specific *Neighbours* influences but Philip says:

> After lunch I always watch *Neighbours*. Soap operas are interesting because there's no limit to the length a story can have – it can go on for months, if it's got some life in it . . . it's fascinating to watch some characters gaining story-potency as others lose it, and to try and work out why it's happening . . . It's all pure story: one thing following another.[6]

There are rather more sophisticated influences on *His Dark Materials* including: the metaphysical poets (especially George Herbert and Andrew Marvell), Plato,[7] Augustine,[8] Dante,[9] Keats,[10] Byron,[11] Wagner,[12] Emily Dickinson,[13] and plenty more. There are hints of voodoo (*zombis*, Spectres and spy-flies) and many biblical ideas, the most significant being the Fall – the first rebellion of humanity against God. Pullman does not believe the Bible, but he values its language and stories nevertheless.[14] The exit from the world of the dead echoes Christ's Harrowing of Hell – a traditional Christian idea of Jesus descending to Hades after his crucifixion in order to proclaim redemption to the dead and to lead out the faithful to eternal life.[15] Pullman, however, inverts this by portraying 'the faithful' as so deluded that they would rather stay in the world of the dead (*AS*, p.336).

However, there are three key influences on much of Pullman's work which he draws attention to in the acknowledgements at the end of *The Amber Spyglass*: Heinrich von Kleist's essay, *On the Marionette Theatre*, John Milton's *Paradise Lost*, and the works of William Blake.

John Milton (1608–1674): *Paradise Lost*

Pullman was sixteen, studying for A-Levels, when he first read *Paradise Lost*.[16] He immediately fell in love with it:

> I found it intensely enthralling, not only the actual story . . . but also the landscapes, the power of the poetry and the extraordinary majesty of the language.[17]

Paradise Lost is a landmark in the development of

English literature. No one had written this kind of epic poem in English before. It's a huge poem written by a blind man as he witnessed the failure of a dream – Milton had supported Cromwell's Protectorate, and passionately opposed the restoration of the monarchy. In that context, Milton wanted to remind people of why the world was in the state it was: life is a mess because it's a fallen world, and it's fallen because there is an enemy both of God and of humanity. Milton retells the story of the first three chapters of Genesis, focusing particularly on the actions of Satan in rebelling against God and instigating the Fall of Adam and Eve. It opens in hell where Satan, once a great angel named Lucifer, and his rebel army are licking their wounds after their rebellion was defeated. They decide that their best strategy is to take revenge by sabotaging the new world that God has created. Satan finds his way to the Garden of Eden – Paradise – and spies on Adam and Eve. He becomes jealous and decides to corrupt them. Having failed to get into the garden once, he enters a snake so that he can gain access undetected by the angel guards. Once inside, he tempts Eve to eat the one fruit which is off-limits to them. Adam follows suit and they immediately become aware and ashamed of their nakedness. Sin and Death, Satan's children, learn of his success so they build a bridge from hell to earth. Now under God's judgement, Adam and Eve are banished from the garden. The archangel Michael explains to them the consequences of their sin for the world, and also the reality of a coming saviour who will rectify the relationship between God and his people. Angels guard the entrance to prevent Adam's and Eve's return.

First disobedience

These themes of rebellion and fall are of enormous importance to Pullman. Given his love of *Paradise Lost* from his teenage years, it is no surprise that he eventually wanted to work it into a story. Dark matter was going to be a major part of his trilogy, so when he was scanning *Paradise Lost* for a phrase that would make a good title, 'His dark materials'[18] leapt out at him. Milton's story of the angelic rebellion against God is the most important element in the backstory of *His Dark Materials*. Lord Asriel is explicitly attempting to conclude what he sees as unfinished business. The trilogy never addresses the question of what has happened to the character of Satan. Pullman's alternative 'creation myth'[19] casts the Sophia – Wisdom – as the instigator of the initial rebellion. This seems to be because Pullman has taken Milton's story and mixed it with the Gnostic ideas of Sophia. In any event, Satan's role is shared by both Lord Asriel and Mary Malone.

Asriel plays the Satanic role of rebel leader, though this time the rebels are not just angels. King Ogunwe says:

> This is the last rebellion. Never before have
> humans, and angels and beings from all the
> worlds, made a common cause. This is the
> greatest force ever assembled. (*AS*, p.222)

However, we don't learn any of this until early in *The Subtle Knife*. Perhaps because of this, Milton's influence on the latter two volumes seems more obvious than it does on *Northern Lights*. We begin *The Amber Spyglass* knowing that the great conflict is drawing near. When the storm does break, the focus is so much on the characters we have been following that the great battle is little more than a rather blurred background. We hear nothing more from the battle once Will and Lyra have escaped into the peace of another world.

Mary Malone, meanwhile, plays Satan's other role of tempter, in the gentle world of the mulefa. In a clever twist, Pullman has another character sneak into the world in an attempt to sabotage the second Fall which is about to happen. Since Pullman unequivocally sees this second Fall as the *right* thing, the ghastly Father Gomez is perhaps more analogous to Satan's sabotaging of Paradise than Mary Malone is. Pullman has turned upside down Milton's sense of who the good guys are.

Satanic reverses

In interviews, Pullman loves to quote William Blake's comment on Milton:

> The reason Milton wrote in fetters when he wrote of angels and God, and at liberty when of devils and hell, is because he was a true poet and of the devil's party without knowing it.[20]

Blake felt that Milton's description of Satan in *Paradise Lost* was much more sympathetic than his description of God, though unwittingly so. Shelley and Byron later took up this idea themselves, as has Pullman who enjoys adding that, 'I am of the Devil's party and I know it.'[21] The problem is that this reading of Milton focuses too strongly on the first four (of twelve) books of *Paradise Lost* (Pullman in fact only read Books I and II when he first encountered it and formed his basic opinions). The other eight books (especially Books V to VIII) significantly reverse the picture. Satan is portrayed in heroic terms – in Books I to IV he boasts about his part in the battle against the forces led by Michael, claiming to have almost defeated them. But in Books V and VI, we discover that he hadn't even come close to this – Milton is deliberately undercutting the heroic ideals. During the battle, an angel, Abdiel (like Balthamos, he is 'not of a high order among angels' – *AS*, p.12) confronts the vastly more powerful Satan and strikes a blow which makes Satan stagger back ten paces. The rebel angels are amazed and furious 'to see / Thus foil'd thir mightiest'[22] by a humble foot soldier. Later, Satan meets Michael in combat. Michael's sword, 'temperd so, that neither keen / Nor solid might resist that edge' (the inspiration for the subtle knife?) slices right through Satan and wounds him deeply – his first experience of intense pain. Rebel angels rush to his defence and carry him back to his chariot where, Milton tells us:

> there they him laid
> Gnashing for anguish and despite and shame
> To find himself not matchless, and his pride
> Humbl'd by such rebuke, so far beneath
> His confidence to equal God in power.[23]

C. S. Lewis[24] says that Satan undergoes 'progressive degradation' during *Paradise Lost*:

> He begins by fighting for 'liberty', however misconceived; but almost at once sinks to fighting for 'Honour, Dominion, glorie and renoune' (VI, 422). Defeated in this, he sinks to . . . ruining two creatures who had never done him any harm, no longer in the serious hope of victory, but only to annoy the Enemy whom he cannot directly attack . . . This brings him as a spy into the universe, and soon not even a political spy, but a mere Peeping Tom leering

and writhing in prurience as he overlooks the
privacy of the lovers, and there described . . .
simply as 'the Devil' (IV, 502) – the salacious
grotesque, half bogey and half buffoon, of
popular tradition. From hero to general, from
general to politician, from politician to secret
service agent, and thence to a thing that peers in
at bedroom or bathroom windows, and thence to
a toad, and finally to a snake – such is the
progress of Satan.[25]

Given Milton's Christian faith, it seems much more likely that Milton initially *wanted* his readers to sympathize
with Satan so that they see the attractiveness of rebellion against God, and how willingly we are led down
that route, *so that* we see more clearly God's mercy
to us.[26]

William Blake (1757–1827)

However, Blake's influence on Pullman goes much
deeper than these views on Milton. The extent of his
influence can perhaps be gauged from the fact that nine
of *The Amber Spyglass* epigraphs (the brief quotations
at the start of each chapter) come from Blake, and the
American edition, curiously, has a longer quotation
from Blake's *America: A Prophecy* in place of the
hymn lines from Robert Grant. Pullman says:

I love Blake in the way I love all great poetry –
because of the sound it makes, and because of
the meanings that follow the sound. I love the
Songs of Innocence and Experience, and
The Marriage of Heaven and Hell, and some
passages from the Prophetic Books.[27]

Songs of Innocence and Experience is probably

Blake's most accessible work. The move from innocence to experience is central in *His Dark Materials*, but it is important to realize that Pullman doesn't mean quite the same thing by the words. Blake's world of *Innocence* is pleasant, sunny, pastoral – it's safe. *Experience*, however, is dark, wild or urban, and hostile. The landscapes of *Northern Lights* fit more naturally with Blake's world of *Experience* than with *Innocence* (it's an adventure story so there has to be danger after all). There are several night-time scenes: the retiring room, Lyra being secretly summoned to the Master's study, escaping from Mrs Coulter, finding Tony Makarios and the escape from Bolvangar. Other landscapes echo *Experience* in their wildness – from the remote fens[28] of East Anglia, through the dark forests of the north, to the wildness of Svalbard. In contrast, the landscape of the mulefa in *The Amber Spyglass* feels distinctly pastoral – it's a gentle, safe world (barring occasional tualapi attacks), which seems to echo the world of *Innocence*.

But for Blake, it's not so much the settings themselves which show the difference between *Innocence* and *Experience* – it's how things are *perceived*. In 'Little Girl Lost' and 'Little Girl Found',[29] for example, the lost girl Lyca and her parents respond to wild animals in opposite ways. She sleeps contentedly while the lion 'gambolled round', whereas her parents are terrified until they come to see the lion with fresh vision. It's perhaps comparable to the ways in which Lyra and the gyptian leaders initially view Iorek Byrnison. Lyra is completely trusting of him, whereas John Faa and even Farder Coram are inclined to believe the story that 'he's a dangerous rogue' (*NL*, p.189). Similarly, when the alethiometer tells Lyra that Will 'is a murderer' (*SK*, p.29) – which would put most people off – Lyra's perception is that *therefore* she can trust him. And when Lyra realizes that her enemies perceive Dust as bad, she concludes that *therefore* it 'must be good' (*NL*, p.397). Perception is also important in, among other things, Lyra's reading of the alethiometer, Will's use of the knife, and Mary's seeing of her dæmon in which she has to maintain a special state of mind combined with 'ordinary seeing at the same time' (*AS*, p.535) – a double vision which Blake strongly believed in.

Violent authority

Which brings us to another key difference: in *Innocence*, authority is protective; in *Experience*, it is cruel and repressive. Although Blake's passionate sense of solidarity with the oppressed leads him to attack several targets (not least commercial interests and the State), it is the Church that bears the brunt of his stinging criticism. Blake portrays it as authoritarian and hypocritical, and he has a deep antipathy to God (at least as Blake sees him expressed in the Old Testament). Like Milton, he focuses especially on the Fall. He often highlights God's punishment of Adam and Eve, not their rebellion, and seems to put the blame for the rift between God and humanity firmly on God. Blake's poem 'Earth's Answer'[30] portrays God as the 'selfish father of men' characterized by 'cruel jealous selfish fear', who makes life on earth 'dread and drear'. It sees his punishment of Adam and Eve as an 'eternal bane' which puts 'free love' into bondage. 'A Poison Tree'[31] goes further to suggest that God was secretly hostile to humanity, and deliberately set a trap into which Adam and Eve would inevitably walk so that he could blame and punish them.

In his 'Prophetic Books',[32] Blake developed an alternative creation myth in which he presented God as vicious tyrant. It may well be that the breadth and complexity of this radical perspective lodged in Pullman's mind, later resulting in him developing an alternative myth of his own. In these books, Blake has two key characters, Urizen (who represents God) and Orc: 'On the one side stands Urizen, a violent, destructive tyrant; on the other side Orc, a violent, destructive rebel.'[33] They could very easily be the Authority and Lord Asriel. Pullman says:

> I certainly wouldn't model any of my characters on any of [Blake's], or on anyone else's for that matter. It would be too limiting. In Blake's own words, 'I must create my own system, or be enslaved by another man's'.[34]

Tyranny and freedom

However, while he may not have modelled his characters on Blake's, nevertheless his perspective closely matches Blake's, and he is open about Blake's influence on him. The parallel between Asriel and Orc extends to the deep ambiguity of character that some people have been surprised at in Lord Asriel. Pullman clearly sees Asriel as on the 'right side' – working to establish the republic of heaven by overthrowing the Authority and his kingdom. Yet at the same time he is just as cold and ruthless as the agents of the Authority – he is prepared to go to any lengths to achieve his goal, including sacrificing Roger. Like the Authority he opposes, Lord Asriel *is* violent and destructive and arrogant. Like Orc, he also carries within him the seed of tyranny which would have expressed itself had he survived the great battle. He has the makings of a megalomaniac when he claims to Mrs Coulter that 'You and I could take the universe to pieces and put it together again' (*NL*, p.396). And Thorold doesn't exactly present him as egalitarian in response to Serafina Pekkala's question about Lord Asriel's intentions:

> You don't think he told me, do you? . . . I'm his
> manservant, that's all . . . He wouldn't confide in
> me any more than in his shaving mug. (*SK*, p.46)

Blake attacks the church for its complicity in tolerating injustice – in 'The Chimney Sweeper',[35] for example, in which a child sweep complains that 'God and His priest . . . make up a heaven of our misery.' In other words, the Church promises heaven to us if we put up with misery now. 'The Garden of Love'[36] focuses on the loss of innocence at the hands of the Church:

> I went to the Garden of Love.
> And saw what I never had seen;
> A Chapel was built in the midst,
> Where I used to play on the green.

It starts with the 'innocent, uninhibited discovery of sexuality between children. However, the speaker is now aware of Church law, and sex is surrounded by bans, punishment and statutes which are enforced by a watchful priesthood.'[37] Now the garden 'that so many sweet flowers bore' has at its centre a closed chapel with 'Thou shalt not' written over the door. The rest of the garden is full of graves . . .

> And priests in black gowns were walking their
>   rounds,
> And binding with briars my joys and desires.

The feeling of joyless, authoritarian lifelessness is unmistakable. The Church's repressive attitude to sexuality is something with which Blake takes particular issue. In response, in *The Marriage of Heaven and Hell*, Blake orders 'the cherub with his flaming sword[38] . . . to leave his guard at [the] tree of life'.[39] He wants to return us to the state of affairs before the Fall – a state of sexual freedom which 'will come to pass by an improvement of sensual enjoyment'. Other poems ('The Blossom' and 'The Sick Rose', for example) make the same point that natural sexuality, free from prudery and religious constraints, is something to be desired.

The echoes of Blake are easily discernible within Pullman's work. Like Blake, Pullman attacks what he sees as a repressive and cruel Church,[40] which feeds people a lie about heaven in order to keep them quiet. He rails against a vicious God who imposes arbitrary and unnatural restrictions on humanity – and especially on our sexuality. It's no accident that Will and Lyra finally express their love for each other in a world where there is no Church, and after the death of the Authority.

Heinrich von Kleist (1777–1811): *On the Marionette Theatre*

Heinrich von Kleist was born in Frankfurt into a family of Prussian soldiers. He dutifully joined the army but left after five years to study science, philosophy and literature. Kleist's confidence in reason was shattered when he discovered the writing of Immanuel Kant, who maintained that human reason cannot discover the true nature of things – we can only rely on appearances. Kleist wrote plays (mostly tragedies) and short stories, but found little recognition. A business failure ruined him, and, with no one producing his plays and the army refusing to take him back, he committed suicide.[41]

A year previously, in 1810, Kleist published his essay *On the Marionette Theatre*.[42] It is a conversation about grace,[43] self-consciousness and the Fall. The narrator of the story[44] meets a friend who is a dancer, and expresses surprise at the dancer's interest in the marionette theatre, calling it a 'vulgar species of an art form'.[45] But the dancer asserts that puppets are more graceful than human dancers. Their advantage, he says, is that the arms and legs are lifeless pendulums, which simply follow the movement of the puppet's centre of gravity – they can therefore never be guilty of affectation. A human, however, is so self-conscious that it's impossible to do anything without some measure of artificiality. The narrator recalls a very graceful teenage boy he had known. The boy had noticed a similarity between his posture and a certain statue, but when the narrator laughed at this he became self-conscious for the first time and soon all his grace was gone. But still the narrator protests that a puppet could never be more graceful than a person.

> [The dancer] countered this by saying that, where grace is concerned, it is impossible for man to come anywhere near a puppet. Only a god can equal inanimate matter in this respect.[46]

To make his point about the benefits of lacking self-consciousness, the dancer recalls a time when he beat a friend in a fencing match. The friend challenged him to try fencing with a bear that was being reared on the friend's farm. The bear was an extraordinary opponent:

> It wasn't merely that he parried my thrusts like

the finest fencer in the world; when I feinted to deceive him he made no move at all. No human fencer could equal his perception in this respect. He stood upright, his paw raised ready for battle, his eye fixed on mine as if he could read my soul there, and when my thrusts were not meant seriously he did not move.[47]

From this the dancer makes the point that 'as thought grows dimmer and weaker, grace emerges more brilliantly and decisively'.[48] The bear is more 'graceful' because it has no self-consciousness. The less self-consciousness there is, the more gracefulness there can be: 'Grace appears most purely in that human form which either has no consciousness or an infinite consciousness. That is, in the puppet or in the god.' This was Pullman's inspiration for Iorek's demonstration that bears cannot be tricked (*NL*, p.226–227). Iorek, of course, is not just any old bear – he is fully conscious, but perhaps (since he has no soul) he is not self-conscious like a human would be.

The dancer says that this problem of self-consciousness is unavoidable 'now that we've eaten of the tree of knowledge.[49] But Paradise is locked and bolted, and the cherubim stands behind us. We have to go on and make the journey round the world to see if it is perhaps open somewhere at the back.'[50] In other words, now that we have partial knowledge and self-consciousness, there is no way back; all we can do is continue pursuing knowledge until it is total. Blake has the same idea when he says, 'If the fool would persist in his folly he would become wise.'[51] 'Only a god can equal inanimate matter,' says the dancer, because 'this is the point where the two ends of the circular world meet.' The narrator asks if this means 'that we must eat again of the tree of knowledge in order to return to the state of innocence?' 'Of course,' replies the dancer, 'but that's the final chapter in the history of the world.'[52]

Full circle

The incompatibility of grace and self-consciousness appears again at the end of the trilogy, after Lyra has become the second Eve and brought about a second Fall. Lyra has reached a new level of consciousness about herself – and her skill with the alethiometer deserts her. Xaphania tells Lyra that she has read it by grace; now she must learn all over again through hard work:

> But your reading will be even better then after a lifetime of thought and effort, because it will come from conscious understanding. Grace attained like that is deeper and fuller than grace that comes freely, and, furthermore, once you've gained it, it will never leave you. (*AS*, p.520)

Here Pullman seems to mix up the way Kleist uses the word grace (talking of a natural ease of doing something) with its theological sense of the undeserved kindness of God. Reading the alethiometer *by grace* sounds theological – and in a sense it is, though Dust, rather than God, has given Lyra her ability. But grace in this sense cannot be earned or worked at; grace in Kleist's sense can be, and he relates this to the Fall. Pullman says:

> Grace is a mysterious quality which is inexplicable in its appearance and disappearance. It's disappearance in Lyra's case symbolises the loss of innocence but the fact

that she can regain it through work and study symbolises the fact that only when we lose our innocence, can we take our first steps towards gaining wisdom.[53]

In other words, having lost her innocence[54] she has lost her grace. When Lyra returns to Oxford the Master recognizes that her 'unconscious grace had gone, and how she was awkward in her growing body' (*AS*, p.544). But by a lifetime of effort she can regain it in a new and better way – she can come back to paradise by the back door.

[1] Pullman, Philip, 'Acknowledgments' in *The Amber Spyglass*, p.549.

[2] One throwaway reference in this respect is to 'the house of the great magician Dr Dee' (*NL*, p.40). This is John Dee (1527–1608), physician to Queen Elizabeth I and alchemist. He was the founder of 'Enochian Magick' which, based on Gnostic sources, was all about talking to angels.

[3] See Appendix: The Science of *His Dark Materials*, for more on dark matter and many worlds. For more on other aspects of science within the trilogy, I recommend Mary and John Gribbin, *The Science of Philip Pullman's His Dark Materials* (Hodder, 2003).

[4] The boatman named Charon ferries the souls of the dead across the River Styx to Hades, the underworld.

[5] See Virgil's *Aeneid* Book III, for example.

[6] Pullman, Philip, author interview on Jubilee Books (www.jubileebooks. co.uk/jubilee/magazine/authors/philip_pullman/interview.asp).

[7] Mary Malone's 'Cave' takes its name from Plato.

[8] Mary Malone is thinking about Augustine's comments on angels (*SK*, p.260).

[9] The World of the Dead has echoes of the great plain of the vestibule of hell in Dante's *Inferno* (Canto III) where the inhabitants are tormented by hornets and gadflies. Perhaps there is deliberate irony in having the stinging Gallivespians riding dragonflies trying to torment the harpies. It's also interesting that the name *Gallivespian* may come from *vespa* meaning *wasp*. The common hornet is *vespa crabro*. Dante also features Charon the boatman, but the boat crossing comes after the great plain.

[10] When telling Lyra about the state of mind necessary for interacting with the 'Cave' (*SK*, p.92) Mary Malone quotes from a letter, which John Keats (1795–1821) wrote in 1871 (www.mrbauld.com/negcap.html). Lyra calls this state of mind 'negative capability' (*AS*, p.484), a phrase borrowed

from Keats' letter although Mary Malone never uses the phrase. Keats' poem 'Ode to a Nightingale' is also quoted as the epigraph for Chapter Twenty Eight in *The Amber Spyglass* (p.390).

[11] The epigraph for Chapter Twenty One of *The Amber Spyglass* (p.291) quotes Lord Byron (1788–1824) in a letter he wrote from Venice in 1817. Byron's sentiments at this point underpin Pullman's approach to writing fiction. Byron says, 'But I hate things all fiction . . . There should always be some foundation of fact for the most airy fabric, and pure invention is but the talent of a liar' (engphil.astate.edu/gallery/byron7.html).

[12] The reforging of the subtle knife perhaps has echoes of Siegfried reforging Siegmund's sword, which had been broken by Wotan in Wagner's *Ring des Niebelungen*.

[13] The epigraphs for three of the chapters in *The Amber Spyglass* come from Emily Dickinson's poems: 'She lay as if at play' in Chapter Four (p.48); 'A shade upon the mind' in Chapter Nine (p.115); and 'I gained it so' in Chapter Twenty (p.284).

[14] Six of the epigraphs from *The Amber Spyglass* are drawn from the Authorised Version (1611) of the Bible: Job 4:15 in Chapter Two (p.11), Exodus 18:3 in Chapter Eight (p.97), 1 Kings 18:44 in Chapter Ten (p.126), Genesis 3:1 in Chapter Seventeen (p.233), John 8:32 in Chapter Twenty Three (p.321), and Ezekiel 16:44 in Chapter Twenty Four (p.339).

[15] The idea has its roots in the New Testament but it was developed and embellished in the apocryphal *Gospel of Nicodemus* (dating from the second or third century AD). For more on this see 'Harrowing of Hell' in *Catholic Encyclopedia* (www.newadvent.org/cathen/07143d.htm).

[16] There are some useful *Paradise Lost* resources on the Internet including www.paradiselost.org, which has the text of the poem, summaries, essays, and other material.

[17] Philip Pullman in an interview with Charles N. Brown at the Lexicon literary convention in Oxford, August 2000. An edited version appeared in 'Philip Pullman: Storming Heaven', *Locus*, vol. 45:6 no.479, December 2000. A longer version of the interview is available online at www.avnet.co.uk/amaranth/Critic/ivpullman.htm.

[18] It comes in Book II, line 916.

[19] The myth is never made explicit in *His Dark Materials*, but Pullman developed it and wrote it down as he went along. It has not been made public, although Pullman has divulged some parts of it in interviews. He intends to include it in *The Book of Dust*.

[20] Blake, William, *The Marriage of Heaven and Hell* in Yeats, W. B. (ed.) *William Blake Collected Poems* (Routledge, 2002), p.165.

[21] Vulliamy, Ed, 'Author puts Bible Belt to the test', *Observer*, 26 August 2001.

[22] Milton, John, *Paradise Lost*, Book VI, line 200.

[23] Milton, *Paradise Lost*, Book VI, lines 327–343.

[24] Philip Pullman says that 'Lewis is a contradictory sort of character for me. I loathe the Narnia books, and I loathe the so-called space trilogy, because

they contain an ugly vision. But when he was talking about writing for children, and about literature in general, Lewis was very, very acute and said some very perceptive and wise things. As a critic . . . I rate him very highly, but I do detest what he was doing in his fiction' (Spanner, Huw, 'Heat and Dust', *Third Way*, Vol. 25 No. 2, April 2002, p.22–26; www.thirdway.org.uk/past/showpage.asp?page=3949).

25 Lewis, C. S., *A Preface to Paradise Lost* (Oxford University Press, 1960), p.99.

26 See Jamie Jensen's 'Perceptions of Satan in Paradise Lost' for a fuller discussion of this (www.honors.sbc.edu/HJSpr03/Jensen2.htm).

27 Pullman, Philip, personal email to the author, 16 June 2004.

28 The 'lonely fen' is actually mentioned in 'Little Boy Found' in the *Songs of Innocence*, but since he is rescued *from* it, the setting seems to belong with *Experience*.

29 Blake, William, *Songs of Experience* in Yeats, W. B. (ed.) *William Blake Collected Poems* (Routledge, 2002), p.67–71.

30 Blake, *Songs of Experience*, p.65–66.

31 Blake, *Songs of Experience*, p.78.

32 Especially *The First Book of Urizen* (1794), *The Song of Los* (1795), *The Book of Ahania* (1795) and *The Book of Los* (1795).

33 Marsh, Nicholas, *William Blake: The Poems* (Palgrave, 2001), p.186.

34 Pullman, Philip, personal email to the author, 16 June 2004.

35 Blake, *Songs of Experience*, p.71.

36 Blake, *Songs of Experience*, p.75.

37 Marsh, *William Blake: The Poems*, p.123.

38 A reference to the angel who blocked a return to Eden for Adam and Eve in Genesis 3:24.

39 Blake, *The Marriage of Heaven and Hell*, p.170.

40 We will consider whether or not this is valid in Chapter 13.

41 He had made a suicide pact with a young married society woman, Henriette Vogel, who was suffering from cancer. They checked into a hotel and went out for a picnic; Kleist shot Henrietta before killing himself. Ironically, it was the ensuing scandal that finally brought his writing to prominence across Europe.

42 Idris Parry's 1981 translation of Heinrich von Kleist's *On the Marionette Theatre* can be found at the back of Nicholas Tucker, *Darkness Visible: Inside the world of Philip Pullman* (Wizard Books, 2003), p.197–207. It is also available online at www.southerncrossreview.org/9/kleist.htm.

43 Kleist uses the word 'grace' in relation to movement, rather than in its theological sense of God's kindness to people who don't deserve it.

44 Kleist tells the story in the first person but it is not clear whether or not this is an account of a real conversation.

45 Kleist, *On the Marionette Theatre*.

46 Kleist, *On the Marionette Theatre*.

47 Kleist, *On the Marionette Theatre*.

[48] Kleist, *On the Marionette Theatre*.

[49] Which armoured bears have never done because they have no soul.

[50] Kleist, *On the Marionette Theatre*.

[51] Blake, *The Marriage of Heaven and Hell*, p.166.

[52] Kleist, *On the Marionette Theatre*.

[53] Pullman, Philip, BBC webchat (www.bbc.co.uk/radio4/arts/hisdarkmaterials/pullman_webchat.shtml).

[54] Not necessarily sexually – see the discussion on this in Chapter 11.

PART TWO

The World(s) of *His Dark Materials*

CHAPTER 5

Northern Lights

The opening of *Northern Lights* is instantly gripping:

> Lyra and her dæmon moved through the
> darkening Hall, taking care to keep to one side,
> out of sight of the kitchen. (p.3)

So many questions clamour for attention within the very first sentence. Who's Lyra? What's a dæmon? Where is this Hall? Why is she so furtive? From the outset there's an air of mystery and adventure. And the mention of the dæmon is unsettling – does it mean 'demon'? Is it evil or good? Why is it '*her* dæmon'? This one sentence is enough to set the tone of the trilogy and give us the sense that Lyra's world is not like ours.

Lyra is 'a barbarian' (p.35), 'a coarse and greedy little savage', and like 'a half-wild cat' (p.37) who prefers adventuring on college roofs, disturbing tutorials, stealing apples and waging war to the more civilized aspects of life in an Oxford college. She's a typical child, living for the moment and full of curiosity. But Lyra is approaching puberty and *His Dark Materials* is, more than anything else, a story about growing up. It's about moving from innocence to experience, and taking responsibility for our actions and destinies. It's about becoming fully conscious and finding true knowledge.

Lyra the liar

Lyra's character, though not her name or any details, had been in Pullman's mind for years. As a child he read *A Hundred Million Francs* by Paul Berna, and was struck by a drawing of some of the characters – including a young girl:

> She was a tough-looking, very French sort of character, with a leather jacket and socks rolled down to her ankles and blonde hair and black eyes, and altogether I thought she was the girl for me. I wouldn't be at all surprised – in fact, now I think about it, it's obvious – to find that the girl on page 34 of *A Hundred Million Francs* is the girl who four decades later turned up in my own book *Northern Lights* . . . where she was called Lyra.[1]

Pullman says Lyra 'had her name from the very beginning. I don't know where it came from.'[2] But perhaps its subconscious origins are, at least partly, from Lyca, the subject of William Blake's poems, 'The Little Girl Lost' and 'The Little Girl Found'.[3] The similarity of sound between 'Lyra' and 'liar' becomes critical in one of the most important moments in Lyra's life in *The Amber Spyglass*. It's entirely appropriate because Lyra sees spinning tales as her greatest talent. She uses this skill to escape the ire of scholars and college servants, as well as to enthral the gang of kids with whom she fights townies, brickburners or gyptians. Her flair for lying becomes invaluable when she finds herself under the watchful eyes of Mrs Coulter and her golden monkey dæmon, then later at Bolvangar and on Svalbard. But once away from Oxford, Lyra seems to respond very positively to integrity when she perceives it in others. She feels that John Faa and Farder Coram must be told only the truth, and she quickly realizes that trying to deceive Iorek Byrnison is futile. It is ironic that Lyra the liar is the one entrusted with an instrument for finding the truth, the alethiometer. It is partly through her encounters with the consciousness behind this instrument that she eventually grows to value truth so highly.[4]

Lyra's moral engagement with the world seems to be complicated by her having a dæmon – though we come to realize that their relationship externalises the internal dialogues which we all experience. Pantalaimon functions in some ways like Lyra's conscience – that's certainly how he comes across at the beginning of the trilogy. But it's not that simple – Lyra has to challenge Pantalaimon's ethics when he advocates keeping their noses out of any attempt to poison Lord Asriel. She tells Pan that they have a duty to stay now they know what the Master intends to do, and asks him, 'You're supposed to know about conscience, aren't you?' (p 9) Without being explicitly told, we realize that Lyra and Pan are one, and yet distinct. They are two aspects of one person, one shared consciousness, knowing each other's thoughts and feelings, and yet in some ways they are two separate beings.[5] Pantalaimon has almost magical shape-shifting abilities[6] – one of many ways in which metamorphosis runs through the story. But hanging over Lyra and Pan is an impending reality that, like Peter Pan, they are not yet ready to face: the time is soon coming when Pan's form will become fixed and Lyra will no longer be a child.

Playing with worlds and words

Dæmons are the biggest difference between Lyra's world and our own, but there are many more and Pullman has plenty of fun with them. Her home is 'the grandest and richest of all the colleges in Oxford' (p.34). Pullman writes:

Jordan College occupies the same physical space in Lyra's Oxford . . . as Exeter College occupies in real life, though rather more of it. I didn't see why I shouldn't make my college the biggest of them all. Jordan . . . has developed in a haphazard, piecemeal way, and for all its wealth, some part of it is always about to fall down, and is consequently covered in scaffolding; it has an air of jumbled and squalid grandeur.[7]

The name Jordan was prompted by an area of our Oxford called Jericho, past which flows the Oxford Canal. Pullman says that although real-life Jericho is 'thoroughly respectable', it 'has always struck me as having a hidden character, more raffish and jaunty altogether, with an air of horse-trading, minor crime, and a sort of fairground Bohemianism. That is the Jericho I describe in the story.'[8] The gyptians who ply the canal and hold fairs at Jericho get their name from *Egyptian* because gypsies (in our world) were first believed to have come from Egypt. Pullman plays a number of similar games with words. For example, Lyra is fond of drinking *chocolatl* – many dictionaries will tell you that this is how the Aztecs pronounced their word for the drink made of cacao beans[9]; synthetic materials (derived from fossil fuel products) are referred to as coal silk; the underground in London is called the *chthonic* railway – chthonic means 'relating to the underworld'. A more involved example is *anbaric* lighting (the main power source being *atomcraft* – nuclear energy), which is supplanting traditional naphtha lamps.[10] It's obvious that *anbaric* means *electric* – but why? Our word *electricity* comes from *electrum*, the Latin name for amber (used in early experiments with static electricity). In Lyra's world they continue to use this Latin name, electrum, for amber (*SK*, p.60). But their word for electricity derives from *anbar*, the Arabic word, which came into English as *amber*. The two root words have been used in opposite ways in the two worlds. There are many more examples, some of which are documented on various Internet fan sites.[11]

One place in Jordan College where naphtha lighting will definitely not be replaced is the Retiring Room into which Lyra's curiosity finally takes her. It's a comfortable, well-furnished room, full of traditions: 'only scholars and their guests were allowed in here, and never females' (p.4); here the Master cooks after-dinner poppy for the scholars.[12]

Lyra barely has time to look around before she is hiding first behind a chair, then in the Retiring Room wardrobe. This was the first idea Philip Pullman had for the story:

> I started with a picture of Lyra hiding in the
> wardrobe, and overhearing things that she
> wasn't meant to hear. And I had pictures of
> other things in the story – the bear in armour,
> and the witches coming up through the clouds.[13]

A number of critics have commented on the parallel between this scene and Lucy hiding in a wardrobe in *The Lion, the Witch and the Wardrobe*.[14] Pullman, who is vehement in his criticism of the *Narnia Chronicles*, insists that it was accidental:

> I didn't notice the parallel till it was too late to
> do much about it. Actually I didn't mind,
> because you could see this story as being a sort
> of riposte to the worldview Lewis puts in front of
> us in Narnia.[15]

Innocence meets experience

Lyra, of course, doesn't go through the wardrobe into another world. But as she stays within it and attends closely to the evening's activities, another world begins to open up – thanks to the arrival of Lord Asriel. Lyra believes him to be her uncle – her only relative after the death of her parents in an air accident. Like Pullman's father, a remote yet glamorous fighter-pilot, Lord Asriel is an occasional figure in Lyra's life, but with a very definite air of glamour. Asriel is described as:

> . . . a tall man with powerful shoulders, a fierce
> dark face, and eyes that seemed to flash and
> glitter with savage laughter. It was a face to be
> dominated by, or to fight: never a face to
> patronize or pity. All his movements were large
> and perfectly balanced, like those of a wild
> animal, and when he appeared in a room like
> this, he seemed a wild animal held in a cage too
> small for it. (p.13)

He's a 'high-spirited man, quick to anger, a passionate man' (p.122). His dæmon, Stelmaria, is a snow leopard: exotic, powerful, graceful and dangerous.[16] Asriel is an explorer, a scientist and a member of the Cabinet Council advising the Prime Minister (p.10). He cares nothing for social status or rank – the gyptians owe him their allegiance because of his help politically, and because of his heroism in saving the lives of two gyptian children (p.136).

Lord Asriel's affair with the high-spirited and passionate Mrs Coulter, and his attempt to hush up the birth of their child, led to him killing Edward Coulter – apparently with scarcely a second thought (p.133). This coldness is a key ingredient in his character. There's no warmth in his interactions with Lyra at Jordan College – perhaps just the barest hint when he tells her about the vast area of college below the ground. The one time in *Northern Lights* when it matters to him that Lyra is his daughter is when she arrives at his house on Svalbard. He is horrified to see her, crying, 'No! No! . . . Get out! Turn round, get out, go! *I did not send for you!*' (p.364). But although he is dismayed, we somehow can't escape the feeling that if Roger wasn't with her, Lord Asriel would even sacrifice his own daughter to make his bridge possible. Nothing and no one will divert him from his great task, though the nature of his mission only becomes clear in *The Subtle Knife*.

Lyra had 'always had a dim sense that . . . somewhere in her life there was a connection with the high world of politics represented by Lord Asriel' (p.37). But in the Retiring Room wardrobe her curiosity is aroused by the overheard conversation, which touches on the biggest issues of the day. Politically, Lyra's world is radically different from our own. Tartars[17] from Siberia are pushing westwards and have invaded Muscovy[18] (p.10); there have recently been the Skraeling[19] wars (*SK*, p.124) in Beringland (Alaska in our world); and warfare in Tunguska (p.192), which is in Siberia (Iorek Byrnison and Lee Scoresby had fought there together). But the political landscape is dominated by the Church. In Lyra's world the Reformation never happened; instead of John Calvin becoming one of the most influential reformers of the sixteenth century, he became pope:

> Ever since Pope John Calvin had moved the seat
> of the Papacy to Geneva and set up the
> Consistorial Court of Discipline, the Church's

power over every aspect of life had been absolute. The Papacy itself had been abolished after Calvin's death, and a tangle of courts, colleges, and councils, collectively known as the Magisterium,[20] had grown up in its place. (p.31)

The Magisterium has a very Jesuit feel to it. The dominant force within it is the Consistorial Court of Discipline, but it's the new General Oblation Board ('a semi-private initiative' directed by Mrs Coulter), which we hear most about in *Northern Lights*. The Magisterium is the government, at least in Europe, and controls almost everything with an iron fist.[21] Even science is under church control: physics is called experimental theology[22] and radical theories are treated as heresy by the church. Lord Asriel causes a stir with his 'photograms' of streams of Dust and of the Aurora (p.21–22). It's immediately apparent that Dust is a controversial subject. Asriel's slides are also controversial because they clearly show the existence of another world. This is an abhorrent idea to the Magisterium, which refers to it as 'the Barnard–Stokes heresy' after the two 'renegade' experimental theologians who proposed that such worlds must exist (p.31–32). By coolly showing his two slides made using the special Dust-sensitive emulsion, Lord Asriel puts himself right at the centre of the controversy and divides the scholars. His slides demonstrate that there is a connection between the Dust the Magisterium so fears, and the heresy of other worlds that it refuses to countenance.

Severing and separation

Lyra's insatiable curiosity has taken her to the edges of enormous political and theological turmoil. In her naïvety she finds it all terribly exciting and wants to join Lord Asriel as he leaves for the north. He refuses, telling her 'the times are too dangerous' (p.29). But it's not until the General Oblation Board swings into operation that Lyra realizes just how close to home danger will come. Children disappearing in other parts of the country makes the basis for a good game, but then Billy Costa disappears, and by the time Lyra and others have spent hours searching, Roger too has gone. Before Pullman tells us about this he introduces us to the work of the Gobblers, or of one in particular – a beautiful woman with a golden monkey dæmon enticing Tony Makarios away from his home and befuddled mother.

This is the point at which Pullman introduces a key strand which runs right through *His Dark Materials* – separation and division. Marina Warner, in her book *Fantastic Metamorphoses, Other Worlds*,[23] says that there are four kinds of metamorphosis in myths, fairy tales and fantasy: *mutating* (a key ability of dæmons), *hatching* (which only happens with Gallivespian dragonflies in *His Dark Materials*), *doubling* (Pullman doubles individuals by giving them dæmons; the Spectres are also doubled when the subtle knife cuts between worlds) and *splitting*. This is the transformation which Pullman makes most use of – he calls it 'binary fission' and says it is 'something in the whole nature of the story, as well as in the underlying structural pattern'.[24]

Again and again, the narrative is pushed on by some form of splitting. At this stage of *Northern Lights* it introduces the clear and present danger of the Gobblers, separating prepubescent children from their homes and families for reasons we cannot yet begin to guess. Pullman takes time to show us how located Tony Makarios is – Limehouse is his home; his mother may not know what's going on, but she remains his mother; running errands and stealing from market traders is his life. But he is torn away from all this for ever, thanks to the magnetism[25] of the woman. Ironically, it is the Master's concern to protect Lyra from the danger of the Gobblers that results in both her own separation from home and substitute families, and her movement towards the heart of the danger. Later at Mrs Coulter's party, Lyra overhears that her new guardian is behind the Gobblers and she flees, separating herself from her new life and, though she doesn't know it, from her mother. Eventually we find out the gruesome nature of the General Oblation Board's experiment at Bolvangar and see that it is splitting once again – the wonderful shape-shifting of the dæmons cruelly cut off by the process of 'intercision'. Each person whose dæmon has been severed has either died or 'has – the well-known consequences of splitting – been evacuated of selfhood and become a zombie'.[26] What the Board doesn't know – but Lord Asriel does – is that this process of severance releases vast amounts of energy. He uses this energy to bridge to another world (another example of 'doubling') and in doing so not only separates himself from his world and his manservant, he also separates Roger from life and Lyra from her friend. It's the pain of this which ultimately drives Lyra to the world of the dead and her own agonizing disconnection from Pantalaimon.

The power of stories
While she's at Bolvangar, Lyra reflects that one of the zombie nurses 'would be able to stitch a wound or

change a blanket, but never to tell a story' (p.240). She contrasts starkly with Lyra's life and energy and story-telling talent. As we saw in Chapter 3, Pullman enjoys putting storytelling in the foreground of his stories, and this is true of *His Dark Materials* too, not least by making his main protagonist an accomplished story-teller herself. In Chapter Three of *Northern Lights*, Pullman describes how the story of the Gobblers grows and develops and mutates once children have begun to disappear (p.45–46). However, the focus on stories within *Northern Lights* is found in the section covering Lyra's time with the gyptians.

The day after Tony Costa and Kerim rescue Lyra from the Turk traders and she is safe on the Costas' boat, she 'clumsily collected her story and shook it into order as if she were settling a pack of cards ready for dealing' (p.108). As Lyra begins her story, Tony cuts in with his own stories of the terrors of the north – Tartars eating children, Nälkäinens, Breathless Ones and *panserb-jørne*.[27] At the Roping, Lyra gets to meet John Faa,[28] lord of the western gyptians, and Farder Coram. Lord Faa is a man with innate authority and great reserves of strength. Lyra recognizes in him something of the qual-ities she has seen in the Master of Jordan and Lord Asriel, and instantly respects him. He may not be edu-cated but he is a wise, brave and effective leader. Farder Coram, Lord Faa's advisor, seems to have little physical strength left, but is knowledgeable and very wise. The depths of Farder Coram are reflected in the extraordi-nary coat of his cat-dæmon, Sophonax. They believe it's important that Lyra knows her own story:

> I'm a-going to tell you a story, a true story. I
> know it's true because a gyptian woman told me,

and they all tell the truth to John Faa and Farder
Coram. So this is the truth about yourself, Lyra.
(p.122)

Why Lord Asriel had wanted Lyra to know nothing of
her true origins is unclear – perhaps just part of his
attempt to keep her away from Mrs Coulter. But as a
result of the untrue story that Asriel made people tell
Lyra, she grew up entirely unaware of her parents and
of how much she owed to Ma Costa and other gyptians.
Now 'Lyra had to adjust to her new sense of her own
story, and that couldn't be done in a day' (p.131). There
are echoes of Pullman's own story here. He started writing *Northern Lights* in the early 1990s, sometime
around, or soon after, the death of his mother. It was
while he was subsequently sorting through her papers
that Philip unearthed things about his parents that he
had never known. His discoveries were not on the scale
of what Lyra is told, but something of the same reori-
entation of perspectives must have taken place.

Grace and authenticity

While Lyra is coming to terms with new stories about
herself, she is also coming to terms with the alethiometer. In a sense the alethiometer is a story-telling instrument. As Lyra frames a question in her mind by point-
ing three of the arrows to symbols, the alethiometer
responds by indicating a sequence of symbols and the
appropriate level of meaning. From the sequence, Lyra
can discern the meaning – a message from the conscious matter of the universe which tells her about past,
present or future. It's an extraordinary experience for
Lyra – 'a sensation of such grace and power that Lyra,
sharing it, felt like a young bird learning to fly' (p.152).

It's more than just a feeling of grace; she is reading it *by* grace (as we saw in Chapter 4). Dust is communicating freely with Lyra by enabling her to see the meanings in a way that is easy, natural, graceful. Instinctively Lyra knows that the alethiometer tells only the truth, and she argues the point passionately when the gyptian leaders are reluctant to try to employ Iorek Byrnison.

Our first encounter with the bear is full of tension:

> Lyra had an impression of bloodstained
> muzzle and face, small malevolent black eyes,
> and an immensity of dirty matted yellowish fur.
> As it gnawed, hideous growling, crunching,
> sucking noises came from it . . . Lyra's heart was
> thumping hard, because something in the bear's
> presence made her feel close to coldness,
> danger, brutal power, but a power controlled by
> intelligence; and not a human intelligence,
> nothing like a human. (p.179)

The pitiful circumstances in which Lyra finds Iorek is once again to do with separation. He is divided from his home and his rightful kingdom; even worse he is cut off from his armour and thus his sense of purpose and dignity. But he is still a creature of integrity and has an extraordinary awareness of the properties of metal, manipulating it with graceful ease. Lyra again witnesses the grace of the bear when she fences with him. We see it again in his confrontation with Iofur Raknison who is marked not by grace but by affectation. Iofur coveted everything about human society – wealth, grandeur, learning – and yearned to have a dæmon. Not for him the uncomplicated life of a *panserbjørn* who makes his own soul by fashioning his armour out of sky (meteoritic) metal. He wanted a dæmon so badly that he carried around a doll as a substitute. Pullman draws very starkly the incongruity of this by his attention to the filth and stench and the uncertain behaviour of Iofur's subjects. Iofur Raknison's pretensions to be human moved him from grace to self-consciousness, and so made him vulnerable to being tricked. The clash of Iorek and Iofur is much more than Iorek regaining his throne, and the way Pullman describes the conflict draws attention to its significance.[29] Here are two competing stories about what armoured bears are; 'two futures, two destinies' (p.349). This is Kleist's contrast of grace *versus* artificiality – or truth *versus* lies:

> Iorek Byrnison . . . was more powerful, more graceful, and his armour was real armour, rust-coloured, bloodstained, dented with combat, not elegant, enamelled, and decorative like most of what she saw around her now. (p.326)

The contrast of authentic with inauthentic is an issue to which Pullman turns again and again. Central to the whole story is the inauthentic authority of the Magisterium and ultimately of the Authority himself. In *Northern Lights*, we only see that of the Magisterium, and this is set off in opposition to two groups of people: the gyptians and the witches.

Gyptians are strong, tough and principled. They are on the fringes of society with their own secret ways and rich traditions, and so they are no friends of the Magisterium. Instead they have a deep goodness, which transcends the moral character of every Magisterium representative we see in the story. As do the witches, who also add in to the mix an alternative spirituality: one which is bound up with the natural world. In their extraordinary but unageing beauty, minimalist clothing despite the cold, unrefined adornment of 'a simple chain of red flowers', and their effortless flying (on branches not broomsticks), everything about the witches speaks of grace. Gyptians and witches (and perhaps even the *panserbjørne* under Iorek's kingship) serve a similar purpose in the story. Pullman wants us to see them as genuine, open, unaffected, wholesome, pure. They have authentic traditions which go back centuries to a time before – in Pullman's view – all the extraneous nonsense of Christianity came in and cut people off from their deep roots. They all show that it's possible – even desirable – to live good lives of integrity entirely independent of such things.

Lyra is without her parents, she's away from the Master and the scholars, so representatives of gyptians and witches provide Lyra with what she needs as she grows up: surrogate parents, role models and perspectives. John Faa and Farder Coram give her new perspectives that enable Lyra to grow up with a true understanding of her past. Serafina Pekkala knows the prophecy about Lyra's future. She cannot tell Lyra, but once they have met, Serafina will do everything in her power to protect Lyra and help her to fulfil the prophecy. It is important that they meet again at the end of the trilogy so that they can testify both to the growth that has taken place and to the fulfilment of destiny.

[1] Pullman, Philip, 'About the Writing' (www.philip-pullman.com/about_the_writing.asp).

[2] Pullman, Philip, 'Philip Pullman's interview transcript' (www2.scholastic.com/teachers/authorsandbooks/authorstudies/authorhome.jhtml?authorID=78&collateralID=6472&displayName=Interview+Transcript).

[3] Blake, William, 'Songs of Experience' in Yeats, W. B. (ed): *William Blake Collected Poems* (Routledge, 2002), p.67–71.

4   We will consider truth, integrity and the part played by the alethiometer in Chapter 12.

5   We will look at dæmons in detail in Chapter 9.

6   Pullman often mentions Pan taking on an ermine form. This was partly inspired by Leonardo da Vinci's 'Lady with an Ermine'. The painting is in the Czartoryskich Museum in Krakow, Poland (www.muzeum-czartoryskich.krakow.pl).

7   Pullman, Philip, 'From Exeter to Jordan', *Register* (Exeter College Association, 2001), p.18. This article is available online at www.oxfordtoday.ox.ac.uk/archive/0102/14_3/03.shtml.

8   Pullman, 'From Exeter to Jordan', p.18.

9   One website on word origins claims that the origin of *chocolate* is a little more complicated than the dictionaries make out. See www.takeourword.com/Issue016.html if you're interested.

10   Naphtha is the name for a group of colourless flammable liquids produced in petroleum or coal tar distillation.

11   E.g. www.bridgetothestars.net (HisDarkMaterials.tk) and www24.brinkster.com/menthapiperita/tgc.htm (HisDarkMaterialsAnnotated.tk).

12   Pullman writes: 'Heaven forfend that the rector of Exeter should feel obliged to serve opium after dinner, but this is an alternative universe, after all. I lifted that dainty detail from the diary of an English lady living in India before the Mutiny, which I'd come across 10 years before while I was looking for something else entirely. I knew I could use it somewhere' (Pullman: 'From Exeter to Jordan', p.18).

13   Philip Pullman in an interview on the Scholastic Teachers website. It has been removed from that site but is available at www.geocities.com/torre_degli_angeli/scholasticinterview.htm.

14   Lewis, C. S., *The Lion, the Witch and the Wardrobe* (Collins, various editions).

15   Philip Pullman in a discussion on Readerville.com (www.readerville.com/WebX?14@65.93OcaX9YecM^7@.ef6c70e/59).

16   Snow leopards are, sadly, in danger of extinction. For more information about snow leopards, see www.snowleopard.org.

17   The Tartars (or Tatars) originally came from Siberia, but the name is used to describe the Mongol invaders of Europe and Asia in the thirteenth century.

18   Muscovy was the predecessor of Russia and existed from the fourteenth to the eighteenth centuries.

19   Skraeling was the Viking name for the Native Americans they encountered in Newfoundland. They were probably Beothuk people, and possibly Miqmac. Since the Skraeling wars in *His Dark Materials* took place in Beringland, it might suggest that the word applies to all natives of North America in the trilogy.

20   *Magisterium* is the word used by the Roman Catholic Church to refer to the authority of the church.

21   We will look at the Church in some detail in Chapter 13.

[22] The background to this phrase is that theology (the study of God) was once thought of as the 'queen of the sciences' – *science* in that sense meaning an area of knowledge. Perhaps also in the background is the famous saying of the astronomer Kepler who referred to his scientific work as 'thinking God's thoughts after him'.

[23] Warner, Marina, *Fantastic Metamorphoses, Other Worlds* (Oxford University Press, 2002).

[24] Philip Pullman, 'There has to be a lot of ignorance in me when I start a story', *Guardian*, 18 February 2002.

[25] She is not literally magnetic, but it seems somehow more than simply her personality. For some curious reason Pullman twice refers to Mrs Coulter having a 'metallic' smell (p.88, 92). Why? 'Now you've got me. I haven't the faintest idea. I think I was trying to convey her powerfully physical presence' (Philip Pullman, personal email to the author, 28 May 2004).

[26] Warner, *Fantastic Metamorphoses, Other Worlds*, p.207.

[27] Pullman says that *panserbjørne* is a 'word I made up from the Nordic languages: the *bjørne* part is bear[s], and *panser* means armour. So putting the two bits together, it was easy to make the word I have now.' In the Point editions from which quotations in this book have been taken, *panserbjørne* (and the singular, *panserbjørn*) has been spelt incorrectly – as *panserbørne*.

[28] John Faa is based on a historical Scottish gypsy family. In 1540 a document of King James V of Scotland mentions 'oure lovit Johnne Faa, Lord und Earle of Littlll Egipt'. In 1611 in Edinburgh, another John Faa was hanged along with three other family members. In 1624 Captain John Faa and some relatives, described as 'all Egyptians, vagabonds, and common thieves', were also hanged in Edinburgh. Their wives and daughters were sentenced 'to be drowned till they be deid' but the King settled for banishing them from Scotland. The descendants of Johnne Faa were the Romany kings and queens, the last being King Charles Faa-Blythe who died in 1902. For more on the Faas see www.electricscotland.com/history/scotsman/gypsies.htm; www.kittybrewster.com/ancestry/anstruther.htm; www.ayrwritersclub.co.uk/the_gypsy_laddie.htm; www.contemplator.com/child/gypsylad.html.

[29] Note Pullman's use of an epic simile on page 350: What begins with 'Like two great masses of rock . . .' gets developed for half a paragraph.

CHAPTER 6

The Subtle Knife

Reading Chapter One of *The Subtle Knife* straight after *Northern Lights* might induce a sense of lostness. The grandeur of Jordan College, the cold beauty of the north, and the feisty young heroine with her extraordinary friends are all missing. Instead we find ourselves in a Winchester housing estate with a boy we've never heard of, struggling to cope with his unbalanced mother. He hasn't even got a dæmon! After one book within an alternative world, Pullman takes us back into 'the universe we know'[1] – and in some ways it feels alien. We've grown used to dæmons communicating personality, but in our world they're nowhere to be seen. And in contrast to Lyra's magical world, Winchester housing estates are, frankly, dull.[2] Chapter Two comes as a relief (despite its sinister beginning): Serafina Pekkala brings a sense of normality, and she goes on to play a major role in this book.

Will power

Will Parry is a troubled, serious boy who is old beyond his years. We first meet him taking his mother to the home of Mrs Cooper. She's a kind old lady who realizes that Will needs help and, in the face of his solemn determination, trusts that he is acting for the best. Clearly Will's mother has mental health problems. She appears to be psychotic,[3] believing that enemies watch her every move. Her psychosis seems to stem from severe depression as a result of her husband, John, disappearing when Will was a baby. Will was just seven when he first realized that he had to look after his mother. Now, five years on, it's part of life – but something is different. He has discovered there *is* real danger and it's not entirely in her mind.

Will doesn't remember his father, but he is a very glamorous figure in Will's mind. A handsome ex-Royal Marine officer who turned to leading scientific expeditions in remote corners of the world, John Parry is the stuff of boyhood heroes. In the hours playing alone acting out dangerous expeditions and daring rescues, Will's father was his imaginary friend. As Will grew, so did the desire to know more about him. There were many unanswered questions: Why had he disappeared? Why are these mysterious men so eager to know about him? Part of the answer is in the writing case where Mrs Parry keeps letters from her husband. But Will doesn't know where she hides it. He wakes in the night, suddenly knowing both that there are intruders in the house, and where the writing case is. This is one of several examples of characters having some extraordinary intuition. This is Dust in action, steering human thinking and attention onto things that are more critical than they realize at the time.[4]

Worlds apart

Having killed one of the intruders, Will flees to Oxford to search for answers. He is confident in his skill at being unobtrusive during the day, but Will knows he must avoid the town centre at night or he will draw attention to himself. He heads towards north Oxford where his attention is drawn to a cat, which behaves strangely before disappearing altogether. Like Will's flash of intuition the previous night, he is receiving a gift of guidance from the Dust:

> Will knew without the slightest doubt that the patch of grass on the other side was in a different world . . . He was looking at something profoundly alien . . . What he saw made his head swim and his heart thump harder, but he didn't hesitate: he pushed his shopping bag through, and then scrambled through himself, through the hole in the fabric of this world and into another.
> (*SK*, p.15–16)

We know about the existence of other worlds from *Northern Lights* – Jordan scholars whisper nervously about the 'Barnard-Stokes' heresy. But until Lord Asriel's audacious experiment with the aurora, it was thought to be mere speculation of a kind the Magisterium is determined to stamp out. Now we realize that Asriel had only found a new – and catastrophic – means of passing between worlds.

Will finds himself in Cittàgazze, the City of Magpies, in precisely the right place for Lyra to literally bump into him. Pullman uses their encounter to further explore the idea of alternative worlds. Although in *Northern Lights* we have seen many ways in which Lyra's world differs from ours, now we see from the other direction: our world and its inhabitants are very strange in Lyra's eyes. She is shocked that Will has no dæmon, and when she enters his world she finds it bewilderingly different. In the centre of Oxford she finds things that are comfortingly familiar – including, apparently, Simon Parslow's initials carved in a stone – but no Jordan College. She feels disoriented, and a photograph in the museum[5] of men identical to the Samoyed hunters who had captured her intensifies the feeling. Lyra is off-guard, resulting in the odious Sir Charles Latrom[6] spotting her.

The alethiometer leads Lyra to Mary Malone, a researcher into dark matter.[7] Lyra is astonished but excited to find a female scholar who knows something about Dust. Mary is flabbergasted by Lyra – especially when she suggests Mary could reprogram 'the Cave' to use words. But the alethiometer had instructed Lyra to give first priority to helping Will find his father. Until this point, Lyra and Will are just acquaintances – all they have in common is their age and the fact that they had met in an alien world. From now on their stories are intertwined. However, instead of obeying the alethiometer, Lyra continues with her own agenda and visits Mary again. This stubborn independence leads to Lyra's first major setback – she ends up alerting the security services to her interest in dark matter and her connection with Will, and, what's more, Sir Charles steals the altheiometer. She later confesses to Will that this was the consequence of her disobedience, and she submits herself to helping him. Will and Lyra are very much equals, but for now Will takes the lead; the new dynamic is part of Lyra's growing-up process.

A Spectre calls

Cittàgazze is alien to both Will and Lyra. It is both beautiful (though decaying)[8] and menacing. It is apparently deserted, but soon they discover the gang of children who roam around free from adult supervision. Their hostility towards the cat Will had followed, and later

towards Will and Lyra, seems extraordinary. Will, however, knows that it is common for people to feel threatened by, and hostile towards, what they don't understand. The far greater menace of Cittàgazze is something they can't see: Spectres which prey on adults,
feeding on their 'conscious and informed interest in the
world' (p.292), sucking the mental life out of them and
leaving them as empty shells. Intriguingly, while
Pullman was writing about Spectres, J. K. Rowling was
writing about dementors draining people of their will to
live.[9] Both writers were expressing something of their
experiences of depression, although Pullman says, 'I
prefer to call it melancholy, or melancholia. It's a horri-
ble condition, I tried to describe it as accurately as I
could.'[10] Pullman's fascination with voodoo may also in
part lie behind the Spectres. Anthropologist Zora Neale
Hurston investigated voodoo in Jamaica and Haiti in the
1930s and questioned someone who described something very similar to a Spectre attack:

> One day you see a man walking the road . . . The
> next day you come to his yard and find him dead
> . . . He is still and silent and does none of the
> things that he used to do. But you look upon him
> and you see that he has all the parts that the
> living have. Why is it that he cannot do what the
> living do? It is because the thing that gave power
> to these parts is no longer there. That is the
> duppy, and that is the most powerful part of any
> man.[11]

The man is now a zombie – undead – and has nothing to
restrain him from evil. He will work as a slave for the
sorcerer who took his spirit – though this idea seems
closer to Bolvangar and the regiment of African *zombis*

than to the Spectres which independently feast on the 'duppies' of living adults.

For the people of Cittàgazze, Spectres are a terrifying mystery. They know what Spectres do, but not why, nor where they come from. Angelica explains to Will and Lyra what happens when a Spectre attacks someone:

> They eat the life out of them there and then . . . At first they know it's happening, and they're afraid, they cry and cry, they try and look away and pretend it ain happening, but it is. It's too late. And no one ain gonna go near them, they on they own. Then they get pale and stop moving. They still alive, but it's like they been eaten out from inside. You look in they eyes, you see the back of they heads. Ain nothing there. (p.62)

Seeing right through to the back of the head is a child's embellishment, but it conveys the utter blankness of victims' expressions. Later, Serafina Pekkala and her companions watch Spectres attack some travellers at a river crossing. The adults all fell victim to their shimmering fate (Serafina, being adult, could see the Spectres), leaving one man standing waste deep in the river, his distraught child still clinging to his back. When the child falls, the father barely responds to the splash and can't engage at all with the reality of his child drowning. Joachim Lorenz, a rider with the party who fled in order to return and care for the children once danger was passed, tells Serafina that there are many more Spectres than previously (p.138–139). This is a consequence of Lord Asriel's experiment, as was the great storm, which happened in this world (p.142).

In *The Amber Spyglass*, we discover more about its devastating consequences – an environmental crisis in Lyra's world, and other worlds out of alignment with each other. Joachim describes his world as it had once been – a place of beauty, plenty and peace – and tells how it all changed three centuries previously. He clearly favours the explanation of Spectres that puts the blame at the door of the Torre degli Angeli, and its guild of philosophers (p.141). Angelica's similar explanation adds a little more detail:

> This Guild man hundreds of years ago was taking some metal apart. Lead. He was going to make it into gold. And he cut it and cut it smaller and smaller till he came to the smallest piece he could get. There ain nothing smaller than that. So small you couldn't see it, even. But he cut that too, and inside the smallest little bit, there was all the Spectres packed in twisted over and folded up so tight they took up no space at all. But once he cut it, bam! They whooshed out, and they been here ever since. (p.153)

At this point Pullman is having fun weaving modern physics together with alchemy and the stuff of horror films to warn against the dangers of pursuing technological progress simply because we *can*, without considering the long-term consequences and whether we *should*. The alchemists sought to turn lead into gold, but without success and before long the idea of chemical elements and atoms was established. In the twentieth century physicists succeeded in splitting the atom – an event that ultimately led to the horrors of Hiroshima and Nagasaki. Subsequent discoveries about subatomic particles led to theories that there are actually ten[12] or eleven[13] dimensions to reality, rather than the four (three plus time) with which we are familiar. These extra dimensions are 'packed in twisted over and folded up so tight they [take] up no space at all'. Pullman uses this idea to create a way for Spectres to be unleashed by the subtle knife. Giacomo Paradisi admits that the creation of the knife was responsible. The Guild of the Torre degli Angeli had probed thoughtlessly into the bonds between the elementary particles, thinking that like financial bonds they could be 'negotiated' (p.196).

Now, after three hundred years of coping with small numbers of Spectres, the world is in chaos with a deluge of them. The Spectres, the great storm and fog, as well as angels flying overhead, are making people anxious. Joachim speculates on what might be happening:

> Something is happening, and we don't know down here what it may be. There could be a war breaking out. There was a war in heaven once, oh, thousands of years ago, immense ages back, but I don't know what the outcome was. It wouldn't be impossible if there was another. But the devastation would be enormous, and the consequences for us . . . I can't imagine it. Though . . . the end of it might be better than I fear. It might be that a war in heaven would sweep the Spectres from this world altogether, and back into the pit they came from. What a blessing that would be, eh! How fresh and happy we could live, free of the fearful blight. (p.144)

This confirms what Thorold told Serafina Pekkala on Svalbard – that Lord Asriel was intent on mounting a rebellion against the Authority (p.48). Joachim's prophetic comments begin to help her (and us) realize that any war in heaven will have enormous repercussions.

Serafina's perspective

It's worth noting at this point that, although Will is the hero of *The Subtle Knife*, Serafina is Pullman's focus in terms of understanding and explaining the cosmic events which are the backdrop to the story. After escaping from the ship where she has played the role of Yambe-Akka[14] and killed the witch who was being tortured, she begins to wonder what Lord Asriel is doing. She perceives that all the upheaval in the world is a direct result of his activities. The fog enveloping the north acts as a metaphor for the uncertainty everyone feels. To find some answers, Serafina first visits Dr Lanselius in Trollesund. He tells her about the Magisterium 'assembling the greatest army ever known' (p.43), including a regiment of *zombis*. Then she discovers Asriel's intentions from Thorold. It's a long time before we're told explicitly what mission awaits the Magisterium's forces, but it is clear once we know Asriel's plans, that these forces will be fighting him.

Thorold's information prompts Serafina to call a clan council. Two guests address the council: Ruta Skadi and Lee Scoresby, the Texan aeronaut.[15] Both expand Serafina's understanding. First, Ruta Skadi recognizes that war is imminent. She has no doubt that the witches should fight against the Magisterium (her stinging criticism is examined in Chapter 14). Second, Lee speaks about Stanislaus Grumman's knowledge of an object that could give more protection to the one who holds it than anything else. He's determined to find it, whatever it may be, and bring Lyra under its protection. Since they all realize that Lyra is central to everything, protecting her is of immense importance. Serafina and twenty other witches head into the Cittàgazze world to find Lyra, while Lee sets off to find Grumman. From this point in the narrative Pullman divides the story into two main strands, one following Serafina who soon finds Lyra and Will, the other following Scoresby. Ruta Skadi sets off with Serafina, but soon leaves to join some angels heading towards Asriel's fortress. Later, after Serafina finds the children and pledges to help them find John Parry, Ruta returns with astonishing news:

> . . . it is the greatest castle you can imagine –
> ramparts of basalt, rearing to the skies, with
> wide roads coming from every direction . . . I
> think he must have been preparing this for a
> long time, for aeons . . . I think he commands
> time, he makes it run fast or slow according to
> his will. And coming to this fortress are warriors
> of every kind, from every world. (p.282)

Ruta also has news for Serafina from an unexpected source – an overheard conversation between some cliff-ghasts. The oldest of all cliff-ghasts tells the others that the impending war will be the greatest ever. Lord Asriel's forces are greater than in the earlier rebellion and better led,[16] but the Authority has an army a hundred times bigger. Asriel has passion and daring and a sense of justice on his side, whereas the Authority's forces are frightened or complacent. But the old cliff-ghast knows of one thing which will mean defeat for the rebellion: 'He hasn't got Æsahættr. Without Æsahættr, he and all his forces will go down to defeat' (p.284–285).

Serafina recognizes that Æsahættr 'sounds as if it means *god-destroyer*' (p.286)[17] – neither she nor Ruta Skadi knows who or what it could be, though they spec-ulate that it might be Lyra. The carelessness of Lena Feldt, one of the witches, prevents Serafina putting one more piece of the puzzle in place. While spying on Mrs Coulter, she hears Sir Charles Latrom/Lord Boreal telling Mrs Coulter that the subtle knife is also known as *teleutaia makhaira* or Æsahættr, to which nothing whatsoever is invulnerable (p.326). But in her absorbed curiosity, Lena Feldt was not sufficiently alert and so fell victim to a Spectre, now under Mrs Coulter's com-mand. Not only did this lapse prevent Serafina under-standing the riddle, it led to the killing of her compan-ions and to Lyra's capture.

Shamanic powers

Meanwhile, Pullman has been developing another major strand of narrative – Lee Scoresby's search for Stanislaus Grumman. First he goes to Nova Zembla[18] to see what he can learn in the bar of the Samirsky Hotel from the trappers and hunters passing through. The more Lee discovers about Grumman, the more mysteri-ous his quarry becomes. He learns that Grumman had been initiated into a Tartar tribe, the Yenisei Pakhtars,[19] and had his skull drilled[20] because he was a shaman. He's told that Grumman took a Tartar name, Jopari, but Lee discovers that it is not a Tartar name at all. He sets out for the Yenisei River to find Grumman or his tribe. When they finally meet, Grumman tells Lee that the name 'Jopari' is simply the Tartars' attempt to pronounce his real name, John Parry. Grumman's revelation that he summoned Scoresby using a ring that had belonged to Lee's mother rattles the aeronaut. Lee demands to know how he had come by it, but Grumman declines to explain, except to say it was thanks to his shamanic powers.

Grumman tells Scoresby that he has learnt about the subtle knife and the Spectre-filled world by travelling there in spirit while in a trance.[21] But he is a sick man from living in an alien world. He intends to use his remaining strength to find the knife bearer, and Lee is to help him. During their journey, Lee witnesses some of Grumman's other shamanic powers, including summoning a wind to carry them into the other world. When they are pursued by zeppelins, Grumman conjures a thunderstorm which destroys one of them. During the night Lee dreams with a vivid intensity of the shaman's work – or perhaps he has some kind of out-of-body experience. He sees Grumman summoning a Spectre to attack a zeppelin pilot who then crashes into the mountainside; then Lee feels himself joining a flock of birds which weigh down a third zeppelin until it crashes. All this seriously drains Grumman's reserves of strength – and profoundly unnerves Lee Scoresby. When the final zeppelin catches up with them at a ravine, Lee holds them off while Grumman goes on through. This Western-inspired last stand by the Texan is one of the great heartbreaking moments of the trilogy, as he and his scrawny, laid-back hare dæmon Hester face their imminent death – and separation. Their very last thought is that they were helping Lyra – by helping Grumman find the knife bearer, Lee believed he was helping the little girl he had come to love so much.

Grumman had made an oath to Scoresby that the knife would protect Lyra, but just hours later Grumman breaks his word. His commitment to Asriel's aims is so great that when the knife bearer blunders into him on top of a mountain in the dark of a wild and windy night, Grumman insists that he go to Lord Asriel to offer the services of the knife. The fight on the mountain is curious, echoing Jacob's night-time fight with an angel in Genesis 32. Will struggles to escape, but although Grumman's strength is failing, he can still grip tightly – he must discover if this is the knife bearer. Once Grumman is sure, he urges the bearer to fight with the knife and kill the Authority. Will wants no part of it, but Grumman's words help to shape Will's sense of himself and his task for some time:

> . . . You're a warrior. That's what you are. Argue with anything else, but don't argue with your own nature. (p.335)

Will is reluctant to see himself in those terms but recognizes the truth in what the man says. Moments later, as Grumman strikes a match, father and son see each other for the first time in twelve years, and – another heartbreaking moment – at the very moment that recognition dawns, they too are separated by the arrow of the vengeful witch whose love Grumman had rejected. As Will descends to the camp, he discovers the two angels who had been protecting his father. The book finishes with another agonizing separation as Will finds that the witches are dead, and Lyra has gone.

Absent fathers

The Subtle Knife is in the difficult situation of being the middle part of a trilogy, with neither the thrill of the new, which comes with an opening volume, nor with the climax of the closing part. It is a mark of Pullman's quality as a writer that he manages to introduce many new elements without losing the essential ingredients of *Northern Lights*, and without the new elements over-whelming. The knife itself, of course, is central to the plot, but the Spectres and the shaman have pivotal roles too. Pullman also wisely develops two of the key supporting characters from *Northern Lights* – Serafina Pekkala and Lee Scoresby – to give them major roles. Pullman works with four separate strands of the story, which he intertwines at stages through the book. First, he connects the thread of Lyra looking for Dust, with the new strand of Will Parry searching for his father. Then he takes the Serafina and Scoresby threads in different directions in order to get two different perspectives on the events that are taking place. Serafina Pekkala gradually pieces together Lord Asriel's role in the impending cosmic conflict. Her story merges with that of Will and Lyra after they have recovered the alethiometer. Lee's story takes him to the mysterious Grumman in an attempt to find something which will protect Lyra, little realizing that it already is protecting her. Grumman brings a shaman's perspective on the knife and the part it will play. Lee's story fades into Grumman's, only to be cut off at the point where it connects with Will's. Pullman has begun to bring together the threads in preparation for the climax in *The Amber Spyglass* – but we've a long way to go yet, so he cleverly divides Will's and Lyra's stories again to leave us with an immense cliffhanger.

The various threads of this story suggest that in terms of theme if not of plot, the two fathers are central to

The Subtle Knife. Yet Lord Asriel doesn't appear in person once, and Stanislaus Grumman doesn't appear until almost two thirds of the way through. However, it is Lord Asriel's implacable opposition to the Authority that is driving the story, and Stanislaus Grumman is the character who most clearly understands what Asriel is doing and why it matters so much. There are some interesting parallels between them. Both were unknown to their children (at least, in Asriel's case, as a father), both have travelled in different worlds and are vehemently opposed to the Authority. Pullman also hints that Asriel, like Grumman, has special powers – recall him 'sending for' a child at the end of *Northern Lights* (*NL*, p.364, 379) and Ruta Skadi's comment about him commanding time. Pullman never develops this but he has nonetheless given these two extraordinary men pivotal roles, which will profoundly impact two critical moments in *The Amber Spyglass*.

---

[1] Though it is, of course, a fictional version of it, and therefore in a sense not the world we know at all. It is, however, a world that is familiar, in that it is like ours in almost all respects.

[2] No offence intended to residents of Winchester. I live near it and it's a fine place, but it doesn't quite compare with Lyra's Oxford or Svalbard for excitement.

[3] Psychosis is having a distorted perception of reality.

[4] We'll return to the subject of Dust in Chapter 10.

[5] The Pitt-Rivers Museum in South Parks Road, Oxford (www.prm.ox.ac.uk), which is accessed through the Oxford University Museum of Natural History (www.oum.ox.ac.uk). See *SK*, p.79.

[6] 'Latrom' is 'mortal' backwards. This doesn't seem greatly significant since everybody in Pullman's stories – including the Authority – is mortal, but perhaps when Lord Boreal chose his pseudonym, he was aware of the need to keep returning to his own world if he wasn't going to sicken and die.

[7] There's more on Mary in the next chapter, and on dark matter in Chapter 11 and the Appendix.

[8] Cittàgazze was inspired by Venice – Pullman has Canaletto's *Portico with Lantern* hanging on his study wall (see www.upenn.edu/ARG/archive/venice/CaMeB10big.jpeg).

[9] Rowling, J. K., *Harry Potter and the Prisoner of Azkaban* (Bloomsbury, 2000).

[10] Pullman, Philip, personal email to the author, 28 May 2004.

[11] Quoted in Warner, Marina, *Fantastic Metamorphoses, Other Worlds* (Oxford University Press, 2002), p.130.

[12] 'String theory' and later 'superstring theory' viewed all fundamental particles as vibrating strings – either loops or open-ended lines. Each string is ten-dimensional with the six extra dimensions (those that we cannot perceive) wrapped up inside the string.

[13] Superstring theory has now evolved into M-theory, which works in eleven dimensions. These multi-dimensional theories are necessary to be able to find some way of combining quantum physics with relativity to arrive at a Theory of Everything. For more information, see 'M-theory, the theory formerly known as Strings' on the Cambridge Relativity website (www.damtp.cam.ac.uk/user/gr/public/qg_ss.html).

[14] In *The Subtle Knife*, Yambe-Akka is the goddess who comes to witches when they die (*SK*, p.41).

[15] He's described as a 'New Dane' (*NL*, p.178). New Denmark was the name used for Canada by the early settlers so the fact that Lee Scoresby is New Dane from Texas suggests that in Lyra's world the USA doesn't exist as such. Lee's name comes from Lee Van Cleef, the actor in Westerns, and William Scoresby, who was a real Arctic explorer (www.whitby-yorkshire.co.uk/scoresby/scoresby.htm).

[16] Is this a tacit – perhaps even subconscious – admission on Pullman's part that Milton really does show Satan as a failure in *Paradise Lost*?

[17] Pullman says 'I made it up from two Norse words meaning God and death' (BBC webchat – www.bbc.co.uk/radio4/arts/hisdarkmaterials/pullman_webchat.shtml).

[18] Novaya Zemlya, an island off the northern coast of Russia.

[19] The Pakhtars appear to be invented by Pullman, as does the Semyonov range of mountains near which they are located (note the similarity of name with the odious Russian priest in *The Amber Spyglass* who is called Semyon Borisovitch (*AS*, p.102). The Yenisei river, however, is one of the major rivers in Siberia, which passes through the Sayan mountains (from which Stanislaus Grumman's dæmon gets part of her name). For information see www.en.wikipedia.org/wiki/Yenisei_River and www.sibirienspezial.com/jenissei/english/jenissej.htm.

[20] The process is called trepanning or trephination, and in Lyra's world it was to let more Dust in. It is not entirely clear why ancient peoples in our world carried out this practice – whether it was for medical or spiritual reasons. See 'Hole in the Head for Bronze Age Chelsea Man' at www.english-heritage.org.uk/default.asp?WCI=NewsItem&WCE=204. There are a small number of people in our times who have trepanned themselves

in order to achieve an altered state of consciousness. For one person's account of this see 'The people with holes in their heads' (from Michell, John F., *Eccentric Lives and Peculiar Notions* (1984)) at www.noah.org/trepan/people_with_holes_in_their_heads.html.

[21] This comes from the Siberian shamans' belief that they can travel to the underworld and the overworld while in a trance.

CHAPTER 7

The Amber Spyglass

The calm and tranquillity of the opening paragraphs of *The Amber Spyglass* come as a surprise after the tension at the close of *The Subtle Knife*, and the trauma of Lyra's disappearance. It's a shift of focus comparable to that between the end of *Northern Lights* and the beginning of *The Subtle Knife*. It reinforces the fact that this is a new book – the story continues, but the end of one volume and the beginning of the next isn't an arbitrary split in the middle of the action. Chapter Two returns to the moments immediately after Will discovered Lyra's disappearance, but Chapter One is days or weeks later. Lyra and Will remain the heroes since this is their story, but we are moving into a new phase. As I noted previously, Pullman has separated the strands of Lyra's and Will's stories in order to maintain tension, and to allow him to introduce new elements into the story. It's not until Chapter Twelve that they are reunited.

Pullman shifts focus so dramatically on the first page that we have no idea where we are or what's happening. The scene is a valley high in the mountains, near the snow line. There are few clues as to where these mountains are. One clue comes in the first sentence: the valley is shaded with rhododendrons. It's enough to locate us somewhere in central or eastern Asia – the Himalayas perhaps. The mention of 'faded silken flags', barley-cakes and dried tea confirm this impression. Pullman describes this peaceful valley at length, not simply to paint the background, but to make us uncertain about where we are in the story. Gradually he zooms in: a path – the deserted cave – a creature at the entrance – a golden monkey – Mrs Coulter.

Now the tension rises as Pullman refrains from telling us about Lyra. We recall that when we last saw Mrs Coulter, she had one of her tame Spectres torture a witch into revealing Lyra's destiny as the second Eve. Once Mrs Coulter had understood this, she realized that she had to destroy Lyra to prevent a second Fall. But now we find her camping in a mountain cave, with a village girl, Ama, bringing her food. Still Pullman remains quiet about Lyra; instead, Ama is passing on the villagers' worried rumours of Mrs Coulter's dangerous companion. Finally we learn that Lyra is alive, though sleeping[1] 'under a spell' (p.4). We're not surprised to learn that in fact her mother is keeping her sedated. What *does* come as a surprise is the disagreement between Mrs Coulter and her dæmon, and the fact that her actions are secret from the Magisterium. Perhaps most surprising is the internal turmoil in a woman who has previously been utterly single-minded.

Mrs Coulter's geographical isolation reflects a more profound isolation. She still wants to prevent Lyra being tempted. But faced with the prospect of annihilating her own daughter, Mrs Coulter's maternal instincts are beginning to wake from their dormant state, and she wants to hide Lyra from the Magisterium (p.148). We don't discover this until much later – and we will be unsure of her motives for a long time, since she becomes a double agent – but this is the first sign that Mrs Coulter is distancing herself from the Magisterium. This takes us back to the theme of separation or binary fission, which we noted in Chapter 5. Already in Chapter One of *The Amber Spyglass* we have Lyra separated from Will, and Mrs Coulter separated from her former allies, as well as being at odds with herself and her dæmon. The first of Lyra's dream fragments (which appear between the first eight chapters) reminds us of another separation which becomes increasingly important in the first half of *The Amber Spyglass*: Roger is cut off from life (p.9). This fragment plants the idea of the world of the dead into the reader's mind; it grows in power and inevitability until Lyra finally gets there.

Angels from the realms of story

Meanwhile, Will has also been finding out about the world of the dead from his new companions, the angels Baruch and Balthamos. They are part of Lord Asriel's coalition – fallen angels, rebels against the Authority. Pullman says:

> There's been a long tradition of seeing the
> 'fallen' angels as being in some way on the
> 'right' side, and I'm just going along with Milton[2]
> and Blake as well as some Gnostic traditions.[3]

Pullman presents them, especially Balthamos, as haughty and unfeeling. They indifferently allowed John Parry to be killed – having led them to the knife bearer, he was no longer useful. It makes for a bad start in their relationship with Will who is distressed at his father's death and Lyra's disappearance. Will, although just a boy, is unfazed by the angels, knowing that with the knife he can call the shots. He insists that they look for Lyra before he will comply with their request to go to Lord Asriel.

Unfortunately an unfallen angel finds them and

summons the Regent who is flying far overhead in 'the Chariot'. They narrowly avoid his spear by escaping to another world. in which Baruch and Balthamos explain to Will that the Authority is not God, but merely the oldest of all angels, and Metatron is his Regent (p.33–34). Metatron is an archangel in Gnostic writings, and the subject of many legends which have come to us via the western esoteric tradition. This is a rich source of inspiration for Pullman who incorporates several of the ideas into his story (see Chapter 14). Pullman says:

> I was guided by what I read of angelic lore in, for instance, Gustave Davidson's *A Dictionary of Angels*, and elsewhere; and also by the needs of the story. If I needed an angel to have been a man at some stage, hey presto! I invented the possibility. There's a lot of making-up in fiction, you know.[4]

His latter comment is curious since one of the main legends about Metatron is that he was once the man Enoch, who the Bible tells us 'walked with God; then he was no more, because God took him away'.[5] It is not, however, a biblical idea – the Bible always sees angels as entirely separate, spiritual beings.[6] In the Metatron legends he is the most powerful angel, so it was a natural step for Pullman to make him the Authority's Regent. It's worth noting in passing that Pullman ignores Jesus.[7] In speaking about Jesus, the Letter to the Hebrews asks, 'To which of the angels did God ever say, "Sit at my right hand until I make your enemies a footstool for your feet?"'[8] The implied answer is 'none' since it is part of an argument for Jesus' superiority to angels.

Will's separation from his father prompts him to ask Baruch and Balthamos, 'what happens when we die?'

They tell him that ghosts go to 'a prison camp' – the world of the dead – not to heaven, which even the churches don't realize is a deception (p.35). Will finds 'his imagination trembling' at this – if it's just another world, the knife can get him in.

Very soon another separation occurs: Baruch flies off to tell Lord Asriel what he and Balthamos had discovered in the Clouded Mountain. He arrives in bad shape but passes on news about Metatron's plans, as well as about the knife, its bearer and Lyra (p.63–66). When the draught from an opening door swirls the angel's loosening particles into the air, Balthamos is immediately aware of Baruch's death. Pullman touchingly conveys the agony of his grief (p.97). The depth of their love for each other is very moving. Many reviewers assume – wrongly in my opinion – that the two angels are homosexual because they love each other 'with a passion' (p.27). Pullman himself is

> . . . constantly amazed at how literal-minded [people] are. People come up to him and say, 'Excuse me, those two angels in *The Amber Spyglass*, are they homosexual?' And he'll say, as evenly as he can, 'No, they love each other, I have no idea of their sexual orientation.'[9]

Since these are angels, it seems entirely reasonable for them to have a profound platonic love for each other at a level of intensity, which is impossible for thoroughly sexual humans to understand.

On the knife edge

Will and Balthamos press on towards Lyra[10] and reach a town on a large river leading directly to the Himalayas. It's here that Will meets Iorek Byrnison and the other armoured bears trying to refuel for their journey in search of a new home. With extraordinary courage and presence of mind, Will races to confront the enormous bear. By slicing up Iorek's helmet, he succeeds in brokering a deal between townspeople and bears, preventing the people's anger from flaring up, and in making himself uninteresting to them afterwards (p.112–113). Iorek is deeply impressed by the boy – and intrigued by the knife.

When Will eventually reaches the cave, his meeting with Mrs Coulter unsettles him, partly because she dazzles him and partly because she brings his mother into the conversation. The rescue of Lyra becomes messy: the Magisterium's forces arrive by zeppelin to kill the girl; Lord Asriel's gyropters arrive to rescue her and his tiny Gallivespian spies fly in from the zeppelins on their dragonflies. Crucially, Will looks at Mrs Coulter as he starts cutting a window and the blade shatters preventing the obvious means of escape. The sight of Lyra's mother brings home to Will his separation from his own mother and breaks his detached yet focused frame of mind. It's too much, too emotional; he becomes disconnected from the knife rather than feeling as if he is at the very tip of it, cutting with his mind as well as the knife, as he had been taught (SK, p.191).

When Will asks Iorek to mend the knife, the bear is reluctant. The ensuing discussion can be seen as an exploration of the ethics of technology, similar to the conversation with Giacomo Paradisi (SK, p.196), but going further in examining the implications. As with all technology, there are side-effects which cannot always be anticipated. Iorek recognizes that the knife is too subtle to fully understand, telling Will that 'the harm it can do is unlimited. It would have been infinitely better if it had never been made,' because 'the knife has intentions too' (p.190).

Lyra insists that, since the knife does exist, it's better to use it responsibly than let it fall into the wrong hands. Iorek acquiesces, recognizing that the bears also use technology, albeit far simpler. But he insists that Lyra consult the alethiometer first since 'full knowledge is better than half-knowledge . . . Know what it is you're asking' (p.192) – a common theme in the trilogy. The alethiometer tells Lyra that the knife is extremely finely balanced; whether the knife brings about good or ill hangs on Will's motives. Within the framework of *His Dark Materials*, this cause and effect relationship comes into play when Will cuts open a fallen crystal litter so he can help the frail old angel within (p.431–432). Will hates killing and would never want to harm such a pathetic creature. So it is Will's motive of compassion that leads to the knife fulfilling its name – Æsahættr, god destroyer (*SK*, p.286) – as the Authority blows away. The scene feels curiously incidental, although the narrative has been heading resolutely in this direction.

After reuniting the knife shards, Iorek is troubled over the wisdom of his actions. Will confesses that he is torn between using the knife to be reunited with his mother, and offering its services to Lord Asriel. Iorek warns him:

> If you want to succeed in this task, you must no longer think about your mother. You must put her aside. If your mind is divided, the knife will break. (p.204)

The world of the dead

With the knife reforged, Will and Lyra, accompanied by the touchy hand-high spies Tialys and Salmakia, can start their journey to the world of the dead. The idea has been growing in Will for some time, and since Lyra had dreamed of finding Roger, they both see the journey as vital – they long to be reunited, even briefly, with Roger and John Parry. The alethiometer confirms their choice, and following its advice of 'Follow the knife,' Will cuts into a world where they find a dead man. He cuts again to escape approaching soldiers, but finds a new world identical in every respect to the one he's in – except for the dead man looking alive and well, though shell-shocked. The man is coming to terms with the fact that he is now a ghost; when he leaves they follow him, joining up with more and more ghosts. As they travel, their surroundings fade away as the ghosts forget the world of the living, which they have left forever.

The travellers arrive in the shantytown 'holding area' of the suburbs of the dead, and find shelter in the home of Peter and his family. It's an awkward meeting since Will, Lyra and the spies arrive without their deaths, whereas they don't understand who the deaths are. Peter explains:

> What we found out when we come here . . . we all brought our deaths with us . . . We had 'em all the time, and we never knew. See, everyone has a death. It goes everywhere with 'em all their life long, right close by . . . the moment you're born, your death comes into the world with you, and it's your death that takes you out. (p.275)

The grandmother's death explains that if they want to cross to the land of the dead, they must call up their deaths, 'say welcome, make friends, be kind, invite your deaths to come close to you, and see what you can get them to agree to' (p.279). But when Lyra sees her death face to face she is terrified – especially that the time of parting from Pantalaimon is imminent. Her death agrees to guide her,[11] and the party comes at last to the jetty to await the boatman. The scene on the shore is one of the most traumatic in the trilogy as Lyra is compelled to leave Pantalaimon behind. The agony of this separation, for both human and dæmon, in which they feel literally torn in two, is horrendous. Lyra's companions fare no better – they discover as they cross the lake that they too are leaving part of themselves behind.

After disembarking, Lyra's torment continues as they are confronted by No-Name the harpy. The loathsome creatures with their foul stench are immune to Gallivespian stings, but no one is immune to their taunting. Lyra's usual strategy of fabrication only succeeds in enraging No-Name. Lyra is shattered by her failure, but has little time to dwell on this, as the little group of living beings is almost immediately surrounded by innumerable ghosts:

> They had as much substance as fog, poor things . . . They crammed forward, light and lifeless, to warm themselves at the flowing blood and the strong-beating hearts of the two travellers.
> (p.311)

The desolation of the place is reinforced by Pullman describing their voices as 'no louder than dry leaves falling'[12] (p.312), and later the ghosts themselves as 'dry leaves scattered by a sudden gust of wind' (p.313). The ghosts agree to help the children find Roger and Will's father. The pity Lyra feels for the ghosts prompts her to suggest using the knife to free the ghosts. The 'true smile, so warm and happy' (p.319) that Will gives her causes a surprising reaction within Lyra. It's her first sensation of falling in love, though she has no idea yet what it means. The harpies are furious that their role, despicable as it is, will be taken from them. In the light of the harpies' response to Lyra's truthful story-telling, the Gallivespians get them to agree to guide the ghosts to the way out in exchange for true stories. With the harpies leading the way, the four travellers, followed by all the ghosts, start out for the best place to cut through into another world.

Dust and destruction

Alongside this narrative, Pullman has been teasing out another thread of the story. We last saw Mary Malone stepping into Cittàgazze (*SK*, p.265), and when we meet her again in *The Amber Spyglass*, she is being guided by the I Ching to yet another world. Everything about this world astounds her: the lava-like roads, the seed-pods from the giant trees, and most of all the mulefa with their curious diamond-framed skeleton – and wheels.[13] Having a scientist in this world gives Pullman the opportunity to explore the subject of evolution. Mary guesses that the various worlds have split off from each other in the past[14] and that evolution had taken a very different course here. Most intriguing is the inter-related evolution of seedpods, and the claw on the mulefa's legs – the mulefa make good use of the pods, but in return crack the pods by riding on them, and care for the seeds. Mary recognizes the centrality of the oil in this, and when the mulefa try to tell her that the oil is connected with wisdom, she begins to see a connection with her work in Oxford (p.135). Tantalizingly, Pullman immediately steers away from making the connection, telling us instead about a tualapi attack. We learn nothing more for several chapters other than a brief comment that the trees are dying.

Mary is astonished to learn from her friend Atal that the mulefa can see shadow particles or *sraf*. Inspired by Atal's description of what sraf looks like, and its similarity to light, Mary sets about making something that will enable her to see it. Through basic technology, craftsmanship and patience, together with some good advice and a little luck,[15] Mary succeeds in making her amber spyglass, which enables her to see with fresh vision. Mary's story seems quite separate from the other strands of the book until this discovery – now Mary can see Dust, the element which is at the centre of all the events. Once she has reached this point, the mulefa, who have been waiting for it, ask for her help with the dying trees. She soon finds that it's connected with a flow of sraf out of the world (p.246–247) – but before she can find a solution the drift turns into a flood.

Mary has no idea why there has been a sudden change, she just sees the effect. Lyra and Will, however, have seen the cause but are unaware of the effect. In the Magisterium's quest to destroy Lyra, they have a two-pronged strategy. One approach is their secret assassin, Father Gomez, who is following Mary's trail. The other is more opportunistic, and comes as a result of Mrs Coulter's visit to Geneva, since she carries some of Lyra's hair in a locket. Stealing it gives the Consistorial Court of Discipline the perfect chance to use a new bomb, which can locate the exact position of the rest of the hair, and somehow target colossal energy to it. The energy needs of the bomb are prodigious – a power station to begin the process, then the extraordinary amount of energy released by severing a dæmon. At the power station in the mountains, Mrs Coulter and Lord Roke manage to create a sufficient diversion for her to escape from being put into the silver cage, and for the golden monkey to rescue all but one hair from the resonating chamber of the bomb. Just as Father MacPhail is preparing to sacrifice himself in the cage, Will is reunited with his father in the world of the dead. The shaman, aware of what is happening, urges Will to shave off the cut hairs from Lyra's head and put them into another world. Will pushes the hairs through a window just as MacPhail twists two wires together and severs his own dæmon. The explosion, which is felt in other worlds, opens up an abyss into which Dust now cascades.

Released and restored

True to the alethiometer's prediction (p.193), the knife has brought about the imminent death of Dust – all the consciousness will flood out of every world into the abyss. After a hazardous journey along the edge of the abyss, Will is eventually able to cut a window out of the world of the dead. The ghosts stream out excitedly and dissolve into the air. As with angels, Pullman's ghosts have *some* physical being – they are not spiritual and non-material; they're still made of particles, but are *very* thin. Later, after dealing with the Spectres in the great battle, Lee Scoresby finally allows himself to drift apart. At this point Pullman seems to go against the oblivion he had been advocating, as 'the last of Lee' comes out 'under the brilliant stars, where the atoms of his beloved dæmon, Hester, were waiting for him' (p.440).

In an audacious attempt to keep Metatron from finding the children's dæmons, and thus controlling the knife bearer, Mrs Coulter again borrows one of Lord Asriel's intention craft. She finds her way to the Regent in the Clouded Mountain and seduces him into following her to the abyss. Although I argued earlier that angels' relationships are platonic, Metatron is portrayed as an angel who had been a sex-crazed man. He longs for contact with human flesh again. Down at the edge of the abyss, she is reunited with Asriel and the two of them sacrifice themselves for Lyra by wrestling the great angel down into the abyss.

In the heat of the battle, Will and Lyra finally reach their dæmons, which are being protected from Spectres by John Parry, Lee Scoresby and other warrior ghosts. They scoop them into their arms, suddenly realizing they have each other's dæmons, and cut through into another world – the world where Mary Malone is worrying over the ebbing tide of sraf. It's not long before they are with Mary in the mulefa village, beginning to recover from their ordeal, though their dæmons are not yet ready to be with them. Some mulefa discover the ghosts leaving the world of the dead and take Mary to see it. The ghost of an old woman tells Mary to 'tell them stories' (p.455) before she dissolves – an injunction which Mary takes to heart and puts into practice the following day. In recounting her own experiences, Mary fulfils her role of tempter without even realizing it. On the next day, as Will and Lyra search for their dæmons, they come to understand their love for each other, and Lyra fulfils her destiny as a second Eve (explored in Chapter

11). The flood of Dust is halted, and it reverts to its age-old patterns of drifting down from space into conscious minds. The knife has also fulfilled the alethiometer's other prediction that it would keep Dust alive.

Star-crossed lovers

Almost as soon as Will and Lyra understand that they want to be with each other forever, they are united once more with their dæmons. But their dæmons bring terrible news: every window opened by the knife creates Spectres, and causes Dust to leak away. They must all be closed – all except the one from the world of the dead. Lyra and Will realize with dismay that they can only live in their own worlds because their dæmons cannot survive in any other (p.512). There are some joyful reunions – with Serafina Pekkala, John Faa and Farder Coram – but always tempered with the anguished realization: once they go home, and the windows are closed, the knife must be destroyed and they will never see each other again. Their final parting is as heart-rending as any other scene in *His Dark Materials*, and the pain of their eternal separation shatters the subtle knife, never to be reforged. Nicholas Tucker comments:

> By making Will and Lyra – like Romeo and Juliet – separate just as they have finally found each other, Pullman also ensures that this first vision of young love remains for ever unsullied by any of the practical difficulties or inevitable disagreements that creep into even the most ideal of human relationships.[16]

But it is not the ending of the story. Xaphania gives them a glimmer of hope, which they barely recognize – she tells them that it would be possible, though very hard work, for them to travel between worlds even with-out windows as Will's father had done. A friend 'has already taken the first steps' (p.523) – we presume Mary after her out-of-body experience. Meanwhile, Will and Mary head off for a good cup of tea before beginning the process of sorting out the messes of their respective situations. Lyra has dinner with the Master and Dame Hannah Relf, and willingly agrees to become a student at St Sophia's, where she can make new friends and begin the process of relearning how to read the alethiometer. And in the final scene in the Botanic Garden, Lyra and Pantalaimon reflect on what they – and Philip Pullman – see as their greatest purpose: to build the republic of heaven.

[1] The quotation at the beginning of Chapter One of *The Amber Spyglass* is from William Blake's 'Little Girl Lost', one of the poems in *Songs of Experience* (Yeats, W. B. (ed.), *William Blake Collected Poems* (London, Routledge, 2002), p.68). Pullman leaves out the first line of the stanza which reads, 'Sleeping Lyca lay . . .'

[2] As I suggested in Chapter 4, this seems to me to be a gross misreading of John Milton's work.

[3] Pullman, Philip, 'Discussion on Readerville.com' (www.readerville.com/ WebX?14@65.93OcaX9YecM^7@.ef6c70e/59).

[4] Pullman, 'Discussion on Readerville.com'. Pullman worked some of his ideas about angels into the text of *His Dark Materials*, but included some more in the *Liber Angelorum*, which is found on the Random House website (www.randomhouse.com/features/pullman/subtleknife/liber.html).

[5] Genesis 5:24, *New International Version*.

[6] For a thorough examination of the idea of angels, see Williams, Peter S., *The Case for Angels* (Paternoster, 2003).

[7] Jesus is mentioned twice in *His Dark Materials*. Both references are from Mary Malone explaining her loss of faith (p.465, 466).

[8] Hebrews 1:13, *New International Version*. The idea of Jesus being at the 'right hand' of God, that is, in the position of utmost importance, occurs frequently in the Bible.

[9] Vincent, Sally, 'Driven by daemons', *Guardian*, 10 November 2001.

[10] Interestingly, Mrs Coulter seems to have managed the journey of several thousand miles in a matter of a few days, whereas Will has to travel at a more modest pace.

[11] We never hear what happens to Lyra's death – does he cease to accompany her throughout life?

[12] There is a strong echo of *Paradise Lost* here which describes Satan's hordes in Hell as 'His Legions, Angel Forms, who lay intrans't / Thick as Autumnal Leaves that strow the Brooks / In Vallombrosa' (Book I, lines 301–303).

[13] Pullman writes: 'I remember a day with my younger son, who was then 15, when we were on holiday in Slovenia, and we were speculating about the business of why no animals had wheels. What would be necessary, biologically, physiologically, for that to be possible? We were walking around Lake Bled, which is a very pretty lake all surrounded by trees, and in two or three hours we had invented the mulefa. At least, we'd got the creatures and the trees and the seed-pods and the wheels. But on their own they would have meant little and added nothing to the story; so then the connection had to be made with Dust and the basic theme of the story, which of course is the difference between innocence and experience' (www. readerville.com/WebX?14@65.93OcaX9YecM^7@.ef6c70e/92).

[14] She says that this is predicted by quantum theory (p.90). This idea is examined in the Appendix.

[15] A recurrence of Pullman's common theme of the need for talent, hard work and luck (see Chapter 3).

[16] Tucker, Nicholas, *Darkness Visible: Inside the world of Philip Pullman* (Wizard Books, 2003), p.179.

CHAPTER 8

Beyond *The Amber Spyglass*

His Dark Materials is developing a life of its own through media other than books. In audio books, apart from the unabridged reading of the trilogy[1] by Pullman and a full cast (a wonderfully absorbing 34 hours), the BBC also produced a radio dramatization[2] in 2003 starring Terence Stamp as Lord Asriel and Emma Fielding as Mrs Coulter. The adaptation by Lavinia Murray got around some of the difficulties of condensing such an extraordinary story into six hours by using Balthamos as a narrator. One small change from the books, which raised some eyebrows among fans, was a name for Mrs Coulter's dæmon – Ozymandias. Pullman wasn't thrilled:

> I didn't choose that name and to be frank I don't think I would have done. I imagine that the scriptwriter did get it from Shelley's poem, but you'd really have to ask her why she went for that name.[3]

Pullman's reason for not giving the golden monkey a name is 'because every time I tried to think of one, he snarled and frightened me. What's more he hardly speaks either.'[4]

Stage and screen

Another adaptation of the trilogy, which shoehorned the story into six hours, was Nicholas Wright's for the

National Theatre.[5] Nick Hytner, the director of the National, said it was 'pouring a petrol station into a pint pot'.[6] But he 'wanted to do a play that spoke as directly to a young audience as a movie at the local multiplex'.[7] It seemed almost impossible to be able to stage such an extraordinary story, but Hytner hadn't even finished reading the trilogy when he decided that he had to do it. He said, 'What seemed immediately stageable were the series of archetypal, highly emotional family conflicts, which I thought were powerful and dramatic and would hold a theatre full of people.'[8] Philip Pullman responded to the news with amazement:

> I was astonished . . . I was absolutely thrilled, of course. Delighted. And simultaneously relieved that it wasn't me having to make it into a play. It was someone else.[9]

Pullman is quite relaxed about his story being retold in a different medium, and by someone else:

> Once a story leaves your desk it goes into the hands of the reader – they see things in it that you didn't think were there. So once you've published a book, you've lost control of it, and if you want to fret about that then don't publish it. But to do something major with it, the main thing was to make sure it got into the best hands. I couldn't think of any better hands than Nicholas Hytner and the National Theatre.[10]

And Pullman was immediately impressed with the actors:

> When I saw [Anna Maxwell Martin] at the read through I was utterly convinced that she was Lyra – she looks like the Lyra I had in my head

and she is very clever in a streetwise way like
Lyra. And Dominic Cooper, who plays Will, is
brilliant.[11]

While they were still rehearsing, Rupert Kaye, Chief
Executive of the Association of Christian Teachers,
denounced the National Theatre for staging the play at
all, and especially at Christmas:

> The National Theatre as a national institution
> has a responsibility to put on a family play over
> the Christmas and New Year season which is
> uplifting, enjoyable and accessible to people of
> all ages and backgrounds. Philip Pullman's story
> is deeply disturbing – it is offensive to Christians
> and will shock and appal people of other faiths
> too.[12]

Hytner, however, was unrepentant:

> I have no problem at all with fundamentalists
> taking offence at Philip's construction of a very
> beautiful and profoundly good mythology. If they
> find his ideas heretical, that's fine. Let's discuss
> it. But the notion of banning is completely
> unacceptable . . . We are not a church. It's not
> the business of the National to celebrate
> Christmas.[13]

Fans are awaiting the film adaptation of *His Dark
Materials* with a mixture of eager anticipation and
apprehension. Scholastic bought the film rights very
early on, and have partnered with New Line Productions
to make the films. Pullman is very pleased that New
Line is involved given their track record with another
three-part epic fantasy, Tolkien's *The Lord of the
Rings*. He was also pleased that Tom Stoppard was
brought in to write the screenplay in late 2002. At the

time of writing (June 2004) a director has not been appointed. Pullman says:

> I hope it will be someone who will take the story seriously and not be intoxicated by all the opportunities for lots of action. At the centre of the story is a very simple thing: a girl and a boy growing up, who realize they love each other.[14]

Discussions are taking place with Chris Weitz, and there are rumours that he will write a new screenplay in place of Stoppard's. Weitz, with his brother Paul, is best known for producing light entertainment films such as *American Pie*. Their most serious film to date is perhaps *About a Boy* based on Nick Hornby's novel. *Empire Online* points out that Peter Jackson would not have seemed an obvious choice to direct *The Lord of the Rings* beforehand, and goes on to point out how keen Weitz is:

> Chris is reportedly so keen to land this job that he wrote a long dissertation detailing how he would tackle the books, which range across several different realities and feature angels, ghosts, Furies, armoured polar bears, a dæmon familiar for every character and the stuff the universe is made of. Weitz' treatment obviously impressed the studio executives as well as author Philip Pullman and screenwriter Tom Stoppard and he is now deep in negotiations for the job.[15]

Pullman says:

> I've seen some of what Chris Weitz has written, and although there are some small areas where we shall have to discuss things, I like the general tendency of what he says.[16]

The Book of Dust

Philip Pullman is, meanwhile, still hard at work – and has stopped giving interviews for a while so that he can get on with his writing. Now he has finished *The Scarecrow and the Servant*, he is finally getting down to work on the long awaited *The Book of Dust*. This will develop further some of the ideas in *His Dark Materials*. In particular, he sees it as a good opportunity to flesh out the 'creation myth', which underpinned the trilogy. This myth is the story of the origin of the Authority, the first angel to condense out of Dust, and his deception of the angels who came afterwards. It talks about 'the Sophia', the angel who became known as Wisdom, and her attempt to unmask the Authority, which resulted in the first angelic rebellion. It also describes how these rebel angels brought 'enlightenment' to the conscious beings of every world, prompting them to declare their independence of God. The churches of every world are, according to the myth, the Authority's way of punishing and controlling the fallen beings. The myth ends at the point where *His Dark Materials* begins – with Lord Asriel preparing a second rebellion. How much more than this story will go into *The Book of Dust* remains to be seen – Pullman is characteristically secretive about its contents, claiming that when he talks too much about things he ends up not writing about them. However, he has said:

> *The Book of Dust* will not be a simple reference book – far from it. I want to go into the background of Lyra's world, and the creation myth that underpins the whole trilogy, and to say something about some of the other characters, and about the alethiometer and the

history of the subtle knife, and so on.

Furthermore I want it to be richly illustrated. It'll be story-driven, not reference-driven, and I'll need to brood over it in silence before I find the right form for it.[17]

Pullman has often said that there are plenty more stories from Lyra's world to be told. He would like to tell the story of Lee Scoresby and Iorek Byrnison fighting together in the Tunguska campaign, for example, and there's a story in the relationship between Serafina Pekkala and Farder Coram. The story about Lyra will be set about four years after the end of *The Amber Spyglass*.

Lyra's Oxford

However, while Pullman was working on material for *The Book of Dust*, he began to realize that it might be good to have some kind of stepping-stone first. He says,

I thought it would be fun to put together some documents and bits and pieces from Lyra's world, such as a map of the Oxford she knows, and as I did, I found a story beginning to take shape.[18]

The story that took shape is just one episode, which probably would have gone into *The Book of Dust*, but editor David Fickling encouraged him to do something more self-contained with it:

I asked Philip if he could do some bits and pieces around the idea of a map and this book grew out of it. He always told me he couldn't write short stories, but it isn't true . . . In my view this new short story is one of the finest pieces of writing that Philip has ever produced.[19]

The short story is called 'Lyra and the Birds' and is found in the book, *Lyra's Oxford*. It's set around two years after Lyra and Will part at the end of *The Amber Spyglass*. The story of Lyra in *The Book of Dust* is likely to be set another two years on again, so 'Lyra and the Birds' looks back to the trilogy as well as ahead to the later work – it acts as 'a sort of bridge'.[20] After *The Book of Dust* Pullman says there will be only one more book about Lyra's world – at Fickling's suggestion there will be a 'little dark-green book' to partner the little dark-red book of *Lyra's Oxford*.

But *Lyra's Oxford* is more than just a single short story:

> We wanted to create an object that was both intriguing and beautiful, and – like the story – was both self-contained and full of references elsewhere. There [is] a map of Lyra's Oxford, like ours but different, and various other bits and pieces; and it [is] illustrated by John Lawrence, the great master of the woodcut.[21]

At the British Book Trade Awards, the Nibbies, in March 2004, *Lyra's Oxford* deservedly won the award for design and production, and David Fickling was voted editor of the year. The 'various other bits and pieces' include the map of Lyra's Oxford, a postcard and other material from Lyra's world. Pullman's delightfully enigmatic preface to *Lyra's Oxford* comments on them:

> The other things might be connected with the story, or they might not; they might be connected to stories that haven't appeared yet. It's not easy to tell.
>
> It's easy to imagine how they might have turned up, though. The world is full of things like that: old postcards, theatre programmes,

> leaflets about bomb-proofing your cellar,
> greetings cards, photograph albums, holiday
> brochures, instruction booklets for machine
> tools, maps, catalogues, railway timetables,
> menu cards from long-gone cruise liners – all
> kinds of things that once served a real and useful
> purpose, but have now become cut adrift from
> the things and the people they relate to.[22]

Some of the things clearly relate to Lyra's world, but others – the postcard from Mary Malone, for one – are from ours. Who knows how these pieces came together, but here they are, stuck together as if they had been tucked into the book for safe keeping. 'All these tattered old bits and pieces have a history and a meaning,' but that meaning is only apparent to the person who put them into the book. The effect is as though we've picked up the book in a second-hand bookshop and been intrigued at what else has come along for the ride. That's exactly the effect Philip Pullman and David Fickling wanted of course – that's part of the reason why the book is clothbound, and John Lawrence's superb woodcuts add to the feeling. It needs to *feel* like a lovely, precious book into which you might tuck some of these things.

Pullman is having lots of fun here. On the reverse side of the map are various advertisements, including one for 'books on travel, archaeology and related subjects'. Several of these fictional publications have connections with the trilogy: we see that Colonel Carborn, who 'made the first balloon flight over the North Pole' (*NL*, p.77) has written a book about his adventure, and that Dr Broken Arrow is an anthropologist as well as an oceanographer (*NL*, p.77). We also discover that the talented Marisa Coulter is a published author – bizarrely on 'The Bronze Clocks of Benin', which seems to be very far removed from the activities of the General Oblation Board. But we do know she spent time exploring in Africa – this is presumably where she came across *zombis* and the magic that created the spy flies.[23] There's a book on 'some curious anomalies in the mathematics' of the *Four Books of Architecture* by one of the world's greatest architects, Andrea Palladio (originator of the Palladian style). The book is by one Nicholas Outram – these are Philip's middle names. The final two books listed also hark back to *Northern Lights*. Jotham Santelia[24] recovered his mind enough to write up his experiences on Svalbard as *A Prisoner of the Bears*, while his Jordan colleague, Trelawney, is the author of *Fraud: an Exposure of a Scientific Imposture* – rather ironic given Santelia's outburst about him (*NL*, p.331).

Perhaps most tantalizing of all the extras, is the information about the cruise of the *SS Zenobia* through the Mediterranean to the Levant (the old name for the countries at the eastern end of the Mediterranean: Lebanon, Israel, and parts of Syria and Turkey). Is this something that will play a part in *The Book of Dust*? We'll have to wait and see. The item which Pullman draws most attention to in the preface is the postcard. It features a very odd collection of images – as its sender, Mary Malone, acknowledges when she writes, 'Such a beautiful city, and they produce a card like this!'[25] Observant readers of the trilogy immediately recognize the hornbeam trees in Sunderland Avenue from Pullman's little drawing for the first chapter in *The Subtle Knife*. We understand the significance of the bench in the Botanic Gardens, and the science building in which Mary works. The picture of a house in Norham Gardens doesn't obviously fit, but Mary says it's round the corner from her flat. Pullman writes:

> . . . it might not have occurred to [Mary Malone] . . . when she sent a postcard to an old friend shortly after arriving in Oxford for the first time, that that card itself would trace part of a story that hadn't yet happened when she wrote it.
>
> Perhaps some particles move backwards in time; perhaps the future affects the past in some way we don't understand; or perhaps the universe is simply more aware than we are.[26]

It is perhaps significant that the preface to *Lyra's Oxford* isn't signed – it doesn't need to be signed, but it often would be. Maybe it only becomes significant because it follows the quotation from Oscar Baedecker. This quotation seems to have the same status as those at the beginning of *Northern Lights* and *The Amber Spyglass* – passages from other writing which influence or shed light on what is to follow. The Baedecker quotation functions in the same way, but it is as much part of the fiction as the story of Lyra and the birds. There is no reference to him anywhere – not even in the British Library or the American Library of Congress. What finally gives the game away is the reference to him on the page apparently from an old Oxford guidebook (inserted just after page 30 of *Lyra's Oxford*) where Baedecker is quoted as referring to 'the coastline Oxford shares with Bohemia'. Perhaps Baedecker is not even of Lyra's world – he certainly isn't from ours. So the preface, sandwiched between fictions, seems to be as fictional as the rest.

The search for meaning

The question that keeps coming back while pondering on all these bits and pieces is, 'What does it all mean?' How does it all fit together? As the preface concludes, 'There are many things we haven't yet learned how to read. The story in this book is partly about that very process.' Is Pullman suggesting that *everything* has some meaning if only we can discern it? Lyra soon confirms this. The story begins with Lyra on the roof of Jordan College again, watching a vast flock of starlings swooping around above the Oxford skyline before roosting in the Botanic Garden. She and Pantalaimon speculate on whether or not their complicated flight path might have some meaning. Pan suggests that it might mean nothing, 'It just is' (*LO*, p.5), but Lyra is adamant that 'Everything means something. We just have to find out how to read it' (p.5–6). After her experiences with the alethiometer, and with the loops and swirls on Mary Malone's computer, perhaps it's not surprising that she holds this conviction so fiercely.

As they ponder this question, the flock begins to attack something. Lyra and Pantalaimon are shocked to realize that it's a witch's dæmon. They help him to escape through the trapdoor into Jordan College and away from the starlings' fury. It transpires that the dæmon is looking for Lyra to get her help in searching for a man called Sebastian Makepeace. The dæmon's witch is sick and needs help from Makepeace. As Lyra investigates the whereabouts of Makepeace, she discovers that he is an alchemist and a former scholar of Merton. Jordan scholar Dr Polstead dismisses him as a nutcase: 'He devoted himself to alchemy – in this day and age!' (p.18). At dinner in St Sophia's,[27] Lyra quizzes an elderly history scholar about alchemy and why it was no longer practised, and is told that Makepeace is the only serious alchemist in two and a half centuries. Lyra's two informants both make connections to the theme of meaning. Dr Polstead believes that, because Sebastian Makepeace is mad, his work and his mumblings to himself have no meaning. The scholar, Miss Greenwood, tells Lyra that the alchemist's name is 'ironic', as he 'was said to be very violent' (p.22) – his name means the opposite of his character.

Lyra and Pantalaimon take the dæmon to Jericho after dinner – but they feel uneasy. There are too many uncertain aspects of what's going on for them to understand. They are suspicious of Makepeace because 'alchemy's nonsense' (p.26). They are suspicious of the witch's dæmon, though they have no real reason beyond the fact that they had never heard of the 'birch oath', which the dæmon had mentioned to them (p.15). And it's a mystery to them why birds keep attacking the dæmon. When they press him to tell them the truth, he explains that Makepeace is the only one who can cure the new sickness that is killing witches but not their dæmons. Lyra's heart goes out to the dæmon, though she suppresses the questions and doubts that still fill her mind. Pullman comments that 'since she and Will had parted two years before, the slightest thing had the power to move her to pity and distress; it felt as if her heart were bruised for ever' (p.30).

When they reach the alchemist's house, Lyra and Pan finally become aware that they are walking into a trap. While Pan struggles with the witch's dæmon, Lyra prepares to face the witch, thinking through how Will, the natural fighter, would act in the situation. She is saved by the extraordinary intervention of another bird, as a swan flies at full speed into the witch, breaking her back. Makepeace and the witch had been lovers; their son had died in the recent war and the witch held Lyra responsible as it was said that the war was fought over Lyra. Lyra claims it was nothing to do with her – it seems that even now she doesn't realize how central a role she played. As they reflect back on the odd behaviour of the birds, Pan realizes that it wasn't random behaviour, but rather they were protecting Lyra. Makepeace confirms this, saying, 'Everything has a meaning; if only we could read it' (p.45–46). The alchemist cannot discern the meaning, but he does tell them, 'It means something about you, and something about the city. You'll find the meaning if you search for it' (p.46). As they return to St Sophia's, they hear a nightingale singing – a sign of peace after the turmoil of the previous hours – and they try to work out the meaning of it all. Pan says, 'It feels as if the whole city's looking after us. So what we feel is part of the meaning, isn't it?'

The story is like the book as a whole – there are several elements that don't seem to fit in or make sense, at least initially. Some of them only make sense when looked at in a different way. Some look back to events which have already taken place, some anticipate events still to come and we won't see the significance of these for some time. It seems highly likely that Sebastian Makepeace (who seems, in the end, to be both sane and peaceful) will play a significant role in *The Book of Dust*[28]; perhaps Dr Polstead and Miss Greenwood will too. Why the city should be looking after Lyra at all remains a mystery – the all-pervasive Dust must still have some purpose in mind for Lyra. Back in *The Amber Spyglass*, as Mary Malone surveys the wreck of her fallen tree, she too is searching for some meaning and finds it in the love of matter for Dust. Pullman's message seems to be that we must search for meaning in this world, our home, and in the matter and consciousness of which it is composed. Lyra's relationship with Oxford seems to be a metaphor for the relationship Pullman thinks we should have with the physical world in which we live:

> The city, their city – *belonging* was one of the
> meanings of that, and *protection*, and *home*.
> (p.48)

We'll explore what kinds of meanings Pullman sees in the world and expresses through his books in Part Three.

[1] Pullman, Philip, *His Dark Materials* (Cover to Cover, 2002). The three volumes each won Audio Publishers Association Audie awards (in 2000, 2001 and 2002).

[2] *Philip Pullman: His Dark Materials Trilogy* (BBC Radio Collection, 2003).

[3] Pullman, Philip, BBC webchat (www.bbc.co.uk/radio4/arts/hisdarkmaterials/pullman_webchat.shtml).

[4] Pullman, Philip, 'Discussion on Readerville.com' (www.readerville.com/webx?14@20.iHImaaLtrtL.0@.ef6c70e/92).

[5] A revival is scheduled from 20 November 2004 until 2 April 2005 – see www.nationaltheatre.org.uk. For more information on staging the production see Robert Butler, *The Art of Darkness: Staging the Philip Pullman trilogy* (National Theatre, 2003) and www.stagework.org.uk.

[6] Quoted in Butler, Robert, *The Art of Darkness: Staging the Philip Pullman trilogy* (National Theatre, 2003), p.76.

[7] Butler, *The Art of Darkness: Staging the Philip Pullman trilogy*, p.6.

[8] Lyall, Sarah, *New York Times*, 25 January 2004.

[9] Quoted in Butler, *The Art of Darkness: Staging the Philip Pullman trilogy*, p.36.

[10] Brunton, Michael, 'You Don't Know How Famous You Are Until Complete Strangers Stop You In The Street To Talk' in *Time* (www.time.com/time/europe/arts/article/0,13716,579063,00.html).

[11] 'Philip Pullman answers your questions' (www.bbc.co.uk/gloucestershire/getfresh/2003/10/philip_pullman_qa.shtml).

[12] Kaye, Rupert, 'Association of Christian Teachers attacks the National Theatre for staging "blasphemous" Philip Pullman play' (www.christian-teachers.org.uk/news/HisDarkMaterials.htm).

[13] Sierz, Aleks, 'Philip Pullman and Nicholas Hytner: Enter the dæmons', *Independent*, 12 December 2003.

[14] Brunton, 'You Don't Know How Famous You Are Until Complete Strangers Stop You In The Street To Talk'.

[15] 'Northern Weitz', 25 May 2004 (www.empireonline.co.uk/site/news/newsstory.asp?news_id=15875).

[16] Pullman, Philip, personal email to the author, 16 June 2004.

[17] Quoted in Eccleshare, Julia, 'Letter from London', *Publisher's Weekly*, 5 March 2001.

[18] Pullman, Philip, 'About the Books: Lyra's Oxford' (www.philip-pullman.com/pages/content/index.asp?PageID=61).

[19] Thorpe, Vanessa and Heawood, Jonathan, 'Pullman brings back Lyra for Oxford mystery', *Observer*, 6 April 2003.

[20] Thorpe and Heawood, 'Pullman brings back Lyra for Oxford mystery'.

[21] Thorpe and Heawood, 'Pullman brings back Lyra for Oxford mystery'.

[22] Pullman, Philip, *Lyra's Oxford* (David Fickling Books, 2003), introductory pages.

[23] Some voodoo traditions are thought to originate with the Dahomey people of Benin.

[24] There is no connection between Jotham Santelia and the city of Sant'Elia in the world of Cittàgazze – Pullman says he was 'just being careless. It's a name I like, and I came back to it forgetting that I'd used it before' (personal email to the author, 28 May 2004).

[25] Pullman, *Lyra's Oxford*, postcard.

[26] Pullman, *Lyra's Oxford*, introductory pages.

[27] St Sophia's may possibly have this name because this is the place where Lyra will continue her process of learning true wisdom. Or it may not.

[28] This is rather a hostage to fortune – if Makepeace doesn't appear in *The Book of Dust* I'll look rather silly. I have *tried* to get Pullman to spill the beans on what's going into *The Book of Dust*, but he remains tight-lipped, saying 'No clues at all. I'm not going to give away the slightest hint' (personal email to the author, 16 June 2004).

PART THREE

Shedding Light on Dark Matter

CHAPTER 9

Dæmons ar
Growing U

Perhaps the most harrowing moment of *His Dark Materials* is when Lyra leaves Pantalaimon to travel to the world of the dead:

> [Lyra] looked back again at the foul and dismal shore, so bleak and blasted with disease and poison, and thought of her dear Pan waiting there alone, her heart's companion, watching her disappear into the mist, and she fell into a storm of weeping. Her passionate sobs didn't echo, because the mist muffled them, but all along the shore in innumerable ponds and shallows, in wretched broken tree stumps, the damaged creatures that lurked there heard her full-hearted cry and drew themselves a little closer to the ground, afraid of such passion.
>
> . . . Lyra was doing the cruellest thing she had ever done, hating herself, hating the deed, suffering for Pan and with Pan and because of Pan; trying to put him down on the cold path, disengaging his cat-claws from her clothes, weeping, weeping. Will closed his ears: the sound was too unhappy to bear. Time after time she pushed her dæmon away, and still he cried and tried to cling.
>
> . . . And she pushed him away, so that he

> crouched bitter and cold and frightened on the
> muddy ground. (*AS*, p.295–298)

We can't quite imagine the depth of pain Lyra experiences because we have no conception of what it means to be inextricably bound up with a creature that is external to us, and yet part of us. I can imagine the pain of leaving the person I most love, possibly never to see them again. But that person is still *not me*; I know what it's like to be away from them; I know that the person exists independently of me. It's the finality of parting that would cause the anguish. But to be sundered from a *part of me* – what would that be like?

The unity of human and dæmon

It's perhaps at this point that we understand even more fully how terrible a place Bolvangar was. Back in *Northern Lights* we realized that to separate a child from his or her dæmon was a terrible thing; we could see Lyra's distress over it. But nearly 800 pages later we are so much more engaged with Lyra and Pantalaimon that we feel the trauma intensely. The oneness of girl and dæmon has become normal to us, as indeed, it has to Will.

We have come to realize that Lyra's sense of herself is as much bound up with Pan as with her own body. She feels no less integrated as a person than Will, who has no visible dæmon. It is Lyra's sense of Will being just as complete as she is that enables her to reason that his dæmon must be inside him. Will is completely unaware of this other part of him – until he discovers 'an agony building inside him' as he leaves the desolate shore with Lyra. He realizes that he does have a dæmon – and he, too, is being torn apart from himself:

Part of it was physical. It felt as if an iron hand had gripped his heart and was pulling it out between his ribs, so that he pressed his hands to the place and vainly tried to hold it in. It was far deeper and far worse than the pain of losing his fingers. But it was mental, too: something secret and private was being dragged into the open where it had no wish to be, and Will was nearly overcome by a mixture of pain and shame and fear and self-reproach, because he himself had caused it.

And it was worse than that. It was as if he'd said, 'No, don't kill me, I'm frightened; kill my mother instead; she doesn't matter, I don't love her,' and as if she'd heard him say it, and pretended she hadn't so as to spare his feelings, and offered herself in his place anyway because of her love for him. He felt as bad as that. There was nothing worse to feel. (*AS*, p.299–300)

Towards the end of *The Amber Spyglass*, Will gets to meet his dæmon, Kirjava,[1] for the first time. He realizes that he'll never forget that meeting, nor the feeling of having Kirjava ripped apart from him before he even knew of her existence.

Dæmons, then, make for a very powerful narrative device within *His Dark Materials*, but what are they?

True companions

Philip Pullman use the dæmons to great effect within *His Dark Materials*, but the idea isn't entirely original to him as he concedes: 'dæmons came into my head suddenly and unexpectedly, but they do have a sort of provenance. One clear origin is Socrates' daimon.

Another is the old idea of the guardian angel.'[2] As Pullman says, the concept of dæmon goes back to the Greeks. A dæmon in that classical sense is 'a spirit, or immaterial being, holding a middle place between men and deities in pagan mythology' or 'one's genius; a tutelary spirit or internal voice; as, the dæmon of Socrates'.[3] You sometimes find dæmon in this classical sense spelt as 'daimon' or 'demon' but there are no evil overtones to this concept. Over time the meaning (and spelling) of the word shifted to have the sense that it does today – an evil spirit. But Pullman draws on the earlier idea and turns it into something visible – the companion animal. Towards the end of *The Amber Spyglass*, Serafina Pekkala reminds Pantalaimon what the primary function of a dæmon is:

> One thing hasn't changed: you must help your humans, not hinder them. You must help them and guide them and encourage them towards wisdom. That's what dæmons are for.
> (*AS*, p.500)

The idea of companion animals who are more than simply animals is an important part of shamanism and witchcraft. Animal familiars are often thought to be able to change shape and to be spirit guides. In tribal shamanism, the spirit travelling while in a trance (*SK*, p.224) is often believed to be in an animal form. In his 1992 television series, *Millennium: Tribal wisdom and the Modern world*,[4] anthropologist David Maybury-Lewis described how Ignacion, a Makuna shaman, became a spirit jaguar under the influence of a hallucinogenic drug. Sir James Frazer, in his famous 1922 book, *The Golden Bough*, also talks about various tribal cultures, which believed in the idea of an external

soul in animals or even stones. Often they believed that
the death of the animal entailed the death of the human
and vice versa.[5] However, neither this nor the Greek
idea of dæmons are quite how Philip Pullman uses
dæmons in *His Dark Materials*, but these things
underpin his invention.

Sally Vincent, writing in the *Guardian* says:

> Your dæmon . . . is the creature of your deepest
> essence; a bird, reptile, insect or animal,
> attached to you by an inevitable thread, like an
> externalised soul. It is your guardian angel, your
> confidante, your conscience, your representative.
> In childhood, while you make the choices that
> form your character, your dæmon changes;
> when you become an adult, it is what you have
> created, and it stays like that until you die. A
> slimy snake, a sly monkey, a fierce tiger, an
> obedient dog, a pussy cat: it's yours. It's you.
> You're never alone with a dæmon.[6]

These descriptions – *externalised soul, guardian
angel, confidante, conscience, representative* – are
partly, but not entirely right. *Externalised soul* is probably the best description, as Iorek Byrnison makes clear
when he tells Lyra that 'a bear's armour is his soul, just
as a dæmon is your soul' (*NL*, p.196). But it doesn't
seem to be the case that the human has no soul and no
conscience apart from the dæmon. That would make
Lyra's separation from Pantalaimon a very different
affair. Neither is it quite right that the dæmon is a
guardian angel, despite Pullman referring to the idea
(he does, of course, include angels as beings in their
own right). *Guardian angels* is suggestive of entirely
separate beings with a responsibility for watching over

and protecting humans. And the dæmon isn't quite a *representative* of the human – except in the case of witches and shamans, whose dæmons can travel far from their humans – although it does represent something about the human. Human and dæmon are fuzzy, over-lapping parts of the same thing; two facets of one being.

And yet they also have some measure of independ-ence. They are physically, although invisibly, bound together. But a dæmon can be active while the human is still, and can move some distance from the human. A child's dæmon can change shape, while the human obviously can't. The human and dæmon are mentally bound together – they each know what the other is thinking ('[Lyra] and Pantalaimon could feel each other's thoughts'; *NL*, p.236), and yet they can also think differently. Think back, for example, to the open-ing scene when Lyra and Pantalaimon sneak into the Retiring Room and see the Master poison the Tokay. Pan argues that 'it's none of our business. And I think it would be the silliest thing you've ever done in a lifetime of silly things to interfere' (*NL*, p.8–9). Lyra doesn't see that they have a choice any more and accusingly says to Pan, 'You're supposed to know about conscience aren't you?' Pantalaimon realizes that he hadn't spotted Lyra's intention of hiding and watching. Lyra tells him off for nagging. There's a suggestion here that the dæmon is, to some extent, the voice of conscience, but clearly Lyra is not without a conscience, despite disagreeing with Pan.

A human and dæmon share physical experiences and are also emotionally bound together, feeling the same way much of the time but not all of it. In the incident just referred to, Lyra and Pantalaimon end up feeling cross, but they are cross with *each other*. Before they are reunited after their agonizing separation, Lyra longs to see Pan and to hold him, but her dæmon keeps his distance from her as a punishment (*AS*, p.502).

The divine paradox

Like the overlapping circles of a Venn diagram, a human and dæmon partly share a consciousness, and partly have separate consciousnesses. Given Philip Pullman's antipathy to Christianity, the great irony of his invention of the dæmon (and the Death) is that he has constructed a rather good model of the Trinity of God. The Trinity is a very difficult concept. It express-es the Christian belief that there is one God, and yet we see God in the Bible in three persons: Father, Son (Jesus Christ) and Holy Spirit. Each of these three persons are fully God, but their unity is such that we cannot say they are three Gods. People often claim that these two aspects of God's nature are contradictory – God cannot be both one and three at the same time. But this isn't the case.

First, it may not be a contradiction but a paradox. A paradox *appears* contradictory but actually expresses some truth that is not obvious. Second, if God is infinite, then we should expect to find aspects of his nature and being, which are beyond our ability to understand. If everything about God was easily comprehended by my limited human mind I would be more likely to agree with those people who argue that Christianity is merely human invention. Third, we accept paradox in other aspects of life, such as the wave–particle duality within modern physics. This holds that electromagnetic waves such as light behave both like waves *and* like particles.

And so do particles like electrons or protons. It all depends on what kind of experiments you do.[7] It goes right against common sense but the physics forces us to see things in this way. It's much the same with God and our understanding of his three-in-one nature.

Pullman's wonderful idea of a human and a dæmon inextricably connected with – indeed, part of – each other is not too dissimilar an idea. When you first read *Northern Lights* the connectedness of Lyra and Pantalaimon (and Pan's shape-changing abilities) seems extraordinary. As we discover more about the way they are two parts of one being, the harder it becomes to understand but the more normal it seems. As I commented above, by the time Lyra is being ferried to the world of the dead, their unity is something we barely stop to think about. The tearing apart of Will's united self brings it home to us forcefully.

The ghosts add in yet another level to the person. Pullman says:

> [Lyra] can think about her body and she can think about her dæmon. Now there must be a third part of her to be doing the thinking, and this is the part I call the ghost . . . The ghost is the part that survives death.[8]

Although we can distinguish between the three parts of her – human, dæmon, ghost – we have to recognize that together they are one being. It's not a perfect model of the Trinity by any means, but it's not a million miles away from it either.

Dæmonic purposes

One of the other ways in which Pullman sometimes uses dæmons – perhaps unconsciously – is to indicate the value he puts on a character, or their potential for redemption. Lord Asriel has Stelmaria, the stunning, graceful and exotic snow leopard; Mrs Coulter has the beautiful but cruel golden monkey; Farder Coram has the double-size cat Sophonax with her fur of extraordinary richness; Stanislaus Grumman has the magnificent osprey Sayan Kötör. By contrast it is revealing that all of the religious characters in *His Dark Materials* have cold-blooded dæmons.[9]

Pullman also uses dæmons to say something about the pain of separation, about depression and about death. It's a rich metaphor, which he uses very creatively. He says, 'right at the end of *Amber Spyglass*, after 1200 or more pages, I was still discovering new things I could do with this human-dæmon link'.[10] While there may be no simple way of describing what a dæmon is, what we can say is that a dæmon is a visible, external part of a person which represents facets of the person's character. They are, perhaps, physical representations of what Stanislaus Grumman calls 'a silent voice in the mind' (*SK*, p.223). These facets of character are not tangible in human beings in our world – we deduce them from a person's actions and words. But Pullman uses this companion creature to bring some aspects of personality to the surface. The existence of dæmons 'was the richest idea I've ever had', says Philip Pullman. 'There were so many different things I could do with it. But it works, and it's actually saying something about the business of being human – it's not just decorative.'[11]

Know yourself

Jerry, the able-seaman on the voyage to Trollesund, tells Lyra that the form of a dæmon tells someone what kind of person he or she is:

> Take old Belisaria. She's a seagull, and that
> means I'm a kind of seagull too. I'm not grand
> and splendid nor beautiful, but I'm a tough old
> thing and I can survive anywhere and always
> find a bit of food and company. That's worth
> knowing, that is. And when your dæmon settles,
> you'll know the sort of person you are . . .
> There's plenty of folk as'd like to have a lion as
> a dæmon and they end up with a poodle. And till
> they learn to be satisfied with what they are,
> they're going to be fretful about it. Waste of
> feeling, that is. (*NL*, p.167)

Pullman says:

> You cannot choose your dæmon, and so no
> matter how much I might like to have a bird or a
> cat or something graceful or elegant, I'd
> probably turn out to have a crab or a slug . . .
> Somebody criticized me for being terribly
> class-ridden and British and snobbish because all
> servants are people whose dæmons are dogs.
> This critic thought that I was saying if your
> dæmon's a dog you have to be a servant. It's not
> like that at all, as Lyra explains elsewhere to Will
> (who doesn't know about dæmons). 'If your
> dæmon turns out to be a dog, that means you're
> the sort of person (and there are plenty of those
> about) who enjoys knowing where they are in a
> hierarchy, who enjoys following orders and
> pleasing the person in charge.' There are people
> like that, and they make good servants. We don't
> have servants any more in our society but we do
> in Lyra's world. If your dæmon is a dog that is a

sign to you that that'd be a career that you'd
enjoy doing and that you'd be good at . . . The
way to find out what your dæmon is, is to ask
your friends to write it down anonymously. Then
you will find out.[12]

Elsewhere he suggests what his own dæmon might be:

I think she's probably a magpie or a jackdaw,
one of these birds that pick up bright shining
things and doesn't distinguish in terms of
shininess between the diamond ring and the Kit
Kat wrapper – just as I don't distinguish in terms
of 'storyness' between Shakespeare and
Neighbours.[13]

Dæmons are usually of the opposite sex – a consequence of the fact that we all have aspects of our per-
sonalities that can be thought of as primarily masculine
and some that are primarily feminine. In *The Subtle
Knife* Stanislaus Grumman tells Lee Scoresby of the
time when he first entered Lee's world and saw his
dæmon for the first time:

I hadn't known of Sayan Kötör here till I entered
[your world].[14] People here cannot conceive of
worlds where dæmons are a silent voice in
the mind and no more. Can you imagine my
astonishment, in turn, at learning that part of my
own nature was female, and bird-formed, and
beautiful? (*SK*, p.223)

The discovery helped him to become more aware of
aspects of his personality that he had sensed only dimly,
if at all. Bernie Johansen, the pastry cook at Jordan
College, is one of the few people with a dæmon of the
same sex. Pullman says:

Occasionally, no doubt, people do have a dæmon

of the same sex; that might indicate homosexuality, or it might indicate some other sort of gift or quality, such as second sight. I do not know. But I don't have to know everything about what I write.[15]

Growing up

Pivotal to *Northern Lights* is the fact that Pantalaimon is able to change his shape – he can be a moth one moment and a wildcat the next and then a sparrow. He can do this because Lyra is still a child. But adolescence is not far off for Lyra and she knows the time will soon come when Pan will change less and less until finally settling into one form for the rest of their life.

This transition from having a dæmon that can change to having a settled dæmon says something about 'the business of being human' – in particular about the business of growing up. For Pullman, this is the central theme of *His Dark Materials*:

I suddenly realized that of course what the whole story is about is growing up. It's about the difference between innocence and experience, between childhood and adulthood.

Lyra asks Jerry the sailor why dæmons have to settle. 'Ah, they always have settled, and they always will,' he replies. 'That's part of growing up. There'll come a time when you'll be tired of his changing about, and you'll want a settled kind of form for him' (*NL*, p.167). Lyra can't believe she would ever want this to happen, but it is inevitable if she is going to stop being a child. The sailor explains that settling dæmons help children develop their self-awareness as they pass through adolescence. Pullman says that dæmons 'symbolise the difference between the infinite plasticity, the infinite potentiality and mutability of childhood and the fixed nature of adulthood'.[16] Millicent Lenz writes:

> Being an adult entails accepting the narrowing of one's potential possible 'shapes', learning to live with a diminishment of the protean possibilities inherent in the child. As the wise seaman implies, there may be some comfort to an adult in having a firmer basis for self-trust and a clearer awareness of limits.[17]

There is, however, a danger that fixed dæmons and this stress on 'the fixed nature of adulthood' shuts down the potential for substantial change of character as an adult. Mrs Coulter goes through something of that process in this story. The Christian experience of conversion is often one of a profound change in character and outlook.

Lyra is very much a self-obsessed child when we first meet her. Her life revolves around escapades on the roofs and in the lanes of Oxford, a constantly shifting array of enemies and allies, and avoiding being worked too hard by her reluctant tutors, the Jordan scholars. She believes that telling an inventive lie is far more satisfying and useful than the truth could ever be. She's a typical child in that she doesn't really know herself – who she is, or what kind of person she is, or what really matters in her life. The changeability of her dæmon reflects the uncertainty, the unsettledness in Lyra.

But as she approaches adolescence – and faces some extremely challenging circumstances – she gets more of a sense of herself. Although she doesn't know what the future has in store for her when she returns to Jordan College at the end of *The Amber Spyglass*, she has some direction and some mature perspectives on life. She has grown up and is rapidly moving towards adulthood. The surprise for me is that this change seems to happen in early adolescence, whereas many adolescents in our world seem to be more confused about their identity and direction in life than they ever were before the onset of puberty.

Embracing change

Like the heroes of so many – perhaps all – great stories, Lyra and Will are on a journey of self-discovery. They set out on their quests as children – extraordinary, strong-willed, resourceful kids maybe, but still children – and in the process of pursuing their goals find something more valuable which they hadn't been looking for: self-knowledge and maturity. The tumultuous events in which they are caught up happen at just the right time for them as they begin to make the transition into adolescence. Of course, this great change in life is also concerned with reaching sexual maturity – something the Church feared but which Lyra and Will embraced (we'll return to this in Chapter 10). For Pullman this transition is perhaps the most important stage of life, in which we move from innocence to experience, childhood to adulthood. And this, more than anything else, is beautifully represented by the imagery of dæmons.

> Will put his hand on hers. A new mood had taken hold of him, and he felt resolute and peaceful. Knowing exactly what he was doing and exactly what it would mean, he moved his hand from Lyra's wrist and stroked the red-gold fur of her dæmon.
>
> Lyra gasped. But her surprise was mixed with

a pleasure so like the joy that flooded through her when she had put the fruit to his lips that she couldn't protest, because she was breathless. With a racing heart she responded in the same way: she put her hand on the silky warmth of Will's dæmon, and as her fingers tightened in the fur she knew that Will was feeling exactly what she was.

And she knew too that neither dæmon would change now, having felt a lover's hands on them. Those were their shapes for life: they would want no other.

So, wondering whether any lovers before them had made this blissful discovery, they lay together as the earth turned slowly and the moon and stars blazed above them. (*AS*, p.527–528)

---

[1] Kirjava means 'multi-coloured'.

[2] 'Achuka Interview' (www.achuka.co.uk/archive/interviews/ppint.php).

[3] *Webster's Revised Unabridged Dictionary*.

[4] See also Maybury-Lewis, David, *Millennium: Tribal wisdom and the Modern world* (Viking Penguin, 1992).

[5] Frazer, James George, *The Golden Bough* (1922) (www.bartleby.com/196/169.html).

[6] Vincent, Sally, 'Driven by dæmons', *Guardian*, 10 November 2001.

[7] The way we resolve this tension is to see the wave in terms of the probability of where a particle is at any moment. See the appendix for more on this.

[8] Quoted in Mooney, Bel, *Devout Sceptics – Conversations on faith and doubt* (Hodder and Stoughton, 2003), p.130.

[9] For example, Fra Pavel has a frog dæmon (*AS*, p.72), Father MacPhail has a lizard (*AS*, p.73), and Father Gomez has a beetle (*AS*, p.80).

[10] Brown, Charles N., 'An interview with Philip Pullman' (www.avnet.co.uk/amaranth/Critic/ivpullman.htm).

[11] Fried, Kerry, 'Darkness Visible: An Interview with Philip Pullman' (www.amazon.com/exec/obidos/tg/feature/-/94589/103-2179560-1236619).

[12] Brown, 'An interview with Philip Pullman'.

[13] Bertodano, Helena de, 'I am of the Devil's party', *Daily Telegraph*, 29 January 2002.

[14] This raises the question of why Will didn't see his dæmon when he entered Lyra's world while searching for her.

[15] Brown, 'An interview with Philip Pullman'.

[16] Pullman, Philip, 'An Introduction to . . . Philip Pullman' in James Carter (ed.) *Talking Books: Children's Authors Talk About the Craft, Creativity and Process of Writing* (Routledge, 1999), p.190.

[17] Lenz, Millicent, 'Philip Pullman' in Hunt, Peter and Lenz, Millicent, *Alternative Worlds in Fantasy Fiction* (Continuum, 2001), p.140.

CHAPTER 10

Dust, Sin and the Fall

At the heart of the plot of *His Dark Materials* is the existence of some very mysterious particles. We first learn about them when Lord Asriel shows some photograms of his recent Arctic expedition to the scholars of Jordan College:

> [Lord Asriel] lifted out the first slide and dropped another into the frame. This was much darker, it was as if the moonlight had been filtered out . . . But the man had altogether changed: he was bathed in light, and a fountain of glowing particles seemed to be streaming from his upraised hand.
>
> 'That light,' said the Chaplain, 'is it going up or coming down?'
>
> 'It's coming down,' said Lord Asriel, 'but it isn't light. It's Dust.'
>
> Something in the way he said it made Lyra imagine Dust with a capital letter, as if this weren't ordinary dust. The reaction of the scholars confirmed her feeling, because Lord Asriel's words caused a sudden collective silence, followed by gasps of incredulity.
>
> (*NL*, p.21–22)

What a great reaction – exactly what Lord Asriel expected. But why do the scholars react like this? It's not simply that they're seeing an image of something that had previously been invisible, but that what they're seeing is extremely controversial. Dust has recently become the subject of intense speculation among experimental theologians (physicists), having been discovered by a Muscovite named Rusakov some years before. Rusakov found that there was a constant flow of previously unknown particles coming from space.[1] These particles interacted with matter in a radically different way from anything that had been studied previously. In particular, he noticed that human beings seemed to attract the particles – but the effect was much stronger in adults than in children. Lord Asriel's photogram shows this clearly:

> [Lord Asriel] indicated the blurred shape of the smaller figure.
>
> 'I thought that was the man's dæmon,' said the Enquirer.
>
> 'No. His dæmon was at the time coiled around his neck in the form of a snake. That shape you can dimly see is a child.'
>
> 'A severed child – ?' said someone, and the way he stopped showed that he knew this was something that shouldn't have been voiced.
>
> There was an intense silence.
>
> Then Lord Asriel said calmly, 'An entire child. Which, given the nature of Dust, is precisely the point, is it not?' (*NL*, p.22)

Dust and sin

Rusakov's discovery was deeply disturbing to the Church authorities – though Pullman doesn't really spell out why. When Lord Asriel explains all this to Lyra, he simply comments that 'discoveries of this sort . . . have a bearing on the doctrines of the church' (*NL*, p.370). But why does the existence of these particles have anything to do with Church doctrine? Rusakov has, apparently, only four significant facts about the particles:

1. They exist.
2. They are elementary particles (they can't be broken down any further).
3. They are attracted to human beings.
4. They are attracted to adults much more than children.

Which of these would cause the Magisterium to suspect Rusakov of possession by an evil spirit (*NL*, p.370)? The mere existence of a new type of elementary particle would hardly do so. However, the fact that the particles are attracted to humans means that they must be bound up with the nature of humanity – and that does relate to theology. What it means to be human is, it seems, something that must be tightly defined in the Magisterium's official doctrines. But again, the simple existence of Rusakov particles reveals little of any consequence about human nature. Only by understanding what those particles are, and the way they affect people, could experimental theologians say anything of note.

The one really significant insight that comes from the discovery of Rusakov particles is that they indicate a major difference between children and adults. Though, since everyone knows that dæmons lose their shape-shifting ability during adolescence, even this is hardly earth-shattering news. However, the Rusakov particles do begin to look like a good candidate for an explanation of *why* dæmons settle. The ambitious Mrs Coulter was the one to guess that there was a connection (*NL*, p.375). Even so, without knowing much more about the nature and action of these particles, there's nothing in this to really make anyone worry. The Magisterium, though, is dogmatic, unthinking and closed-minded – it is no surprise that they responded like this (we'll look more fully at Pullman's portrayal of the Church in Chapter 13).

NB .   **Genesis reloaded**

After their knee-jerk response to Rusakov's work, the Magisterium needed to work out how it fitted in with their doctrines. The answer seemed obvious: these particles were the physical evidence for original sin. Lord Asriel explains this to Lyra by referring her to Genesis 3. He reads the passage in which Adam and Eve, having been tempted by the Serpent, break God's command not to eat from the tree of the knowledge of good and evil. Theologians call this first rebellion against God 'the Fall'.

What Asriel reads is very different from the real text of Genesis 3. In Lyra's world everyone has a dæmon, so Pullman inserts new material and changes a little of the original to reflect this. He uses the 1611 Authorised Version of the Bible because he loves its rich and poetic language.[2] Here is the passage in question – the material deleted from the real Genesis 3 is shown with a line through it, and Pullman's inserted text is in italics:

> And the woman said unto the serpent, We may eat of the fruit of the trees of the garden:
> But of the fruit of the tree which is in the midst of the garden, God hath said, Ye shall not eat of it, neither shall ye touch it, lest ye die.
> And the serpent said unto the woman, Ye shall not surely die:
> For God doth know that in the day ye eat

thereof, then your eyes shall be opened, *and
your dæmons shall assume their true forms,*
and ye shall be as gods, knowing good and evil.
And when the woman saw that the tree was good
for food, and that it was pleasant to the eyes,
and a tree to be desired to ~~make one wise~~ *reveal
the true form of one's dæmon,* she took of the
fruit thereof, and did eat, and gave also unto her
husband with her; and he did eat.
And the eyes of them both were opened, ~~and
they knew that they were naked~~ *and they saw
the true form of their dæmons, and spoke
with them.*
*But when the man and the woman knew their
own dæmons, they knew that a great change
had come upon them, for until that moment it
had seemed that they were at one with all the
creatures of the earth and the air, and there
was no difference between them:*
*And they saw the difference, and they knew
good and evil; and they were ashamed,* and
they sewed fig leaves together, ~~and made themselves aprons~~ *to cover their nakedness.*[3]
(Genesis 3:2–7)

Inserting around 50% more material is a fairly significant alteration to the original. Since many young people
reading *His Dark Materials* have no idea what Genesis
3 actually says, I can't help wondering how many of
them either begin to wonder whether dæmons are real
but invisible, as for Will, or assume that Pullman has
invented the whole quotation! This tampering with the
text is a difficult issue for many Christians. They believe
the Bible to be communication from God himself and as

such it has a very special status – it should be left with nothing added and nothing taken away. Philip Pullman, of course, values the Bible as nothing more than a work of literature. He doesn't especially revere it, and so feels no qualms about changing it to suit his purposes. Christians may not like it, but it's unreasonable to expect an atheist to worry about this – especially since this passage is part of a work of fantasy fiction, and is set in another world.

Returning to the point Lord Asriel was making, his theology is correct when he tells Lyra, that this 'was how sin came into the world . . . sin and shame and death'. But he also tells her it was 'the moment their dæmons became fixed'. In other words, there is a connection between sin and settled dæmons. As far as the Magisterium is concerned, if dæmons first settled when humans first fell, then a settled dæmon *must* be something to do with sin. And if Rusakov particles cluster around adults with settled dæmons, then *they* must be to do with sin too.

Original sin

However, the phrase 'original sin' doesn't simply refer to the first human act of rebellion against God. It is the belief that every human being since is caught up in it. Christians disagree about how this actually works[4] but they agree that, since Adam, sin – rebellion – is part of our *nature*, not just what we *do*. Sin is a word that many people misunderstand. It has connotations of Victorian morality, or of 'naughty' things we do (which we find rather enjoyable). In fact, *sins* are specific acts (or thoughts), which are contrary to God's nature as utterly pure and holy. *Sin* is a fundamental, innate attitude of rebellion against God. As the reformers said: we are not sinners because we sin, we sin because we are sinners.

> [Christians] agree on the universality, solidarity, stubbornness and historical momentum of sin. That is to say, all serious Christians subscribe to the generic doctrine of corruption, the centrepiece of which is the claim that even when they are good in important ways, human beings are not *sound*.[5]

That doesn't mean that there's no good in us – Christians also believe that humans are made in the image of God, and therefore it is also in our nature to be good. In a sense good is more fundamentally part of our nature than bad, but both are very much part of life for every one of us. These parallel convictions of good-ness *and* sinfulness explain the paradox of human nature.

Since this affects *all* human beings, there is no age distinction. We talk easily about the innocence of children – and at some levels they are innocent but they already have this bias in their nature. Surely no one who has had children should be surprised at this – their capacity to do the wrong thing manifests itself at a remarkably young age.

Rebellion against God has consequences. The Bible's position is that there is no greater crime than to rebel against the creator and sustainer of the universe, whose very nature defines what is good. Adam's first sin brought about death – his spiritual death was immediate; his physical death came later on. Part of God's judgement on him (and all humanity) was that he would 'return to the ground, since from it you were taken; for dust you are and to dust you will return'.[6] This phrase was the origin of the Magisterium's name for Rusakov particles: Dust. Incidentally, Lord Asriel's comments about this verse – that the translation is disputed because the text is corrupt, and that it could mean God is admitting his own sinfulness (*NL*, p.373) – are unjustified. I have yet to find any commentator arguing for an alternative translation of 'to dust you will return'.[7] And the idea that this could have any reference at all to God's nature has no basis whatsoever outside Pullman's fictional world.

It's clear that the Magisterium is in error because it has misunderstood the doctrine of original sin – sin doesn't start at puberty, it is part of every human being long before then. Therefore, the fact that Dust is attracted to humans from adolescence onwards shows not that it is evidence *for* original sin, but that it cannot be to do with original sin at all. The Magisterium had hastily jumped to a wrong conclusion about the nature of Rusakov particles. It was also wrong to give the name Dust to Rusakov particles, since Adam was made from the dust of the ground *before* the Fall, not from Dust falling from space. Having made these mistakes, the Magisterium has backed itself into a corner from which it can only ever view Dust as bound up with sin and evil.

Severing the sin problem

In the minds of the Church authorities, then, the influx of Dust, the settling of a dæmon, and sin itself are firmly linked with adolescence. And, therefore, they are implicitly linked with sexuality. Mrs Coulter certainly hints strongly at this in what she tells Lyra at Bolvangar:

> Dust is something bad, something wrong,
> something evil and wicked. Grown-ups and
> their dæmons are infected with Dust so
> deeply that it's too late for them. They can't
> be helped . . . Your dæmon's a wonderful friend
> and companion when you're young, but at
> the age we call puberty . . . dæmons bring
> all sort of troublesome thoughts and
> feelings, and that's what lets Dust in.
> (*NL*, p.284–285)

Having spotted the connection between dæmons, Dust and adolescence, Mrs Coulter began to wonder whether children could be insulated from the effects of Dust before adolescence kicks in. If so, would that prevent them from becoming sinful? And if Dust is linked with a dæmon taking on its settled form, might the solution be to sever that powerful bond between human and dæmon? Mrs Coulter certainly thought so, not least because of her experience of *zombis* in Africa – unquestioningly obedient slaves who have lost their own will as a result of being separated from their dæmons. She knew it was possible, she was desperate for power, and the Magisterium was frightened of what Rusakov had discovered. So they quickly took up her suggestion that a new body – the General Oblation Board – conduct some experiments on children.

As far as Mrs Coulter was concerned, it is all in a good cause; the end justifies the means:

> . . . a quick operation on children means they're
> safe from it. Dust just won't stick to them ever
> again. They're safe and happy . . . A quick little
> operation . . . and you're never troubled again.
> And your dæmon stays with you, only . . . just

       not connected . . . like a wonderful pet, if you
       like. (*NL*, p.284–285)

However, her reaction when she finds her own daughter in the silver cage shows that the end she is pursuing is not altruistic but deeply personal. Mrs Coulter wants power, status and influence rather than the ultimate good of the children – that is simply how she rationalizes it all to herself. Lyra spots the inconsistency and asks, 'if it was so good, why'd you stop them doing it to me? If it was good you should've let them do it. You should have been glad' (*NL*, p.284). Her mother never quite answers the question. It's clear that Mrs Coulter is protecting her daughter from the very thing which she claims is so beneficial.

By now Lyra's conviction that Dust isn't actually bad is growing. She's seen her mother's double standards. She's seen what this terrible machinery has done to Tony Makarios, and knows it's all wrong. She's seen the vapid nurses with their 'blank and incurious' dæmons, who contrast sharply with the powerful, intelligent, energetic people she admires so much – John Faa, Farder Coram, Lord Asriel, even Mrs Coulter (though Lyra's former admiration for her has evaporated by this point in the narrative). She has no clue as to the real nature of Dust, but it seems nobody else has either. At the end of *Northern Lights*, Lyra realizes that if everyone she *doesn't* trust perceives Dust to be a *bad* thing, it's probably the opposite – and she and Pantalaimon set out to search for it.

The Magisterium becomes aware of Lyra and learns about the witches' prophecy. But it takes them until *The Amber Spyglass* before they finally have the all-important detail:

> The child . . . is in the position of Eve, the wife
> of Adam, the mother of us all, and the cause of
> all sin . . . if it comes about that the child is
> tempted, as Eve was, then she is likely to fall.
> On the outcome will depend . . . everything. And
> if this temptation does take place, and if the
> child gives in, then Dust and sin will triumph.
> (*AS*, p.71)

For the Magisterium, this is unmitigatedly terrible. Having made a connection between Dust and original sin, they can only see a 'triumph' of Dust as the worst possible outcome. And now they know that Lyra is to reprise Eve's role, they perceive that they are facing the most critical moment in the world's history since the first Fall. Their solution is as callous as Bolvangar: Lyra must be stopped at all costs.

Off the leash

We, of course, have known about Lyra's destiny since the witch Lena Feldt confessed it to Mrs Coulter (*SK*, p.328). If it is true that Lyra is a second Eve, then it looks rather as if the Magisterium was right after all: Dust is to do with sin. But if Dust is good, and Dust is sin, then doesn't that mean that 'sin' is also good?

This takes us right to the heart of the reversal that underpins the whole of *His Dark Materials*. Philip Pullman portrays the Magisterium and God as unremittingly bad, and he sees all that the Magisterium opposes as wholesome and good. In Christian thinking, the Fall was the undoing of humanity – the moment at which we rebelled against God and became outcasts. Pullman doesn't accept the account of the Fall as historical, but it *represents*, for him, one of the greatest moments in human history. Like Lord Asriel, he thinks of Adam and Eve 'like an imaginary number, like the square root of minus one: you can never see any concrete proof that it exists, but if you include it in your equations, you can calculate all manner of things that couldn't be imagined without it' (*NL*, p.372–373).[8] During an Australian radio discussion he said:

> I just reversed [the traditional view of the Fall]. I thought wasn't it a good thing that Eve did? Isn't curiosity a valuable quality? Shouldn't she be praised for risking this? It wasn't, after all, that she was after money or gold or anything – she was after knowledge. What could possibly be wrong with that?[9]

Pullman sees Adam and Eve before the Fall as God's lapdogs,[10] clever pets which trot around the Garden of Eden doing exactly as they're told, with no freedom and no will of their own. In contrast, the act of taking the fruit was an act of self-determination, of freedom. This was the moment at which humanity took responsibility for itself and its destiny. This was the moment at which we cast off God's shackles and grew up so that we could stand on our own two feet. This was the moment at which we became wise.

Freedom and constraint

Pullman's characterization of what happened is partly right but he also misreads the situation. The world in which Adam and Eve lived was not one of constraints, but one of great freedom:

> The LORD God took the man and put him in the Garden of Eden to work it and take care of it.

And the LORD God commanded the man, 'You
are free to eat from any tree in the garden; but
you must not eat from the tree of the knowledge
of good and evil, for when you eat of it you will
surely die.'[11]

It is clear that those first people had some positive
responsibilities – work and caring for their environment
is mentioned in this extract. They are also responsible
to rule in God's place – to be stewards of the earth,[12] to
be fruitful,[13] to investigate and develop.[14] All of this suggests very strongly that Adam and Eve were being treated like very responsible and capable adults, not like lapdogs. They had enormous freedom and only one restriction: 'you must not eat from the tree of the knowledge
of good and evil'. The very fact that God gives them this
command is evidence that they had the ultimate freedom of choosing whether to listen to God or to some
other voice. They aren't *prevented* from eating from
the tree of the knowledge of good and evil, or *programmed* not to do so, but *commanded* not to – it's
their moral choice to obey or not. There may be nothing special about the tree apart from the fact that this
was the one they shouldn't eat from – a test case tree.[15]
It was the *disobedient act* of eating from the tree that
brought them knowledge of good and evil, not some
supernatural property of the fruit itself.

The serpent first put doubts into Eve's mind, asking
her, 'Did God really say "You must not eat from any tree
in the garden"?'[16] This is not at all what God said – the
restriction was eating from *one* tree, not *any* tree. Eve
answers him correctly at first, but then for some reason
adds her own exclusion on top: ' . . . and you must not
touch it, or you will die.'[17] Then the serpent moves to a

flat denial of what God had said – 'You will not surely die . . .'[18] – before finally misrepresenting God and his motivations: 'For God knows that when you eat of it your eyes will be opened, and you will be like God, knowing good and evil.'[19] This is partially true: God did know that their eyes would be opened and that they would know good and evil. But they would not be like God because they would neither see like he sees, nor know good and evil like he does. Their eyes were opened – to see their nakedness, and they were ashamed of it. Until then human relations had been characterized by absolute openness, honesty and love – they could be free to be naked as they had nothing to hide. From that point on relationships would be characterized by shame, deception, blame and exploitation – and their impulse to cover themselves was the sign of their new situation. They did come to know good and evil – but from the inside, experientially, because they had embraced evil – that which is inconsistent with God's utterly pure and holy nature.

Adam and Eve fell for the scepticism, the denial and the misrepresentation. For the first time they perceived themselves as cheated out of some freedom and insight, which they now felt ought to be theirs. They wanted complete autonomy – the absolute freedom to make their own choices, to decide for themselves what was right and wrong, to make themselves, rather than the God who made them, the centre of their worlds. They wanted God's role for themselves. But it was the wrong kind of autonomy and freedom. They had been given so much, but by grasping after that little bit more, they threw away much of what they had. Human existence would never be the same again.

Pullman commends Eve for embracing freedom and knowledge, suggesting that her motivation was simple curiosity. But he ignores the fact that true freedom is structured and always at least a little constrained. To go beyond that is to embrace anarchy which undermines the good that was already being appreciated. I could say that I resent the restriction my skeleton puts on my movements. I can't slide through narrow gaps or even touch my right elbow with my right wrist. But the restrictions go with the territory and my skeleton is in fact what liberates me. If I disposed of it and its constraints I would be a lump of quivering blubber on the floor.

By identifying Dust with sin, and then showing us that Dust is such a good thing, Philip Pullman turns the traditional understanding of sin on its head. Instead of it being the height of human arrogance – rebellion against God, it becomes something every wise person should embrace. It's still rebellion against God, but Pullman suggests that this is exactly the right thing to do. Like the serpent, Pullman has misrepresented God (a theme we'll return to in Chapter 13) and encouraged us to wrest control away from him. Since Pullman frequently says, 'I am of the Devil's party and I know it',[20] I suspect he'd be rather pleased at the comparison.

---

[1] In our world, diseases were once thought to have come from space in a constant inflow – which is where we the word *influence* from, as well as *influenza*.

[2] Pullman says, 'I know the Bible very well. I know the hymns and the prayer book very well – and this is the old, authorized King James Version of the Bible, and the 1662 Book of Common Prayer that used to be used in

English churches . . . I love the language and the atmosphere of the Bible and the prayer book' (Odean, Kathleen, 'The story master', *School Library Journal*, 1 October 2000; www.schoollibraryjournal.com/article/ca153054). Elsewhere he talks of the 'dreadful, barren language that disfigures the forms of service they have now' (Spanner, Huw, 'Heat and Dust', *Third Way*, Vol. 25 No. 2, April 2002, p.22–26; www.thirdway .org.uk/past/showpage.asp?page=3949).

[3] Interestingly, this last change suggests that, although Philip is scathing about modern translations of the Bible, he evidently sees at least *some* need for updating the language for a modern audience.

[4] See 'Sin' in Ferguson, Sinclair and Wright, David (eds), *New Dictionary of Theology* (IVP, 1988), p.641–643 and Blocher, Henri, *Original Sin* (Leicester: Apollos, 1997).

[5] Plantinga, Cornelius, *Not the Way It's Supposed to be: A Breviary of Sin* (Apollos, 1995), p.33.

[6] Genesis 3:19, *New International Version*.

[7] Some commentators do disagree with the majority in that they take 'to dust you will return' as something that was always inevitable for Adam, even before his rebellion. In other words, he would have died whether he sinned or not, and the judgement on him is that work will now be difficult for him until that time. Most see physical death as being part of God's judgement and a consequence of being expelled from Eden. But this difference of opinion is over what the words imply, not over the translation itself. See Gordon Wenham, *Word Biblical Commentary: Genesis 1–15* (Word, 1987), p.83 for more details.

[8] The square root of any number, when multiplied by itself (squared) gives you the number you started with. The square root of 9 is 3, so 3 x 3 = 9. But what number, when multiplied by itself gives the answer –1? It's impossible since multiplying two positive numbers gives a positive result as does multiplying two negative numbers. The square root of –1 is therefore called an 'imaginary number' and it's vital for solving certain equations.

[9] *Faith and Fantasy*, Australian Broadcasting Company Radio National, 24 March 2002 (www.abc.net.au/rn/relig/enc/stories/s510312.htm). The same ideas come at the end of his 'Republic of Heaven' essay (Pullman, Philip, 'The Republic of Heaven', *Horn Book Magazine*, November/December 2001, p.655–667).

[10] Watkins, Tony, 'In conversation with Philip Pullman' (www.damaris.org/content/content.php?type=5&id=357).

[11] Genesis 2:15–17, *New International Version*.

[12] Genesis 1:26.

[13] Genesis 1:28.

[14] Genesis 2:19–20.

[15] There is nothing to suggest that it was an apple tree – this is a common misconception.

[16] Genesis 3:1.

[17] Genesis 3:3.

[18] Genesis 3:4.

[19] Genesis 3:5.

[20] For example, see Bertodano, Helena de, 'I am of the Devil's party', *Daily Telegraph*, 29 January 2002.

CHAPTER 11

Consciousness, Wisdom and the Second Fall

In *The Subtle Knife*, the alethiometer leads Lyra to an Oxford physicist in our world who is researching into dark matter. Dark matter is one of the great mysteries of modern physics – Pullman says it is 'intoxicatingly exciting'.[1] It's possible to calculate the mass of the universe – how much stuff there is – but most of it can't be accounted for. What this means is that we can see stars, planets and gas clouds, but not enough of them. If you calculate the mass of everything we can see, it only adds up to a fraction of what we know must be out there. This was first spotted in the 1930s but it was only in the 1970s that scientists started to realize that only seriously large amounts of hidden matter could account for some of their observations. Now astrophysicists are trying to find out what and where this mysterious missing mass is, because it will help to confirm theories about the universe's origins and structure. Estimates vary but something between around 90 and 99 per cent of the stuff in the universe is invisible. Nobel Prize-winner Carlo Rubbia says 'All the visible objects in the Universe . . . only account for 0.5% of the total, so the Universe as we know it is only a side-show.'[2]

Some of our universe is missing

This missing stuff is known as dark matter because there's no detectable light coming from it, whereas we see stars and galaxies by the light coming from them. At the end of the twentieth century, and in the first two or three years of the twenty-first century, the leading candidate – the one Pullman builds into *His Dark Materials* – was vast numbers of tiny particles. These particles hardly interact with the normal matter of which everything around us is made. This means that millions of them are passing through you each second. Coincidentally, I'm writing this chapter on the first anniversary of the opening[3] of a major British research facility for detecting these particles: Boulby Underground Laboratory. Its detectors are more than a kilometre underground, which it's hoped will soon yield some answers.[4]

Dr Mary Malone is spared the rigours of going deep underground dressed in miner's gear to do her experiments. She and her colleague Oliver Payne have managed to solve the riddle of the missing matter in the comfort of their laboratory by using an electromagnetic field to deflect all the particles that they're not trying to detect. Dark matter particles aren't affected by electromagnetism so they get through. But their pioneering research has produced startling results:

> '. . . our particles are strange little devils and
> no mistake. We call them shadow-particles,
> Shadows . . . You know what? They're conscious.
> That's right. Shadows are particles of
> consciousness.' (*SK*, p.91–92)

Here Philip Pullman has brilliantly woven two of the greatest puzzles of modern science – dark matter[5] and the nature of consciousness – into one very powerful element within his narrative. He has just enough of the real science to make it all sound quite plausible – but he says it's best not to research it too deeply because it would stop him feeling free to develop the ideas as he sees fit. To combine the two *and* link them with the difficult transition from childhood to adolescence is a stroke of genius, and one of the reasons why this trilogy works so incredibly well at several different levels.

The mystery about consciousness is that we really don't have much of a clue how it works. We know *that* we think and feel – but how? We understand a lot about the physical processes within brains, but very little about how those physical processes end up as thoughts. As I sit at my computer writing this chapter, electrical signals are buzzing around my brain, passing from neurone to neurone. We know that the signals in certain areas of the brain are predominantly to do with vision or fine motor control, and a scan of my brain would indicate high levels of activity in those regions as a result of what I'm seeing on screen and the movement of my fingers as I type. There would be activity over many other parts of the brain too. Some of this activity controls my body's basic functions and I'm never aware of it; some of it causes this chapter to form into words on the screen. But *how* electrical signals result in the business of thinking and actually results in a written chapter, is an enigma. It's a mystery how this lump of soggy grey matter in my head gives me the sense of being me. Why is my brain conscious? This riddle is known as the mind–body problem – the mind is my experience, awareness and thought; the body includes my physical brain; the problem is because we can't understand how the two interact. This issue is profoundly interesting to brain scientists, psychologists, philosophers, cyberneticists, and others.

For many scientists working in the area, the solution lies entirely within the physical structures and processes of the brain – a 'materialist' approach. This is in sharp contrast to the traditional idea of the mind being closely connected with the soul which is somehow separate from the brain – an approach known as dualism. Although Pullman believes that the physical universe is the only reality, his solution to the problem of consciousness in *His Dark Materials* is not materialistic as we might expect, but dualistic. To some extent, it's dualist because of dæmons, though as we have seen in Chapter 9, they can't really be thought of as being an external soul, despite many critics seeing them in this way. A far more significant way in which Pullman takes a dualistic line is his use of Dust. By making shadows the 'particles of consciousness' he has a system in which consciousness comes from outside.

Focused consciousness

This understanding of consciousness does present a significant problem for the narrative, however. If Dust is the stuff of consciousness and cascades down on humans in far greater quantities *after* adolescence, the implication would appear to be that children are not fully conscious *until* adolescence. At that point these particles of consciousness start streaming into them, and their dæmons settle into a fixed form. As far as Dust is concerned, that's when the person really seems to come alive. But on that basis we would expect children to have more in common with an adult whose dæmon has been severed – we would expect them to be zombies. The reality is very different of course. Lyra and Will are as conscious and as fully alive as any adult.

Stanislaus Grumman helps to make it a little clearer when he explains to Lee Scoresby the Spectres' lack of interest in children:

> The Spectres feast as vampyres feast on blood, but the Spectres' food is attention. A conscious and informed interest in the world. The immaturity of children is less attractive to them. (*SK*, p.292)

Pullman explains:

> Of course children are conscious. But I think that a different kind of self-awareness, self-consciousness, comes to us all at adolescence. It's partly sexual in origin, of course. But it coincides with a sudden and passionate interest in other things – science, poetry, art, music, religion, politics.[6]

Reaching adolescence in Cittàgazze was an altogether deadlier process than it was in Lyra's Oxford, but the underlying change is the same. In one world a dæmon becomes fixed; in another the Spectres have something new to feed on. Behind both of these phenomena lies the huge increase in Dust settling on the person. As the adolescent matures, 'a conscious and informed interest in the world' grows. Unlike the child whose attention is drawn in many different directions, the adult is more focused. When Mary Malone first sees sraf, she sees a golden haze around all of the mulefa's objects and a slightly stronger haze around one of the mulefa children. What marked him out was that the golden sparkles were in little currents and eddies which swirled around him. His mother, however, had much stronger currents that were 'more settled and powerful' (*AS*, p.244). So Dust may be the stuff of consciousness, but there's clearly a high value on directed consciousness.

This raises the question of which comes first – a rising influx of Dust, or a focused consciousness? Does the increase in Dust change someone, and make them mature? Or does a maturing person attract more Dust? If Dust is particles of consciousness, it would suggest that the Dust must come first. But at the end of *The Amber Spyglass*, the angel Xaphania tells Lyra and Will that conscious minds produce Dust:

> 'Understand this,' said Xaphania: 'Dust is not a constant. There's not a fixed quantity that has always been the same. Conscious beings make Dust – they renew it all the time, by thinking and feeling and reflecting, by gaining wisdom and passing it on.' (*AS*, p.520)

We also know that Dust remains associated with objects that have been changed in some way by conscious beings – the trepanned skulls in the museum, for example. So Dust collects around people, especially adults with focused minds; it lingers on objects produced by them; and more Dust is produced by them. In other words, it's a symbiotic relationship between conscious beings and Dust. This becomes very clear when we discover about the mulefa's symbiotic relationship with the wheel trees. When Mary Malone tries to explain her work to Atal, she is astonished to discover that her mulefa friend is well ahead of her. Mary asks if the mulefa know where it comes from. 'From us, and from the oil,' replies Atal, adding, '. . . without the trees it would just vanish again. With the wheels and with the oil it stays among us' (*AS*, p.235). After explaining the mulefa version of the Fall, Atal makes the symbiosis very explicit:

> . . . when the children were old enough, they
> began to generate the sraf as well, and as they
> were big enough to ride on the wheels, the sraf
> came back with the oil and stayed with them.
> (*AS*, p.237)

Pullman confirms the intertwined nature of conscious
beings and Dust:

> Dust permeates everything in the universe, and
> existed before we individuals did and will
> continue after us. Dust enriches us and is
> nurtured in turn by us; it brings wisdom and it is
> kept alive by love and curiosity and diligent
> enquiry and kindness and patience and hope.
> The relationship we have with Dust is mutually
> beneficial. Instead of being the dependent chil-
> dren of an all-powerful king, we are partners and
> equals with Dust in the great project of keeping
> the universe alive. It's a republican relationship,
> if you like, not a monarchical one.[7]

It's alive!

It's clear both from these comments, and from many
incidents in the trilogy, that the particles of Dust are not
simply the raw materials of consciousness, but are conscious themselves. The particles seem to have a kind of
collective consciousness, rather than at an individual
level (and given the vast numbers of Rusakov particles,
it's probably as well). Dust can think for itself and interact with intelligent brains in a number of ways. The
most obvious of all examples of this within *His Dark
Materials* is the alethiometer. Lyra begins to suspect
that it works by Dust while watching the Aurora
at Trollesund (*NL*, p.183). It's Dust that directs the

swinging needle in its journey around the symbols which decorate the alethiometer's rim.

Mary Malone deduces that her 'shadows' are conscious (*SK*, p.92), but is shocked when, at Lyra's suggestion, she reconfigures the software of her computer, the Cave, and gets messages in English directly from the particles[8] she is investigating (*SK*, p.258–262). Later, in the mulefa's world, Mary realizes that the I Ching is another means of communication from this mysterious consciousness (*AS*, p.83–85), though Lyra worked that out very quickly when she visited Mary's office and saw the chart on the door (*SK*, p.99).

Pullman makes the connection not only between the alethiometer and the I Ching, but with other methods of divination. He says: 'The alethiometer comes about because of my fascination with symbolic images of the Renaissance and earlier. I thought it would be interesting to invent a little machine to come up with symbolic answers.'[9] His ideas for the alethiometer were influenced by 'the notion behind or underneath the Tarot':

> The notion that you can tell stories, you can ask and answer questions, and so on, by means of pictures . . . What did influence [me] were those extraordinary devices they had about the middle of the sixteenth century – emblems, emblem books. There was a great vogue for these things. The first emblem book, I think, was published in 1544 in Italy. The idea was that you had a little moral . . . a little piece of wisdom encapsulated in a verse, usually Latin, usually doggerel, and a sort of motto, and illustrating those there was a picture . . . They're all rather everyday little things, like 'look before you leap', or, 'penny

wise, pound foolish' . . . but given this extraordinary semi-surrealist air by being pictured in emblem form in these rather curious little woodcuts . . . So I invented the alethiometer using a mixture of conventional symbols . . . and ones I made up . . . And then I discovered, in a book of emblems in the Bodleian Library, something rather similar. It looked as though somebody had actually drawn the alethiometer. But what had happened was that in this particular emblem book, which was published in about 1620, somebody had invented a way of fortune-telling. You were supposed to cut this thing out, and you put a pencil or a stick through the middle of it, and you twirl it . . . and wherever it falls . . . refers you to a number inside the book, and you look that up, and that's the answer to your question. So people were using this sort of thing in that sort of way. And then, of course, there's the Tarot . . . there's the Chinese I Ching – all sorts of ways of divination. There are dozens and dozens of ways of interrogating the universe, basically, and the alethiometer is the one I made up for this book.[10]

When I asked Pullman to explain what he meant by 'interrogating the universe', he replied:

Perhaps 'interrogating' is too fierce a word (not least in view of the pictures we've seen from Iraq recently). I should have said something like 'respectfully questioning'. Human beings have got lots of ways of doing this; as well as the ones I mentioned, there is astrology, palm-reading,

> etc. I don't think these things give true answers;
> but what they might do – especially the more
> intellectually complex or enigmatic ones – is
> help you focus your question more precisely. So
> the answer you seem to be getting from them is
> actually coming from you. Probably.[11]

Within the context of *His Dark Materials*, all these are means by which Dust communicates. It's clear that Dust can also communicate more directly, though more intuitively. I commented earlier (Chapter 6) on Will's sudden intuition about the intruders in the house and the location of the writing case. Will seems to run into Lyra in Cittàgazze entirely by accident, but after the fight with Tullio on top of the Torre degli Angeli, we realize that something had brought him here. Giacomo Paradisi tells Will that he was destined to be the knife-bearer. When we also learn the importance, both to the story and to Will, of Stanislaus Grumman, we again see some kind of invisible force at work. The force is, of course, Dust. It has guided Will using inquisitive cats, apparent accidents, even the theft of the alethiometer by Sir Charles Latrom, all to bind Will's path with Lyra's. And Dust guides them both on their path to growing maturity, reaching its zenith at the point at which they recognize their love for each other in the grove. Somehow this reverses the flow of Dust and revitalizes the vast multiplicity of worlds. We'll return to this shortly, but for now we need to note that expressing their love wasn't just focused attention, but a new level of self-consciousness.[12] It's this self-awareness that coincides with their dæmons fixing on their final forms – they know who they are and what they want in life.

A second Fall

As we saw in Chapter 9, the theme of growing up is very significant to Philip Pullman – it is a change from innocence to experience. This theme is central to much of Pullman's work. In *The Broken Bridge*, *The Butterfly Tattoo*, the Sally Lockhart Quartet, and even *The Firework-maker's Daughter*, the central characters all leave a stage of innocence and find wisdom. In particular, they come to understand who they are and where they're going in life. Pullman often identifies this with a growing independence of thought, and in both *The Butterfly Tattoo* and *His Dark Materials*, he ties this in with the Fall.

We saw in the previous chapter that Pullman inverts the traditional understanding of the Fall, seeing it as a good thing. As he sees it, all Eve was after was knowledge, and 'what could possibly be wrong with that?'[13] Throughout *His Dark Materials* we have a growing sense of Lyra having some cosmic significance, from the Master's dark hints (*NL*, p.32), through to the moment when Father Gomez is despatched to kill her (*AS*, p.71, 74–75). We learn that we are heading towards a second Fall – a second occasion in which the future of everything would hang in the balance. Pullman knew from the outset that he 'would use a variation on the temptation motif, when Lyra falls in love . . . but here it's seen from another angle, through other eyes, this moment of revelation and sudden understanding, sudden self-consciousness, knowledge'.[14] The moment itself is beautifully captured by Pullman, and yet is also an anti-climax considering that the entire trilogy has been building towards some critical point. There is drama – Father Gomez is heading in their direction, rifle in hand; if it wasn't for Balthamos' reappearance like Lee (Robert Vaughn) after regaining his nerve in *The Magnificent Seven*,[15] all would have been lost – but this is slightly removed from the 'Fall' itself.

The moment of 'temptation' is further removed – it happens the day before, when Mary describes her experience of falling in love. She remembered that as a child she had fallen in love with a boy who put some marzipan[16] in her mouth. Years later, as a nun researching in physics, she had met, and enjoyed the company of, a man at a restaurant. Suddenly the taste of marzipan had brought her earlier experiences flooding back. It was the key to her starting a brief affair with the man and throwing off her Christianity. As she tells this story Lyra experiences some new sensations:

> She felt as if she had been handed the key to a great house she hadn't known was there, a house that was somehow inside her, and as she turned the key, deep in the darkness of the building she felt other doors opening too, and lights coming on . . . She didn't know what it was, or what it meant, or where it had come from: so she sat still, hugging her knees, and tried to stop herself trembling with excitement. *Soon*, she thought, *soon I'll know. I'll know very soon.* (*AS*, p.468, 471)

The following day, Lyra and Will go searching for their dæmons, taking a packed lunch including some 'sweet thirst-quenching red fruits' (*AS*, p.481). When they stop to eat in a grove of trees, they are edgy and hesitant; the food has no taste to it – until Lyra deliberately takes one of the red fruits and, replaying both Mary's childhood incident and Eve offering fruit to Adam, puts it to Will's lips. It's all so lovely and natural – two young people who are growing up fast and who have been through hell together, falling in love. Pullman tells this story in a beautiful, tender way, and invests their first kiss with very powerful emotions. He is often asked if Lyra and Will made love, but he insists it is none of his business: 'I don't know what they did. I wrote about the kiss – that's what I knew happened. I don't know what else they did. Maybe they did, maybe they didn't. I think they were rather young to, but still . . .'[17] Elsewhere he says, 'My imagination withdrew at that point. If you want to follow them under the tree and watch what happens, you must bear the responsibility for what you see. Personally, I think privacy is a fine and gracious thing. I describe a kiss: and there are some turning-points in life for which a kiss is quite enough.'[18]

Innocence and experience

In an interview for *Third Way*, he sets out the difference between the Fall of Will and Lyra, and the Fall of Adam and Eve:

> But of course the Satan figure is Mary Malone . . . and the temptation is wholly beneficent. She tells her story about how she fell in love, which gives Lyra the clue as to how to express what she's now beginning to feel about Will, and when it happens they both understand what's going on and are tempted and they (so to speak) fall – but it's a fall into grace, towards wisdom, not something that leads to sin, death, misery, hell – and Christianity.[19]

Perhaps this is why the 'Second Fall' feels anti-climactic – for me, at least. The parallels aren't strong enough.

Although Pullman says that Mary Malone is the 'Satan figure', she doesn't quite *tempt* Lyra. The serpent of Genesis 3 questions and denies what God has said, and misrepresents God's character. Mary simply 'tells them stories'. By recounting her own emotional development, she gives Will and Lyra the insight that unlocks their own feelings for each other, and the freedom to express those feelings. For Eve the fruit represented wisdom and autonomy; for Lyra it represented the deepest feelings of her heart. Adam and Eve were knowingly acting in disobedience to God; Lyra and Will were simply acting out of love for each other. The Bible contrasts the initial innocence of Adam and Eve with their subsequent guilt; Pullman contrasts innocence with wisdom. He does the same in *The Butterfly Tattoo*:

> We're not innocent; we *know* . . . The Garden
> of Eden – you know that story? The tree of
> knowledge of good and evil . . . Before you eat
> the fruit you're innocent, whatever you do is
> innocent because you don't understand. Then
> you eat it. And you're never innocent again. You
> know now. And that's painful; it's a terrible thing
> . . . Losing that innocence is the first step on the
> road to real knowledge. To wisdom if you like.
> You can't get wisdom till you lose that
> innocence. (p.155–156)

Pullman says that before eating the fruit we are innocent, naïve and ignorant. Taking the step towards knowledge and wisdom may be very difficult and painful (though not for Will and Lyra – their pain is still to come) but is essential if we are ever going to find it. Here he is drawing on Kleist and Blake (both discussed in Chapter 4). Will and Lyra are, metaphorically, eating the fruit a second time and beginning the process of returning the world to a state of innocence. Which brings us back to where we started this chapter. Will and Lyra have turned their backs on innocence, and have turned the ebbing tide of Dust, the myriad mysterious particles which are the very stuff of consciousness. They are stepping over the threshold into maturity – Mary sees them as 'children-no-longer-children' as they return to the village (AS, p.497). They have become fully self-conscious, their dæmons are about to settle, and they have no doubt about what they want in life. They don't yet realize that their deepest desire – to be together – will be thwarted, but they know they must work at building the republic of heaven wherever they are. Pullman thus equates this goal with their pursuit of wisdom. What this means in practice we will consider in Chapter 14.

---

[1] Dodd, Celia, 'Debate: Human nature: Universally acknowledged', The Times, 8 May 2004

[2] Gehmlich, Pierre, 'Dark matter "found within decade"', 9 April 2004 (news.bbc.co.uk/1/hi/sci/tech/3614127.stm).

[3] The opening was on 28 April 2003.

[4] For more information see Whitehouse, David, 'Science in the underworld', 28 April 2003 (news.bbc.co.uk/1/hi/sci/tech/2981837.stm).

[5] The appendix of this book has more on the real science of dark matter.

[6] Pullman, Philip, personal email to the author, 13 May 2004.

[7] Reply by Pullman in a discussion on the Readerville website (www.readerville.com/WebX?14@216.M6d8aZSiqFu.17@.ef6c70e/28).

[8] The responses Mary gets confirm that it is Shadows/Dust/dark matter, which is communicating with her (SK, p.259), but then they call themselves angels – 'structures' or 'complexifications' of Dust (SK, p.260).

[9] Reply by Pullman in a discussion on the Readerville website (www.readerville.com/webx?14@207.TcfXaajhstu.0@.ef6c70e/92).

[10] Brown, Charles N, 'An interview with Philip Pullman' (www.avnet.co.uk/amaranth/Critic/ivpullman.htm).

[11] Pullman, Philip, personal email to the author, 13 May 2004.

[12] Self-consciousness in the positive sense of self-awareness, rather than awkwardness.

[13] 'Faith and Fantasy', Australian Broadcasting Company Radio National, 24 March 2002 (www.abc.net.au/rn/relig/enc/stories/s510312.htm).

[14] Weich, Dave, 'Philip Pullman Reaches the Garden' (www.powells.com/authors/pullman.html).

[15] Weich, 'Philip Pullman Reaches the Garden'.

[16] 'Ah! Marchpane!' exclaims Lyra (*AS*, p.467). Marchpane was the Old English name for marzipan.

[17] Spanner, Huw, 'Heat and Dust', *Third Way*, Vol. 25 No. 2, April 2002, p.22–26 (www.thirdway.org.uk/past/showpage.asp?page=3949).

[18] Philip Pullman in a discussion on the Readerville website (www.readerville.com/WebX?14@216.M6d8aZSiqFu.18@.ef6c70e/30).

[19] Spanner, 'Heat and Dust'.

CHAPTER 12

Truth, Integrity and the Alethiometer

Philip Pullman has a passion for stories and storytelling as we saw in Chapter 3. But it is Pullman's most ambitious work, *His Dark Materials*, which explores their importance most fully. In particular, it is here that he makes the strongest and clearest case for the importance of *truthful* stories.

Truth seems to be something that Lyra doesn't initially value very highly. She talks her way out of trouble with the scholars and college servants. She lies to her uncle Asriel when he comes to enquire about her progress, and where she plays. She maintains her position of power within the various games and feuds that shape her life, by telling stories. For example, she convinces Roger that she is not afraid of Gobblers by telling him:

> I'd just do what my uncle done last time he came to Jordan. I seen him. He was in the Retiring Room and there was this guest who weren't polite, and my uncle just gave him a hard look and the man fell dead on the spot, with all foam and froth round his mouth. (*NL*, p.46–47)

When Roger is doubtful, having not heard about this in the kitchens, Lyra weaves another layer into her story, claiming Lord Asriel had done the same to some Tartars who had captured him and tied him up ready to 'cut his guts out'. Lyra tells such stories with glee, as well as a complete disregard for the truth. Roger isn't at all sure about it, which highlights the effect Lyra achieves with her stories. She uses them to exploit the fact that she connects with the worlds of academia and politics as well as with the worlds of the college servant children and the townies. Her fanciful stories about the dashing Lord Asriel enable her to reflect some of his glamour and mystique onto herself. Roger, and presumably others, strongly suspect that Lyra is making things up, but are not sure that they're in a position to disagree. Besides, it's more fun if such things *might* be true. In this incident, as probably in many others, the story is 'too good to waste' (*NL*, p.47), and they act it out using sherbet dip to get some authentic foaming at the mouth.

Deception and discretion

At Mrs Coulter's party Lyra finds telling half-truths harder than outright lies, but it's not long before she has to rely on her lying skills. Having escaped from the party, she finds herself the focus of attention of a man in a top hat. Lyra tells the man that she is going to meet her father, a murderer, and that she has his spare clothes in her bag. She manages to slip away into the crowd when she diverts the man's attention with her claim that her father is approaching and looking angry. Much later at Bolvangar, Lyra turns herself into Lizzie Brooks, a 'slow, dim-witted and reluctant' (*NL*, p.239) eleven-year old. Now she is lying both with what she says and with her whole nature, using her small stature to make herself seem 'shy and nervous and insignificant' (*NL*, p.240). Lying is so habitual to Lyra that she often invents stories even when she doesn't need to. When Lyra, Will and the Gallivespians spend the night in the suburbs of the dead, Lyra embroiders one of her fanciful stories for her host in response to his question about their origins:

> 'I'll tell you all about it,' said Lyra.
>
> And as she said that, as she took charge, part of her felt a little stream of pleasure rising upwards in her breast like the bubbles in champagne. And she knew Will was watching, and she was happy that he could see her doing what she was best at, doing it for him and for all of them. (AS, p.276)

The only reason for Lyra to make up her extraordinary story is to avoid having to admit why she is trying to get to the world of the dead. The people and their deaths lap it up, and it's such an engaging tale that Will and the spies are drawn into colluding with the invention: Will affirms what Lyra says, and Salmakia adds details of her own. Chevalier Tialys eventually rebukes Lyra:

> You're a thoughtless, irresponsible lying child.
>
> Fantasy comes so easily to you that your whole nature is riddled with dishonesty . . . (AS, p.280)

It's not that Lyra can't tell the truth, of course, just that Pullman presents her as instinctively lying in all kinds of situations. There are many times when we see Lyra telling the truth – very often, as we noted in Chapter 5, when she is speaking to people whom she senses have real integrity. This first happens after Lyra has been rescued by Billy Costa and Kerim, and Ma Costa wants to know what had happened to the young girl of whom she was so fond. All the enmity between Lyra and the gyptians – which she pretended was deadly serious, but was of course very playful – has gone, and Lyra responds to the down-to-earth goodness of the gyptian woman by telling the truth (or much of it).

Faa sighted

Later, at the Byanroping, Lyra sees Lord Faa for the first time – a man with 'nothing to mark him out but the air of strength and authority he had' (*NL*, p.115). He's strong in every way, straightforward, perhaps even rough and ready. He doesn't have the learning of Farder Coram but he comes across powerfully as a man with great integrity, a man with a strong moral sense who encourages other gyptians to have the same standards. When Raymond van Gerrit questions rescuing the land-loper children, John Faa makes clear the implications of what Raymond is asking and suggests that he is 'a better man than that' (*NL*, p.117). In the second assembly John Faa has to rebuke van Gerritt again, this time reminding him that Lyra is the daughter of Lord Asriel, a man to whom they owe much. Faa is a man to whom duty matters more than money, insisting that although there's a thousand-sovereign bounty for Lyra's capture, none of the gyptians should even think about handing her over: 'Anyone tempted by those thousand sovereigns had better find a place neither on land nor on water. We en't giving her up' (*NL*, p.116). John Faa shows his integrity, too, in conceding his ignorance about what the Gobblers are doing, and admitting that rescuing the children will be difficult and dangerous. When Lyra gets to talk to Lord Faa and Farder Coram in the parley room, she tells him everything 'more slowly than she'd told the Costas, but more honestly too. She was afraid of John Faa, and what she was most afraid of was his kindness' (*NL*, p.120). The delightful

Farder Coram, and, indeed, the vast majority of the gyptians, are also presented as deeply honourable and trustworthy people.

Here, of course, Pullman is deliberately reacting against the stereotype many people in the real world have about gypsies, whether referring to travellers or true Romanies. Peter Hitchens, writing in the *Spectator*, seems to imply that this is a mark of Pullman's leftist moral degeneracy, claiming that 'much of his thinking could . . . have been taken from the pages of the *Guardian*, or from politically correct staffroom conversation in a thousand state schools. Among the good characters in his trilogy are gypsies, an African prince,[1] a homosexual angel and a renegade nun.'[2] This extraordinary sweeping comment from Hitchens implies that the four good characters he mentions should all be considered bad. Whatever opinion one has on Africans and gypsies, homosexuality and apostasy,[3] it is a profoundly shallow view of human nature that sees the people concerned as only qualifying to be bad characters in a story.

Bear necessities

When Lyra meets the witches' consul, Dr Lanselius, she tells him the truth, not because of her sensing *his* integrity, but because she felt that his dæmon sensed the lack of honesty in what Farder Coram was saying (*NL*, p.173). The dynamic in the development of her relationship with Iorek Byrnison includes both her responding to his integrity, and her feeling that he could see right through her. She quickly realizes the utmost faithfulness of the bear, even given the dreadful circumstances in which he finds himself ('I must work till sunset . . . I gave my word this morning to the master here. I still owe a few more minutes' work'; *NL*, p.196) and uses this to dissuade him from killing one of the sentries at the priest's house (*NL*, p.199). Lee Scoresby is in no doubt about the quality of Iorek's character:

> All bears are true, but I've known Iorek for years, and nothing under the sky will make him break his word. Give him the charge to take care of [Lyra] and he'll do it, make no mistake.
> (*NL*, p.207)

Again and again we see Iorek Byrnison as a model of honesty and faithfulness in the way he behaves. Having given his word to obey Lord Faa, he will not take Lyra to the village where she finds Tony Makarios unless Lord Faa instructs him to. And once Iorek had been commanded to care for Lyra, he keeps doing so until he has accompanied her almost to the very northern tip of Svalbard when a thin ice bridge across a fissure prevented him going any further. There comes a moment when Lyra realizes that the armoured bear can read her in an uncanny way. Iorek gives her a startling demonstration that bears cannot be tricked (an incident straight out of Kleist's *On the Marionette Theatre* – see Chapter 4):

> He seemed to know what she intended before she did, and when she lunged at his head, the great paw swept the stick aside harmlessly, and when she feinted, he didn't move at all. She became exasperated, and threw herself into a furious attack . . .
>
> Finally, she was frighted and stopped . . . 'I bet you could catch bullets,' she said, and threw

the stick away. 'How do you *do* that?'

'By not being human,' he said. 'That's why you could never trick a bear. We see tricks and deceit as plain as arms and legs. We see in a way humans have forgotten.' (*NL*, p.227)

Philip Pullman draws a very stark contrast between Iorek Byrnison and the ursine usurper, Iofur Raknison. Iorek exemplifies all that is good about the noble *panserbjørne* because of his integrity as a bear – he is true to his nature. Iofur, however, has brought about a period of great uncertainty in the Svalbard kingdom as a result of his lack of integrity. He wants to be like the humans and has instituted a programme of 'modernization' and development that has left his subjects no longer knowing how to act or even how to think – they can no longer be true to themselves. What's more, Iofur wants to be a human complete with dæmon, and by denying his bear nature so radically he becomes vulnerable to Lyra tricking him. The great confrontation between the two bears is a powerfully tense moment in which Pullman pits not simply two bears against each other, but two ways of life and two moralities. It's not just a bear hero who wins, but integrity as a way of living. Iorek's great dilemma as to whether he should repair the subtle knife or not comes down to whether or not to do so would be consistent with his bear nature. Afterwards he's not sure he's done the right thing:

'Maybe I should not have mended it. I'm troubled, and I have never been troubled before, never in doubt. Now I am full of doubt. Doubt is a human thing, not a bear thing. If I am becoming human something's wrong, something's bad. And I have made it worse . . . I think I have

      stepped outside bear nature in mending this
      knife. I think I have been as foolish as Iofur
      Raknison. Time will tell. But I am uncertain and
      doubtful.' (*AS*, p.201–202)

His deep uncertainty springs from the fact that he is now caught up in affairs which are a long way from the concerns of the bears. He is caught up in a crisis that reaches far beyond the world, never mind his kingdom, and which has implications for all fully conscious creatures in all the worlds. Suddenly he no longer has clear bear-like criteria against which to measure his actions. And yet, he still acts – and worries – with extraordinary integrity.

The importance of being honest

Lyra seems to be strongly affected by her encounters with characters who are so full of integrity – not just John Faa and Iorek Byrnison but others including Farder Coram, Lee Scoresby, Serrafina Pekkala, and of course Will. They don't prompt Lyra to have a sudden change of heart about her reliance on lying. But we do see her being challenged, helped and even unnerved by them. What finally does bring about a moment of transformation is her encounter with creatures who seem to be the embodiment of everything that stinks, physically and morally. In what are some of the most heart-wrenching scenes in *His Dark Materials*, Lyra succeeds in getting to the world of the dead, though at great personal cost. She arrives feeling scared, heartbroken and more vulnerable than ever. But when the harpy attacks, she knows she has her great skill to fall back on – some fantastic tale will get her and Will and the spies out of danger:

'What do you want with us?' said Lyra.

'What can you give me?'

'We could tell you where we've been, and maybe you'd be interested, I don't know. We saw all kinds of strange things on the way here.'

'Oh, and you're offering to tell me a story? . . . Try, then,' said No-Name.

And even in her sickness and pain, Lyra felt that she'd just been dealt the ace of trumps . . . [Her] mind was already racing ahead through the story she'd told the night before, shaping and cutting and improving and adding: *parents dead; family treasure; shipwreck; escape* . . . (*AS*, p.307)

The response from the harpy is rapid, unexpected and terrifying. She flies at Lyra, tearing out some of her hair, and screaming at her:

'Liar! Liar! Liar!'

And it sounded as if her voice was coming from everywhere, and the word echoed back from the great wall in the fog, muffled and changed, so that she seemed to be screaming Lyra's name, so that *Lyra* and *liar* were one and the same thing. (*AS*, p.308)

Lyra is desolate. Having wrenched herself away from Pantalaimon, now the one skill she felt she could rely on has let her down:

She gave a shudder and took a long shaky breath, and her eyes focused on him, full of a wild despair.

'Will – I can't do it any more – I can't do it! I can't tell lies! I thought it was so easy – but it

        didn't work – it's all I can do, and it doesn't
        work!' (*AS*, p.309)

Will is quick to point out that she does have another skill – one which is both extremely rare and hugely significant for the future of all the worlds. She can read the alethiometer. This points out a paradox with which Lyra has been living for some time. On the one hand she prides herself in being an accomplished liar; on the other she has access to – and passes on – truth through her reading of the golden compass. The word *alethiometer* means 'truth meter', and almost from the very beginning Lyra has been convinced that it is entirely truthful. Yes, her invented stories have got them out of scrapes, but attending to the instructions of the alethiometer may have avoided the need for it in the first place. Now, having realized the failure of lying and the success of truth, she is ready for her transformation. A little later, the ghosts crowd around Lyra and beg her to tell them about the world of life, the sunshine and wind. She is apprehensive but Will, who was always committed to truth, encourages her to be honest. She uses her same storytelling skills to tell true stories, evoking the sensations of living, and at the end is startled to see the harpies all listening intently. The chevalier Tialys quizzes them about what has made the difference:

        'Answer my questions truly, and hear what I
        say, and then judge. When Lyra spoke to you
        outside the wall, you flew at her. Why did you do
        that?'

        'Lies!' the harpies all cried. 'Lies and
        fantasies!'

        'Yet when she spoke just now, you all listened,

everyone of you, and you kept silent and still.
Again, why was that?'

'Because it was true,' said No-Name. 'Because
she spoke the truth. Because it was nourishing.
Because it was feeding us. Because we couldn't
help it. Because it was true. Because we had no
idea that there was anything but wickedness.
Because it brought us news of the world and the
sun and the wind and the rain. Because it was
true.' (*AS*, p.332–333)

The Authority had given the harpies 'power to see the
worst in everyone'. The worst has been their constant
diet, and now their 'blood is rank with it', their 'very
hearts are sickened' (*AS*, p.331). But there was no alternative; it was all they had. Now they are incensed at the
possibility of Lyra taking even that away by opening a
way out for the ghosts, but they also realize for the first
time that there is something better. Tialys brokers a
deal, by which the harpies will become the guides,
rather than guardians, for the dead, and in return will
have the right to demand from people true stories. The
injunction on all future ghosts to 'tell them stories' is
eventually passed on to Mary Malone by the ghost of an
old woman as she leaves the window which Will ultimately opens into the world of the mulefa. Mary takes
this to heart in her relationship with Will and Lyra. It is
her recounting the true story of her past which crystal-
lizes the feelings of the children, allowing them to
express their love for each other and so restoring the
inflow of Dust into the worlds. Lyra's economy with the
truth is a part of her impish nature, but perhaps the
most important way in which she matures during the
trilogy is her embracing of truthfulness, which happens

at the lowest point of her life. It is a turning point not only for Lyra, but for the entire narrative of *His Dark Materials*.

Fantastic truth

Philip Pullman is clearly a writer who puts an extremely high value on truth and integrity. This comes through the kinds of characters that many of his heroes are, and through parts of the narrative (especially in *His Dark Materials*), particularly in some of the transformations which characters experience and in the focus on the importance of truth-telling. But Pullman wants to communicate truth at a deeper level than that – he wants his stories to be truthful. That doesn't mean that he believes he is writing true stories – he's a fiction writer, and a writer of fantasy fiction at that – but that he believes the stories he tells are truthful about human beings. In an interview on the Scholastic website he referred to *His Dark Materials* as 'stark realism'.[4] It was a provocative comment to make about books featuring dæmons, talking bears and other universes. Philip explains what he meant by it on his own website:

> That comment got me into trouble with the
> fantasy people. What I mean by it was roughly
> this: that the story I was trying to write was
> about real people, not beings that don't exist like
> elves or hobbits. Lyra and Will and the other
> characters are meant to be human beings like
> us, and the story is about a universal human
> experience, namely growing up.[5]

Although there are non-human characters which play a very prominent part in the story, it is first and foremost about Lyra and Will, and perhaps secondly about Lord

Asriel and Mrs Coulter. Iorek Byrnison, Serafina Pekkala, Tialys and Salmakia, and others are in supporting roles. Pantalaimon is important too – his animal forms should not distract us from remembering that dæmons are intended to say something important about the nature of human beings, as we discussed in Chapter 9. Pullman continues:

> The 'fantasy' parts of the story were there as a picture of aspects of human nature, not as something alien and strange. For example, readers have told me that the dæmons, which at first seem so utterly fantastic, soon become so familiar and essential a part of each character that they, the readers, feel as if they've got a dæmon themselves. And my point is that they have, that we all have. It's an aspect of our personality that we often overlook, but it's there. That's what I mean by realism: I was using the fantastical elements to say something that I thought was true about us and about our lives.[6]

Pullman disdains much of the fantasy he has read, including Tolkien's abidingly popular *Lord of the Rings*,[7] because it doesn't seem to him to say anything very interesting about people and their psychology. In a debate on morality in fiction at the 2002 Edinburgh International Books Festival, he said that: 'Fantasy, and fiction in general, is failing to do what it might be doing. It has unlimited potential to explore all sorts of metaphysical and moral questions, but it is not . . . My quarrel with fantasy writing is that it is such a rich seam to be mined, such a versatile mode, that is not always being used to explore bigger ideas.'[8] He argued that fiction should deal with big issues, including death. On

Pullman's own website, however, he appears to contradict this when he says that children's literature *doesn't* have a duty to deal with big issues. 'The only duty it has is best expressed in the words of Dr Johnson: "The only aim of writing is to help the reader better to enjoy life, or better to endure it."'[9] But helping people to enjoy or endure life does still fit with his conviction that the business of writing stories is profoundly moral: 'You can't leave morality out unless your work is so stupid and trivial and so worthless that [nobody] would want to read it anyway.'[10]

So Philip Pullman wants his fiction to be true in that it deals honestly with human psychology and with difficult issues of morality. In many respects he succeeds admirably at this: Lyra and Will are very believable characters who have some very real struggles, for example. But there are weaknesses too. One is Lyra's response to Roger's death. After the trouble Lyra goes to to rescue Roger from Bolvangar, at the end of *Northern Lights* she doesn't seem too distraught at his death, more angry with her father. Yes, she felt 'wrenched apart with unhappiness' (*NL*, p.397) but within moments she is fired up at the thought of discovering the source of Dust. This doesn't feel psychologically true – an eleven-year-old's playmate has just been killed by her father and she jumps off to pursue Dust in another world just five minutes later? Roger's death is referred to quite matter-of-factly in *The Subtle Knife*, and it isn't until *The Amber Spyglass* that we begin to see Lyra's anguish over his fate – and then only because of her drug-induced hallucinatory glimpse into the world of the dead. More seriously for many people, Pullman's portrayal of the Church is deeply prejudiced and unfair – a subject we will consider in the next chapter.

Still, despite the weaknesses, *His Dark Materials* and much of Pullman's other work is often very insightful into human nature and does place a high value on some vital human qualities: integrity and honesty are central; curiosity and a love of the physical world are important too. And because the situations within which he places his characters are so full of moral issues, almost anyone who reads his books will find themselves asking some searching questions as a result.

---

[1] Ogunwe is, in fact, a king, not a prince (*AS*, p.66).

[2] Hitchens, Peter, 'A labour of loathing', *Spectator*, 18 January 2003.

[3] Giving up on one's faith.

[4] 'Philip Pullman in his own words' (www.scholastic.co.uk/zone/spyglasshome/amber_philip.html). Terry Pratchett says that referring to *His Dark Materials* as 'stark realism' rather than fantasy shows 'that Mr Pullman – a nice chap, by the way – has certainly grasped one requisite for being a successful fantasy writer' (www.dcs.gla.ac.uk/SF-Archives/Ansible/a175.html).

[5] Pullman, Philip, 'About the Writing' (www.philip-pullman.com/about_the_writing.asp).

[6] Pullman, 'About the Writing'.

[7] When I think about the fantasy that I've read . . . I have to say that it's pretty thin . . . Inventiveness a-plenty – no shortage of strange creatures and made-up languages and broad landscapes . . . but that kind of thing is not hard to make up . . . But there isn't a character in the whole of *The Lord of the Rings* who has a tenth of the complexity, the interest, the sheer fascination, of even a fairly minor character from *Middlemarch*, such as Mary Garth. Nothing in her is arbitrary; everything is necessary and organic, by which I mean that she really does seem to have grown into life, and not to have been assembled from a kit of parts. She's surprising. It's not just character drawing, either; it's moral truthfulness. I can't remember anything in *The Lord of the Rings*, in all that vast epic of heroic battles and ancient magic, that titanic struggle between good and evil, that even begins to approach the ethical power and the sheer moral shock of the scene in Jane Austen's *Emma* when Mr Knightley reproaches the heroine

for her thoughtless treatment of poor Miss Bates. Emma's mortification is one of those eye-opening moments after which nothing is the same. Emma will grow up now, and if we pay attention to what's happening in the scene, so will we. That's what realistic fiction can do, and what fantasy of the Tolkien sort doesn't (Pullman, Philip, *Writing Fantasy Realistically*, Sea of Faith National Conference, 2002; www.sofn.org.uk/Conferences/pullman2002.htm).

[8] Quoted in Chrisafis, Angelique, 'Pullman lays down moral challenge for writers', *Guardian*, 12 August 2002.

[9] Pullman, 'About the Writing'.

[10] Quoted in Chrisafis, 'Pullman lays down moral challenge for writers'.

CHAPTER 13

The Magisterium and the Authority

His Dark Materials made Philip Pullman the focus of a certain amount of controversy. For some time the three volumes sold strongly without attracting the hostility that was greeting J. K. Rowling's books in some circles. Pullman suspects that Harry Potter initially diverted the general public attention away from him:

> I've been surprised by how little criticism I've got. Harry Potter's been taking all the flak . . . the people – mainly from America's Bible Belt – who complain that Harry Potter promotes Satanism or witchcraft obviously haven't got enough in their lives. Meanwhile, I've been flying under the radar, saying things that are far more subversive than anything poor old Harry has said. My books are about killing God.[1]

Pullman doesn't beat about the bush on this: he says, 'I'm trying to undermine the basis of Christian belief',[2] though elsewhere he claims that he's 'not making an argument, or preaching a sermon or setting out a political tract: I'm telling a story.'[3] He insists he didn't set out to offend Christians. However, 'before too long I realised I was telling a story which would serve as a vehicle for exploring things which I had been thinking about over the years. Lyra came to me at the right stage of my life.'[4]

Throughout *Northern Lights* it seems as though only the Church is in Pullman's sights, but early in *The Subtle Knife*, Lord Asriel's manservant Thorold tells Serafina Pekkala that Asriel is 'aiming a rebellion against the highest power of all. He's gone a-searching for the dwelling place of the Authority Himself, and he's a-going to destroy him' (*SK*, p.48).

Secret history

A key bone of contention for Pullman is the issue of authority, which is of course why Pullman gives God the title of 'The Authority'. There is a sense in which the Authority and the Magisterium are just manifestations of misused power. But given Pullman's comments quoted above, it seems clear that he does have religion – rather than authority generally – in his sights. The Authority's title distances him in the reader's mind from the Christian God; it doesn't feel like Pullman is talking about the same being. But in case we fail to make the connection, Balthamos spells it out:

> The Authority, God, the Creator, the Lord,
> Yahweh, El, Adonai, the King, the Father, the
> Almighty – those were all names he gave himself.
> He was never the creator. He was an angel
> like ourselves – the first angel, true, the most
> powerful, but he was formed of Dust as we are.
> (*AS*, p.33)

How can 'God' be an angel? In Pullman's underlying 'creation myth', matter became conscious of itself and generated Dust. Some of it 'condensed' into the first angel – a being of pure Dust. This new being was fully conscious, and when he began to see other angels condensing out of the Dust he realized what an opportunity he had. Since he came first, he could tell the subsequent angels that he was God and had created them. The angels loved and obeyed him, but the Sophia (Wisdom), the youngest and most beautiful angel, discovered the truth about the Authority who subsequently expelled her. There was an angelic rebellion, but the Authority defeated it and imprisoned the rebels in one of the many worlds. The Sophia told them about the Authority's lies to human beings (and conscious beings in other worlds), and the rebels escaped to bring enlightenment, wisdom and full consciousness to the poor creatures under the Authority's rule.

This myth draws heavily on second-century Gnosticism, but also inverts it. Gnosticism is all about *gnosis* – knowledge, in particular secret, esoteric knowledge open only to a privileged few. For the early Gnostics, the secret knowledge about reality was that the world was not created by God, but by an evil Demiurge (a lesser or false god); the true God is unreachable and unknowable. The Gnostics believed that matter is essentially evil, but Sophia, one of the angelic beings, managed to put a spark of true spiritual nature (*pneuma*) into human beings. Pullman doesn't believe this but sees it as a good story with 'immense explanatory power: it offers to explain why we feel . . . *exiled* in this world, *alienated* from joy and meaningfulness and the true connection we feel we must have with the universe'.[5] Where Pullman turns this on its head is in the attitude towards the physical. Gnosticism sees it as evil; Pullman sees it as something to be enjoyed and celebrated.

Pullman's myth also draws on *Paradise Lost*'s angelic war, Satan's escape from his prison, and his tempting of Adam and Eve. By recasting God as the demiurge impostor, Pullman transforms him into the bad guy, and casts the rebels (including the Sophia) as the good guys. On this view, the Fall is a good thing (see Chapters 10 and 11). This is an ideal scenario for Pullman: a materialist universe, which has found its own wisdom fighting off the deceptions and impositions of a 'god' who is really nothing of the sort. Archbishop Rowan Williams points out that:

> Someone [the demiurge or the Authority] is
> trying to pull the wool over your eyes . . . and
> wisdom is an unmasking . . . If you have a view
> of God which makes God internal to the
> universe, that's what happens.[6]

Williams is saying that if you see God merely as part of the physical universe, then you automatically see him as a deceiver. The historically orthodox Christian understanding of God and the universe only works if God is transcendent.

The death of God

Pullman says that 'the Authority . . . is an ancient *idea* of God, kept alive artificially by those who benefit from his continued existence'.[7] He believes that for sensible people, 'the old assumptions have withered away . . . the idea of God with which I was brought up is now perfectly incredible'.[8] So God should be eliminated. In the real world, Pullman thinks the *idea* of God should be abandoned; in his imagined worlds, where the Authority is merely an angel, he can kill him off. He makes much of the fact that the Authority is getting old – early on he walks in the Garden with Adam and Eve, but eventually he is the 'Ancient of Days'.[9] So Pullman portrays him as now 'demented and powerless', fearful, miserable and light as paper ('in other words he has a reality which is only symbolic'[10]). Will cuts open his crashed crystal litter to help him out:

> The aged being could only weep and mumble in fear and pain and misery, and he shrank away from what seemed like yet another threat . . . in the open air there was nothing to stop the wind from damaging him, and to their dismay his form began to loosen and dissolve. Only a few moments later he had vanished completely, and their last impression was of those eyes, blinking in wonder, and a sigh of the most profound and exhausted relief. Then he was gone: a mystery dissolving in mystery. (*AS*, p.431–432)

In interviews, Pullman stresses the 'profound and exhausted relief' – he wants this to be seen as an act of compassion for a being who has had enough. For the being in *His Dark Materials* this is perfectly reasonable. But that being is *not* the God of the Bible.

The Bible is clear that God exists eternally and is unique. He is the creator of everything, and made human beings in his image. That means we are fully conscious not because we have rebelled against an angelic upstart, but because we reflect our creator. That much comes from the first chapter of the Bible. It's clear from elsewhere in the Bible that God is not simply different in *degree* from the angels – he's not just older and more powerful – but that he is radically different in his very *nature*.[11] It's also clear that he is not remote from his creation, threatened by it, or vindictive towards it; rather he is intimately involved in it moment by moment,[12] compassionate towards it,[13] and longing for both humans and the whole creation to find redemption.[14]

Repellent religion

Rowan Williams writes:

> What the story makes you see is that if you believe in a mortal God, who can win and lose his power, your religion will be saturated with anxiety – and so with violence. In a sense, you could say that a mortal God needs to be killed . . . And if you see religious societies in which anxiety and violence predominate, you could do worse than ask what God it is that they believe in. The chances are that they secretly or unconsciously believe in a God who is just another inhabitant of the universe, only more powerful than anyone else. And if he is another inhabitant of the universe, then at the end of the day he just might be subject to change and chance like everything else.[15]

The Church in Lyra's world – and especially its ruling body, the Magisterium – is indeed 'saturated with anxiety and so with violence'. It is a singularly repellent institution. The Church's 'power over every aspect of life' was 'absolute' (*NL*, p.31) and had been since the time of Calvin, who Pullman rather mischievously makes the last Pope in Lyra's world. In reality, John Calvin did live in Geneva but far from being Pope, he was one of the most significant figures in the Reformation. To have him as the end of the papal line signals clearly that in Lyra's world there was no Reformation. This makes it easy for Pullman to portray the Church as authoritarian, with a history of Inquisitions and the kinds of theological manoeuvring which provoked the Reformation in our world. Early in *Northern Lights* we learn about the Magisterium's interference in 'experimental theology', and later of its interrogation of Rusakov 'under the rules of the Inquisition' (*NL*, p.371). John Faa also tells Lyra about rumours that the Office of Inquisition is to be re-instituted (*NL*, p.128). These references to the Inquisition carry connotations of ruthlessness and violence.

The Church is responsible for the atrocity of Bolvangar by tacitly accepting the General Oblation Board's Experimental Station. The fact that Mrs Coulter can insist on the torturing of a captured witch (in the presence of various clerics including a Cardinal, and Fra Pavel, the Consistorial Court of Discipline's alethiometrist) suggests that the Magisterium is fully supportive of her. But the Board and its activities are sufficiently removed from the Magisterium to be denounced if necessary. The feeling evoked by the scenes on the boat is of unmitigated cruelty. Later in *The Subtle Knife*, the troubled times bring Ruta Skadi to meet with Serafina Pekkala and her clan. When Serafina invites her to address their council that evening, the visitor says:

> Sisters . . . let me tell you . . . who it is that we must fight . . . It is the Magisterium, the church. For all its history . . . it's tried to suppress and control every natural impulse. And when it can't control them, it cuts them out. Some of you have seen what they did at Bolvangar. And that was horrible, but it is not the only such place, not the only such practice. Sisters, you know only the

north: I have travelled in the south lands. There
are churches there, believe me, that cut their
children too, as the people of Bolvangar did –
not in the same way, but just as horribly – they
cut their sexual organs, yes, both boys and girls
– they cut them with knives so that they shan't
feel.[16] That is what the church does, and every
church is the same: control, destroy, obliterate
every good feeling. So if a war comes, and the
church is on one side of it, we must be on the
other, no matter what strange allies we find
ourselves bound to. (*SK*, p.52)

In *The Amber Spyglass*, we meet Semyon Borisovitch,
the disgusting, drunk, witch-hating, and possibly pae-
dophilic priest (*AS*, p.102–107), and, in an outrageous
slur on a real historical figure, we are told that John
Calvin was responsible for ordering the deaths of children (*AS*, p.217).[17] The Magisterium also shows callous
cruelty with its solution to the problem of Lyra once it
learns that she is a second Eve. The President of the
Consistorial Court of Discipline, Father Hugh MacPhail,
proposes to have her hunted down and killed. The 'blaz-
ing-eyed' fanatic, Father Luis Gomez is quick to volunteer having already done sufficient masochistic penance
in advance to offset the guilt of killing someone (*AS*,
p.75).[18] He is to stop at nothing to achieve his goal – but
he's on his own; the Magisterium will disown him if he
is ever discovered.

Blurring fact and fiction

Now, all this is so strongly anti-church as to be offen-
sive to many people within the real-world Church. But
His Dark Materials is *fantasy* literature. The Church

Pullman describes is in another world; it is not the Church in our world. And yet something about the passion with which Pullman denounces it, and the fact that the Magisterium has not one single redeeming feature, leaves one feeling that the contempt is still directed at the real-world Church, even if the specific criticism is only within the realm of fiction. Pullman confirms this impression when he says very similar things about the real-world Church in interviews. In a discussion on Readerville.com he was asked why all the Magisterium characters are bad. He replied:

> That was due to a flaw in my artistry, no doubt.
> But I was trying to hit a target that deserved
> hitting, and there's no merit in pulling punches
> when important issues are at stake. Anyway,
> every time I thought I was overdoing it, up came
> another scandal about brutal monks mistreating
> children in Irish schools, or sadistic nuns
> tormenting children in Scottish orphanages, to
> name but two that came up recently. These
> things do happen.[19]

Pullman's view of Christian history is profoundly negative. At times he concedes that there have been some very positive aspects:

> I'm fascinated by the history of religious thought
> and the structures of religious life. It was a
> natural thing to write about, because it
> encapsulates so much of the best as well as the
> worst of what human beings have done.[20]

He also happily affirms that there are many good Christian people. But the overall tenor of his assessment is still rather jaundiced. He says that his antipathy towards the Church comes from history:

It comes from the record of the Inquisition, persecuting heretics and torturing Jews and all that
sort of stuff; and it comes from the other side,
too, from the Protestants burning the Catholics.
It comes from the insensate pursuit of innocent
and crazy old women, and from the Puritans in
America burning and hanging the witches – and
it comes not only from the Christian Church but
also from the Taliban.

Every single religion that has a monotheistic
god ends up by persecuting other people and
killing them because they don't accept him.
Wherever you look in history, you find that. It's
still going on.[21]

Elsewhere he says:

The God who dies is the God of the burners of
heretics, the hangers of witches, the persecutors
of Jews, the officials who recently flogged that
poor girl in Nigeria who had the misfortune to
become pregnant after having been forced to
have sex – all these people claim to know with
absolute certainty that their God wants them to
do these things. Well, I take them at their word,
and I say in response that that God deserves
to die.[22]

Pullman's antagonism towards religion generally, and
Christianity in particular, certainly doesn't seem to be
motivated by bad personal experiences of it. His grandfather's influence was very positive, and he admits that
his early experiences of church gave him a love for the
Bible, or at least, the Authorised Version of 1611:

All through my childhood, I went to church
every Sunday. I went to Sunday school. I know

the Bible very well. I know the hymns and the
prayer book very well – and this is the old,
authorized King James Version of the Bible,
and the 1662 Book of Common Prayer that used
to be used in English churches, and the old
hymns that used to be sung. When I go into a
church now, I don't recognize the language. It's
sort of modern and it's flat and it's bureaucratic
and it's derivative . . . In attempting to be
inclusive and friendly, it becomes awfully . . .
jolly and I can't bear that. But I love the language and the atmosphere of the Bible and the
prayer book.[23]

But this does not mean that he believes it. He continues:

I don't say I agree with it . . . Since growing up
and since thinking about it, I've come to realize
that the basis on which these belief systems were
founded isn't there. I no longer believe in the
God I used to believe in when I was a boy. But I
do know the background very well, and I will
never escape it. So although I call myself an
atheist, I'm certainly a Christian atheist and even
more particularly, a Church of England . . .
atheist. And very specifically, a 1662 Book of
Common Prayer atheist. I can't escape these
influences on my background, and I would not
wish to.[24]

It's interesting that he would not wish to escape these
influences, but they are influences at a literary, artistic,
perhaps emotional level, rather than at the level of
belief. However, I would argue that this background
also continues to have a profound influence on Pullman
at a moral level too.

Pullman's Christian values?

Many of the values Pullman champions in his books are thoroughly Christian. We saw in the previous chapter how committed he is to notions of truth and integrity. He is also a great believer in courage, love, freedom, responsibility, duty, curiosity and tolerance.

Pullman is correct to point out that in history and around the world today, there are all too many expressions of Christianity which are far removed from these values. But these values are nevertheless a core part of Christian behaviour when it is lived with integrity and in faithfulness to God. Everybody – Christian or otherwise – has lapses and fails to live up to his or her own standards. When so-called Christians depart significantly from Christian values, it shows that their faith is not a heart matter – not a relationship with a living God, but merely the inspiration for their own invented religion, which superficially looks like genuine Christianity.

Pullman is also correct to say that these values are not *distinctively* Christian. One interviewer, Huw Spanner, asked Philip about the source of values: 'Where in a world without God does [the] sense of "ought" come from?' Pullman's response was vigorous:

> I'm amazed by the gall of Christians. You think
> that nobody can possibly be decent unless
> they've got the idea from God or something.
> Absolute bloody rubbish! Isn't it your experience
> that there are plenty of people in the world
> who don't believe who are very good, decent
> people? [25]

When Spanner pressed him on where the values come from, Pullman continued:

> For goodness' sake! It comes from ordinary

human decency. It comes from accumulated human wisdom – which includes the wisdom of such figures as Jesus Christ. Jesus, like many of the founders of great religions, was a moral genius, and he set out a number of things very clearly in the Gospels which if we all lived by them we'd all do much better. What a pity the Church doesn't listen to him![26]

Morality in a godless universe

Pullman's comment that Christians 'think that nobody can possibly be decent unless they've got the idea from God or something', misses the point. Spanner was not suggesting that each person's moral sense comes *directly* from God; nor was he denying that many non-Christians, including atheists, are deeply moral people. Pullman himself is a good example. The question is, why is there *any* sense of ought, *any* moral value, in a world without God? Why is it possible to talk about 'ordinary human decency' at all? How do we give such a phrase any meaning?

Pullman's view is that it is through 'accumulated human wisdom'. But *human* wisdom, accumulated or otherwise, has nothing transcendent about it. In other words, there's no objective basis for it, nowhere to ground it. On what basis do we decide that 'Jesus, like many of the founders of great religions, was a moral genius'? Which 'founders of great religions' do we include in the category of 'moral genius', and which do we exclude – and why? Is it simply that we *like* the moral positions of Jesus, Zarathustra, Siddharta Gautama, Mohammed, or Guru Nanak,[27] but we don't like the moral positions of Sun Myung Moon,[28] Joseph

Smith Jr.,[29] Charles T. Russell,[30] or L. Ron Hubbard?[31]

Perhaps it is the *accumulation* of wisdom over the centuries which allows us to see that some moral positions work well and others don't. But if we really were accumulating wisdom, surely we should be seeing an improvement in the moral foundations of society. Yet as I write this chapter it's exactly ten years since the genocide in Rwanda – 800,000 people killed in 100 days. Since then we've seen massacres in the former Yugoslavia, East Timor, Sierra Leone, Liberia and elsewhere. The supposedly morally upstanding forces of the West are currently facing allegations of abusing Iraqi prisoners. How much did we learn from the slaughter of six million Jews at the hands of the Third Reich? Why doesn't our 'accumulated human wisdom' prevent such things happening? Simply because it is human wisdom with no objective basis.

If morality is simply determined by humans, then why should one powerful group listen to the rest of the world? Or why should one individual listen to anyone else, when self-interest clashes with the 'herd morality' of society? If moral principles are simply the customs of wise human beings, then someone who chooses to reject those morals is doing nothing more serious than being an individualist, a non-conformist. Pullman himself is against the moral anarchy that would result from people making their own moral decisions without reference to everybody else – he believes there are genuine moral principles. But in a world without God it seems to be extremely difficult to find any objective basis for those principles; they become arbitrary.

Christians are not claiming a monopoly on morality and values. But they believe that morality only functions because it has an objective basis in the character of God, *whether or not* anybody believes in him. Pullman rejects the existence of God yet clings to moral principles – but basing these simply on 'accumulated human wisdom' isn't good enough. Besides which, Pullman is a materialist – he believes this world is all there is. So where does his cherished freedom come from? If there is nothing other than a physical universe then *everything* Pullman does or thinks is a result of physical processes. Everything is a result of his genetic inheritance or of physical influences from outside his body. But these two are a result of prior physical processes. Everything is deterministic – there is no freedom. As Will Provine, professor of biological sciences and the history of biology at Cornell University, insists:

> Humans are comprised only of heredity and environment, both of which are deterministic. There is simply no room for the traditional concepts of human free-will. That is, humans do make decisions and they go through decision-making processes, but all of these are deterministic. So from my perspective as a naturalist, there's not even a possibility that human beings have free will.[32]

It's not sufficient to bring in quantum effects within the human brain to answer this problem either – all that does is introduce complete randomness into the mix. The only way humans can be genuinely free to make real moral choices is if something outside the physical system of the universe gives us that freedom – if there is a God.

But Pullman doesn't believe there is a God – or at least, he says he's seen no evidence of God; he doesn't rule out the possibility that God may exist somewhere very remote from human life. The Christian response is that the evidence is all around – a world of magnificent beauty and diversity; a world of freedom and moral responsibility; a world in which even today the vast majority of people believe in the existence of the super-natural[33]; and in particular there is the historical textual evidence of the life, death and resurrection of Jesus of Nazareth. It is possible to explain such things away with alternative theories, but the question is which explanation best fits *all* the evidence – a materialistic, deterministic universe; or a God who is intimately involved with his creation? A rationalist man like Philip Pullman sees the idea of God as 'now perfectly incredible',[34] but as Will says, 'You think things have to be *possible*? Things have to be *true!*' (*SK*, p.337).

[1]   Meacham, Steve, 'The shed where God died', *Sidney Morning Herald*, 13 December 2003.

[2]   Wartofsky, Alona, 'The Last Word', *Washington Post*, 19 February 2001.

[3]   Spanner, Huw, 'Heat and Dust', *Third Way*, vol. 25 no. 2, April 2002, p.22–26.

[4]   Meacham, 'The shed where God died'.

[5]   Pullman, Philip, 'The Republic of Heaven', *Horn Book Magazine*, November/December 2001, p.657.

[6]   Pullman, Philip and Williams, Rowan, 'The Dark Materials debate: life, God, the universe . . .', *Daily Telegraph*, 17 March 2004.

[7]   Pullman, Philip, 'Discussion on Readerville.com' (www.readerville.com/WebX?14@216.M6d8aZSiqFu.17@.ef6c70e/28).

[8]   Pullman, 'The Republic of Heaven', p.655.

[9]   Pullman, Philip, *His Dark Materials: The Myth* (unpublished).

[10] Pullman and Williams, 'The Dark Materials debate: life, God, the universe . . .'.

[11] See Hebrews 1 for one discussion of Jesus the Son of God's superiority to angels.

[12] See Hebrews 1:3 for example.

[13] For example, see Psalm 111 and Psalm 145.

[14] See Romans 8:19–23.

[14] Williams, Rowan, 'A near-miraculous triumph', *Guardian*, 10 March 2004.

[16] Male circumcision is a central part of the religious practices of Jews and Muslims; it is generally performed expertly and carries little or no health risk. Female circumcision, also known as Female Genital Mutilation (FGM), is a cultural practice, *not* a religious one (though there is some controversy within Islam about two sayings of Mohammed which are interpreted as approving of the practice). It is a barbaric practice intended to preserve a girl's virginity by preventing or reducing any sexual feeling, and it carries very severe health risks. For more information, see www.religioustolerance.org/fem_cirm.htm.

[17] Since John Calvin is a real historical figure in our world, it's important to remember at this point that Pullman is writing about a fictional John Calvin in another world. The Calvin in our world was never guilty of such a thing.

[18] The idea of pre-emptive absolution is Pullman's invention – it is not an idea accepted in any orthodox, mainstream church.

[19] Pullman, 'Discussion on Readerville.com' (www.readerville.com/WebX?14@216.M6d8aZSiqFu.18@.ef6c70e/30).

[20] Pullman, 'Discussion on Readerville.com' (www.readerville.com/WebX?14@216.M6d8aZSiqFu.11@.ef6c70e/111).

[21] Spanner, 'Heat and Dust'.

[22] Pullman, 'Discussion on Readerville.com' (www.readerville.com/WebX?14@216.M6d8aZSiqFu.17@.ef6c70e/28).

[23] Odean, Kathleen, 'The story master', *School Library Journal*, 1 October 2000 (www.schoollibraryjournal.com/article/ca153054).

[24] Odean, 'The story master'.

[25] Spanner, 'Heat and Dust'.

[26] Pullman says: 'Jesus is a very interesting character, whom the Christian church in all its branches has completely misunderstood – more truthfully, misrepresented – for two thousand years. In almost every respect his actual words directly contradict what churches tell us – about the family, to take one obvious and current example. To hear the church, you'd think that Jesus was completely obsessed by the question of homosexuality and what a threat it was to the family. But he never mentions homosexuality, and his view of families was that you should leave them behind entirely. And so on. My view of him, of course, would say that he was not God at all, but a man – a man of genius, a great moral teacher and storyteller, but only a man – who died. The resurrection was a story made up later in order to consolidate the authority of the new and shaky structure of the church, and to bolster the fantasies of Paul about the imminent end of the world' (personal email to the author, 16 June 2004).

[27] Zarathustra (Zoroaster in Greek) (probably around 1500 BC) was the founder of Zoroastrianism; Siddharta Gautama (563–483 BC) was the founder of Buddhism; Mohammed (AD 570–632) was the founder of Islam; and Guru Nanak (AD 1469–1539) was the founder of Sikhism.

[28] Sun Myung Moon (born 1954) is the founder of the Unification Church. Moon and his followers have frequently been accused of manipulative recruiting techniques, deception and brainwashing. Moon was convicted of tax fraud in 1982 and is alleged to have links with extremist right-wing organizations and arms manufacturers. While I was writing this chapter it was announced that Moon, while in the US Senate, had declared himself Messiah, and claimed that 'communist leaders such as Marx and Lenin, who committed all manner of barbarity, and dictators such as Hitler and Stalin, have found strength in my teachings, mended their ways and been reborn as new persons' (Julian Borger, 'Moonie leader "crowned" in Senate', *Guardian*, 24 June 2004). See also en.wikipedia.org/wiki/Sun_Myung_Moon.

[29] Joseph Smith Jr. (1805–1844) was the founder of The Church of Jesus Christ of Latter Day Saints (Mormons). He was accused of being a charlatan, and many of his early associates turned against him, not least because of his practice of polygamy. The Mormon Church is accused of being authoritarian, deceptive and oppressive of women, as well as secretly continuing to encourage polygamy. See en.wikipedia.org/wiki/Church_of_Jesus_Christ_of_Latter-day_Saints and www.irr.org/mit/Default.html.

[30] Charles T. Russell (1852–1916) was the founder of the Jehovah's Witnesses (although this is disputed by some). He too is accused of being a charlatan and not only lost a libel suit when contesting such allegations, but perjured himself in the process. It has a history of failed prophecies (it has prophesied the end of the world at least six specific dates). See en.wikipedia.org/wiki/Jehovah's_Witnesses and www.watchtowerinformationservice.org.

[31] L. Ron Hubbard (1911–1986) was the founder of the Church of Scientology. Hubbard, a science fiction writer and convicted thief, is said to have been a pathological liar, a fraud, a cheat, a wife-beater, alcoholic and drug-addict. The Church of Scientology has repeatedly been accused of mind control, exploitation, espionage, intimidation, violence, and even murder. See en.wikipedia.org/wiki/Scientology and www.clambake.org.

[32] Quoted in Stannard, Russell, *Science and Wonders: conversations about science and belief* (Faber & Faber, 1996), p.60.

[33] Victoria Nelson argues that many secular people have a deep, unconscious belief in the transcendent, which is why science fiction and fantasy are such popular genres in both literature and film; *The Secret Life of Puppets* (Harvard University Press, 2003).

[34] Pullman, 'The Republic of Heaven', p.655.

CHAPTER 14

The Republic of Heaven

To the characters within the story, Lord Asriel is the hero, mounting a justifiable rebellion against a malevolent and sadistic usurper. By the time Mrs Coulter joins him, we have still not learned what he has in mind to replace the Authority's regime. Interestingly, we never hear it from Asriel himself; it is King Ogunwe who reveals the aims to Mrs Coulter as they descend the staircase deep into the adamant[1] tower. After shocking her with news that the Authority was not eternal (*AS*, p.221), Ogunwe explains to her:

> We haven't come to conquer, but to build . . .
> I am a king, but it's my proudest task to join
> Lord Asriel in setting up a world where there
> are no kingdoms at all. No kings, no bishops,
> no priests. The kingdom of heaven has been
> known by that name since the Authority first set
> himself above the rest of the angels. And we
> want no part of it. This world is different. We
> intend to be free citizens of the republic of
> heaven. (*AS*, p.222)

Republic or revolution?

King Ogunwe is committed to the ideals of the new republic, but I wonder whether he has perhaps been taken in by Lord Asriel. As we noted in Chapter 4, Lord Asriel's high-handed attitude to his manservant seems stereotypically aristocratic rather than republican.

Thorold can only guess at his master's plans despite nearly forty years of service (*SK*, p.47). Even in his relationship with his commanders, although they are free to speak their minds, Asriel is very much in charge. Ruta Skadi tells Serafina Pekkala that Lord Asriel 'lives at the centre of so many circles of activity, and he directs them all' (*SK*, p.282). It feels less like a democracy in the making than an embryonic tyranny. Perhaps I'm doing Lord Asriel a disservice, but he has shown that he will do anything to get what he wants (think of little Roger 'crying and pleading, begging, sobbing and Lord Asriel [taking] no notice except to knock him to the ground' (*NL*, p.391)). Why does the heroic visionary leader never once articulate what his vision is? Ruta Skadi's breathless report of her visit to Asriel emphasizes not the great future ahead, but that to rebel is 'right and just' because of the 'hideous cruelties . . . all designed to destroy the joys and the truthfulness of life' (*SK*, p.283). The Gallivespians also seem more focused on defeating the Authority than on what follows. Lord Asriel's aim does seem to be conquering not building.

Most major characters seem distanced from Lord Asriel's cause, being concerned to protect Lyra above everything: Lee Scoresby, Serafina Pekkala and Iorek Byrnison (who also wants to avenge Lee Scoresby's death – *AS*, p.45) are involved in the war but there's no sense of them thinking ahead to the republic of heaven. When Mrs Coulter changes sides, she too wants only to protect Lyra. Even Lord Asriel finally sees that the future of the republic depends on his daughter remaining alive (*AS*, p.397), and wonders whether it might actually exist primarily to serve a higher cause: helping her (*AS*, p.399).

An organic republic

The one significant character who clearly believes in the republic of heaven ideal is Stanislaus Grumman. From the perspective of the whole narrative, the shaman shows himself to be the most insightful man in the story. He tells Will and Lyra:

> Your dæmon can only live its full life in the
> world it was born in. Elsewhere it will eventually
> sicken and die. We can travel, if there are
> openings into other worlds, but we can only live
> in our own. Lord Asriel's great enterprise will fail
> in the end for the same reason: we have to build
> the republic of heaven where we are, because for
> us there is no elsewhere. (*AS*, p.381–382)

This is the first time that Will and Lyra hear the phrase 'republic of heaven'. Far from being committed to 'Lord Asriel's great enterprise', their minds are entirely on other things – Dust, Will's father, rescuing Lyra, reaching the world of the dead, bringing 'salvation' to the ghosts – before at last becoming wrapped up with each other. Later, when Will and Lyra are trying to come to terms with the traumatic realization that they cannot stay together, Will recalls his father's words:

> He said we have to build the republic of heaven
> where we are. He said that for us there isn't any
> elsewhere . . . I thought he just meant Lord
> Asriel and his new world, but he meant us, he
> meant you and me. We have to live in our own
> worlds . . . (*AS*, p.516)

Despite their distress they recognize that, for the good of each other and of all the dead, they must part. And every window except the one for the dead must be closed. Will and Lyra both assume that their duty is to build the republic of heaven. Though this is not spelled out explicitly, the final words of the story drive home its importance.

'The republic of heaven' is a powerful phrase[3] that Pullman has used extensively in real life (suggesting that he *does* see *His Dark Materials* as having a message despite claiming the contrary – see p.21). In one interview he said:

> The most important questions of all are the big religious ones: Is there a God? What is our purpose? And so on . . . If there are lessons to be learned in the fantasy world, we have to see how to put them to use in our real lives . . . the theme, if you like, of *His Dark Materials* is the search for a way of looking at . . . big religious questions which might be called republican. My own belief is that God is dead, but that we need heaven nonetheless; and since it's no longer possible to believe in a Kingdom of Heaven, we shall have to create a republic.[4]

Or take these comments from another interview:

> We're used to the kingdom of heaven; but you can tell from the general thrust of the book that I'm of the devil's party, like Milton. And I think it's time we thought about a republic of heaven instead of the kingdom of heaven. The king is dead. That's to say I believe that the king is dead. I'm an atheist. But we need heaven nonetheless, we need all the things that heaven meant, we need joy, we need a sense of meaning and purpose in our lives, we need a connection with the universe, we need all the things that the kingdom of heaven used to promise us but failed

> to deliver. And, furthermore, we need it in this
> world where we do exist – not elsewhere,
> because there ain't no elsewhere.[5]

These remarks clearly show that when Pullman writes
about Will and Lyra building the republic of heaven, he
thinks it is something we should do in the real world.
Again he blurs the boundary between fiction and reality, as with his critique of the church and of God. But
what does 'the republic of heaven' really mean?

Stay in your own world

Several aspects come out of Xaphania's conversation
with Will and Lyra. I have already touched on the first:
they must build the republic of heaven in their own
worlds. Pullman feels strongly about this in the real
world too – 'there ain't no elsewhere'. There are two
sides to this. First, Pullman (strongly echoing Blake[6]) is
celebrating the physical world. In passage after passage
in *His Dark Materials*, Pullman brilliantly evokes different worlds and stresses the importance of their physical natures. One example is Will's and Lyra's exit from
the world of the dead:

> . . . it was the sweetest thing they had ever seen.
> The night air filled their lungs, fresh and clean
> and cool; their eyes took in a canopy of dazzling
> stars,[7] and the shine of water somewhere below
> . . . (*AS*, p.382)

Part of Pullman's celebration of the physical is his focus
on growing up, especially with regard to sexuality (see
Chapter 9). Pullman rejoices in all the physical sensations that come with Will and Lyra's love – their kisses,
the feelings within them, even the sensations of their
picnic (*AS*, p.491–492).

In his essay, 'The Republic of Heaven', Pullman says:

> The republic of Heaven . . . enables us to see this real world, our world, as a place of infinite delight, so intensely beautiful and intoxicating that if we saw it clearly then we would want nothing more, ever. We would know that this earth is our true home, and nowhere else is.[8]

The other side of 'there ain't no elsewhere' is the denial of any spiritual reality or afterlife. It's the corollary of his denial of God's existence. Pullman says that 'the most important subject I know . . . is the death of God and its consequences'.[9] I find it fascinating that Pullman finds what he doesn't believe in 'the most important subject' he knows. By the death of God, he means the death of the *idea* of God. He continues: 'The idea that God is dead has been familiar, and has felt true, to many of us for a long time now . . . the old assumptions have all withered away . . . the idea of God with which I was brought up is now perfectly incredible.'[10] There are many highly intelligent people who would find such comments patronizing since they do not find it remotely incredible.

Face up to responsibilities

A second aspect of the republic of heaven is the importance of bearing responsibilities even at great personal cost. 'A great wave of rage and despair' (*AS*, p.521) sweeps over Will but he still faces the 'bleak rocks' (*AS*, p.522) of his obligations. Responsibilities require commitment, and Lyra now faces a lifetime of relearning to read the alethiometer. Will and Lyra could learn to travel to other worlds 'in spirit' as Will's father did in his trances (*SK*, p.224; *AS*, p.523). But it will require long practice and work – a familiar theme in Pullman's stories. The windows must be closed partly so that Will and Lyra don't waste their lives: 'if you thought that any [windows] still remained, you would spend your life searching for one, and that would be a waste of the time you have. You have other work than that to do, much more important and valuable, in your own world' (*AS*, p.524).

This all entails selflessness and sacrifice. After they have parted, Lyra reflects on this – she or Will would gladly have lived in an alien world, 'But then we wouldn't have been able to build [the republic of heaven]. No one could, if they put themselves first' (*AS*, p.548). Nicholas Tucker remarks that this is a 'final temptation for Will and Lyra to put their own good above everything else . . . Lyra, the second Eve, resists the temptation of selfishness, and this time Pullman is on her side'.[11] The need for selflessness is one of the most powerful moral lessons of the trilogy as well as several of his other stories. He says:

> Putting your own feelings first and insisting on
> expressing them, no matter what the cost, is not
> a republican virtue.[12]

Make more Dust

The third aspect that Xaphania highlights is the particular responsibility to make more Dust:

> Conscious beings make Dust – they renew it all
> the time, by thinking and feeling and reflecting,
> by gaining wisdom and passing it on. And if you
> help everyone else in your worlds to do that, by
> helping them to learn and understand about
> themselves and each other and the way

> everything works, and by showing them how to
> be kind instead of cruel, and patient instead of
> hasty, and cheerful instead of surly, and above
> all how to keep their minds open and free and
> curious . . . Then they will renew enough to
> replace what is lost through one window.
> (*AS*, p.520)

It's worth noting that all this is very close to what Pullman sees as the process of growing up. The children must help others grow so that Dust is constantly replenished. Growth involves thinking and feeling (rational and intuitive), self-analysis, and understanding. This is the search for meaning, which is the central theme of *Lyra's Oxford*. We'll return to this shortly. 'Gaining wisdom' is discovering the right way to live. Pullman singles out kindness, patience, cheerfulness, and having open, inquiring minds. Lyra reflects on this in the Botanic Garden:

> We have to be all those difficult things like
> cheerful and kind and curious and brave and
> patient, and we've got to study and think, and
> work hard, all of us, in all our different worlds
> . . . (*AS*, p.548)

Pullman frequently stresses the importance of belonging:

> In the republic we're connected in a moral way
> to one another, to other human beings. We have
> responsibilities to them, and they to us. We're
> not isolated units of self-interest in a world
> where there is no such thing as society; we can-
> not live so.[13]

These values are as important to citizens of the kingdom of heaven as they are to citizens of the republic. As Pullman said on *The South Bank Show*:

An honest reading of the story would have to
admit that the qualities that the stories celebrate
and praise are those of love, kindness, tolerance,
courage, open-heartedness, and the qualities that
the stories condemn are: cruelty, intolerance,
zealotry, fanaticism . . . well, who could quarrel
with that?[14]

These good qualities are indeed seen throughout the
trilogy. But is it really true that the stories condemn
'cruelty, intolerance, zealotry, fanaticism'? Well, up to a
point. I have commented before on Lord Asriel's
ambiguity. He shows little of these positive qualities,
except courage, but he exemplifies cruelty (to Roger),
zealotry and fanaticism. The Church is accused of these
things but Asriel is equally guilty. He's guilty of intolerance too. Thorold tells Serafina he's 'seen a spasm of
disgust cross his face when they talk of the sacraments,
and atonement and redemption, and suchlike'
(*SK*, p.47).

Many commentators have seen Pullman's own attack
on Christianity as fanatical and intolerant. It's hard to
escape the feeling from some passages in *His Dark
Materials* that Pullman is expressing his own deep
hatred of the real Church. Pullman seems to register a
spasm of disgust himself when he blasts C. S. Lewis'
stories. He calls *The Narnia Chronicles* (based on
Christian ideas), 'one of the most ugly and poisonous
things I've ever read', 'vile', 'life-hating', 'nauseating
drivel', 'loathsome',[15] 'disgusting',[16] and 'containing a
view of life so hideous and cruel I can scarcely contain
myself when I think of it'.[17] When I first witnessed
Pullman talking about Lewis I was startled at the anger
with which he spoke. It's a very strong reaction to

a mere *story*, even if it is perhaps over-revered by some. Yes, it contains some serious flaws, but the real problem seems to be that it is a story that expresses a worldview completely antithetical to Pullman's. His 'paroxysm of loathing'[18] feels distinctly intolerant.[19]

Make your own choices

The republic of heaven also includes the need to make one's own choices. Will and Lyra reluctantly choose to part without Xaphania laying it on them as their duty. Will later tells Xaphania:

> *I* shall decide what I do. If you say my work is fighting, or healing, or exploring, or whatever you might say, I'll always be thinking about it, and if I do end up doing that I'll be resentful because it'll feel as if I didn't have a choice, and if I don't do it, I'll feel guilty because I should. Whatever I do, I will choose it, no one else.
>
> (*AS*, p.524–525)

Will has responsibilities to build the republic of heaven but he insists on his absolute autonomy. Xaphania (who at this point seems to represent the highest wisdom) underlines the importance of autonomy when she replies to Will that he has 'already taken the first steps towards wisdom'. This is a key lesson within the story – you must freely choose your own path because you are answerable only to yourself. Will and Lyra are both fiercely independent and insist on making their own decisions. Will made the same point in his final conversation with his father's ghost:

> You said I was a warrior. You told me that was my nature, and I shouldn't argue with it. Father,

you were wrong. I fought because I had to. I
can't choose my nature, but I can choose what I
do. And I *will* choose, because now I'm free.
(*AS*, p.440)

Here Pullman touches on the tension between our
genes determining who we are, and the freedom to
act differently. For Pullman, not only can we transcend
our genetic inheritance, we have a responsibility to
do so. But as I noted in Chapter 13, in a materialist
universe (which Pullman believes in) such freedom
is an illusion. There is a further tension in
Pullman's thinking here. Lyra can only fulfil her
destiny by acting freely. This kind of destiny is not at all
the predetermined outcome of a purely physical
universe, since Lyra could fail to fulfil her destiny if
she knew what it was. Pullman has to smuggle in this
kind of destiny with the witches' prophecies and
the alethiometer's leadings. These things are tied in
with the intentions of Dust, which becomes a dualistic
substitute for God. God, as the Bible describes him,
is not found in *His Dark Materials,* while the god-sub-
stitute that Pullman puts in his place is so much part of
the system that he cannot act sovereignly over
the whole of it (and is not eternal). So to bring a
sense of destiny without God, Pullman presents
Dust as omnipresent and omniscient. While not
omnipotent, Dust can still direct the affairs of material
creatures in order to fulfil its intentions and desires.
Dust may be God-like but there is no sense of account-
ability to this pseudo-deity. Xaphania endorses
Will's autonomy rather than instruct him in 'interrogating the universe'[20] so he can find out what Dust would
have him do.

Myth and meaning

There is another important dimension to the republic of heaven which does not come out in the conversation with Xaphania, but which underpins the whole of *His Dark Materials*. That dimension is *myth*, which is related to the issue of *meaning*.[21] Pullman wrote his underlying 'creation myth' to help him get the story of *His Dark Materials* right. But myths are needed in the real world too:

> We need a story, a myth that does what the traditional religious stories did. It must *explain*. It must satisfy our hunger for a *why* . . . there are two kinds of *why*, and our story must deal with both. There's the one that asks *What brought us here?* and the other that asks *What are we here for?*[22]

For Pullman, the answer to the first question is evolution by natural selection, which he recognizes as a purposeless process. But his response is to say that purpose has arisen through consciousness: 'Now we are here, now we are conscious, we make a difference.'[23] Again, in a materialist universe, how can you ever know if consciousness includes freedom?[24] And if not, how can we make a difference? Part of the second question is to do with how we discern good and bad, right and wrong. He says that 'what shuts out knowledge and nourishes stupidity is wrong; what increases understanding and deepens wisdom is right'.[25] Another part of the question is to do with what happens when we die. That issue is very much bound up with the issue of the meaning of life.

Pullman says:

> I think we need this thing which I've called joy. I

might also have called it Heaven. What I'm referring to is a sense that things are right and good, and we are part of everything that's right and good. It's a sense that we're connected to the universe. This connectedness is where meaning lies; the meaning of our lives is their connection with something other than ourselves.[26] The religion that's now dead did give us that, in full measure: we were part of a huge cosmic drama, involving a Creation and a Fall and a Redemption, and Heaven and Hell. What we did *mattered*, because God saw everything, even the fall of a sparrow. And one of the most deadly and oppressive consequences of the death of God is this sense of meaningless[ness] or alienation that so many of us have felt in the past century or so.[27]

Connection regained

Pullman admits that a Christian worldview makes sense of life. So where does meaning come from if there is no God? Later he adds:

Part of the *meaning* that I've suggested we need, the sense that we belong and we matter, comes from the moral and social relations that the republic of heaven must embody.[28]

The importance of belonging, and of being part of a bigger story, shapes the end of *His Dark Materials*: Will returns to his world with Mary who tells him that, 'if you'll let me, I'll be your friend for the rest of our lives' (*AS*, p.540). Lyra returns home with Serafina Pekkala; later she can develop a new kind of relationship with the Master and Dame Hannah Relf. But it's more than human relations:

> Part of the sense of wider meaningfulness that
> we need comes from seeing that we have a con-
> nection with nature and the universe around us,
> with everything that is *not* human as well.[29]

Mary Malone realizes what Christianity offered:

> This was the very thing she'd told Will about
> when he asked if she missed God: it was the
> sense that the whole universe was alive, and that
> everything was connected to everything else by
> threads of meaning. When she'd been a
> Christian, she had felt connected too; but when
> she'd left the Church, she felt loose and free and
> light, in a universe without purpose. (*AS*, p.473)

But then comes her realization that the physical world
was trying to hold back the flood of Dust:

> Matter *loved* Dust. It didn't want to see it go.
> That was the meaning of this night, and it was
> Mary's meaning too.
>
> Had she thought there was no meaning in life,
> no purpose, when God had gone? Yes, she had
> thought that.
>
> 'Well, there is now,' she said aloud, and again,
> louder: 'There is now!' (*AS*, p.476)

Both Mary's conclusion and Pullman's own comments
have a distinctly mystical, spiritual feel – it sounds like
New Age monism.[30] Pullman is a convinced materialist,
but he does nevertheless seem to be drawn towards the
mystical with his reliance on Gnostic and other esoteric
ideas, and references to shamans, voodoo and angels.

Embracing oblivion

The same sense comes in the description of ghosts'
atoms merging again into the cosmos. Pullman is clear

that there is no continuation of existence beyond death, but he smuggles in the same mystical feeling to mask the bleakness of this materialist view.

The ghost of a martyred girl denounces the faith by which she lived and died, and welcomes Lyra's message as one of hope:

> Even if it means oblivion . . . I'll welcome it,
> because it won't be nothing, we'll be alive again
> in a thousand blades of grass and a million
> leaves, we'll be falling in the raindrops and
> blowing in the fresh breeze, we'll be glittering in
> the dew under the stars and the moon out there
> in the physical world which is our true home and
> always was. (*AS*, p.336)

And at the end of the story, Will tells Lyra:

> I *will* love you for ever . . . and when I find my
> way out of the land of the dead I'll drift about
> for ever, all my atoms, till I find you again . . .

She replies:

> I'll be looking for you, Will, every moment, every
> single moment. And when we do find each other
> again we'll cling so tight that nothing and no
> one'll ever tear us apart. Every atom of me and
> every atom of you . . . We'll live in birds and
> flowers and dragonflies and pine trees and in
> clouds and in those little specks of light you see
> floating in sunbeams . . . (*AS*, p.526)

To talk about atoms being conscious in this kind of way – since they are not particles of Dust – is mystical non-sense, which serves only to make the prospect of oblivion more palatable.

The ideals of the republic of heaven (celebrating and making the most of this world, responsibility, wisdom, moral behaviour, selflessness) sound great, but the underlying framework – the myth – is a worldview of materialist determinism with no genuine freedom (despite the claims for autonomy) and a destiny of oblivion, however much it is dressed up in mystical ideas. We will unpack this a little more in the next chapter.

[1] The double meaning of *adamant* is surely intentional – Lord Asriel's fortress is both made of an exceptionally hard stone, and is immoveable, unshakeable and impenetrable.

[2] While dissolving into the cosmos may not seem like salvation, within the framework of the narrative it is certainly presented in this way – the ghosts experience a liberating release.

[3] The idea is not original to Pullman. A book called *The tableau or, heaven as a republic* by a John George Schwahn was published in America in 1892. More recently, David Boulton's *Gerrard Winstanley and the Republic of Heaven* was published in 1999 – a year before *The Amber Spyglass*.

[4] Pullman, Philip, interview on Kidsreads.com, 12 December 2001 (www.kidsreads.com/authors/au-pullman-philip.asp).

[5] Brown, Charles N., 'An interview with Philip Pullman' (www.avnet.co.uk/amaranth/Critic/ivpullman.htm).

[6] In 'The Republic of Heaven' (*Horn Book Magazine*, November/December 2001, p.664), Pullman calls Blake 'one of the founding fathers of the republic of Heaven' and quotes some lines from *The Marriage of Heaven and Hell*: 'How do you know but ev'ry Bird that cuts the airy way, / Is an immense world of delight, clos'd by your senses five?.' Blake also wrote 'To see a world in a grain of sand, / And a heaven in a wild flower; / Hold infinity in the palm of your hand, / And eternity in an hour' ('Auguries of Innocence' in Yeats, W. B. (ed), *William Blake Collected Poems* (Routledge, 2002), p.88).

[7] Dante also comments on the stars when he leaves Hell: 'I beheld through a round aperture / Some of the beauteous things that Heaven doth bear; / Thence we came forth to rebehold the stars' (Dante Alighieri, *Inferno*, Canto XXXIV).

[8] Pullman, Philip, 'The Republic of Heaven', *Horn Book Magazine*, November/December 2001, p.664.

[9] Pullman, 'The Republic of Heaven', p.655.

[10] Pullman, 'The Republic of Heaven', p.655.

[11] Tucker, Nicholas, *Darkness Visible: Inside the world of Philip Pullman* (Wizard Books, 2003), p.181.

[12] Pullman, 'The Republic of Heaven', p.663.

[13] Pullman, 'The Republic of Heaven', p.664.

[14] Pullman, Philip, *The South Bank Show*, 9 March 2003 (www.southbankshow.com/coming_shows/show/17).

[15] All from Pullman, Philip, 'The Darkside of Narnia', *Guardian*, 1 October 1998.

[16] Bertodano, Helena de, 'I am of the Devil's party', *Daily Telegraph*, 29 January 2002.

[17] Wagner, Erica, 'Courageous and dangerous: a writer for all ages', *The Times*, 23 January 2002.

[18] Wagner, 'Courageous and dangerous'.

[19] For an evaluation of Pullman's critique of C. S. Lewis, see www.damaris.org/Pullman.

[20] Brown, 'An interview with Philip Pullman'.

[21] Myth in this sense means a story (which may or may not be true) that explains a worldview, or some feature of the world

[22] Pullman, 'The Republic of Heaven', p.665.

[23] Pullman, 'The Republic of Heaven', p.665.

[24] If the universe is a purely physical system, the only factors which affect the movement of electrical signals in my brain are my genes and my environment (both of which are deterministic in a purely physical system), and quantum fluctuations (which are entirely random). Therefore, my thoughts are either *determined* or *random*. In either case, how can I possibly know whether my thoughts are *true* or *reliable*? My beliefs about the nature of the universe, my brain and determinism (or randomness) would themselves be completely determined or completely random. As the biologist J. B. S. Haldane remarked, 'In order to escape from the necessity of sawing away the branch on which I am sitting, so to speak, I am compelled to believe that mind is not wholly conditioned by matter.' And that is possible *only* if there is something beyond the material.

[25] Pullman, 'The Republic of Heaven', p.666.

[26] This is a key idea within *Lyra's Oxford* – see Chapter 8.

[27] Pullman, 'The Republic of Heaven', p.656.

[28] Pullman, 'The Republic of Heaven', p.664.

[29] Pullman, 'The Republic of Heaven', p.664.

[30] Monism can mean two things. First, the belief that everything is the same kind of stuff. Pullman is a monist in this sense in that he believes only in the physical world and rejects any spiritual dimensions. The second is more mystical: the belief that 'reality is one unitary organic whole with no independent parts' (Merriam-Webster Online Dictionary; www.m-w.com/cgi-bin/dictionary?book=Dictionary&va=monism).

Once Upon a Time Lasts For Ever

Pullman, as we have seen, is a master storyteller above all else. From the deceptively simple retelling of classic fairy tales through to the epic of *His Dark Materials*, Pullman revels in the joy of storytelling and writing about stories:

> My intention is to tell a story – in the first place because the story comes to me and wants to be told . . . I am the servant of the story – the medium in a spiritualist sense, if you like – and it feels as if, unless I tell this story, I will be troubled and pestered and harried by it and worried and fretted until I do something about it. The second reason I do it is that I enjoy the technical business of putting a story together in a way that excites and gives pleasure to an audience. The third reason is that I need to earn a living – and there is another range of reasons beyond that which might include at some point the desire to make sense of the world and my experience of it and give a sort of narrative account of why things are as they are.[1]

But Pullman also contends that: 'All stories teach, whether the storyteller intends them to or not. They teach the world we create. They teach the morality we live by.'[2] His stories teach the things included in what he refers to as 'another range of reasons'. We have considered Pullman's insistence that stories must have some truth about them – they must be psychologically true, telling us about ourselves and our place in the world. When Lyra finally tells true stories in the world of the dead, the harpies find themselves drawn to it. This is something they have longed for and needed all their long lives without ever realizing it, but their deep, unsatisfied hunger had spewed out in venom and filth and hatred. Tialys persuades them to guide every ghost to the window to oblivion in return for true stories. Pullman comments:

> The implication is that we have to engage with life, or else. We have to notice the world. If we spend our lives doing nothing but watching television and playing computer games, we will have nothing to tell the harpies in the world of the dead, and there we will stay.[3]

Pullman loves life, and through his stories he urges all of us to engage with it. He wants readers who are still in the process of growing up to discover the focus of their lives, and to pursue their ambitions with determination and hard work, making the most of their talents and every opportunity life throws at them. He wants them to develop their autonomy, setting their own course and seeking all the wisdom the world can offer. This is the world Pullman creates in his books, and the morality he lives by. It's an extremely positive vision of life.

A convincing mistake?

But while Pullman's stories are life-affirming, he faces up to the hard side of life too – including the harsh realities of separation and of death. The way his protagonists respond teaches important lessons about handling difficulty and tragedy. But as we saw in the previous chapter, Pullman tries to put a very positive spin on his materialist convictions in the oblivion of death. John Faa summarizes this:

> To know that after a spell in the dark we'll come out into a sweet land like this, to be free of the sky like the birds, well, that's the greatest promise anyone could wish for. (*AS*, p.532)

How can this be the greatest promise anyone could wish for? Which is a greater promise – the republic of heaven's promise of complete nothingness, or the kingdom of heaven's offer of eternal life? But Pullman has rejected the possibility of king or kingdom and all that comes with it.

His Dark Materials is a narrative of extraordinary scope and brilliance, but those critics who claim that he loses his focus in the third volume do perhaps have something of a point. There are times when the story feels uneasily like the background for the philosophical and theological ideas, rather than the ideas forming the backdrop to the story. Now and again Pullman seems to take his eyes off his overriding goal of telling the story, rather than teaching a message. Leonie Caldecott claims that 'he commits the cardinal sin of fiction, whereby an author, instead of embedding the moral of his story in the text as a whole, contents himself with putting it on the lips of a protagonist'.[4] This is certainly true when Pullman has Mary Malone describe her loss of faith to Will and Lyra:

> I thought physics could be done to the glory of God, till I saw there wasn't any God at all and that physics was more interesting anyway. The

Christian religion is a very powerful and
convincing mistake, that's all. (*AS*, p.464)

It feels like he strains a little too hard to keep empha-
sizing his humanist views in opposition to Christian
ideas. As I suggested in Chapter 13, the picture of both
God and the Church that Pullman paints in *His Dark
Materials* is a straw man, which would matter far less
if he didn't keep saying the same things in interviews.
While Pullman is deeply critical – and rightly so – of the
many failings of the Christian Church over the years,
he does have a strong tendency to stress only the negative aspects and to downplay the positives. In his interview for *Third Way*, he agrees with Mary Malone
that Christianity is a 'powerful and convincing mistake',
saying:

It's a very good story. It gives an account of
the world and what we're doing here that is
intellectually coherent and explains a great deal
. . . The Christian story gives us human beings a
very important and prominent part. We are the
ones who Jesus came to redeem from the
consequences of sin . . . It is a very dramatic
story and we are right at the heart of it, and a
great deal depends on what we decide.[5]

But then he dismisses this story on the grounds that it
doesn't 'gel at all with the more convincing account that
is given by Darwinian evolution – and the scientific
account is far more persuasive intellectually'.[6] He
quickly moves on to argue that belief in a single God is
a 'very good excuse for people to behave very badly'. It
is certainly true that belief in God has been – and continues to be – used as a good excuse to justify oppres-
sion, warfare and genocide. But this is true of *any* pow-

erful belief system – or, indeed, of any system at all. There are always people who will attempt to use a system to their own ends, regardless of how consistent or inconsistent they may be with the underlying ethics. In fact the history of the last century includes terrifying atrocities at the hands of explicitly atheistic regimes – atrocities that are out of all proportion to anything the Christian Church has ever done.[7] On the other hand, the impact of Christianity on the world's education, healthcare and social reforms has been incalculable.[8] On one side we see 'the general human tendency to exalt one doctrine above all others',[9] and on the other we see the committed followers of Christ making an impact on their world.

A tale of two kingdoms

In Pullman's attack on the kingdom of heaven then, he misrepresents history and misreads the Bible to create a caricature of Christianity, inverting all the categories in the process. He makes God out to be a cruel and vindictive impostor who is part of the universe not its transcendent creator; he presents the rebellious human grasping after autonomy as a search for wisdom; and thus redefines 'sin' as good. Within the narrative world of *His Dark Materials* this is internally coherent, if rather overplayed. As Rowan Williams points out, this is what happens if you have a 'mortal God, who can win and lose his power'.[10] But when Pullman plays this card so frequently and blatantly within the story, and then makes exactly the same points in interviews, it all feels rather intolerant, as I suggested in Chapter 14. The irony is that this is the exact opposite of one of the major moral lines of *The Amber Spyglass*. Scott

Masson, an English lecturer at Durham University, writes:

> Lyra and Will *personally* exhibit the courage, loyalty, honesty and fairness that incite our genuine admiration . . . However, . . . these virtues seem to bear no relation to the idea of ultimate good, which is only really revealed in the final instalment of the trilogy. The powers of good and evil . . . give way to the 'higher virtue' of tolerance in Pullman's earthly eschatology. And this leaves the reader ice-cold, the dull sensation that is the residue of a virtue divested of sacrificial, atoning love. Much as one would expect of one enamoured of the virtue of the Enlightenment god (which Pullman tries to foist onto Christianity), we are left with a complacent, abstract and wholly intellectual virtue. The irony is heavy indeed, though I suspect that it will escape most readers.[11]

Nicholas Tucker writes that 'at base *His Dark Materials* is a strongly humanist text, celebrating the abiding existence of human courage and essential goodness'.[12] Well yes, but the worldview underpinning *His Dark Materials* is bleak. The physical world is all there is; there ain't no elsewhere. So we are here through the purposeless, deterministic processes of evolution by natural selection and nothing more. Somehow, this process has led to us having consciousness, personality and genuine freedom of thought and action, although *every* physical process involved is deterministic. That consciousness brings purpose and meaning to us – and perhaps to the entire universe. We must live good lives, connected to other people and the universe; in particular we must be open-minded and tolerant, which is seeking after wisdom. We must live in such a way that we have a story to tell. When we die, our personal consciousness ceases to exist but our atoms can be reused in a beautiful world of which we are already a vital part. This rather reminds me of the Authority – emaciated, weak, fragile, paper-thin, and offering no real hope.

It's hard to see how this gives much of a base for those Pullmanic virtues of curiosity, kindness, courage and determination. And it's hard to see the grounds for Pullman's optimism in human nature, especially given our history – why do we have any essential goodness? It all relies on that leap of 'There is now' – meaning and purpose has come, in Pullman's view because of consciousness. We are back at the Fall with Milton, Blake and Kleist again, and Pullman's conviction that moving from innocence to experience, seizing autonomy, declaring independence, becoming masters of our own destiny was the best possible thing we could – or can – do.

As Pullman concedes in the quotation above, the Christian worldview is an 'intellectually coherent' view of the world. I strongly dispute his claim that the 'scientific account is far more persuasive intellectually' because that scientific account is so limited. Science cannot *begin* to answer fundamental questions like 'Is there a God beyond the physical universe?' or 'Why are we here?' Science deals in mechanisms not metaphysics. The Christian worldview includes the reality of a spiritual realm[13]; it sees humans as created by God in his image, giving us consciousness, personality, *genuine* freedom, purpose, meaning, and a spiritual dimension. Kleist was right that we cannot return to Paradise, we can only go forwards, but wrong to suggest that we can come to it again through a back door, and eat again of the tree of knowledge of good and evil. The second decisive moment in human history is not a second Fall, but the undoing of the first Fall in the death and resurrection of Jesus Christ.

There's a curious parallel between this and the 'Fall' of Lyra and Will. I commented in Chapter 10 that it didn't *seem* like a Fall – responding to Mary's account of her own experiences, they discover the emotional language and freedom to both recognize and express their love for each other. From the point of view of the story's sympathies they do *exactly the right thing*, and it brings about a new age in human history. From the point of view of the Christian story, Jesus did exactly the right thing when he gave himself up to be killed on a cross, also bringing about a new age in human history.[14]

Pullman sees Jesus as little more than a teller of great stories, and dismisses his claims to be God's Son. Yet for Christians, Jesus' death and resurrection open up the possibility of redemption through a relationship with him, and the prospect of eternity with him, rather than oblivion. The Christian conviction is that God the Father has given all authority to the risen Jesus, not to an angelic Regent; Jesus is the King and the Bible contrasts his Kingdom not with a republic, but with another kingdom: 'the kingdom of darkness.'[15] Many Christians reading *His Dark Materials* want to distance themselves from both the Magisterium and the Authority, but believe that wisdom is ultimately found in the person of the King of Heaven, not in building the republic of heaven.

Nevertheless, despite these objections to the underlying worldview of *His Dark Materials*, there is much to be enthusiastic about. Philip Pullman's books are, as I have said repeatedly, fabulous, wonderful celebrations of some of the richest aspects of life – the 'absolute preciousness of the here and how',[16] the innate qualities of human beings, the values that should be part of every good life, the need to keep on growing in wisdom and understanding because we're not yet what we can be. These are common to the vast majority of Pullman's work so far. His editor, David Fickling, quotes Pullman as saying, 'telling and listening to stories is what makes us human', and adds, 'It defines us . . . stories are at the foundation of what we call civilisation.'[17] Philip Pullman's stories will be chewed over for years. While the philosophical and theological issues pass many readers by, nobody can fail to be inspired by his stories of gutsy heroines and heroes exemplifying values which sadly often feel in short supply. As Pullman himself says, 'Once upon a time lasts forever.'[18]

[1] Spanner, Huw, 'Heat and Dust', *Third Way*, vol. 25 no. 2, April 2002, p.22–26.

[2] Pullman, Philip, 'Carnegie Medal acceptance speech' (www.randomhouse.com/features/pullman/philippullman/speech.html).

[3] Pullman, Philip, 'Writing Fantasy Realistically', Sea of Faith National Conference, 2002 (www.sofn.org.uk/Conferences/pullman2002.htm). It is interesting to note when Bel Mooney asked Pullman if he believes in any form of life after death, he replied, 'I believe pretty well what I've described . . . I believe in something like what happens in the world of the dead (Mooney, Bel, *Devout Sceptics – conversations on faith and doubt* (Hodder and Stoughton, 2003), p.131).

[4] Caldecott, Leonie, 'Paradise Denied: Philip Pullman and the uses and abuses of enchantment', *Touchstone*, 2003 (www.touchstonemag.com/docs/issues/16.8docs/16-8pg42.html).

[5] Spanner, 'Heat and Dust'.

[6] Spanner, 'Heat and Dust'. When I interviewed Pullman, he seemed surprised that there are Christians who see a process of evolution as compatible with belief in God as a creator. This is a contentious issue within Christian circles – especially in the USA. Some argue that the scientific theories of origins are an explanation of the way God works; some argue that aspects of the science point clearly to the need for some original creative act; others argue that the science is completely wrong and needs to be completely reinterpreted.

[7] Nazism may have made use of Christian ideas, but its heart was thoroughly atheistic (based as it was on the thinking of Nietzsche and a misreading of Darwin's theory of evolution by natural selection), and it was responsible for the deaths of six million Jews; Stalin had millions of people killed; Pol Pot had a million or more killed in Cambodia. Pullman's response to this is fascinating: 'They functioned psychologically in exactly the same way [as religions]. They had a sacred book that provided an explanation of history which so far transcended every other explanation as to be unquestionable. There were the great prophets – Marx, Engels, Lenin, Stalin, Mao Tse-Tung – men so far above the human race that they might as well be exalted as gods. They were treated in just the same way as the Pope. Every word they said, every thing they touched, was holy; their bodies had to be preserved and filed past in reverential silence. The fact that they proclaimed that there was no God didn't make any difference: it was a religion, and they acted in the way any totalitarian religious system would' (Spanner, 'Heat and Dust').

[8] See, for example, Randall, Ian, 'Evangelicals And Social Reform', *Light and Salt – The Care Review*, Volume 9, Issue 2, December 1997 (www.care.org.uk/resource/ls/ls971201.htm) or see the summaries of the actions of many individuals at www.spartacus.schoolnet.co.uk/religion.htm.

[9] Spanner, 'Heat and Dust'.

[10] Williams, Rowan, 'A near-miraculous triumph', *Guardian*, 10 March 2004.

[11] Masson, Scott, 'Philip Pullman's His Dark Materials Trilogy', *The Glass*, No. 15, Spring 2003, p.19–23.

[12] Tucker, Nicholas, *Darkness Visible: Inside the world of Philip Pullman* (Wizard Books, 2003), p.167.

[13] Materialist theologian Don Cupitt chides Pullman for 'clinging to the apparatus of supernaturalism' (www.sofn.org.uk/Conferences/pullman2002.htm).

[14] In some ways, the voluntary self-sacrifice of Mrs Coulter and Lord Asriel also parallels Jesus' sacrificial death: they realize that it is only through their death that Lyra can be safe and the ultimate victory won. It is also their death that brings about the destruction of their greatest enemy, Metatron.

[15] Colossians 1:13 (*New Living Translation*).

[16] Bertodano, Helena de, 'I am of the Devil's Party', *Sunday Telegraph*, 27 January 2002.

17   Fickling, David, 'Narrative Heaven: The Editor's Tale – The Patrick Hardy
     Lecture 2001', *Signal* 97, January 2002.
18   Pullman, 'Carnegie Medal acceptance speech'.

APPENDIX:

The Science of
His Dark Materials

Philip Pullman loves science. He says it 'was one of
those things . . . that I was fascinated by at home, and
turned off by at school'.[1] He struggles with mathematics so could never be a scientist, but he loves science
'for the stories that are told about it'.[2] His fascination
with the subject and its stories led him to include quite
a lot of science in *His Dark Materials*. He sees it in
terms of the background to the story he's really trying
to tell, and it was important to him that he got it sufficiently right to 'make the reader feel that the background was solid enough not to fall over when anyone
leant against it'.[3] At the same time, he didn't want to be
over-zealous about it – he wanted the freedom to invent
things too. He says:

> My test was always: 'I don't know very much
> about this, but I do know something, and if I
> read this in a novel, would it make me think that
> the writer knew at least as much as I did, and
> wasn't a complete fool?'[4]

He has done remarkably well to include so much science and to give it that sense of solidity. This is confirmed by the fact that highly respected science writers,
Mary and John Gribbin, were able to write an entire
book on the subject: *The Science of Philip Pullman's
His Dark Materials*.[5] Their book is written at a level to

suit teenage readers of the trilogy and is therefore very accessible.

Despite the existence of the Gribbins' excellent book, I wanted to include an appendix on the science here, partly because with a background in physics myself I would feel it was missing otherwise, but more importantly because the Gribbins have not really dealt with some of the philosophical ideas which are associated with the science, and certainly haven't dealt with the objections to some of them. There is much more to be said than can be written in one short appendix, so I have concentrated briefly on just two physics-related aspects of the science, which play a significant role in *His Dark Materials*.

Dark matter

Dark matter has been one of the greatest mysteries of modern science for three decades. Since the 1970s scientists have been trying to track down vast quantities of the universe, which our telescopes and detectors can't see. We know it's there somewhere from studying the behaviour of galaxies – they just don't behave in a way that fits what we can see. The only way of making it all work is if there's a lot of matter, which is currently invisible to us. The searchers divided into two main camps: at one extreme, astronomers busied themselves looking for MACHOs (Massive Astrophysical Compact Halo Objects) – big lumps of stuff like small, dense stars (brown dwarfs) or enormous black holes, or even large numbers of planets. All these things are difficult to see at any distance because they don't radiate much, if any, electromagnetic radiation – hence the name 'dark matter'. As the sensitivity of our equipment increased significantly, some enormous but far-off objects were identified.[6] They do make some contribution to the missing mass of the universe, but nowhere near enough.

At the other extreme, physicists started looking for tiny particles that could make up the missing mass. There were two rival ideas – hot dark matter and cold dark matter. The particles at the centre of the hot dark matter theory are large neutrinos, huge numbers of which must have been created in the Big Bang. They are thought of as 'hot' because they must be travelling at nearly the speed of light. Cold dark matter theorists – who now seem to be winning the day[7] – were looking for a new kind of particle altogether: WIMPs Weakly Interacting Massive Particles. If WIMPs behaved like the ordinary matter that makes up everything we see, they would be easy to find – but they don't. Normal (baryonic) particles interact with each other in four ways: the strong and weak nuclear forces, electromagnetism, and gravity. Gravity isn't generally a big deal with tiny particles because they don't have much mass – the other three forces are what stick everything together. Gravity only becomes significant when a lot of matter is collected in one place – except when it comes to WIMPs. WIMPs are non-baryonic and they *only* interact with normal baryonic matter by gravity, which is why they are *weakly interacting*. They are *massive* particles because they have a much greater mass than that of a proton or neutron. In the world of particle physics, that makes them enormous – but because they only interact by gravity they're just about impossible to spot.

Therein lies the problem: the only time we can detect one is if it bumps into the nucleus of an atom in the detector, and because both WIMPs and nuclei are rather miniscule, that won't happen very often. While we're waiting for one to make its presence felt, all kinds of other particles and cosmic rays could be smashing into the detection equipment and obscuring the results. The solution is to place the detectors deep underground. That way the earth's crust shields out all the more obvious particles, leaving only the WIMPs shooting deep underground. In the United States, the Cryogenic Dark Matter Search (CDMS II)[8] is carrying out its research at the bottom of a mine in Minnesota, while Britain has the Boulby Underground Laboratory,[9] also in a mine more than a kilometre deep. At the time of writing CDMS II had failed to find evidence of WIMPs, though their first results showed that there would be less than one WIMP interaction every 25 days within each kilogram of the detector material.[10]

Although WIMPs became the main contender for an explanation of dark matter, in the last few years the situation has become more complicated. In the late 1990s cosmologists started to realize that the expansion of the universe was accelerating, not slowing down. Some cosmic force was driving it apart. They began to think in terms of dark energy as well as dark matter. In 2001 NASA launched a new satellite – the Wilkinson Microwave Anisotropy Probe (WMAP) – to measure the cosmic microwave background radiation more accurately than ever before. This background radiation is the 'echo' of the Big Bang, and by studying it closely scientists expect to clarify much of their understanding about the early universe. WMAP results from 2003 confirm that a mere 4% of the universe is composed of atoms, and only 23% is dark matter. Which leaves a colossal 73% of the universe in the form of *dark energy*[11] (energy and matter are, of course intricately linked in Einstein's famous equation, $E=mc^2$). This is an even bigger mystery than dark matter.

There are dissenters who claim that our models of how the universe began and developed (a Big Bang followed by a period of rapid inflation) are completely wrong. They see dark matter and dark energy as a quick fix, which avoids revising the widely held inflationary theory. If WIMPs can't be found it may begin to look as though they have a point. The difficulty for the objectors is that there don't seem to be any good alternatives to inflationary theory at present. Mainstream cosmologists are reluctant to drop their current model of the origin of the universe without having something else to replace it with. They also point to the impressive accuracy of WMAP results and claim that 'dark energy is unassailable now'.[12]

Multiple universes

The idea of multiple universes is very trendy in the worlds of cosmology and quantum physics at present. But many people don't realize that the multiple universe ideas in these two branches of physics are quite different.

Cosmology

The first area of physics in which people are talking about multiple universes is in cosmology. Some models of the early inflation of the universe suggest that the Big Bang gave rise to a number of universes, rather like bubbles coming off the surface of a boiling liquid. We live in one bubble but there could be many more beyond the limits of ours. They remain entirely separate (though Michio Kaku suggests that 'dark matter may be the presence of a neighbouring universe that we cannot see'[13]). But there are also many good inflationary theories that *don't* predict multiple universes, and we're not yet at a point where we can say that one model rather than another is right. Among others, Stephen Hawking and the Astronomer Royal, Martin Rees, believe that there are other bubble universes besides our own which are different in a few, or maybe in many, respects.

In his book, *Just Six Numbers: The Deep Forces That Shape the Universe*,[14] Rees explores some of the amazingly delicate balances of the universe that make it possible for us to be here. For example, he discusses the ratio of the electromagnetic forces between atoms to the force of gravity between them. If this ratio was only very slightly lower, only a tiny universe could exist for a very short period of time. There's exactly the right amount of material in the universe to enable stars and galaxies to form without the whole thing collapsing back on itself. The rate of expansion is just right. Rees focuses on six, but astrophysicist Hugh Ross lists many more.[15]

The idea that the universe is finely balanced to make human life on earth possible is called the *anthropic principle*. The *strong* version of the anthropic principle says that the universe has been *designed* this way to make life possible. The *weak* anthropic principle says we just *happen* to live in a universe that is balanced in this way.[16] It may be that we were just lucky that it all worked, or it may be that there are other universes where things are a little different. One universe might be expanding just a little too fast to produce conditions favourable for life. Another may expand more slowly and collapse back on itself before life ever formed. After examining these anthropic balances, Rees has to decide which way he's going – with the strong or weak versions of the anthropic principle. He presents the choice starkly: either he has to accept the existence of God, or he has to assume there are other universes and we just happen to live in the one that resulted in us. He admits that he chooses the latter because he doesn't want to believe in the former:

> If one doesn't accept the 'providence' argument, there is another perspective, which – though still conjectural – I find compellingly attractive.
> This may not seem an 'economical' hypothesis – indeed, nothing might seem more extravagant than invoking multiple universes – but it is a natural deduction from some (albeit speculative) theories.[17]

It rather seems that his emotional – or theological – preference for bubble universes, rather than design, is what makes him lean towards some inflationary models rather than others.

Quantum physics

The second area in which the idea of multiple universes comes up is in quantum physics. As with the bubble universes of cosmology, the idea only arises in *some* interpretations of quantum physics, not all. The mathematics of the quantum world have never been seriously challenged since the 1920s and 1930s when it was developed – although it has been significantly refined since then. But there are a number of ways of *interpreting* what the mathematics mean in practice. The standard way of understanding quantum physics is called the Copenhagen Interpretation because it was developed by physicists working there, and others who came to meet with them, in the late 1920s – Werner Heisenberg, Niels Bohr, Max Born and Erwin Schrödinger being the most notable. Two of its key features are:

- Heisenberg's Uncertainty Principle, which says that there's a fundamental limit to how accurately we can measure certain pairs of quantities at the quantum level. For example, it's impossible to measure both the position and the speed of a particle accurately. You can pin down its position but you won't have a clue about the speed, or you can know how fast it's going but not know quite where it is.

- Bohr's complementarity of waves and particles, which says that, at a quantum level at least, everything can be thought of as waves *or* particles. We think of light as waves and can do many experiments that demonstrate this (a diffraction grating like the surface of a CD, for example, produces bands of colour because the waves are split by the grating and then interfere with each other as they recombine). But there are also experiments that show just as clearly that light is particles – photons (Einstein first demonstrated this with the photoelectric effect). On the other hand, different experiments can show electrons behaving as particles or as waves.

The solution was to start thinking of everything as a wave that doesn't exist in one particular position. It has a 'wave function', which describes the probability of finding a particle at each position. The particle could be anywhere along the wave but we don't know where. When the detecting apparatus spots a particle, the wave function collapses – it has a 100% probability of being where it is, and a 0% probability of being anywhere else. It's impossible to really understand this. Richard Feynman, one of the greatest geniuses ever in the world of physics and winner of a Nobel Prize for his further development of quantum theory, said that 'nobody understands quantum mechanics . . . Do not keep saying to yourself . . . "But how can it be like that?" because you will go down the drain into a blind alley from which nobody has yet escaped. Nobody knows how it can be like that.'[18] So, we haven't got much of a clue what's really going on at a quantum level. Quantum physics is riddled with paradoxes, both mathematically and experimentally. Bohr's interpretation of it all was that nothing was real until you looked at it, or measured it.

But in 1957 Hugh Everett proposed a radically different interpretation of quantum mechanics. He suggested that there is a parallel universe for every quantum possibility. So a wave function collapses one way, to leave a particle in position X, in our world. But at that moment another world comes into existence in which *everything* is exactly the same *except* the wave function collapses differently to leave a particle in position Y. And since quantum effects are a crucial part of the workings of the brain, each time we make a decision, reality splits into more parallel universes. We are only aware of the decision we did take, and the path we are on. But on Everett's view, there are other versions of me who are only aware of *their* decisions. Once a world splits off, it goes on a path of its own, and the two worlds become increasingly divergent. Time is no longer going in a straight line, but branches off into a tree that is constantly expanding. Some of the scientists who advocate this 'Many Worlds Interpretation', including Stephen Hawking, see it as just a way of doing the mathematics, rather than as a real situation of a rapidly mushrooming number of universes. Others believe these other universes really do come into existence. One of the most enthusiastic exponents of the Many Worlds Interpretation is Oxford physicist David Deutsch, who says, 'Physical reality is the set of all universes evolving together.' He calls it the *multiverse*. This is the interpretation of quantum physics[19] that you will recognize from *His Dark Materials*.[20]

It's important to understand that this is a radically different notion from the bubble universes of cosmology. The bubbles all arise out of the initial inflation of the universe. The parallel universes of the Many Worlds Interpretation are constantly coming into existence. There may be only one inflationary bubble universe among many that has the right conditions to support life, but in the Many Worlds Interpretation there are uncountable billions of parallel universes almost identical to ours.

Many worlds, five problems

However, it seems to me that there are some very fundamental questions that need to be asked about these multiple universe ideas. First, how can we ever know? Science writer Martin Gardner wrote:

> The stark truth is that there is not the slightest shred of reliable evidence that there is any

universe other than the one we are in. No
multiverse theory has so far provided a
prediction that can be tested.[21]

How *could* a prediction of other universes ever be tested (and no, a really sharp knife won't actually help us
on this)? By definition, we cannot scientifically verify
anything beyond this universe. And if there's no way of
testing the predictions, how useful a theory is it? Karl
Popper, the philosopher of science, argued that all good
scientific theories must be capable of being proved false
– and there's no way of falsifying an idea about something which is inaccessible to us.

Second, science has an important principle known as
Occam's Razor,[22] which says that simple explanations
are preferable to complicated ones. Occam's Razor is
often misused by not taking into account all the available evidence, so a simple explanation at one point may
turn out to be over-simplistic when other evidence is
included. However, an exponentially increasing number
of universes seems to violate this principle to an
extraordinary degree.

Third, and related to this, is the problem about where
all the stuff comes from. Two principles of physics are
the conservation of mass and the conservation of energy. In the day-to-day world, the amount of stuff you
have remains the same no matter what processes you
put it through. You may melt some ice into water and
then boil it into steam, which you then lose into the air,
but the same molecules are still around somewhere.
Energy is conserved in a similar way. When you put fuel
into your car, it has a certain amount of energy stored
in it. Some of that energy gets turned into the kinetic
(moving) energy of the car, a small amount becomes

sound energy, and a lot is wasted as heat energy (note that this isn't talking about *saving* energy, but that the amount of energy in the system is conserved, or remains the same). We can combine the two for the universe as a whole with Einstein's famous equation $E=mc^2$, but still the total amount of mass-energy remains the same. Where does the mass-energy for a rapidly increasing number of new universes come from?

Fourth, if you have countless billions of universes you can use it to explain absolutely anything because there are always other worlds where things are different. It provides such an easy way out of finding explanations that the whole process of science becomes devalued – all the results, all the conclusions and theories are particular to some universes and not others. It actually begins to render science *unintelligible*.

Fifth, most proponents of the Many Worlds Interpretation admit that it excludes any idea of free will. You never really make a choice, the universe splits so that one of you is in a universe in which you took one course of action, and another of you is in a universe in which you took the other course. Although terrorists flew aeroplanes into the World Trade Centre in the world(s) in which you are reading this book, there are other worlds in which they did not do such a heinous thing. They didn't *choose*, they just *felt like* they were choosing. Note the statement of value I included – why is it right to describe the events of 9/11 as 'heinous'? Why do we see the action of the terrorists as morally reprehensible? If there are many worlds, they *did not choose* to do what they did, and therefore their actions *have no moral value*. We cannot say that a world in which the Holocaust never happened is preferable to a world in which it did, because both outcomes must have happened; the state of affairs *just is*. All our talk about morality is just words and we have no choice about saying them or thinking them. But the words mean nothing, on this view, because everything is determined – including what you think about morality and multiple universes. It's my conviction that morality does matter, that it's not illusory, and neither is my perception of having genuine freedom. And the only way I see that the universe can be non-determinist and include genuine freedom is if there is a God to whom we are morally accountable.

Martin Gardner summarizes.

> Surely the conjecture that there is just one universe and its Creator is infinitely simpler and easier to believe than that there are countless billions upon billions of worlds, constantly increasing in number and created by nobody. I can only marvel at the low state to which today's philosophy of science has fallen.[23]

Philip Pullman, however, isn't trying to argue for the science, or an interpretation of it. He's simply telling a story and using some current ideas of science to give him stage scenery that has some substance. Fantasy writers have written about alternative worlds for a long time, and will continue to do so regardless of whether or not real science supports their ideas.

[1] Pullman, Philip, 'Science: a very short introduction' in Gribbin, Mary and Gribbin, John, *The Science of Philip Pullman's His Dark Materials* (Hodder, 2003), p.xv.

[2] Pullman, 'Science: a very short introduction', p.xvi.

[3] Pullman: 'Science: a very short introduction', p.xviii.

[4] Pullman: 'Science: a very short introduction', p.xviii–xix.

[5] Gribbin, Mary and Gribbin, John, *The Science of Philip Pullman's His Dark Materials* (Hodder, 2003).

[6] See, for example, 'First sighting of dark matter', 22 March 2001 (physicsweb.org/article/news/5/3/10/1).

[7] See 'Hot gas reveals cold dark matter,' *CERN Courier*, Vol. 43 No. 6 (July/August 2003) (www.cerncourier.com/main/article/43/6/12).

[8] See the CDMS II website (cdms.berkeley.edu/experiment.html).

[9] See the UK Dark Matter Collaboration website (hepwww.rl.ac.uk/UKDMC/ ukdmc.html).

[10] 'Dark matter remains at large', 5 May 2004 (physicsweb.org/article/news/ 8/5/3/1).

[11] See the very informative WMAP website for more information (map.gsfc.nasa.gov/index.html); the results are summarized at map.gsfc.nasa.gov/m_mm/mr_limits.html.

[12] Frenk, Carlos, quoted in 'Biggest map of Universe clinches dark energy', *New Scientist*, 28 October 2003 (www.newscientist.com/news/ news.jsp?id=ns99994314).

[13] Kaku, Michio, 'Parallel universes live chat', BBC (www.bbc.co.uk/ science/space/spacechat/livechat/michio_kaku.shtml).

[14] Rees, Martin, *Just Six Numbers: The Deep Forces That Shape the Universe* (Weidenfeld & Nicolson, 1999).

[15] See Ross, Hugh, 'Design and the Anthropic Principle' (www.reasons.org/ resources/apologetics/design.shtml?main).

[16] For more on this see Craig, William Lane, *Barrow and Tipler on the Anthropic Principle vs. Divine Design* (www.leaderu.com/offices/ billcraig/docs/barrow.html).

[17] Rees, *Just Six Numbers*, p.150.

[18] Quoted in Gribbin and Gribbin, *The Science of Philip Pullman's His Dark Materials*, p.77.

[19] For an analysis of the two interpretations of quantum physics mentioned here and two other interpretations, see Sinclair, James Daniel, 'The Metaphysics of Quantum Mechanics' (www.reasons.org/resources/apologetics/other_papers.shtml?main#metaphysics_of_quantum_mechanics).

[20] Duetsch talks about 'shadow particles' which are the counterparts of 'tangible particles' in our world, but Mary Malone uses the term 'shadow particles' only to talk about dark matter.

[21] Gardner, Martin, 'Multiverses and Blackberries', *Skeptical Inquirer*, Vol. 25 no. 5, September/October 2001 (www.csicop.org/si/2001-09/ fringe-watcher.html).

[22] The principle is named after William of Ockham (c.1285–1349), a Franciscan monk who said, *'Entia non sunt multiplicanda praeter neccessitatem'* – 'entities are not to be multiplied beyond necessity'.

[23] Gardner, 'Multiverses and Blackberries'.

Bibliography

This is a select bibliography listing just a few of the many books and articles related to Philip Pullman. A fuller bibliography is available from Damaris Publishing's *Dark Matter: a thinking fan's guide to Philip Pullman* website: www.damaris.org/Pullman.

Due to the nature of the Internet, we cannot guarantee that the URLs given for online articles will remain correct, or even that the articles will remain accessible via the Internet. All URLs were correct as of July 2004

Books by Philip Pullman

The Haunted Storm (London: NEL, 1972)

Galatea (London: Victor Gollancz, 1978)

Using the Oxford Junior Dictionary: A Book of Exercises and Games, illustrated by Ivan Ripley (Oxford: Oxford University Press, 1979)

Ancient Civilizations, illustrated by Gary Long (Exeter: Wheaton, 1981)

The Ruby in the Smoke (Oxford: Oxford University Press, 1985); Revised edition (London: Puffin, 1987)

The Shadow in the North (London: Penguin 1988); first published as *The Shadow in the Plate* (Oxford: Oxford University Press, 1986)

Spring-Heeled Jack: A Story of Bravery and Evil, illustrated by David Mostyn (London: Doubleday, 1989)

The Broken Bridge, (London: Macmillan, 1990)

How To Be Cool (London: Macmillan, 1990)

Frankenstein. Adapted from the novel by Mary Shelley (Oxford: Oxford University Press, 1990)

Count Karlstein or The Ride of the Demon Huntsman, illustrated by Patrice Aggs (London: Doubleday, 1991) first published as *Count Karlstein*, illustrated by Diana Bryan (London: Chatto & Windus, 1982)

The Tiger in the Well (London: Penguin, 1991)

The Butterfly Tattoo (London: Macmillan Children's Books, 2001). First published as *The White Mercedes* (London: Pan Macmillan, 1992)

Sherlock Holmes and the Limehouse Horror (Walton-on-Thames: Thomas Nelson, 1992)

The New Cut Gang: Thunderbolt's Waxwork, illustrated by Mark Thomas (London: Viking, 1994)

Northern Lights (London: Scholastic, 1995; Published in the USA as *The Golden Compass*. New York: Knopf, 1996)

The Wonderful World of Aladdin and the Enchanted Lamp, illustrated by David Wyatt (London: Scholastic, 1995)

The Firework-maker's Daughter, illustrated by Nick Harris (London: Doubleday, 1995)

The New Cut Gang: The Gas-Fitter's Ball, illustrated by Mark Thomas (London: Viking, 1995)

The Tin Princess (London: Penguin, 1994)

Clockwork or All Wound Up, illustrated by Peter Bailey (London: Doubleday, 1996)

The Subtle Knife (London: Scholastic, 1997)

Mossycoat, illustrated by Peter Bailey (London: Scholastic, 1998)

Pullman, Philip and Hardcastle, Nick (eds), *Detective Stories* chosen by Philip Pullman, illustrated by Nick Hardcastle (London: Kingfisher, 1998)

I Was a Rat . . . or The Scarlet Slippers, illustrated by Peter Bailey (London: Doubleday, 1999)

The Amber Spyglass (London: Scholastic, 2000)

Puss in Boots, illustrated by Ian Beck (London: Doubleday, 2000)

Lyra's Oxford (Oxford: David Fickling Books, 2003)

The Scarecrow and the Servant (London: Doubleday, 2004) (not yet published when *Dark Matter: A thinking fan's guide to Philip Pullman* went to press)

Other works

'Achuka Interview: Philip Pullman' (www.achuka.co.uk/archive/interviews/ppint.php)

Alderson, Brian, 'Compass, Knife and Spyglass', *New York Times*, 19 November 2000

Barger, Jorn, 'Philip Pullman resources on the web' (www.robotwisdom.com/jorn/pullman.html)

BBC webchat (www.bbc.co.uk/radio4/arts/hisdarkmaterials /pullman_webchat.shtml)

Bertodano, Helena de, 'I am of the Devil's Party', *Daily Telegraph*, 29 January 2002

Billen, Andrew, 'A Senile God? Who would Adam and Eve it?', *The Times*, 21 January 2003

Billington, Michael, 'Literary epic feels the squeeze', *Guardian*, 5 January 2004

Bobby, Susan, 'What Makes a Classic? Dæmons and Dual Audience in Philip Pullman's *His Dark Materials*', *Alice's Academy*, Vol. 8, Issue 1, 2 January 2004 (www.the-looking-glass.net/rabbit/v8i1/academy1. html)

Brown, Charles N., 'An interview with Philip Pullman' (www.avnet.co.uk/amaranth/Critic/ivpullman.htm). An edited version appeared in 'Philip Pullman: Storming Heaven', *Locus*, vol. 45:6, no.479, December 2000

Brunton, Michael, 'You Don't Know how Famous You are Until Complete Strangers Stop You in the Street to Talk', *Time* (www.time.com/time/europe/arts/article/0,13716,579063,00.html)

Butler, Robert, *The Art of Darkness: Staging the Philip Pullman trilogy* (London: National Theatre, 2003)

Butler, Robert, 'The epic task of staging Pullman,' *Daily Telegraph*, 4 November 2003

Caldecott, Leonie, 'Paradise Denied: Philip Pullman and the Uses and Abuses of Enchantment', *Touchstone*, 2003 (www.touchstonemag.com/docs/issues/16.8docs/16-8pg42.html)

Chabon, Michael, 'Dust and Dæmons', *New York Review of Books*, Vol. 51, No. 5, 25 March 2004

Chrisafis, Angelique, 'Pullman Lays Down Moral Challenge for Writers', *Guardian*, 12 August 2002

Costa, Maddy, 'Kid's Stuff', *Guardian*, 22 August 2001

Couchman, David, 'Philip Pullman's *His Dark Materials*: A Not-so Subtle Knife', *Facing the Challenge* (www.facingthechallenge.org/pullman.htm)

Couchman, David, 'The Empty Vision', *Facing the Challenge* (www.facingthechallenge.org/lewis.htm)

Curtis, Nick, 'Spotlight on Pullman's Dark', *Evening Standard*, 2 January 2003

Dante Alighieri, *Inferno* (www.gutenberg.net/etext97/0ddcl10.txt)

Dirda, Michael, 'The Amber Spyglass', *Washington Post*, 29 October 2000

Dodd, Celia, 'Human Nature: Universally Acknowledged', *The Times*, 8 May 2004

Eccleshare, Julia, 'Rational Magic', *Guardian*, 28 October 2000

Eccleshare, Julia, 'Letter from London', *Publishers Weekly*, 2 December 2002

Ezard, John, 'Narnia books attacked as racist and sexist', *Guardian*, 3 June 2002

Faith and Fantasy, Australian Broadcasting Company Radio National, 24 March 2002 (www.abc.net.au/rn/relig/enc/stories/s510312.htm)

Fitzherbert, Claudia, 'This Author is Original and Also Dangerous', *Daily Telegraph*, 23 January 2002

Flesch, William, 'Childish Things', *Boston Globe*, 13 June 2004

Fried, Kerry, 'Darkness Visible: An Interview with Philip Pullman' (www.amazon.com/exec/obidos/tg/feature/-/94589/103-2179560-1236619)

Gevers, Nick, 'Northern Lights by Philip Pullman', Infinity Plus, 24 July 1999 (www.iplus.zetnet.co.uk/nonfiction/northern.htm)

Gevers, Nick: 'The Subtle Knife by Philip Pullman' Infinity Plus, 24 July 1999 (www.iplus.zetnet.co.uk/nonfiction/subtle.htm)

Gibbons, Fiachra, 'Epic Children's Book takes Whitbread', Guardian, 23 January 2002

Greene, Mark, 'Poisoned Pen', Christianity + Renewal, April 2002 (www.christianityandrenewal.com/archapr2002d.htm)

Grenier, Cynthia, 'Philip Pullman's Dark Materials', Crisis, October 2001 (www.crisismagazine.com/october2001/feature4.htm)

Gribbin, Mary and Gribbin, John, The Science of Philip Pullman's His Dark Materials' (London: Hodder Children's Books, 2003)

Harnett, Seán, 'Fast Food Fantasy', Spike (www.spikemagazine.com/0602amberspyglass.htm)

Hitchens, Peter, 'This is the most dangerous author in Britain', Mail on Sunday, 27 January 2002. A copy of the article is online at pers-www.wlv.ac.uk/~bu1895/hitchens.htm

Hitchens, Peter, 'A labour of loathing', Spectator, 18 January 2003

Humphrys, John, 'An Atheists' Creed Could be the Saving of the Church', The Sunday Times, 18 August 2002

Hunt, Peter, Children's Literature (Oxford: Blackwell, 2001)

Jefferson, Margo, 'On Writers and Writing: Harry Potter for Grown-Ups', *New York Times*, 20 January 2002

Johnson, Sarah, 'His Dark Materials: The Subtle Knife', *The Times*, 1 December 1997

Johnson, Sarah, 'Narnia for the Nineties', *The Times*, 18 October 1997

Johnson, Sarah, 'On the Dark Edge of Imagination', *The Times*, 18 October 2000

Jones, Dudley, 'Only Make-Believe? Lies, Fictions, and Metafictions in Geraldine McCaughrean's *A Pack of Lies* and Philip Pullman's *Clockwork*' , *The Lion and the Unicorn*, 23.1, January 1999, p.86 96

Jones, Nicolette, 'The Garden of Earthly Delights', *The Sunday Times*, 30 October 2000

Jones, Nicolette, 'What Shall We Tell the Children?', *The Times*, 18 July 1996

Kaye, Rupert, 'Association of Christian Teachers attacks the National Theatre for staging "blasphemous" Philip Pullman play' (www.christian-teachers.org.uk/news/HisDarkMaterials.htm)

Kaye, Rupert, 'Association of Christian Teachers critiques Philip Pullman's attempt to besmear Christianity, undermine the Church and attack God' (www.christian-teachers.org.uk/news/PhilipPullman.htm)

Kellaway, Kate, 'A Wizard with Worlds', *Observer*, 22 October 2000

Kellaway, Kate, 'Pullman Class', *Observer*, 2 November 2003

Kemp, Peter, 'Master of his universe', *The Sunday Times*, 19 October 1997

Kleist, Heinrich von, *On the Marionette Theatre* (1810) (www.southerncrossreview.org/9/kleist.htm)

Krehbiel, Greg, 'Philip Pullman's His Dark Materials', *Journeyman*, Vol. 1, No. 1, September 2001 (www.crowhill.net/journeyman/Vol1No1/Darkmaterials.html)

Langton, Jane, 'What is Dust?', *New York Times*, 19 May 1996

Lenz, Millicent, 'Philip Pullman', in Hunt, Peter and Lenz, Millicent, *Alternative Worlds in Fantasy Fiction* (London: Continuum, 2001), p.122–169

Lister, David, 'Children's book wins Whitbread top prize', *Independent*, 23 January 2002

Logie, Thea, 'Pullmeister RAQ' (urchin.earth.li/cgi-bin/twic/wiki/view.pl?page=PullmeisterRAQ)

Lopez, Barry, *Arctic Dreams: Imagination and Desire in a Northern Landscape* (London: Harvill Press, 1999)

Lyall, Sarah, 'The Man Who Dared Make Religion the Villain', *New York Times*, 7 November 2000

Lyall, Sarah, 'Staging the Next Fantasy Blockbuster', *New York Times*, 25 January 2004

Mann, Jessica: 'A Paradise Without God', *Sunday Telegraph*, 5 November 2000

Marin, Minette, 'What happens to the Kingdom of Heaven when God is killed?', *Daily Telegraph*, 21 October 2000

Marr, Andrew, 'Pullman does for atheism what C. S. Lewis did for God', *Daily Telegraph*, 24 January 2002

Masson, Scott J., 'Philip Pullman's *His Dark Materials* Trilogy', *The Glass*, Number 15, Spring 2003, p.19–23 (www.freenetpages.co.uk/hp/clsg/Glass15.pdf)

McCrum, Robert, 'Not for children', *Observer*, 22 October 2000

McCrum, Robert, 'Daemon Geezer', *Observer*, 27 January 2002

McDonagh, Melanie, 'Reading too Much into Narnia Tales', *Daily Telegraph*, 5 June 2002

McSporran, Cathy, 'The Kingdom of God, the Republic of Heaven: Depictions of God in C. S. Lewis's *Chronicles of Narnia*, and Philip Pullman's *His Dark Materials*' (www.sharp.arts.gla.ac.uk/e-sharp/articles/autumn_2003/Cathy_McSporran-Kingdom of_God.htm)

Meacham, Steve, 'The shed where God died', *Sidney Morning Herald*, 13 December 2003 (www.smh.com.au/articles/2003/12/12/1071125644900.html?from=storyrhs)

Milton, John, *Paradise Lost* (www.dartmouth.edu/~milton/reading_room/pl/note/index.shtml)

Mitchison, Amanda, 'The art of darkness', *Daily Telegraph*, 3 November 2003

Moloney, Daniel P., 'An Almost Christian Fantasy', *First Things*, 113, May 2001, p.45–49 (www.firstthings.com/ftissues/ft0105/reviews/moloney.html)

Mooney, Bel, *Devout Sceptics – Conversations on faith and doubt* (London: Hodder and Stoughton, 2003), p.122–133

Nelson, Victoria, *The Secret Life of Puppets* (Cambridge, Mass: Harvard University Press, 2003)

Odean, Kathleen, 'The story master', *School Library Journal*, 1 October 2000 (www.schoollibraryjournal.com/article/ca153054)

Parsons, Wendy, and Nicholson, Catriona, 'Talking to Philip Pullman: An Interview', *The Lion and the Unicorn*, 23:1 January 1999, p.116–134

Pattison, Darcy, 'Letter to the editor', *Horn Book Magazine*, March/April 2002, p.333

'Philip Pullman answers your questions' (www.bbc.co.uk/gloucestershire/getfresh/2003/10/philip_pullman_qa.shtml)

'Philip Pullman' in *Jubilee Books* (www.jubileebooks.co.uk/jubilee/magazine/authors/philip_pullman/interview.asp)

'Philip Pullman' in *Kidsreads.com*, 12 December 2001 (www.kidsreads.com/authors/au-pullman-philip.asp)

'Philip Pullman in Readerville', 5–9 February 2001 (www.readerville.com/webx?14@223.shZGaf9Fsuu.0@.ef6c70e/0)

'Philip Pullman' on *The South Bank Show*, 9 March 2003 (www.southbankshow.com/coming_shows/show/17)

'Philip Pullman Scholastic Interview Transcript' (www.geocities.com/torre_degli_angeli/scholasticinterview.htm)

Potton, Ed, 'Garden-Shed Visionary', *The Times*, 24 January 2002

Pullman, Philip, 'An Introduction to . . . Philip Pullman' in James Carter (ed), *Talking Books: Children's Authors Talk About the Craft, Creativity and Process of Writing* (London: Routledge, 1999), p.178–195

Pullman, Philip and Williams, Rowan, 'The Dark Materials debate: life, God, the universe . . . ' (with Rowan Williams), *Daily Telegraph*, 17 March 2004

Pullman, Philip, 'The Darkside of Narnia', *Guardian*, 1 October 1998

Pullman, Philip, 'Fire and Ice: Children's Literature in the New Millennium', *Youth Library Review*, Issue 28, Spring 2000 (www.la hq.org.uk/groups/ylg/archive/ylr28_4.htm)

Pullman, Philip, 'From Exeter to Jordan', *Register* (Exeter College Association, 2001), p.18 (This article is available online at www.oxfordtoday.ox.ac.uk/archive/0102/14_3/03.shtml)

Pullman, Philip, 'Invisible Pictures', *Signal 60*, September 1989, p.160–186

Pullman, Philip, 'Let's Write it in Red: The Patrick Hardy Lecture', *Signal 85*, January 1998, p.44–62

Pullman, Philip, 'Picture Stories and Graphic Novels' in Reynolds, Kimberley and Tucker, Nicholas (eds), *Children's Book Publishing Since 1945* (Aldershot: Scholar Press, 1998), p.110–132

Pullman, Philip, 'Responsibility and the Storyteller', *New Humanist*, 1 March 2002 (www.newhumanist.org.uk/volume117issue1_more.php?id=296_0_14_0_C)

Pullman, Philip, *The Firework-maker's Daughter, and how she became a play, and then a book, and then another play* (www.sheffieldtheatres.co.uk/education/productions/fireworkmaker/pullman.shtml)

Pullman, Philip, 'The Republic of Heaven', *Horn Book Magazine*, November/December 2001, p.655–667

Pullman, Philip, 'There has to be a lot of ignorance in me when I start a story', *Guardian*, 18 February 2002

Pullman, Philip, 'Why I don't Believe in Ghosts', *New York Times*, 31 October 2003

Pullman, Philip, *Writing Fantasy Realistically*, Sea of Faith National Conference, 2002 (www.sofn.org.uk/Conferences/pullman2002.htm)

Rabinovitch, Dina, 'His Bright Materials', *Guardian*, 10 December 2003

Reynolds, Nigel, 'Dæmons Leap into Limelight as Pullman's Dark Fantasy Takes Life on Stage', *Daily Telegraph*, 3 January 2004

Roberts, Susan, 'A dark agenda?' (www.surefish.co.uk/culture/features/pullman_interview.htm)

Robinson, Karen, 'Dark Art of Writing Books That Win Minds', *The Sunday Times*, 27 January 2002

Ross, Deborah, 'Philip Pullman: Soap and the serious writer', *Independent*, 4 February 2002

Said, S. F., 'Why Philip Pullman should win the Whitbread tonight', *Daily Telegraph*, 22 January 2002

Shackleford Tise, Mary, 'Philip Pullman, Writer of Stories', 12 October 1998 (www.delanet.com/~ftise/pullman.html)

Sharkey, Alix, 'Heaven, Hell, and the Hut at the Bottom of the Garden', *Independent on Sunday*, 6 December 1998

Shaviro, Steven, 'The end of Childhood, Beginning' (www.thestranger.com/2000-12-14/books.html)

Sierz, Aleks, 'Philip Pullman and Nicholas Hytner: Enter the dæmons', *Independent*, 12 December 2003

Snelson, Karin, 'It's No Fantasy' (www.amazon.com/exec/obidos/tg/feature/-/79470/104-2884940-7655910)

Spanner, Huw, 'Heat and Dust', *Third Way*, vol. 25 no. 2, April 2002, p.22–26 (www.thirdway.org.uk/past/showpage.asp?page=3949)

Squires, Claire, *Philip Pullman's* His Dark Materials *Trilogy* (London: Continuum, 2003)

Thomson, Stephen, 'The Child, the Family, the Relationship. Familiar Stories: Family, Storytelling, and Ideology in Philip Pullman's *His Dark Materials*' in Lesník-Oberstein, Karin (ed.), *Children's Literature: New Approaches* (Basingstoke: Palgrave Macmillan, 2004) (not yet published when *Dark Matter: A thinking fan's guide to Philip Pullman* went to press)

Thompson, Bob, '"Dark Materials," Bright Promise', *Washington Post*, 14 December 2003

Thorpe, Nick, 'The anti-Christian fundamentalist', *The Sunday Times*, 4 August 2002

Tonkin, Boyd, 'Whitbread Award: An inevitable victory for a dark and complex fable', *Independent*, 23 January 2002

Tucker, Nicholas, 'Paradise lost and freedom won', *Independent*, 28 October 2000

Tucker, Nicholas, *Darkness Visible: Inside the world of Philip Pullman* (Cambridge: Wizard Books, 2003)

Veith, Gene Edward, 'Atheism for Kids', *World*, 22 June 2002

Vincent, Sally, 'Driven by daemons', *Guardian*, 10 November 2001

Vulliamy, Ed, 'Author puts Bible Belt to the test', *Observer*, 26 August 2001

Wagner, Erica, 'Divinely Inspired', *The Times*, 18 October 2000

Wagner, Erica, 'Courageous and Dangerous: A Writer for All Ages', *The Times*, 23 January 2002

Walter, Natasha, 'A Moral Vision for the Modem Age', *Independent*, 24 January 2002

Warner, Marina, *Fantastic Metamorphoses, Other Worlds* (Oxford: Oxford University Press, 2002)

Wartofsky, Alona, 'The Last Word', *Washington Post*, 19 February 2001

Weich, Dave, 'Philip Pullman Reaches the Garden' (www.powells.com/authors/pullman.html)

Weinberg, Anna, 'Are you there, God? It's me, Philip Pullman', *Book*, November/December 2002 (www.bookmagazine.com/issue25/inthemargins.shtml)

Welborn, Amy, 'His Dark Materials' (www.amywelborn.com/reviews/pullman.html)

Welch, Frances, 'Jesus was like the Buddha and Galileo', *Sunday Telegraph*, 19 November 2000

Williams, Rowan, 'A near-miraculous triumph', *Guardian*, 10 March 2004

Wood, N., 'Paradise Lost and Found: Obedience, Disobedience, and Story-telling in C. S. Lewis and Philip Pullman', *Children's Literature in Education*, 32:4, p.237–259

Yeats, W. B. (ed.), *William Blake Collected Poems* (London: Routledge, 2002)

Useful websites

Philip Pullman's website – www.philip-pullman.com – contains a number of articles (and links to more) which have been cited in this book and are not relisted here.

The Random House website – www.randomhouse.com/features/pullman – contains much information about Pullman and his books including his additional material about the alethiometer, the *Liber Angelorum*, and his Carnegie Medal acceptance speech.

Damaris Publishing's *Dark Matter: a thinking fan's guide to Philip Pullman* website: www.damaris.org/pullman (see also articles and study guides on Damaris' CultureWatch site – www.CultureWatch.org)

National Theatre – www.nationaltheatre.org.uk and www.stagework.org.uk

BridgeToTheStars.net – www.bridgetothestars.net

His Dark Materials.org – www.hisdarkmaterials.org

His Dark Materials: An Unofficial Fansite – www.darkmaterials.com

Dark Adamant – www.geocities.com/darkadamant

HisDarkMaterialsAnnotated – www24.brinkster.com/menthapiperita/tgc.htm

Index

About the author

Tony Watkins spent several years teaching physics and mathematics in a girls' school before joining the Universities and Colleges Christian Fellowship (UCCF) as a staff worker in the south of England. He joined The Damaris Project (the precursor to the Damaris Trust) as Project Co-ordinator when it was launched in 1996.

Since the formation of Damaris Trust in 2000 he has been Managing Editor of CultureWatch (a Damaris website which engages with the media from a Christian perspective for a secular readership) as well as heading up the Damaris Workshop programme and CultureWatch groups. He is also a member of the writing team for *Connect Bible Studies* and contributed to the previous book in this series, *Matrix Revelations: A thinking fan's guide to the Matrix trilogy*.

Tony and his wife, Jane, have three boys, Charlie, Oliver and Philip, and live in Southampton.

Matrix Revelations:

A thinking fan's guide to the Matrix Trilogy

edited by Steve Couch

In depth analysis of the *Matrix* films, ranging from
the science fiction and comic book influences
to the philosophical and religious themes that
underpin the films. A book for people who love
the films and don't just fast-forward from one
action scene to the next.

Includes chapters by Tony Watkins.

> 'A multi-faceted, rich, illuminating and
> serious exploration of the Matrix film
> trilogy, and the major ideas behind it.'
>
> **Mark Greene**
> *London Institute for Contemporary Christianity*

www.damaris.org/matrix

Multiple Choice Questions

MRCP Part 1

For Churchill Livingstone:

Publisher: Laurence Hunter
Project Editor: Barbara Simmons
Copy-editor: Alison Bowers
Project controller: Nancy Arnott
Design direction: Erik Bigland

Multiple Choice Questions

MRCP Part 1

H L C Beynon BSc MD MRCP
Consultant Physician
Department of Rheumatology
Royal Free Hospital
London

J B van den Bogaerde MBChB PhD (Cantab) FCP (SA) MMed Int MRCP
Professor of Physiology
University of Pretoria
South Africa;
Reader in Physiology
St Mark's Hospital
Harrow

K A Davies MA MD FRCP
Senior Lecturer and Honorary Consultant
Department of Medicine
Imperial School of Medicine at the
Hammersmith Hospital
London

Foreword by

Mark J Walport MA PhD FRCP FRCPath
Professor of Medicine, Chairman of the Division of Medicine, Imperial College
School of Medicine and Hammersmith Hospital, London

SECOND EDITION

**CHURCHILL
LIVINGSTONE**

EDINBURGH LONDON NEW YORK PHILADELPHIA SAN FRANCISCO SYDNEY
TORONTO 1998

CHURCHILL LIVINGSTONE
A Division of Harcourt Brace and Company Limited

Churchill Livingstone, 1-3 Baxter's Place, Leith Walk, Edinburgh EH1 3AF

© Longman Group Limited 1991
© Churchill Livingstone, a division of Harcourt Brace and Company Limited 1998
 is a registered trademark of Harcourt Brace and Company Limited.

First edition 1991
Second edition 1998

ISBN 0443 056919

British Library of Cataloguing in Publication Data
A catalogue record for this book is available from the British Library.

Library of Congress Cataloging in Publication Data
A catalog record for this book is available from the Library of Congress.

Medical knowledge is constantly changing. As information becomes available,
changes in treatment, procedures, equipment and the use of drugs become
necessary. The author and publisher have, as far as it is possible, taken care to
ensure that the information given in the text is accurate and up-to-date.
However, readers are strongly advised to confirm that the information,
especially with regard to drug usage, complies with current legislation and
standard of practice.

Produced by Addison Wesley Longman China Limited, Hong Kong
EPC/01

Foreword To The Complete MRCP

The MRCP examination aims to test a broad range of clinical skills and background knowledge at an early stage of training in general medicine. The Part 1 examination provides an assessment of general medical knowledge and the written Part 2 assesses the ability to interpret clinical data and to identify those physical signs that can readily be photographed.

The format of the examination is influenced by the large number of candidates and the necessity to provide a test of uniform standard. Multiple choice questions (MCQs) provide a standardised assessment of knowledge. Studies conducted in disciplines other than medicine have shown that MCQs provide a discriminator of abilities that correlates with other tests such as the writing of essays. Animated discussion of the answers to multiple choice questions posed in the examination often engenders paranoia about the ambiguity or idiocy of particular questions. In reality, the answers to clinical questions are rarely black and white, as demanded by MCQs. However, the occasional obscure or ambiguous question that slips into the exam will be detected during marking of the papers and will not be used again. Such questions will only damage individual candidates if the fury tho engender at tho timo disturbs a balanced approach to answering the remainder of the questions. The 'grey' cases and photographic questions provide tests that approximate more closely to the reality of the bedside and probe comprehension of relevant clinical physiology and pathology.

This series of three books has been written by a team of physicians who have not yet forgotten the agonies of the MRCP examination and who participate actively in teaching others who are about to confront the same hurdle. These books provide stimulating examples of the types of question encountered in all three sections of the MRCP examination, and provide an entertaining and informative journey through many of the highways and byways of medicine.

London 1998   M.J.W.

Preface

This is the first book in the series 'The Complete MRCP' and is
complementary to books 2 and 3. Book 3 covers the photographic
interpretation section and Book 2 covers the data interpretation and
case histories section of Part 2 of the MRCP exam.

This book contains 300 MCQs which cover common Part 1 MRCP
examination topics. Expanded answers supplemented by relevant
lists of differential diagnosis are given as an aid to revision. We
would also recommend candidates revising for Part 1 of the
examination to utilise the other two books in the series which,
although directed at Part 2 of the exam, contain in their expanded
answers information relevant to Part 1.

We hope this series will be both stimulating and helpful for
candidates preparing for the examination.

We gratefully acknowledge the contribution of Dr C Marguerie to
the first edition of this book.

1998

H.L.C. Beynon
J.B. van den Bogaerde
K.A. Davies

Questions

Answers begin on p. 57

1 Regarding prostate cancer:
a) PSA screening is recommended for men above 50 years.
b) PSA screening is specific for prostate cancer.
c) Digital examination provides added diagnostic accuracy.
d) Most men with prostate cancer will not die as a direct consequence of the cancer.
e) GNHR analogues reduce androgen secretion.

2 Adenocarcinoma of the colon:
a) Is caused by a single gene mutation.
b) May be associated with diets rich in fats.
c) The p53 oncogene mutation makes adenomas malignant.
d) The COX 2 (cyclooxygenase 2) gene is overexpressed in a majority of adenocarcinomas of the colon.
e) Screening for cancer by faecal occult blood tests is recommended.

3 A right-handed 70-year-old man has a brain scan which reveals a lesion that has damaged his left angular and supramarginal gyrus. On examination you would expect the following:
a) Dysphasia.
b) Inappropriate affect.
c) Finger agnosia.
d) Constructional apraxia.
e) Difficulty with left–right discrimination.

4 The Eaton–Lambert syndrome
a) Is most commonly associated with an adenocarcinoma of the lung.
b) Generally spares the lower limbs.
c) Is helped by guanidine hydrochloride.
d) Commonly affects the ocular muscles.
e) Shows fatiguability only if repeated electrical stimulation is used.

5 Thrombolytic therapy using streptokinase:
a) Is indicated in all patients with chest pain and widespread ST-segment elevation on the ECG.
b) May be associated with bradycardia and hypotension during reperfusion.
c) Should be repeated if chest pain and ECG abnormalities recur 1–2 weeks after the initial episode.
d) May be associated with the development of a fever, rash, arthritis, or renal impairment, mediated by immune complexes.
e) Is contraindicated in pregnancy.

6 Deep venous thrombosis:
a) Is always found in patients presenting with pulmonary embolism.
b) Should lead to long term anticoagulation if recurrent.
c) Should be prevented in surgical patients by twice daily injection of low molecular weight heparin.
d) May occur in patients with homocystinuria.
e) Is reliably clinically diagnosed.

7 Prescribing in renal failure:
a) Gentamicin is contraindicated.
b) In chronic renal failure patients, hypocalcaemia usually requires long-term therapy with cholecalciferol.
c) Erythromycin may cause a rise in serum creatinine when administered to patients receiving cyclosporin.
d) Indomethacin may cause significant impairment of renal function.
e) In diabetic patients receiving chronic ambulatory peritoneal dialysis, subcutaneous insulin therapy is the treatment of choice.

8 Which of the following may present with diarrhoea?
a) Carcinoid syndrome.
b) Thyrotoxicosis.
c) Primary hyperparathyroidism.
d) Conn's syndrome.
e) Cystic fibrosis.

9 The following are true of hypertension:
a) Most hypertensives in the developed world have satisfactory blood pressure control.
b) Potassium restriction is important in blood pressure control.
c) Increased left ventricular mass is more important than smoking as a predictor of mortality.
d) Hypercholesterolaemia, increased left ventricular mass, smoking and impaired glucose tolerance result in more than 10-fold increase in mortality if combined with hypertension.
e) β blockers do not reduce left ventricular mass.

10 Regarding inflammatory bowel disease:
a) Enteral diets are as effective as steroids in ulcerative colitis.
b) Cyclosporine is used in treatment.
c) Azathioprine is often effective in allowing withdrawal of corticosteroids.
d) Anti-TNF antibodies have been shown to be of use against Crohn's disease.
e) Enteral diets have been successfully used in treatment of Crohn's disease.

11 Contraindications to performing a transcutaneous liver biopsy include:
a) An INR of 1.5.
b) Biliary obstruction.
c) Portal hypertension.
d) Infection with *Echinococcus granulosus*.
e) Haemangioma.

12 Chronic granulomatous disease:
a) Is an autosomal dominant condition.
b) Is characterised by abnormal bacterial phagocytosis.
c) Recurrent streptococcal infections are usual.
d) May be diagnosed by the nitroblue tetrazolium test.
e) Is compatible with a normal life-expectancy.

13 Pityriasis rosea:
a) Is caused by a fungus.
b) The organism is best isolated by skin scrapings.
c) A herald rash typically precedes a generalised eruption.
d) Predominantly affects distal extremities.
e) Should be treated with topical steroids.

14 Which of the following are causes of Raynaud's disease?
a) Cervical rib.
b) Systemic sclerosis.
c) Syringomyelia.
d) Pneumatic drill.
e) Ankylosing spondylitis.

15 Regarding non-alcoholic steatohepatitis:
a) This is seen in less than 5% of liver biopsies.
b) It is a recognised complication of jejunoileal bypass.
c) AST and ALT may be raised.
d) Steroids are a recognised cause.
e) Cirrhosis is seldom associated.

16 Regarding infective diarrhoea:
a) Cryptosporidia are resistant to chlorine treatment.
b) Cryptosporidia diarrhoea is treated effectively with antibiotics.
c) *G. lamblia* typically produce a bloody diarrhoea.
d) Cyclospora commonly causes diarrhoea in healthy young people.
e) *E. coli* can cause diarrhoea and renal failure.

17 Following a partial gastrectomy the following are true:
a) The patient is at an increased risk of developing fractures.
b) Gallstones are more common.
c) Patients have an increased risk of aspiration pneumonia.
d) Megaloblastic anaemia is a well-recognised complication.
e) Renal stones are more common.

18 In Mycoplasma pneumoniae infections the following are recognised complications:
a) Endocarditis.
b) Cerebellar ataxia.
c) Pancreatitis.
d) Thrombocytopenia.
e) Acute glomerulonephritis.

19 The following conditions are X-linked recessive:
a) Haemophilia B.
b) Vitamin D-resistant rickets.
c) Complete testicular feminisation.
d) Wilson's disease.
e) Deficiency of hypoxanthine guanine phosphoribosyl transferase.

20 The following statements are true of a thrombocytopenia:
a) Platelet growth factor can be given in malignancy-associated thrombocytopenia.
b) Heparin is a cause of thrombocytopenia.
c) Quinine does not cause thrombocytopenia.
d) DIC is usually associated with the thrombocytopenia of TTP.
e) Thrombocytopenia of ITP is caused by IgM anti-platelet antibodies.

21 The following statements are true of insomnia:
a) The diagnosis of chronic insomnia requires a history of sleeplessness.
b) β blockers are not implicated in insomnia.
c) Thyroid hormone replacement does not cause insomnia.
d) Zolpidem does not work through the GABA pathway.
e) Melatonin is of no proven benefit in insomnia.

22 In Behçet's syndrome:
a) There is a positive family history in 30% of cases.
b) Erythema nodosum is common.
c) Early morning stiffness is a typical presenting feature.
d) Abdominal pain and diarrhoea occur in approximately 10% of cases.
e) Papilloedema is rare.

23 Aplastic anaemia:
a) Is a disease of old people.
b) Is usually associated with drugs.
c) Has an immunological aetiology in some.
d) Bone marrow transplant is used in most patients.
e) Immunosuppression is not useful in therapy.

24 A double blind trial is planned to compare the utility of cyclophosphamide and cyclosporin in the treatment of lupus nephritis. The main reasons for randomising patients are:
 a) So that the number of subjects in each group will be identical.
 b) So that the two patient groups will have similar prognostic features.
 c) So that the sample may be compared with a known group of patients with similar disease characteristics.
 d) So that the investigator does not known in advance what therapy which patient will receive.
 e) To prevent the clinician knowing which drug the patient is on.

25 Terfenadine:
 a) Is an effective H1 histamine blocker.
 b) May cause reduction of the QT interval on the ECG.
 c) Is metabolised mainly by the liver.
 d) Is a drug whose metabolism may be inhibited by the co-administration of grapefruit juice.
 e) Should be used with caution in patients receiving macrolide antibiotics.

26 The effect on gut transit time of two different laxatives A and B is compared on two samples of patients using the unpaired t-test:
 a) The null hypothesis assumes that there will be a significant difference between the two groups.
 b) The number of patients in each group must be the same.
 c) The degree of freedom is given by n-2 where n is the total number of people in the trial.
 d) If $p < 0.05$ for a given value of t then the null hypothesis is refuted
 e) The assumption is made that the observations are normally distributed.

27 The following are frequent causes of a serum alpha-fetoprotein level greater than 10 times the normal upper limit:
 a) A seminoma.
 b) Metastatic carcinoma of the liver.
 c) Hepatoma.
 d) Cirrhosis of the liver.
 e) Oat-cell tumour of the lung.

28 Which of the following may be associated with an underlying malignancy?
 a) Acanthosis nigricans.
 b) Necrolytic migratory erythema.
 c) Bullous pyoderma gangrenosum.
 d) Granuloma annulare.
 e) Erythema gyratum repens.

29 HIV infection, true or false:
a) In the latent phase patients make few HIV particles.
b) Infected T cells survive for a month in infected patients.
c) CD4 counts are the best predictor of disease progression.
d) Needle stick injury leads to infection in 0.3%.
e) Nucleoside analogues reduce needle stick infectivity.

30 Cholesterol lowering:
a) Statins reduce mortality in patients with previous infarctions.
b) Statins reduce cholesterol in a linear fashion.
c) Bile acid sequestrants are difficult for patients to tolerate.
d) Niacin therapy is limited by side-effects.
e) The NCEP (National Cholesterol Education Programme) guidelines recommend reduction of LDL to below 3.36 if two risk factors are present.

31 A case control study is designed to analyse a suspected hypothetical association between the development of a brain tumour and anti-migraine treatment. This study:
a) Can derive an estimate of the risk of an individual developing the condition as a consequence of the treatment.
b) Will demonstrate that any association found is likely to be causal.
c) Will need controls who are chosen at random from the general population.
d) Will necessitate careful follow-up of a group of patients receiving migraine treatment, and a not treated control group.
e) Will not give biased results if all the patients have been carefully assessed in a hospital outpatient department.

32 The following are true of patients with ankylosing spondylitis:
a) There is a family history in 25% of cases.
b) Cardiac conduction defects are a recognised association.
c) Affects females more commonly than males.
d) Some patients are at risk of leukaemia.
e) They have an increased risk of developing the cauda equina syndrome.

33 The following are associated with a raised plasma volume and a normal red cell volume:
a) Stress.
b) The third trimester of pregnancy.
c) A prolonged period spent at high altitude.
d) Cirrhosis of the liver.
e) Congestive cardiac failure.

34 The seventh cranial nerve:
a) A lower motor neurone weakness of the facial nerve may result in ptosis.
b) Intolerance of loud noises may occur with lower motor neurone lesions.
c) Carries taste sensation from the posterior third of the tongue.
d) Sarcoidosis is a recognised cause of bilateral lower motor neurone lesions.
e) An upper motor neurone lesion may result in tears during salivation (crocodile tears, gustatory lacrimation).

35 Regarding geriatric care:
a) A third of the health budget is spent on the elderly.
b) Care becomes more expensive above the age of 80.
c) NSAIDs are more dangerous in elderly patients.
d) NSAID use results in a doubling of hospitalisation in the elderly.
e) Untreated asymptomatic bacteriuria increases mortality of the elderly.

36 Regarding type II diabetes:
a) A third of diabetics with no history of heart disease have coronary artory stenosis.
b) Women with type II diabetes do not have an increased incidence of ischaemic heart disease.
c) Diabetic cardiomyopathy is always ischaemic in nature.
d) Insulin stimulates sodium excretion.
e) Insulin increases aldosterone levels.

37 True or false in coeliac disease.
a) IgG anti-endomysial antibodies are found in coeliac disease.
b) DR4 is commonly found.
c) Whole gliadin molecules are recognised by T cells.
d) Rectal gluten challenge is diagnostic.
e) Villous atrophy recovers after gliadin withdrawal.

38 In Strongyloides stercoralis infections:
a) The patient may present with malabsorption.
b) The infection is acquired after drinking contaminated water.
c) Infection is commoner in war veterans from the Western Desert.
d) Thiabendazole therapy is often employed.
e) The risk of septicaemia following immunosuppression is increased.

39 **A man presents with fatigue and weight loss.** On examination his pulse is a regular 100/min, his JVP is raised with a rapid y-descent and rises further on inspiration. He has hepatomegaly, ascites and ankle oedema.
   a) Superior vena cava obstruction should be excluded urgently.
   b) The systolic blood pressure is likely to decrease on expiration.
   c) The findings are consistent with constrictive pericarditis.
   d) The presence of Q-waves or a bundle branch block would suggest a restrictive cardiomyopathy.
   e) You would expect a wide pulse pressure.

40 **The following statements are true:**
   a) Tetracycline is bactericidal.
   b) Ceftazidime is active against *Pseudomonas aeruginosa*.
   c) Aztreonam is the choice antibiotic for *Proteus mirabilis* pneumonia.
   d) Gentamicin is active against *Staphylococcus aureus*.
   e) Metronidazole is the treatment of choice for acute amoebic dysentery.

41 **Regarding motor neurone disease:**
   a) The incidence is 1 per million per year.
   b) 50% of patients will die in 3 years.
   c) Aspartine is neurotoxic.
   d) Glutamate binds to the N-methyl D asparate (NMDA) receptor.
   e) Riluzole has been used with demonstrated benefit.

42 **HIV/AIDS — true or false:**
   a) Gancyclovir can be started when CD4 count falls below 150 cells per µl in HIV-infected patients.
   b) Lamivudine and zidovudine combination results in reduced drug resistance to zidovudine.
   c) Anal herpes produces characteristic anal ulcers.
   d) Pancreatitis is an uncommon complication of AIDS.
   e) Gastric bleeds are common in HIV infected patients.

43 **Regarding gastrointestinal bleeding:**
   a) Early sclerotherapy prevents bleeding in patients with grade IV variceal disease.
   b) Sclerotherapy results in reduced mortality when compared to medical therapy, in patients with bleeding varices.
   c) Faecal blood testing is positive for up to 12 days after an acute gastric bleed.
   d) Gastric bleeding does not cause red blood per rectum.
   e) Inflammatory bowel disease commonly causes rectal bleeding in the elderly.

44 Gynaecomastia may be caused by:
a) Chlorpromazine.
b) Nitrofurantoin.
c) Mumps.
d) Interstitial cell carcinoma of the testes.
e) Phenytoin.

45 A third heart sound:
a) May occur in pregnancy.
b) May be caused by constrictive pericarditis.
c) Never occurs with atrial fibrillation.
d) If louder during inspiration indicates a right ventricular source.
e) Suggests a cardiomyopathy when detected in a 35-year-old man with a resting bradycardia.

46 A patient has a cardiac arrest; and despite apparently normal electrical activity no cardiac output is detectable. The following are true:
a) The patient may have had a pulmonary embolism.
b) Atropine is useful.
c) Defibrillation should be attempted before giving any drugs.
d) The patient may have a pneumothorax.
e) Calcium chloride is useful if the patient is hypocalcaemic.

47 A patient presents with a broad complex tachycardia, rate 160 beats/min. The following suggest ventricular tachycardia rather than a supraventricular mechanism:
a) A history of angina.
b) Capture beats.
c) An Irregular rhythm.
d) Left axis deviation.
e) Q waves in VI.

48 The following are true:
a) The assignment of racial group is a nominal variable.
b) A histogram is a useful way of showing how a particular variable is changing in respect to time.
c) The mean of a large sample is invariably greater than the median value.
d) The mean of a large sample will always increase in size as the size of the sample increases.
e) The interquartile range is a useful measure of the spread of the distribution.

49 A study was performed in a group of 100 patients attending the Rheumatology Outpatients Department with Raynaud's phenomenon. The aim was to evaluate the utility of measuring anti-C1q antibodies in the diagnosis of SLE. Of patients who had positive anti-C1q antibodies, 22 had lupus while 31 did not. Of patients with negative anti-C1q antibodies, 7 had lupus while 40 did not.
   a) The sensitivity of the anti-C1q antibody test for diagnosis of lupus in this population is 22/29.
   b) The specificity of a positive anti-C1q antibody test for diagnosis of lupus is 22/71.
   c) Predictive value of this particular test might be different if patients presenting with a facial flush were studied.
   d) The positive predictive value of the test in the Raynaud's population here is 22/53.
   e) The specificity of this test is dependent upon the prevalence of lupus in the test population.

50 The following drugs are recognised causes of cholestatic jaundice:
   a) Chlorpromazine.
   b) Chlorpropamide.
   c) Nitrofurantoin.
   d) Methyltestosterone.
   e) Isoniazid.

51 The following are recognised causes of cancer in man:
   a) Vinyl chloride.
   b) Phenacetin.
   c) Cytomegalovirus.
   d) Sawdust.
   e) Schistosomiasis.

52 Polycythaemia rubra vera is associated with:
   a) A raised ESR and plasma viscosity.
   b) Pruritus.
   c) Haemorrhage.
   d) A raised leukocyte alkaline phosphatase (LAP).
   e) Raised erythropoietin levels.

53 A 60-year-old man presents with weakness and depression. His plasma osmolality is 255 mosmol/kg and urine osmolality 330 mosm/kg.
   a) A history of a recent road traffic accident is relevant.
   b) He is at risk of grand mal convulsions.
   c) A chest X-ray should be obtained.
   d) Treatment with amitriptyline may be responsible.
   e) Oral demeclocycline is appropriate first line therapy.

54 Superior vena cava obstruction:
   a) May be caused by an aortic aneurysm.
   b) May present with syncope.
   c) Should be treated with local radiotherapy before embarking on invasive tests.
   d) May be caused by Kaposi's sarcoma.
   e) May be caused by a seminoma.

55 Absolute contraindications to thrombolytic therapy include:
   a) Proliferative diabetic retinopathy.
   b) Major surgery in the last month.
   c) A recent liver biopsy.
   d) A cerebrovascular accident 6 months before.
   e) Traumatic cardiopulmonary resuscitation.

56 True or false:
   a) Carotid endarterectomy is not recommended in asymptomatic patients.
   b) Thrombolytic therapy is of use in all acute stroke patients.
   c) Combined therapy is optimal for epilepsy.
   d) Sodium valproate may also be used in restless legs syndrome.
   e) Interferon α is recommended for patients with multiple sclerosis.

57 Concerning nutrition:
   a) Protein calorie malnutrition is rare in hospital patients of developed countries.
   b) Cholestyramine causes reduced absorption of water-soluble vitamins.
   c) Metformin may inhibit B_{12} absorption.
   d) Isoniazid can lower tryptophan levels.
   e) Malnourished people have low lymphocyte levels.

58 True or false:
   a) Diarrhoea is present when 5 or more stools per day are passed.
   b) Faecal fat should not exceed 7 g per day.
   c) Diarrhoea is a well recognised complication in patients with systemic sclerosis.
   d) β blockers can cause diarrhoea.
   e) Artificial sweeteners reduce flatus.

59 Regarding autoimmune thyroiditis:
   a) Atrophic thyroiditis is the end stage of Hashimoto's disease.
   b) CD4 T cells in Graves' disease thyroids are oligoclonal.
   c) Anti-TSH antibodies are rare in atrophic thyroditis.
   d) 20% of Down's syndrome patients have autoimmune thyroid disease.
   e) Low iodine intake increases the population levels of autoimmune thyroid disease

60 Glucagonomas:
a) Are generally benign.
b) May be associated with necrolytic migratory erythema.
c) Typically show glucose intolerance.
d) May present with steatorrhoea.
e) Arise in the γ-cells of the pancreas.

61 The following drugs may cause pulmonary fibrosis:
a) Bleomycin.
b) Methotrexate.
c) Amiodarone.
d) Nitrofurantoin.
e) Phenytoin.

62 Which of the following are true?
a) Nail pitting is a feature of lichen planus.
b) Blue nails are seen in Darier's disease.
c) Yellow nails may be associated with an increased incidence of respiratory infections.
d) There is a recognised association between hypoplastic nails and the nephrotic syndrome.
e) Koilonychia is a recognised feature of folic acid deficiency.

63 Hyperprolactinaemia
a) May be associated with myxoedema.
b) Produces a low testosterone level.
c) May be caused by L-dopa therapy.
d) Can cause impotence in men.
e) May be caused by metoclopramide.

64 The following are tick-borne diseases:
a) A polio-like syndrome in children.
b) Louping-ill.
c) Mediterranean typhus.
d) Erythema chronicum migrans.
e) Q fever.

65 Cryoglobulinaemia:
a) Blood samples taken for the investigation of suspected cryoglobulinaemia should be rapidly cooled to facilitate the precipitation of the cryoglobulin.
b) May be associated with an underlying myeloproliferative disorder.
c) Polyclonal antibodies with rheumatoid factor activity are characteristic of type II cryoglobulinaemia.
d) Very low levels of C3 and C4 are typically found in patients with mixed essential cryoglobulinaemia.
e) Is often associated with membranous glomerulonephritis and renal impairment.

66 Thromboembolism in pregnancy, true or false:
a) Is commoner in the first trimester.
b) Factor I, II, VII and IX are raised.
c) Protein C and S are reduced.
d) V/Q scanning exposes the fetus to high levels of irradiation.
e) Subcutaneous heparin is used in the second trimester.

67 Regarding obesity:
a) Exercise, diet and behavioral therapy result in sustained weight loss in 50% of patients.
b) Obesity is the leading cause of preventable death in developed countries.
c) A body mass index of 29 to 30 predicts a 60% increase in mortality.
d) Even small weight loss is associated with benefit.
e) 1/1000 patients on dexfenfluramine develop pulmonary hypertension.

68 The following is true of blood transfusion:
a) Autologous blood transfusion is the most common type of transplant.
b) Graft versus host reaction can occur following a transfusion.
c) Febrile, non haemolytic reactions to blood occur in fewer than 1/1000 blood transfusions.
d) Platelet transfusion is useful in patients with DIC.
e) Transfusion reactions are usually against ABO blood group antigens.

69 Which of the following are true?
a) Basophilic stippling is seen in β-thalassaemia.
b) Heinz bodies are characteristic of glucose-6-phosphate dehydrogenase deficiency.
c) Target cells occur in hypersplenism.
d) Cabot's rings may be seen in red cells in a peripheral blood film after splenectomy.
e) Howell–Jolly bodies are a feature of coeliac disease.

70 Human Leukocyte Antigens (HLA):
a) Are encoded by genes on chromosome 7.
b) The gene products of loci A, B and C are called class II antigens.
c) HLA B27 is associated with a 20-fold increased risk of developing ankylosing spondylitis.
d) Narcolepsy is associated with HLA DR3.
e) Behçet's disease is associated with HLA A3 in Caucasians.

71 True or false:
a) Natural killer cells kill via an MHC-directed mechanism.
b) Perforins are produced by macrophages.
c) CD2 on T cells binds to LFA1 molecules on target cells.
d) CD8 and CD4 cells kill via the Fas/APO-1 system.
e) CD8 cells kill virally-infected cells.

72 True or false:
a) 50% of men between 60 and 79 have substantial prostate enlargement.
b) 5 alpha reductase inhibitors may be used to decrease bladder outflow obstruction in patients with prostatic enlargement.
c) Alpha-1 antagonists reduce bladder sphincter muscle contraction.
d) There is a direct relationship between size of prostate and urinary stream.
e) Cancer and prostate hyperplasia can occur together.

73 Regarding H. pylori:
a) *H. pylori* may cause gastric cancer.
b) Duodenal ulcer is negatively associated with gastric cancer.
c) *H. pylori* causes multifocal atrophic gastritis.
d) Proton pump inhibitor therapy without *H. pylori* eradication may predispose to multifocal atrophic gastritis.
e) *H. pylori* contributes to Barrett's oesophagus.

74 Cocaine abuse:
a) Is primarily confined to the lower social classes, and may be associated with the abuse of opiates as well.
b) Cocaine is well absorbed from the GI tract.
c) Physical dependence is common, and withdrawal symptoms may be severe.
d) May result in a toxic psychosis, mydriasis and hypertension.
e) May be complicated by the development of gangrene.

75 Lymphocytes:
a) T cells rosette with sheep red cells via the CD2 antigen.
b) Hairy cell leukaemia cells express the CD11 antigen.
c) CD8 cells recognise antigen bound to class II MHC molecules.
d) CD3 positive cells are B cells.
e) T-cytotoxic cells are usually CD4 positive.

76 Drugs in pregnancy:
a) Tetracycline is contraindicated.
b) Aspirin is commonly used in the treatment of patients with high titre anticardiolipin antibodies.
c) Anticoagulation with warfarin may be required in early pregnancy in patients with recurrent thromboses.
d) Sulphonylurea therapy may be useful in the management of gestational diabetes in cases where insulin is not needed.
e) Prednisolone and dexamethasone may be safely administered in pregnancy, if indicated, as they are metabolised by placental 11β-dehydrogenase to inactive keto-forms.

77 Infectious mononucleosis syndrome:
a) Is exclusively caused by Epstein–Barr virus.
b) Splenomegaly is seen in 10% of patients.
c) IgM antibodies against viral capsid antigen (VCA) are diagnostic of acute infection with Epstein–Barr virus.
d) Atypical lymphocytes may be confused with leukaemic cells.
e) Hepatitis is not a feature of Epstein–Barr virus infection.

78 The following are true:
a) DNA oligonucleotide hybridisation to fragments of digested DNA run on a gel is called a Western blot.
b) Restriction length polymorphisms use DNA-specific enzymes to digest DNA at different nucleotide sequences, thus producing a unique pattern for each individual.
c) PCR methodology is specific, but not sensitive.
d) Polymorphism is defined as an allelic frequency of 10%.
e) Nucleotide sequence variation in proximity to a gene results in linkage disequilibrium.

79 Concerning Mycobacterium avium intracellulare :
a) *Mycobacterium avium Intracellulare* (MAI) is the third most common infection in HIV-infected individuals in developed countries.
b) MAI is less common than *M. tuberculosis* in Africa.
c) Prophylaxis is instituted when the CD4 count is < 100.
d) Resistance to azithromycin is infrequent.
e) Headache is the chief side-effect of clarythromycin.

80 Regarding Creutzfeldt–Jacob disease:
a) RNA particles transmit the disease.
b) Cooking reliably kills the infectious agent.
c) The disease is invariably fatal.
d) There is no association with BSE (bovine spongiform encephalopathy).
e) Killing cattle older than 30 months should eradicate BSE.

81 Regarding Creutzfeldt–Jacob disease:
a) Conventional CSF examination is normal.
b) May be inherited disease as an autosomal dominant trait.
c) Amyloid plaques may be seen.
d) All people in the general population are susceptible to the disease.
e) A CT scan is useful in confirming the diagnosis.

82 The following is true of pancreatitis :
a) Alcohol is the most common cause of acute pancreatitis in the UK.
b) In the UK all patients should receive broad spectrum antibiotics.
c) Ascaris infestation may cause acute pancreatitis.
d) Chronic pancreatitis is usually associated with gallstones.
e) Antioxidants may be useful in treating chronic idiopathic pancreatitis.

83 Pneumonia:
a) Is the most common infective cause of death in the developed world.
b) In elderly patients Gram-negative pneumonias are common.
c) Less than 50% of patients with pneumonia are treated at home.
d) Pleuritic pain is a poor prognostic sign.
e) A poor white cell response is an ominous sign.

84 True or false?
a) Deficiency of terminal pathway complement components is commonly associated with SLE.
b) Immune complexes usually initiate the alternative pathway of complement activation.
c) Measurement of immune complexes by a C1q-binding assay is particularly useful in monitoring patients with SLE.
d) Complement levels are usually low in pregnancy.
e) Hypocomplementaemia is a bad prognostic sign in severely ill patients with multi-organ failure.

85 True or false?
a) Complement receptor type 1 (CR1) is found only on red blood cells.
b) CR1 is important in the transport of immune complexes in the circulation.
c) CR2 is the receptor on lymphocytes which binds Epstein–Barr virus.
d) An inherited deficiency of erythrocyte CR1 is common in SLE patients.
e) Deficiency of complement receptors CR3 and CR4 predisposes affected subjects to life-threatening viral infections.

86 On review in outpatients a patient with rheumatoid arthritis is noted to have a haemoglobin of 10 g/dl. The plasma iron level is 5 mmol/L (normal range: 12–30 mmol/L), the TIBC 45 mmol/L (normal range: 50–80 mmol/L). The following are true:
a) Blood loss is the most likely diagnosis.
b) A prescription of oral iron 200 mg 8-hourly would be appropriate.
c) The ferritin is likely to be raised.
d) Erythropoietin levels are likely to be low.
e) A bone marrow biopsy stained for iron will certainly show decreased deposits in reticuloendothelial cells.

87 CAH: true or false?
a) Congenital adrenal hyperplasia (CAH) is usually an autosomal dominant condition.
b) 17-hydroxylase deficiency is the commonest variant.
c) Masculinisation of female infants with CAH may result in mistaking them for males.
d) Salt loss and hypotension are major features of CAH due to 11-β-hydroxylase deficiency.
e) 21-hydroxylase deficiency will result in a very high serum ACTH, and reduced 17-oxosteroid levels in the urine.

88 True or false:
a) Multiple sclerosis affects approximately one million people worldwide.
b) TH2 cells are responsible for myelin damage.
c) Immunomodulation reverses damage to myelin sheaths.
d) Interferon β prevents functional deterioration over the long term.
e) Magnetic resonance can accurately show areas of disease activity.

89 Regarding calcium antagonists:
a) Short acting calcium blockers are associated with an increased risk of cardiac events.
b) Long acting calcium blockers should not be used to treat hypertension.
c) The risk of gastrointestinal haemorrhage is not increased.
d) Nifedipine is associated with the highest risk of cardiac events in patients with angina
e) β blockers are preferable to calcium antagonists when treating patients with angina.

90 Regarding idiopathic thrombocytopenia purpura:
a) The incidence is 13 per million.
b) 50% of adults will achieve spontaneous remission.
c) Bone marrow examination is essential to confirm the diagnosis.
d) A platelet count of less than 50 000 is an absolute indication for hospitalisation.
e) Splenectomy should never be performed in these patients with a platelet count of less than 10 000.

91 Autoantibodies:
a) Anti-mitochondrial antibody is 70% sensitive for primary biliary cirrhosis.
b) Transplacental transfer of antibodies in mothers with certain autoimmune diseases may cause neonatal heart block.
c) Anti-neutrophil cytoplasmic antibodies cause Wegener's granulomatosis.
d) Anti-centromere antibodies are specific for mixed connective tissue disease.
e) Scl-70 is a specific autoantibody for systemic lupus erythematosus.

92 A 46-year-old woman presents with a history of taking 33 paracetamol tablets:
a) Hyperpyrexia, tinnitus, and hypokalaemia are common in such patients.
b) A normal prothrombin time ratio at 24 hours suggests that serious liver toxicity is unlikely to supervene.
c) Initial levels of > 300 mg/L or 100 mg/L at 12 hours are a bad prognostic sign.
d) N-acetylcysteine increases urinary excretion of the drug.
e) Liver failure is very unlikely to occur following an overdose of this size.

93 There are recognised antidotes for the following drug overdoses:
a) Imipramine.
b) Dextropropoxyphene.
c) Digoxin.
d) Lorazepam.
e) Ibuprofen.

94 The following drugs are secreted in significant quantities in breast milk:
a) Amiodarone.
b) Metronidazole.
c) Indomethacin.
d) Amoxycillin.
e) Phenytoin.

95 Which of the following are appropriate treatments?
a) *Pneumocystis carinii*: co-trimoxazole.
b) *Streptococcus viridans* endocarditis: benzyl penicillin and gentamicin.
c) Chlamydial infection: tetracycline
d) Cytomegalovirus retinitis: ganciclovir
e) Mycoplasma pneumoniae: erythromycin.

96 Anti-fungal agents:
a) Ketoconazole interacts with cyclosporin.
b) Systemic candidiasis should be treated with clotrimazole.
c) Histoplasmosis may be treated with ketoconazole.
d) Fluconazole is used prophylactically in neutropenic patients.
e) Deep-seated Aspergillus infection responds well to ciprofloxacin treatment.

97 The following are true of amiodarone and the lung:
a) Patients need to be on long-term therapy to develop this complication.
b) Autoantibodies are aetiologically important.
c) Old age predisposes to this condition.
d) Symptoms may mimic congestive cardiac failure.
e) Lamellar inclusion bodies are typical.

Question 98–101

98 True or false:
 a) Symptoms and severity of left ventricular failure are directly related.
 b) Patients with diastolic dysfunction have a normal sized heart.
 c) Exercise in patients with heart failure reduces mortality.
 d) Hydralazine, isosorbide dinitrate, or ACE inhibitors should not be used in combination.
 e) Low sodium is a contraindication to ACE inhibitor therapy.

99 Prophylactic therapy:
 a) Routine antibiotic prophylaxis for dental surgery is indicated in all renal transplant patients.
 b) Prophylaxis with flucloxacillin is recommended before patients with prosthetic heart valves undergo dental procedures under local anaesthetic.
 c) Combination therapy with parenteral gentamicin and amoxycillin is indicated in patients with prosthetic heart valves prior to cystoscopy.
 d) Antimalarial therapy should be started 24 hours before travel to an endemic area.
 e) Long-term therapy with penicillin or tetracycline is indicated in children who undergo splenectomy.

100 Malaria:
 a) Benign malaria is usually caused by *Plasmodium ovale*.
 b) Primaquine is used in the therapy of malaria caused by *Plasmodium malariae*, in order to reduce the risk of relapse due to chronic hepatic carriage of parasites.
 c) Proguanil is now the drug of choice for the treatment of acute chloroquine-resistant Falciparum malaria.
 d) Chloroquine may be given as a chemoprophylactic agent in pregnancy.
 e) Plasma concentrations of quinine may be elevated in patients receiving long-term cimetidine therapy.

101 True or false?
 a) Stevens–Johnson syndrome represents the severe systemic form of erythema marginatum.
 b) Pemphigoid is characterised by the formation of subepidermal blisters.
 c) IgA antibodies may be found directed against the epidermal basement membrane in dermatitis herpetiformis.
 d) Dapsone may be used to treat dermatitis herpetiformis.
 e) Herpes gestationis usually presents in the first trimester of the first pregnancy.

102 True or false?
a) The so-called 'maternity blues' have a peak incidence at 6 weeks post partum.
b) Tricyclic antidepressants are usually required in the treatment of 'maternity blues'
c) Puerperal psychosis complicates approximately 1 in 1000 deliveries.
d) Delusions do not occur in puerperal psychosis.
e) A history of previous puerperal psychosis is an indication for a therapeutic abortion.

103 A man of 75 is referred because of falls; his BP is 190/100 lying down and 170/80 standing:
a) A thiazide diuretic would be appropriate treatment.
b) He may have Parkinson's disease.
c) He may have had a recent myocardial infarction.
d) Increased alcohol ingestion would explain the clinical findings.
e) You would suspect hypoglycaemia in a diabetic.

104 An immunology laboratory has developed a new antibody test for the diagnosis of scleroderma.
a) A sensitivity of 95% means that 5% of patients with scleroderma will be antibody negative for the new test.
b) A specificity of 80% indicates that 20% of patients who are antibody negative will actually have the disease.
c) A positive predictive value of 83% implies that 17% of antibody positive subjects will not suffer from scleroderma.
d) The predictive value of the new antibody test will not be influenced by the prevalence of scleroderma in the patient population.
e) The sensitivity of the new antibody test will be directly affected by the prevalence of scleroderma in the population studied.

105 When patients seroconvert to HIV:
a) They are more infectious.
b) They may already have developed cytotoxic lymphocytes against the virally infected cells.
c) Antibodies to HIV are unlikely to develop until 20–25 weeks after the onset of symptoms.
d) Development of symptomatic primary infection suggests that a patient is more likely to develop AIDS within 3–5 years.
e) The fall in CD4 lymphocytes is offset by a rise in CD8 positive cells, so patients do not become lymphopenic.

106 Recognised features of idiopathic thrombocytopenic purpura (ITP) include:
a) A normal platelet lifespan.
b) A palpable spleen in the majority of cases.
c) Absence of megakaryocytes in the bone marrow.
d) A poor response to corticosteroids in the majority of cases.
e) Lymphadenopathy.

107 Recognised features of Hodgkin's disease include:
a) Bone pain.
b) A low relapse rate following treatment of the nodular sclerosing type.
c) Pruritus.
d) An autoimmune haemolytic anaemia.
e) Pel–Ebstein fever.

108 Which of the following may be associated with hyposplenism?
a) Coeliac disease.
b) Howell–Jolly bodies.
c) Primary biliary cirrhosis.
d) Idiopathic thrombocytopenic purpura.
e) Schizocytes.

109 Causes of a raised serum creatine kinase include:
a) Intramuscular injection.
b) Polymyalgia rheumatica.
c) Lobar pneumonia.
d) Polymyositis.
e) Hypothyroidism.

110 The affinity of haemoglobin for oxygen:
a) Is greater for HbA than HbF.
b) Is reduced by a fall in temperature.
c) Is increased by a rise in pCO_2.
d) Is greater in HbS than HbA.
e) Is increased by a fall in RBC 2,3 DPG.

111 Recognised features of sarcoidosis include:
a) Erythema multiforme.
b) Proteinuria.
c) Keratoconjunctivitis sicca.
d) Atrioventricular block.
e) Bone pain.

112 The following are recognised features of the sleep apnoea syndrome:
a) An abnormal EEG.
b) Chronic hypercapnoea.
c) Arterial desaturation.
d) Nocturnal enuresis.
e) Cyclical changes in the RR interval of 40–80 ns in a continuous ECG recording.

113 Crohn's disease is more likely than ulcerative colitis if:
a) Crypt abscesses are seen in a bowel biopsy.
b) The patient has pyoderma gangrenosa.
c) The patient has bowel haemorrhage sufficient to require transfusion.
d) The sigmoidoscopy is normal.
e) The patient has clubbing.

114 Cystic fibrosis:
a) Is characterised by a restrictive pattern of ventilation.
b) Should be treated with continuous antibiotics.
c) Patients may develop portal hypertension.
d) Patients have a predisposition to develop hypertension.
e) Patients may have abnormalities of their cilia.

115 Methaemoglobinaemia:
a) May be treated with methylene blue.
b) Can be caused by salazopyrine.
c) Will be associated with cyanosis if the methaemoglobin concentration is greater than 2 g/dl.
d) If chronic is likely to produce symptoms related to polycythaemia.
e) Is associated with a reduction in oxygen affinity.

116 Which of the following are true?
a) Infection with tetanus protects against further tetanus.
b) Typhoid vaccination will prevent typhoid infection.
c) BCG vaccine is best given subcutaneously.
d) Hepatitis B vaccine is a live attenuated vaccine.
e) A live attenuated hepatitis A virus vaccine is of use in protecting travellers against hepatitis A infection.

117 The following features of a murmur suggest an underlying cardiac defect:
a) A soft ejection systolic murmur in pregnancy.
b) Associated with a thrill.
c) Diastolic component.
d) Change with posture.
e) Heard only in the neck.

118 A woman has secondary amenorrhoea, hirsutism and a raised serum testosterone level. Which of the following are possible causes?
a) Self-administration of testosterone.
b) Anorexia nervosa.
c) Polycystic ovaries.
d) Hilar cell tumour of ovary.
e) Testicular feminisation.

119 Low molecular weight heparin preparations:
a) May be administered on a once daily basis.
b) Are generally monitored by the partial thromboplastin time.
c) Have a role in the management of the primary antiphospholipid syndrome.
d) Have a very unpredictable dose response relationship.
e) May be given orally.

120 Regarding the inflammatory response:
a) Complement activation is an important component of acute inflammation.
b) In chronic inflammation lymphocytes predominate.
c) Type IV hypersensitivity results in an acute inflammatory reaction.
d) Gout results from the stimulation of mononuclear cell infiltration by uric acid crystals.
e) IL1, IL6 and TNF are important inflammatory cytokines.

121 Which of the following are true?
a) The presence of a third sound suggests mitral stenosis is severe.
b) Fixed splitting of the second sound is suggestive of an ASD.
c) Reversed splitting of the second sound is heard in patients with HOCM.
d) Wide splitting of the second sound is associated with a left bundle branch pattern in the ECG.
e) Splitting of the first sound generally suggests pulmonary valve disease.

122 Motor neurone disease:
a) Is a cause of absent knee jerks and extensor plantars.
b) Abdominal reflexes are lost early.
c) Urinary retention and constipation are common.
d) Rarely affects the oculomotor nerve.
e) Death usually occurs within 2–4 years of presentation.

123 Extrinsic allergic alveolitis:
a) The presence of precipitating antibodies is diagnostic.
b) Wheezing is common.
c) Typically shows a fall in the FEV_1/FVC ratio.
d) May be helped by the prescription of a suitable face mask.
e) There is generally a peripheral eosinophilia.

124 In acute lymphoblastic leukaemia:
a) HbF may be raised at the time of diagnosis.
b) Patients may present with osteoporosis.
c) Blasts with B-cell markers account for 30% of cases.
d) Cranial irradiation is not performed until the patient is in remission.
e) Girls have a better prognosis than boys.

125 The following are true in leukaemia:
a) Promyelocytic leukaemia may present with disseminated intravascular coagulation.
b) Auer rods suggest acute lymphoblastic leukaemia.
c) Gum hypertrophy is a feature of acute monocytic leukaemia.
d) Widespread skin infiltration is a feature of erythroleukaemia.
e) Trisomy 8 is a common chromosome abnormality in AML.

126 Chronic myeloid leukaemia:
   a) Has a peak onset between 50 and 60 years.
   b) One third of patients develop a blast crisis which responds to acute lymphoblastic leukaemia treatment.
   c) Leukocyte alkaline phosphatase is high in the abnormal cells.
   d) Myelocytes, promyelocytes and neutrophils are prominent in the peripheral film.
   e) Patients may present with arterial thrombosis.

127 Regarding viral hepatitis:
   a) Hepatitis B, C, D and E result in chronic liver disease.
   b) 50% of chronic liver disease in developed countries is caused by hepatitis B.
   c) Interferon β is used to treat chronic viral hepatitis (B and C).
   d) 50% of patients with hepatitis C develop cirrhosis.
   e) Infection with hepatitis D is sufficient to cause cirrhosis.

128 A patient has a macrocytosis (MCV 102 fl) and a normoblastic bone marrow. The following are recognised causes:
   a) Cytotoxic drug therapy.
   b) Hypothyroidism.
   c) Pregnancy.
   d) A recent gastrointestinal bleed.
   e) Jejunal diverticulosis.

129 In the management of acute liver failure:
   a) Lactulose should be given.
   b) The patient is best managed at 45°.
   c) Plasmapheresis is useful.
   d) Renal impairment is a recognised late feature.
   e) Hyperventilation reduces cerebral oedema.

130 The irritable bowel syndrome is characterised by:
   a) Nocturnal diarrhoea.
   b) The passage of mucus.
   c) Abdominal pain which may wake the patient at night.
   d) Abdominal pain relieved by defecation.
   e) A sensation of incomplete evacuation.

131 The following are associated with hirsutism:
   a) Carbamazepine.
   b) Anorexia nervosa.
   c) Depot progesterone.
   d) Anabolic steroids.
   e) Porphyria cutanea tarda.

132 The following are recognised causes of osteoporosis:
   a) Early menopause.
   b) Thyrotoxicosis.
   c) Marfan's syndrome.
   d) Heparin.
   e) Turner's syndrome.

133 Which of the following may be associated with osteomalacia/ rickets?
a) Proximal myopathy.
b) Bone tenderness.
c) Galactosaemia.
d) Cystinuria.
e) A high plasma phosphate.

134 Paget's disease:
a) Is common in China.
b) Is primarily a disease of osteoblasts.
c) May be associated with spinal cord compression.
d) Is usually associated with an elevated serum calcium.
e) Calcitonin may be used for severe bone pain.

135 In gastric (MALT) lymphoma:
a) There is a strong association with *H. pylori* infection.
b) Characteristic lymphoepithelial cells are present.
c) Gastrectomy is the treatment of choice for most patients.
d) Early disease is treated with *H. pylori* eradication.
e) Associated paraproteinaemia is rare.

136 Paraproteinaemia:
a) Is common in elderly patients.
b) Usually requires treatment in patients over the age of 70.
c) May be associated with a peripheral neuropathy.
d) May be associated with cryoglobulinaemia.
e) Can result in systemic complement activation.

137 Which of the following are recognised features of homocystinuria?
a) Low IQ.
b) Upward dislocation of the lens.
c) Aortic valve disease.
d) Osteopetrosis.
e) Recurrent thrombotic episodes.

138 Which of the following are true?
a) Hartnup disease may present with pellagra.
b) Cystinosis is a cause of the Fanconi syndrome.
c) Renal transplantation is contraindicated in cystinosis.
d) Penicillamine is used in the treatment of cystinuria.
e) Cystine stones are radio-opaque.

139 Which of the following are true of visceral leishmaniasis?
a) Positive leishmanian skin test.
b) Hypogammaglobulinaemia is common.
c) Neutrophilia is usual.
d) General hyperpigmentation is a recognised association.
e) The diagnosis may be confirmed by splenic aspiration.

140 Lepromatous leprosy:
a) Is caused by a Gram-negative coccus.
b) Is characterised by a strongly positive lepromin test.
c) Thickened peripheral nerves are typical.
d) Hypertrichosis is a recognised feature.
e) Erythema nodosum leprosum may be expected to complicate treatment in approximately 50% of patients.

141 The following are true in patients with sickle-cell disease:
a) The presence of a spleen suggests homozygous sickle-cell disease.
b) Proliferative retinopathy may develop.
c) The oxygen dissociation curve is shifted to the left.
d) Isosthenuria may occur.
e) A severe chest syndrome is the commonest cause of death in all age-groups.

142 A solitary pulmonary nodule is observed on a chest X-ray. The following statements are true:
a) In a patient with seropositive rheumatoid arthritis the nodule is likely to be benign.
b) A calcified nodule excludes malignancy.
c) If on fluoroscopy the shadow does not move with respiration, it is not within the lung.
d) Although likely to be benign in a non-smoking man of 25, yearly chest radiographs are still appropriate.
e) If infection with *Echinococcus granulosus* is suspected, then percutaneous biopsy is the appropriate means of obtaining material for culture and histology.

143 A diagnosis of pre-eclampsia at 36 weeks would be supported by:
a) An increase in blood pressure of 30/15 mmHg compared to the booking value.
b) Epigastric pain.
c) An elevated blood uric acid level.
d) A primigravida pregnancy.
e) Proteinuria of 2 g a day.

144 In glucose-6-phosphate dehydrogenase deficiency:
a) The red blood cells may contain Heinz bodies.
b) Haemolysis may occur after ingestion of vitamin K.
c) Presentation with neonatal jaundice is common.
d) Females are more frequently affected than males.
e) RBC glutathione levels are raised.

145 Wilson's disease:
a) Commonly presents with a manic depressive illness.
b) May result in retinal abnormalities.
c) Serum copper levels are high.
d) Urine copper levels rise in response to penicillamine.
e) Is inherited as an autosomal dominant trait.

146 Recognised causes of generalised pruritus include:
a) Haemolytic jaundice.
b) Iron deficiency anaemia.
c) Hypothyroidism.
d) Morphine.
e) Tabes dorsalis.

147 Warfarin:
a) Anticoagulant effect may be inhibited by allopurinol therapy.
b) Anticoagulant effect is reduced by rifampicin.
c) There is an increased risk of bleeding with concomitant aspirin therapy due to inhibition of dicoumerol metabolism.
d) In a patient with a prosthetic heart valve, overdose of the drug should be treated with intravenous vitamin K.
e) Therapy should be monitored by regular measurement of the partial thromboplastin time.

148 Which of the following are true?
a) The incidence of Turner's syndrome is 0.3/1000 live births.
b) Lymphoedema is a recognised feature of Turner's syndrome.
c) Patent ductus arteriosus is the commonest cardiac abnormality seen in Turner's syndrome.
d) Patients with Noonan's syndrome have Turner's phenotype.
e) Pulmonary stenosis is the commonest cardiac abnormality seen in Noonan's syndrome.

149 An elderly lady has generalised lymphadenopathy, a mild anaemia and a raised WBC containing 50 × 10⁹/L lymphocytes:
a) Basket cells are likely to be present.
b) She may have a raised conjugated bilirubin.
c) She has an increased risk of shingles.
d) She may have cold agglutinins.
e) Hypergammaglobulinaemia would be expected.

150 *Listeria monocytogenes:*
a) Is an intracellular parasite.
b) Can multiply at 4°C.
c) May present with purulent conjunctivitis.
d) May be transmitted transplacentally.
e) Infection is best treated with sulphonamides.

151 The TLCO is increased in:
a) Goodpasture's syndrome.
b) Polycythaemia rubra vera.
c) Asthma.
d) The Eisenmenger syndrome.
e) Cirrhosis.

152 The following can occur in acquired haemolytic anaemia:
a) Target cells.
b) Increased urobilinogen.
c) Bone pain.
d) Methaemalbuminaemia.
e) Increased conjugated bilirubinaemia.

153 Which of the following are true of *Pneumocystis carinii*?
a) May be carried asymptomatically.
b) Is a recognised cause of hepatomegaly.
c) Pneumonitis is usually associated with a productive cough.
d) Pneumonitis is invariably accompanied by an elevated lymphocyte count.
e) The suspected diagnosis of pneumocystis pneumonia may be confirmed serologically.

154 The common peroneal nerve:
a) Is a branch of the femoral nerve.
b) Supplies the tibialis posterior muscle.
c) The superficial branch supplies the skin over the first dorsal interspace.
d) Innervates the extensor hallucis longus via nerve root L4.
e) A common peroneal nerve palsy leads to weakness of ankle eversion.

155 True or false?
a) Diabetes is a recognised cause of a mononeuritis multiplex.
b) A painful asymmetrical proximal motor neuropathy is more commonly seen in insulin-dependent compared to non-insulin-dependent diabetics.
c) In a diabetic, third nerve palsy pupillary function is affected early.
d) Postprandial diarrhoea is a recognised feature of diabetic autonomic neuropathy.
e) Diabetics are predisposed to compression neuropathies.

156 Which of the following are true of filariid infections?
a) *Wuchereria bancrofti* is transmitted by the Chrysops fly.
b) Brugian filariasis is a recognised cause of hydrocele.
c) Calabar swellings are characteristic of onchocerciasis.
d) Blindness is the commonest serious complication of onchocerciasis.
e) Praziquantel is the drug of choice in the treatment of loiasis.

157 Bacterial meningitis:
a) Pneumococcal meningitis has a mortality rate in excess of 20%.
b) Petechial haemorrhages are pathognomonic of *Neisseria meningitidis*.
c) Kernig's and Brudzinski's signs are sensitive clinical tests.
d) *Haemophilus influenzae* is the commonest cause in pre-school children.
e) Benzylpenicillin is the drug of choice for Haemophilus meningitis.

158 Oligoclonal bands in the CSF can occur in:
a) Hypothyroidism.
b) Sarcoidosis.
c) Systemic lupus erythematosis.
d) Subacute combined degeneration of the cord.
e) Subacute sclerosing panencephalitis.

159 Which of the following may be associated with a low CSF glucose concentration?
a) Subarachnoid haemorrhage.
b) Mumps meningitis.
c) Amoebic meningitis.
d) Multiple sclerosis.
e) Sarcoidosis.

160 Benign intracranial hypertension:
a) Is characterised by large ventricles on CT scanning.
b) Commonly presents with epilepsy.
c) May present with visual obscurations.
d) May be associated with severe loss of vision in 10% of cases.
e) May be treated with corticosteroids.

161 Which of the following are true of antiglomerular basement antibody disease?
a) Lung haemorrhage primarily occurs in smokers.
b) Lung haemorrhage may be precipitated by infection.
c) Classically occurs in old men.
d) Is associated with the HLA type DR2.
e) Is a cause of rapidly progressive glomerulonephritis.

162 PCR (polymerase chain reaction):
a) Needs knowledge of the DNA sequence of the flanking regions of the templates in order to design appropriate primers.
b) Can be used reliably in diagnosing herpes simplex, or tuberculous infection of the CSF.
c) Usually results in the production of a double stranded gene product.
d) Needs multiple copies of the DNA template.
e) Facilitates prenatal diagnosis on a single embryonic cell.

163 In diffuse systemic sclerosis:
a) Raynaud's phenomenon is rare.
b) Interstitial lung disease is a significant cause of morbidity or mortality.
c) Antibodies to SCL70 and to endothelial cells may be detected.
d) Treatment with high dose oral steroids may be associated with scleroderma renal crisis.
e) Angiotensin-converting enzyme inhibitors are useful in the management of hypertension in patients with this condition.

164 Hyperuricuria is often associated with:
a) Diuretics.
b) Xanthinuria.
c) Pre-eclampsia.
d) An increased MCV.
e) Crohn's disease.

165 Which of the following are true?
a) Pseudomembranous colitis is caused by *Clostridium perfringens*.
b) Pseudomembranous colitis may be treated with metronidazole.
c) Clostridium food poisoning is usually associated with severe vomiting.
d) Gas gangrene is a recognised complication of surgery to ischaemic limbs.
e) Hyperbaric oxygen may be used in the treatment of gas gangrene.

166 The following are recognised features of pulmonary embolism:
a) Syncope.
b) A normal chest X-ray.
c) Inversion of the T wave in ECG leads 1–4 suggests a large pulmonary embolus.
d) Right bundle branch block pattern.
e) Is rare during pregnancy.

167 The following increase the risk of avascular necrosis:
a) HbSC disease.
b) Thiemann's disease.
c) Alcoholism.
d) Pregnancy.
e) Achondroplasia.

168 Phaeochromocytoma:
a) The cervical sympathetic chain is the commonest extra-adrenal site.
b) Glycosuria may be demonstrated in one-third of patients during an acute hypertensive episode.
c) Patients may exhibit postural hypotension.
d) Adrenaline levels are suppressed by the administration of pentolinium.
e) When the patient is prepared for surgery beta-blockers should be introduced prior to alpha-blockade.

169 Syringomyelia/syringobulbia:
a) The majority of cases are associated with an Arnold–Chiari-type malformation.
b) May cause wasting of the small hand muscles.
c) Sensory loss on the face is confined to the area around the nose and mouth.
d) May lead to a Charcot arthropathy of the shoulders.
e) Episodes of coughing may lead to clinical deterioration.

170 Which of the following conditions are recognised causes of a spastic paraparesis?
a) Parasagittal cranial meningioma.
b) General paralysis of the insane.
c) Guillain–Barré.
d) Poliomyelitis.
e) Friedreich's ataxia.

171 Cataracts may be associated with:
a) Galactosaemia.
b) Hypoparathyroidism.
c) Rheumatoid arthritis.
d) Prolonged use of corticosteroids.
e) Long-standing uveitis.

172 Hypercalcaemia:
a) Hyperparathyroidism is the commonest cause in hospitalised patients.
b) Commonly occurs with disseminated carcinoma of the prostate.
c) Due to malignancy is often associated with a hyperchloraemic metabolic acidosis.
d) May be treated with intravenous saline and thiazide diuretics.
e) Pamidronate is effective in cases of hypercalcaemia associated with malignancy.

173 Lyme disease:
a) The VDRL is usually positive.
b) Erythema chronicum migrans is seen in 10% of cases.
c) Is a recognised cause of facial palsy.
d) Typically produces a symmetrical small joint polyarthritis.
e) May lead to prolongation of the PR interval.

174 Glue sniffing:
a) Is commoner in girls than boys.
b) Is associated with a haemolytic anaemia.
c) Is a cause of renal tubular acidosis.
d) Can lead to rhabdomyolysis.
e) Prolonged abuse can lead to cerebellar degeneration.

175 Regarding lung function: which of the following statements are true?
a) The residual volume is the volume of air remaining in the lungs at the end of a normal expiration.
b) The average male has an inspiratory reserve volume of 800 ml.
c) The vital capacity is greater in the erect than the supine position.
d) The expiratory reserve volume is greater than the inspiratory reserve volume.
e) The FEV_1/FVC ratio is typically reduced in restrictive airways disease.

176 The following are recognised associations of anticardiolipin antibodies:
a) Subarachnoid haemorrhage.
b) Chorea.
c) An increase in the prothrombin time.
d) Livedo reticularis.
e) Thrombocythaemia.

177 CNS disease in association with HIV:
a) Neuropathology due to infection with HIV can be identified in 90% of patients who die of AIDS.
b) The commonest manifestation in adult patients is encephalopathy.
c) May cause a myelopathy.
d) May be due to a direct neurotoxic effect of viral products.
e) May cause a painful peripheral neuropathy.

178 True or false:
a) In the development of atheroma, low density lipoproteins may activate endothelial cells.
b) Plaque formation takes place in the tunica media.
c) Accelerated coronary disease occurs more slowly in cardiac transplant recipients who are HLA matched with their donor.
d) Mononuclear cells which have migrated into the intima from the blood stream are transformed into foam cells following uptake of low density lipoprotein.
e) Smooth muscle proliferation is an important factor.

179 In myocardial infarction:
a) Inferior infarction is associated with mural thrombus.
b) Troponin C and I levels after infarction predict mortality.
c) Papillary muscle rupture is a recognised complication of infarction.
d) Ventricular rupture is a rare cause of mortality after infarction.
e) Right ventricular infarction usually shows more than 2 mm elevation of ST segments of leads V1 and V2.

180 Which of the following are true?
a) *Neisseria meningitidis* is a Gram-negative rod.
b) Asymptomatic nasal carriage of meningococci is common.
c) Visible petechiae are present in less than 20% of cases of meningococcal meningitis.
d) Sulphonamides are the antibiotic of choice for meningococcal prophylaxis.
e) Intravenous chloramphenicol is the antibiotic of choice for acute meningococcaemia.

181 Which of the following are true?
a) Acetylcholine is the neurotransmitter released at all sympathetic ganglia.
b) Acetylcholine acts on muscarinic receptors at the anomalous sympathetic nerve effector junction.
c) Acetylcholine is metabolised primarily by pseudocholinesterase in the synaptic cleft.
d) Noradrenaline acts at muscarinic receptors.
e) White rami communicantes carrying sympathetic nerves leave the spinal cord from C1 to L2.

182 The following are true of autonomic neuropathy:
a) Can occur as part of an acute Guillain–Barré syndrome.
b) Forms part of the Shy–Drager syndrome.
c) Is a recognised complication of Chagas' disease.
d) During the Valsalva manoeuvre on releasing the expiratory pressure the blood pressure immediately overshoots.
e) Leads to a reduction in the heart rate response to deep breathing.

183 Which of the following are true of familial Mediterranean fever?
a) Abdominal pain is the commonest presenting symptom.
b) Attacks usually last for several weeks.
c) Is a recognised cause of splenomegaly.
d) May be treated with colchicine.
e) The onset of nephrotic syndrome is associated with a good prognosis.

184 Which of the following are true of amyloidosis?
a) Bronchiectasis may lead to AL amyloid deposition.
b) AA amyloid usually presents with proteinuria.
c) 50% of cases of AA amyloid die within 5 years of diagnosis.
d) Macroglossia is a feature of AA amyloidosis.
e) Beta 2 microglobulin is the primary component of amyloid fibrils in cases of haemodialysis arthropathy.

185 Alport's syndrome: true or false
a) Females are more frequently affected than males.
b) Haematuria is the commonest presenting feature.
c) Conductive deafness is common.
d) Serum complement levels are usually low.
e) Commonly leads to end stage renal failure in females.

186 Anderson–Fabry disease:
a) Is inherited in an autosomal recessive fashion.
b) Results from a deficiency of the enzyme hexosaminidase A.
c) Can present in childhood with pain and paraesthesiae in the extremities.
d) Is associated with a psoriatic-type rash.
e) Is a recognised cause of renal failure.

187 **Diabetic nephropathy:**
a) Occurs in over 80% of type 1 insulin-dependent diabetics.
b) Initially leads to an increase in the glomerular filtration rate.
c) Microalbuminuria is often an early clinical finding.
d) Immunofluorescence shows linear deposits of IgG along the capillary basement membrane.
e) Haemodialysis is the treatment of choice for end stage renal disease.

188 **Which of the following are true?**
a) The plasma urea level may be increased by tetracyclines.
b) The plasma creatinine may be disproportionately elevated in comparison with the urea following a gastrointestinal bleed.
c) With a urine flow rate of less than 2 ml/min, up to 70% of the filtered urea may be reabsorbed by the tubules.
d) Liver failure is associated with a low plasma urea level.
e) Due to renal reserve the plasma creatinine level does not rise much until the glomerular filtration rate falls to approximately 15 ml/min.

189 **Which of the following are true?**
a) Hypernatraemia is usually due to a gain in extracellular sodium ions.
b) Diabetes insipidus is a cause of hypernatraemia.
c) Hyperlipidaemia may be associated with a low plasma sodium level.
d) The nephrotic syndrome is a cause of hypotonic hyponatraemia.
e) Rapid correction of hyponatraemia may be complicated by the development of central pontine myelinolysis.

190 **Polio virus:**
a) Transmission occurs primarily by respiratory droplet spread.
b) 10% of those infected with the virus will develop paralytic poliomyelitis.
c) Tonsillectomy increases the incidence of bulbar involvement.
d) The majority of outbreaks are due to type 2 polio virus strain.
e) Salk inactivated polio vaccine is routinely used for immunisation purposes in the United Kingdom.

191 **T cells:**
a) Are principally implicated in host defence against bacterial infections.
b) Typically are CD3 positive.
c) Produce interferon gamma as the main cytokine.
d) Are predominantly involved in type I and II hypersensitivity reactions.
e) CD4/CD8 ratio varies between normal subjects.

192 Wernicke's encephalopathy:
a) Is due to pyridoxine deficiency.
b) Can occur in hyperemesis gravidarum.
c) Is commonly associated with a peripheral motor neuropathy.
d) In acute cases is associated with petechial haemorrhages in the region of the mamillary bodies.
e) May be precipitated in a susceptible individual by a large glucose load.

193 Recognised associations of chronic alcohol abuse include:
a) Hepatocellular carcinoma.
b) Mesangial IgA glomerulonephritis.
c) An increased incidence of ischaemic heart disease.
d) Avascular necrosis of the femoral head.
e) An increased risk of lymphomas.

194 Which of the following are recognised causes of raised plasma triglyceride levels?
a) Nephrotic syndrome.
b) Hypergammaglobulinaemia.
c) Hyperthyroidism.
d) Chronic renal failure.
e) Thiazide diuretics.

195 In the Fredrickson/WHO classification of hyperlipidaemic states, which of the following statements are true?
a) Plasma VLDL is elevated in type IIa.
b) Type IIa is inherited in an autosomal dominant fashion.
c) Type I is associated with an increased risk of ischaemic heart disease.
d) Lipaemia retinalis can occur in type IV hyperlipidaemia.
e) Tendon xanthomas are typical of type IIa hyperlipidaemia.

196 Which of the following are associated with hydrocephalus?
a) Arnold–Chiari syndrome.
b) Intraventricular haemorrhage.
c) Möbius syndrome.
d) Down's syndrome.
e) Dandy Walker syndrome.

197 Good control of diabetes in pregnancy:
a) Is achieved by the use of oral biguanides.
b) Maintains blood glucose of 10–12 mmol/L.
c) Reduces the incidence of polyhydramnios.
d) Decreases fetal hyperinsulinism.
e) Is best monitored by testing the urine four times a day.

198 In bereavement:
   a) Delayed grief is said to occur if more than 2 weeks elapse before grieving begins.
   b) Anger is a common manifestation of the normal grief reaction.
   c) The bereaved will often search for the lost person.
   d) Diarrhoea may occur during the acute reaction.
   e) Mortality of surviving widowers is lower than their married counterparts.

199 Recognised side-effects of Ecstasy (methylenedioxymethylamphetamine) are:
   a) Fulminant hyperthermia.
   b) Disseminated intravascular coagulation.
   c) ADH secretion.
   d) Interaction with lithium.
   e) Liver damage.

200 Which of the following statements regarding glomerulonephritis are correct?
   a) The nephrotic syndrome is the commonest presenting feature of acute diffuse exudative proliferative glomerulonephritis (post-streptococcal GN).
   b) Respiratory tract infections may be followed by macroscopic haematuria in cases of mesangial IgA disease.
   c) Hypertension is common in patients with a diffuse proliferative crescentic glomerulonephritis.
   d) On urine microscopy, dysmorphic red blood cells are suggestive of glomerulonephritis.
   e) In general a renal biopsy should be performed in all cases of suspected glomerulonephritis occurring in adults.

201 Membranoproliferative glomerulonephritis:
   a) Is common in children.
   b) Type 1 is associated with subepithelial deposits.
   c) Type 2 is associated with C3 nephritic factor.
   d) May be associated with crescent formation.
   e) Does not normally lead to end stage renal failure.

202 Recognised causes of optic atrophy include:
   a) Leber's disease.
   b) Syphilis.
   c) Giant cell arteritis.
   d) Vitamin B_{12} deficiency.
   e) Myasthenia gravis.

203 Which of the following may be associated with tunnel vision?
   a) Abetalipoproteinaemia.
   b) Papillitis.
   c) Refsum's disease.
   d) Tabes dorsalis.
   e) Papilloedema.

204 Reiter's syndrome:
a) May be triggered by *Shigella flexneri*.
b) Arthritis typically involves the upper limbs in a symmetrical fashion.
c) Circinate balanitis is usually painful.
d) Enthesopathy is common.
e) Rarely progresses to a chronic arthritis.

205 Acute intermittent porphyria:
a) Is inherited in an autosomal dominant fashion.
b) Commonly presents in childhood.
c) Is associated with photosensitivity.
d) May be associated with a peripheral motor neuropathy.
e) Delta aminolaevulinic acid levels are only high during an acute attack.

206 Which of the following are true of porphyria cutanea tarda?
a) Increased skin fragility may occur in isolation.
b) Commonly leads to alopecia.
c) Is often associated with hepatomegaly.
d) May be treated with regular blood transfusions.
e) High urine levels of delta aminolaevulinic acid occur.

207 True or false?
a) Neurological symptoms do not occur in variegate porphyria.
b) β-carotene is used in the treatment of variegate porphyria photosensitivity.
c) Diazepam is contraindicated in acute intermittent porphyria.
d) Phenytoin is the anticonvulsant of choice in acute intermittent porphyria.
e) Chloroquine may be used in the treatment of non-acute porphyrias.

208 Which of the following statements are true?
a) Impaired skin hypersensitivity (type IV) to candida is a recognised consequence of malnutrition.
b) The calorific requirement of a hypercatabolic patient is of the order of 2000 kcal in 24 hours.
c) Hypercatabolic patients require up to 12 g of nitrogen in 24 hours.
d) Ketosis is a common finding in hypercatabolic patients.
e) Lactose is the predominant energy source in standard enteral feeds.

209 Recognised first-rank symptoms of schizophrenia include:
a) Short-term memory loss.
b) Visual hallucinations.
c) Thought broadcasting.
d) General apathy.
e) Primary delusions.

210 Which are true of depression?
a) Men are affected more commonly than women.
b) In mild illness difficulty in falling asleep is often a problem.
c) Nihilistic delusions may occur.
d) Patients may present with an inability to concentrate and retain facts.
e) Tricyclic antidepressants would be expected to work within 7 days.

211 Which of the following are true?
a) Refusal to maintain body weight above the minimum for height and age is used as a diagnostic criterion for anorexia nervosa.
b) Axillary and pubic hair may be lost in anorexia nervosa.
c) Painless enlarged parotid glands is often an early sign in bulimia nervosa.
d) Tricyclic antidepressants have been used with success in the treatment of bulimia nervosa.
e) The prognosis for anorexia nervosa is better than for bulimia nervosa.

212 Alzheimer's disease:
a) Is associated with the presence of neurofibrillary tangles in the cerebral cortex.
b) Is a rare cause of progressive presenile dementia.
c) There is an increased incidence in Down's syndrome.
d) Usually presents with mild cerebellar signs.
e) The EEG often shows diffuse slow wave activity.

213 The following are associated with sideroblastic anaemia:
a) Chronic alcohol ingestion.
b) Antituberculous chemotherapy.
c) Rheumatoid arthritis.
d) Lead poisoning.
e) A raised haemoglobin F.

214 The following are true of clinical trials:
a) In a single-blind clinical trial the doctor is usually unaware of the specific treatment being administered.
b) In general a placebo response is more likely if the placebo is coloured blue rather than red.
c) Fewer patients are required in a parallel design clinical trial compared to a crossover trial.
d) Crossover trials are useful in looking for short-term symptomatic relief of chronic conditions.
e) Crossover trials are best used for drugs with a short duration of onset of action.

215 The following are true of HIV:
a) HIV virus only binds to CD4 molecules.
b) HIV can be transmitted in a cell-free form.
c) A low CD4 count is pathognomic of HIV.
d) Western blot is more sensitive than ELISA in diagnosing HIV.
e) Optimal pharmacological therapy can result in reversal of low CD4 cell count.

216 Toxocariasis:
a) The adult worms live in the intestine of sheep.
b) Man is infected by larvae which enter through the skin.
c) Patients may present with a squint.
d) Is associated with an eosinophilia.
e) Is a recognised cause of hepatomegaly.

217 The following are recognised features of toxoplasma infections:
a) Generalised tender lymphadenopathy.
b) Splenomegaly.
c) Peripheral neuropathy.
d) Cerebral calcification visible on plain skull X-ray.
e) A positive Sabin–Feldman dye test.

218 Pityriasis versicolor:
a) Is caused by a virus.
b) The rash is non-pruritic.
c) Lesions heal with hyperpigmentation.
d) Is treated with topical 5-iodo-deoxyuridine.
e) Infrequently recurs.

219 Pulmonary eosinophilia:
a) Is associated with a peripheral blood eosinophil count > 400 mm^3.
b) May be caused by sulphonamides.
c) Due to *Aspergillus fumigatus* may be associated with proximal bronchiectasis.
d) Due to helminth infection is usually accompanied by a normal serum IgE level.
e) Cryptogenic pulmonary eosinophilia typically responds slowly to corticosteroids.

220 Recognised causes of photosensitivity include:
a) Chlorpromazine.
b) Tetracyclines.
c) Frusemide.
d) Chlorpropamide.
e) Nalidixic acid.

221 Normal pregnancy is associated with:
a) An elevated blood urea.
b) An elevated uric acid level.
c) An elevated fasting blood sugar.
d) Decreased serum albumin.
e) Decreased serum lipids.

222 Gastro-oesophageal reflux disease (GORD):
   a) Affects quality of life as severely as stable angina.
   b) H2 antagonists are as good as proton pump inhibitor therapy in achieving relief of symptoms.
   c) Affects about 10% of the general population.
   d) May lead to malignancy.
   e) May be responsible for angiogram-negative chest pain.

223 Which of the following statements are true?
   a) The precision of an assay is the way in which repeated observations conform to themselves.
   b) The accuracy of an observation is the closeness of the observation to the quantity intended to be measured.
   c) A sensitive assay is one where there are few false positives.
   d) The incidence of a disorder is the percentage of the population suffering from the disorder at any one time.
   e) The higher the specificity, the less useful a test is for screening.

224 Anxiety neurosis:
   a) May present with palpitations.
   b) Tetany may occur.
   c) May be complicated by unprovoked panic attacks.
   d) Patients may complain of poor memory.
   e) Is usually associated with a poor prognosis.

225 Recognised complications of ulcerative colitis include:
   a) Sclerosing cholangitis.
   b) Pancreatitis.
   c) Venous thrombosis of the legs.
   d) Gastrocolic fistula.
   e) Carcinoma of the bile duct.

226 Cholera:
   a) The underlying organism is a Gram-positive shaped rod.
   b) In endemic areas attack rates are highest in adults.
   c) Achlorhydria renders individuals susceptible to the disease.
   d) Enterotoxin inhibits glucose-facilitated transport across the epithelial cell.
   e) The mean sodium concentration in stool is lower in adults than children.

227 Helicobacter pylori:
   a) Was first recognised in pathology samples more than 100 years ago.
   b) Is involved in the aetiology of 90% of duodenal ulcers.
   c) In the UK 80% of the general population is infected.
   d) Metronidazole resistance is rarely reported in the UK.
   e) All patients with duodenal ulcer need *H. pylori* eradication.

228 Which of the following statements are true?
a) The presence of an internuclear ophthalmoplegia is strongly suggestive of multiple sclerosis.
b) An internuclear ophthalmoplegia is usually due to a lesion affecting the medial lemniscus.
c) A lesion of the right vestibular apparatus will typically produce nystagmus which is maximal on looking to the right.
d) A right cerebellar hemisphere lesion will typically produce nystagmus which is maximal on looking to the left.
e) Vertical nystagmus may be induced by phenytoin toxicity.

229 Barrett's oesophagus:
a) Refers to deep penetrating peptic ulcers which occur in the squamous epithelium of the lower oesophagus.
b) Strictures do not occur.
c) The condition is pre-malignant.
d) The commonest complication is massive haemorrhage.
e) Treatment should always consist of surgical excision.

230 Primary pulmonary hypertension:
a) Primary pulmonary hypertension can be associated with pericardial disease.
b) An autosomal recessive inheritance is seen is some patients.
c) Pulmonary artery pressure falls during exercise.
d) Raised endothelin levels have been implicated in pathogenesis.
e) A response to calcium antagonists is compatible with 95% 5-year survival

231 Skin tumours:
a) Malignant melanomas are the commonest malignant skin tumours in this country.
b) Xeroderma pigmentosum predisposes to the development of malignant skin tumours in skin exposed to UV light.
c) Basal cell carcinomas near the nose and ear are best treated by radiotherapy.
d) Hutchinson's melanotic freckle may develop into an invasive melanoma.
e) The Breslow level is the most important prognostic indicator in malignant melanoma.

232 Parasuicide and suicide:
a) Parasuicide is commonest in females whereas suicide is commoner in males.
b) Epileptics have an increased risk of attempted suicide.
c) Parasuicide is often preceded by heavy alcohol consumption.
d) Extensive premeditation suggests a serious suicide attempt.
e) 50% of parasuicide patients have an underlying serious psychiatric illness.

233 Huntington's chorea:
a) Is typically inherited as an autosomal dominant condition.
b) Atrophy of the caudate nucleus is typical.
c) Symptoms commonly present between the ages of 20 and 30 years, with a change in personality.
d) Epilepsy is common in juvenile onset disease.
e) Tetrabenazine may be used to control chorea.

234 The following diseases are caused by abnormal DNA triplets:
a) Friedreich's ataxia
b) Fragile X syndrome
c) Sly syndrome
d) Machado Joseph disease
e) Hunter's syndrome

235 In coarctation of the aorta:
a) A diastolic murmur may be heard over the spine.
b) Hypertension may be refractory to therapy.
c) An apical click may be heard on auscultation in the aortic area.
d) Tricuspid stenosis may accompany the defect in approximately 50% of patients.
e) Surgical correction in adults cures hypertension in 90% of cases.

236 Pneumoconioses:
a) Asbestosis is associated typically with apical lung fibrosis.
b) Eggshell calcification of the hilar lymph nodes is characteristic of silicosis.
c) There is a significant increase in infection with *Mycobacteria* in asbestosis.
d) The radiological features of berylliosis may resemble those seen in sarcoidosis.
e) Calcification is common in coal workers' pneumoconiosis.

237 Mitral valve disease:
a) Mitral incompetence may be caused by methysergide.
b) Mixed mitral valve disease is a recognized complication of rheumatic heart disease.
c) Mitral prolapse is the commonest cause of mitral incompetence in the developed world.
d) Surgery can be deferred in a patient with mitral incompetence if ejection fraction is 50%.
e) Patients with heart failure and mitral incompetence have 90% mortality without surgery.

238 Q fever (*Coxiella burnetii*):
a) May manifest as infective endocarditis.
b) Is a recognised cause of hepatic granulomas.
c) A rash is usual.
d) May be effectively treated with benzyl penicillin.
e) Antibodies to phase 1 antigens are elevated during the acute illness.

239 Haemochromatosis:
a) Is inherited as an autosomal dominant.
b) Diabetes, hepatomegaly and skin darkening is seen in the majority of patients.
c) May present with pain affecting the metacarpo-phalyngeal joints.
d) HLA H, a class I-like gene, is linked to the disease.
e) Males are affected five times more often than females.

240 Pemphigus vulgaris:
a) Is associated with antibodies to the epidermal basement membrane.
b) Pemphigus usually presents between 20 and 30 years of age.
c) Pemphigus rarely involves the mucous membranes.
d) The blisters heal with scarring.
e) Is best treated with low doses of prednisolone.

241 Which of the following statements are true?
a) The spinal cord extends from the foramen magnum to the lower border of the second lumbar vertebra.
b) Pain and temperature are carried in the dorsal columns of the spinal cord.
c) Extrinsic spinal cord compression is associated in the early stages with marked sensory signs.
d) The Brown–Séquard syndrome is characterised by contralateral loss of pain and temperature below the level of the lesion.
e) A lumbar myelogram should be performed in all patients with an acute spastic paraparesis.

242 True or false?
a) Pyridoxine deficiency results in pellagra.
b) Hypercarotenosis results in yellow sclerae.
c) Edentulous patients with scurvy do not have bleeding gums.
d) Acrodermatitis enteropathica is associated with manganese deficiency.
e) Bitôt's spots are a feature of nicotinamide deficiency.

243 Regarding the carcinoid syndrome:
a) Symptoms only occur if hepatic secondaries are present.
b) Flushing may be accompanied by oedema.
c) Mitral regurgitation is a recognised complication.
d) Coeliac disease may elevate urinary 5-HIAA levels.
e) Somatostatin analogues may be used to treat diarrhoea.

244 Herpes simplex encephalitis:
a) May be associated with normal cerebrospinal fluid.
b) Is usually associated with visible herpetic lesions on the nose.
c) Predominantly affects the temporal lobes.
d) Idoxuridine is the drug of choice.
e) The EEG is characteristic.

245 Benign essential tremor:
   a) Is worse at rest.
   b) Is often relieved by alcohol.
   c) May be treated with propranolol.
   d) Is inherited in an autosomal recessive fashion.
   e) Is due to a lesion in the subthalamic area.

246 For a population which is normally distributed:
   a) The mean will be greater than the mode.
   b) The median is that value which occurs most frequently.
   c) The standard deviation is obtained by squaring the variance.
   d) 68% of the population would be expected to lie within +/– 1 SD of the mean.
   e) 5% would be expected to lie 2 SD below the mean.

247 Membranous glomerulonephritis:
   a) Usually presents with proteinuria.
   b) Microscopic haematuria is common.
   c) In 90% of cases is idiopathic in nature.
   d) May be associated with gold treatment.
   e) Rarely progresses to end stage renal failure.

248 Systemic vasculitis:
   a) Is always associated with a positive ANCA.
   b) May occur in association with viral infections.
   c) Is usually limited to small arteries.
   d) May be associated with hypocomplementaemia.
   e) Is unlikely to involve the renal vasculature in the absence of cutaneous lesions.

249 The secretion of gastric acid:
   a) Is inhibited by somatostatin.
   b) Is dependent on parietal cells.
   c) Is higher in women than in men.
   d) May be stimulated by acetylcholine, histamine, and amino acids.
   e) Gastrin is produced by G cells in the antrum.

250 Which of the following syndromes are associated with an increased risk of malignancy?
   a) Gorlin–Goltz syndrome.
   b) Epiloia.
   c) Tylosis.
   d) Ataxia telangiectasia.
   e) Chediak–Higashi syndrome.

251 Which of the following investigations support a diagnosis of prerenal failure in an oliguric patient?
   a) A urinary Na of > 20 mmol/L.
   b) A urine osmolality of 280 mosmol/L.
   c) A urine to plasma urea ratio of > 20.
   d) A urine to plasma osmolality ratio > 1.1.
   e) Urinary sediment containing red cell counts.

252 Which of the following are normal findings in pregnancy?
a) A rise in the cardiac output of 1.5 L/min during the first trimester.
b) A short apical diastolic murmur.
c) A third heart sound.
d) A pulmonary ejection murmur.
e) A right ventricular heave.

253 Acute fatty liver of pregnancy:
a) Usually has a good outcome.
b) Abdominal pain is rare.
c) Is often associated with fatty infiltration of the renal tubules.
d) Pyrexia is typical.
e) Is characterised by very high levels of transaminases.

254 Regarding primary biliary cirrhosis:
a) 95% of patients are female.
b) Anti-mitochondrial antibodies are present in up to 75% of patients.
c) Alkaline phosphatase may be elevated in the face of normal bilirubin levels.
d) Pruritus can occur in the absence of jaundice.
e) Osteoporosis is often seen.

255 Regarding melatonin:
a) Maximum melatonin secretion is at night.
b) Melatonin is essential to normal testicular function.
c) Melatonin is a free radical scavenger.
d) Albinos have higher levels of melatonin production.
e) Melatonin may be of use in treating jet lag.

256 Pulmonary alveolar proteinosis:
a) Is associated with an obstructive lung defect.
b) Secondary infection with nocardia is common.
c) Bilateral hilar lymphadenopathy is typical.
d) Should be treated with corticosteroids.
e) May be treated with bronchoalveolar lavage.

257 Regarding intracranial aneurysms:
a) 1% of the general population have aneurysms.
b) Repeat bleeds from a second aneurysm are uncommon.
c) Intracranial aneurysms are more dangerous than extracranial aneurysms.
d) A third of patients have headaches weeks before rupture.
e) Magnetic resonance scanning is useful after aneurysmal surgery.

258 Recognised complications of rheumatoid arthritis include:
a) Obliterative bronchiolitis.
b) Heart block.
c) Photosensitive skin rash.
d) Distal sensory neuropathy.
e) Generalised lymphadenopathy.

259 Recognised X-ray changes of rheumatoid arthritis include:
a) Juxta-articular osteosclerosis.
b) Sacroiliitis.
c) Geodes.
d) Marginal erosions.
e) Calcification of entheses.

260 The following are true of epilepsy therapy:
a) Sodium valproate is teratogenic.
b) Lamotrigine may be associated with hepatic dysfunction.
c) Vigabantrin is useful as a first line agent against seizures.
d) Gabapentin is used in partial seizures.
e) Benzodiazepines have long term anti-epileptic effects.

261 The following drugs have clinically important first pass hepatic metabolism:
a) Amitryptyline.
b) Pethidine.
c) Labetolol.
d) Ethyloestradiol.
e) Pentazocine.

262 The following are consistent with hypokalaemia:
a) Peaked P waves.
b) *Torsades de points* arrhythmia.
c) ST-segment elevation.
d) A shortening of the PR interval.
e) U waves.

263 A prolonged QT interval is associated with:
a) Myxoedema.
b) Renal failure.
c) Tricyclic antidepressants.
d) Amiodarone.
e) Hypermagnesaemia.

264 Hypothermia is associated with:
a) Muscular rigidity.
b) Hyperglycaemia.
c) A diuresis.
d) J waves on the ECG.
e) Shortened QT interval.

265 The following are associated with pulmonary hypertension:
a) Sickle-cell disease.
b) Scleroderma.
c) Adulterated rapeseed oil ingestion.
d) Appetite suppressants.
e) Cirrhosis.

266 The following are true:
a) Interleukin-1 acts on neutrophils, monocytes and lymphocytes, causing them to be retained in sites of inflammation.
b) Th 1 cells produce interleukin-2.
c) Th 2 cells produce interleukin-4 and 10.
d) Tumour necrosis factor is produced by neutrophils.
e) γ-interferon induces the expression of class II HLA molecules on the surface of cells.

267 The following are recognised features of Legionnaires' disease:
a) Gastroenteritis.
b) Rhabdomyolysis.
c) Splenomegaly is common.
d) Cold agglutinins.
e) Lymphopenia.

268 Regarding arrhythmias after myocardial infarction:
a) Bradycardia is an ominous sign.
b) Second degree block usually requires pacing.
c) Type I heart block has a worse prognosis than type II heart block.
d) Ventricular fibrillation is found in about 5% of infarction victims.
e) Sotalol reduces mortality post infarction.

269 With regard to the pupil, which of the following are true?
a) The Marcus Gunn phenomenon results from a lesion of the parasympathetic effector nerve fibres.
b) The Argyll–Robertson pupil of syphilis will dilate in response to atropine.
c) Holmes–Adie pupils are commoner in women.
d) Adrenaline 1:1000 will dilate the pupil in a Horner's syndrome due to a lesion below the superior cervical ganglion.
e) Dilated pupils are a feature of a pontine bleed.

270 Urinary calcium:
a) Excretion is reduced by parathyroid hormone.
b) Excretion is increased by metabolic acidosis.
c) Excretion is increased by phosphate depletion.
d) Excretion is principally determined by proximal tubular function.
e) Reabsorption is principally active.

271 The following are characteristic of type A lactic acidosis:
a) Hypercapnoea.
b) Hypertension.
c) Anion gap 10–18 mmol.
d) Base deficit > – 5 mmol.
e) Chloride > 110 mmol.

272 Clear, fresh urine becoming coloured may be seen in:
a) Homocystinuria.
b) Haemolytic anaemia.
c) Pentosuria.
d) Laxative abuse.
e) Porphyria variegata.

273 In the treatment of a pregnant woman with Graves' disease:
a) Thyroxine crosses the placenta.
b) The fetus may be affected by transplacental carriage of IgM autoantibodies.
c) Carbimazole is contraindicated.
d) The mother may require thyroxine supplements.
e) Plasma exchange is the treatment of choice.

274 Concerning atrial fibrillation:
a) Atrial fibrillation is the most common of the sustained tachyarrhythmias.
b) Is a recognised complication of carcinoma of the bronchus.
c) May occur with acute pericarditis.
d) Aspirin and warfarin show equal efficacy in preventing strokes.
e) Transoesophageal echo monitoring produces substantial benefit during cardioversion.

275 Chondrocalcinosis may be associated with:
a) Hyperthyroidism.
b) Haemochromatosis.
c) Paget's disease.
d) Hypoparathyroidism.
e) Osteoarthritis.

276 True or false:
a) Genomic imprinting was first discovered in patients with genetic diseases.
b) Autosomal genes are imprinted.
c) DNA splicing is responsible for imprinting.
d) Amniocentesis is performed later than chorionic villous sampling.
e) If RFLPs on both sides of a mutant gene are found, the chance of inheritance of the same mutant gene is much higher.

277 True or false?
a) The normal sagittal diameter of the cervical spine is 10 mm.
b) Cervical spondylotic changes are maximal at C1/C2.
c) An L4/5 disc lesion usually affects the L4 nerve root.
d) Infraspinatus innervated by the subscapular nerve is responsible for externally rotating the shoulder.
e) Knee extension is mediated by the hamstring muscles which are innervated by L5.

278 The following are true of Paget's disease:
a) Paget's disease is found in 10% of patients over 55.
b) Osteosclerotic bone enlargement is seen in Paget's disease and prostate cancer.
c) Arthritic pain is common.
d) Patients with radiologically defined disease have abnormal alkaline phosphatase values.
e) Biphosphonates are the treatment of choice.

279 Concerning the kidney:
a) Movement of the diaphragm in respiration causes movement of the kidney of the order of 3–5 cm.
b) Toldt's fascia is the weak anterior leaf of Gerota's fascia.
c) The pelvis of the kidney lies between the renal vein and main renal artery.
d) Ureteric duplication with ectopic ureter is easily seen on intravenous pyelography.
e) Crossed renal ectopia occurs in 1:7000 births.

280 Defecation:
a) The initial stimulus for defecation is the distension of the rectum with faeces.
b) The urge to defecate first occurs when the pressure in the rectum is about 20 mmHg.
c) Defecation is a spinal reflex that can be voluntarily inhibited by keeping the internal sphincter contracted.
d) Distension of the stomach by food frequently causes a desire to defecate.
e) Faecal incontinence during coughing or sneezing is called urge incontinence.

281 Micturition:
a) Follows stimulation of the sympathetic nerves to the bladder.
b) Depends on the integrity of a lumbar spinal reflex arc.
c) Bladder filling without a rise in pressure until the bladder is almost full is a normal occurrence and is a manifestation of the law of Laplace.
d) The normal voiding pressure is 70 mmHg.
e) Urine remaining in the male urethra after micturition is expelled by several contractions of the bulbocavernosus muscle.

282 The following are true:
a) Digitalis has an inotropic action in patients in sinus rhythm.
b) Digitalis decreases quality of life of patients with cardiac failure.
c) Digitalis may increase the risk of myocardial infarction.
d) Digitalis increases arrhythmic deaths in treated patients.
e) Digitalis decreases mortality of patients with cardiac failure.

283 Which of the following may be associated with a low level of C3?
a) Post-streptococcal glomerulonephritis.
b) Idiopathic membranous glomerulonephritis.
c) Cryoglobulinaemia.
d) Minimal change glomerulonephritis.
e) Infective endocarditis.

284 Which of the following are causes of a positive R wave in lead V1?
a) Wolff-Parkinson-White type A.
b) An inferior myocardial infarction.
c) Left bundle branch block.
d) Digoxin toxicity.
e) Kartagener's syndrome.

285 In the blood supply of the heart:
a) Dominance refers to the origin of the posterior (inferior) interventricular artery.
b) Although variable the sinoatrial node is more often supplied by the left coronary artery.
c) The left ventricle is supplied totally by the left coronary artery.
d) The atrioventricular node is supplied by the inferior interventricular artery in most cases.
e) Major conduction disturbances in anterior infarctions imply substantial myocardial damage.

286 In the bronchial tree and thorax:
a) Inhaled liquids are more likely to enter the apical segment of the right lower lobe.
b) The right main bronchus is more vertical than the left main bronchus.
c) The carina usually lies in the midline.
d) The pulmonary ligaments stablise the lung roots.
e) The surface marking of the oblique fissures can be taken as approximately the line of the fifth rib.

287 Which of the following are true?
a) Hypokalaemia does not occur in systemic acidosis.
b) Hyperkalaemia is a recognised side-effect of captopril.
c) Hyperkalaemia may be associated with periodic paralysis.
d) Hyperventilation may persist for some time after bicarbonate has been given to correct a systemic acidosis.
e) A neutrophilia accompanying a metabolic acidosis strongly implies a bacterial infection.

288 Recognised causes of a salt-losing nephropathy include:
a) Analgesic abuse.
b) Tuberculosis.
c) Polycystic disease.
d) Sickle-cell disease.
e) The recovery phase of acute tubular necrosis.

289 Which of the following are true?
a) In adults salicylate toxicity is associated with a respiratory acidosis.
b) Nikethamide is a recognised cause of a respiratory acidosis.
c) Pulmonary oedema may give rise to a respiratory alkalosis.
d) Ankylosing spondylitis is commonly associated with a respiratory alkalosis.
e) Dextropropoxyphene may be associated with a respiratory alkalosis.

290 Clinical features of hypothalamic lesions include:
a) Anorexia.
b) Hypoprolactinaemia.
c) Hypothermia.
d) Somnolence.
e) A bitemporal hemianopia.

291 Which of the following are true?
a) Plasma ACTH levels are high in cases of adrenal adenoma.
b) Cortisol levels in Cushing's disease suppress with a low-dose dexamethasone suppression test.
c) Conn's syndrome is characterised by a hypokalaemic metabolic acidosis.
d) Transsphenoidal hypophysectomy is associated with rhinorrhoea in 70% of cases.
e) Ketoconazole may be useful in suppression of cortisol after radiation for pituitary tumour.

292 Assessing patients with ischaemic heart disease:
a) Exercise electrocardiography is of value in patients with unstable angina.
b) Hot spots during an exercise 201-thallium scan indicate ischaemic areas.
c) A fall in the ejection fraction during exercise is associated with a worse prognosis.
d) A maximal exercise ECG should be performed 10 days after an uncomplicated anterior wall myocardial infarction.
e) Coronary angiography has a mortality rate of 1%.

293 Atrial septal defects:
a) The majority are ostium secundum defects.
b) The incidence of bacterial endocarditis is greater for ostium secundum than primum defects.
c) A mitral diastolic murmur is usually present in ostium secundum defects.
d) Ostium secundum defects are usually asymptomatic in childhood.
e) An ostium secundum defect in adult life may present with atrial fibrillation.

294 Neurological features of hypothyroidism include:
a) Carpal tunnel syndrome.
b) Hoffman's syndrome.
c) Proximal myopathy.
d) Ataxia.
e) Deafness.

295 Recognised features of dystrophia myotonica include:
a) Hypertrichosis.
b) Cardiomyopathy.
c) Hypogonadism.
d) Hypoglycaemia.
e) Low IQ.

296 Osteogenesis imperfecta:
a) Blue sclerae are always present.
b) May be associated with deafness.
c) In childhood is a differential diagnosis of child abuse.
d) Is primarily a disease of elastin.
e) Serum acid phosphatase is often elevated.

297 A woman with Vitamin-D-resistant rickets seeks genetic counseling; which of the following are correct?
a) 25% of her offspring will be affected.
b) A male child has a 50% chance of being affected.
c) All daughters will be carriers.
d) Affected daughters have a more severe disease than affected sons.
e) Affected children can be diagnosed at birth.

298 Antituberculous therapy:
a) Side-effects with isoniazid are more commonly seen in fast acetylators.
b) 'Rifampicin flu' is usually seen in people taking rifampicin on a daily basis.
c) Red–green colour impairment is often an early sign of ethambutol-induced optic neuritis.
d) Ethambutol accumulates in renal failure.
e) Hyperuricaemia is a recognised side-effect of pyrazinamide.

Question 299–300

299 Which of the following are recognised causes of a painful myopathy?
a) Osteomalacia.
b) Hypokalaemia.
c) Cushing's syndrome.
d) *Trichinella spiralis.*
e) Heroin abuse.

300 In Epstein–Barr infections:
a) The atypical mononuclear cells are B cells.
b) Autoimmune haemolytic anaemia is well recognised.
c) Thrombocytopenic purpura may occur.
d) Patients may present with abdominal pain.
e) Transient rises in creatinine are common.

Answers

Answer to question 1

b) **False**
c) **True**
d) **True**
e) **True**

Prostate cancer incidence has doubled in the last 5 years, and by the year 2010 prostate cancer will be the leading cause of cancer death in men. There has been no survival benefit demonstrated by prostate-specific antigen screening, therefore routine screening at this stage is not recommended. Recent data has shown that informing men of the risks and benefits of screening results in fewer men choosing to be screened. Another problem is that more than 60% of those with a raised PSA have benign disease. The cost and emotional burden of further examination on these patients is substantial. A combination of digital examination and PSA will provide a diagnostic sensitivity of more than 90%.

Therapy is either radical prostatectomy for localised disease, or medical therapy with gonadotrophin hormone release analogues, which reduce androgen secretion. Magnetic resonance imaging and PSA levels may be useful predictors of outcome (< 10 ng/ml having a better outcome, and > 20 a poor outcome). Neither medical nor surgical therapy has shown a clear benefit as far as survival is concerned, although some surgeons in the USA consider radical prostatectomy to be the treatment of choice in patients with non-metastatic disease. Castration is an effective and inexpensive way of hormone reduction, but is associated with emotional problems.

a) **False**
b) **True**
c) **True**
d) **True**
e) **True**

Colon cancer has been shown to require a series of mutations leading to adenoma, and then carcinoma. The adenomatosus polyposis coli (APC) gene results in normal mucosa undergoing adenomatous change, and is mutated in patients with polyposis coli and in up to 50% of patients with adenocarcinoma of the colon. Mutations to the p53 and the ras gene cause adenomas to progress to a more malignant phenotype, but in the absence of a mutant APC gene, they will not cause carcinogenesis.

Paneth cells have been shown to produce phospholipase A2, which has also been implicated in the genesis of colon cancer. This enzyme digests intraluminal fats, converting them to prostaglandins and leukotrienes. COX 2 (cyclooxygenase 2) is overexpressed in more than 85% of adenocarcinomas, and there may be a role for specific COX 2 inhibitors. We do know that NSAIDs may lower incidence of adenocarcinoma.

Colorectal cancer is the second commonest malignancy, resulting in 16 000 deaths per year in the UK. Cancer screening reduces colon cancer deaths, and although the optimal screening is 5 to 10 yearly colonoscopic examination in patients over the age of 50, this is not feasible. Faecal occult blood is however cheaper, and new sensitive tests are recommended for screening. A large study has shown a 15% reduction in death from colorectal cancer.

Answer to question 3

a) **True**
b) **False**
c) **True**
d) **True**
e) **True**

Parietal lobe signs depend on whether the dominant or non-dominant hemisphere is affected. Most patients, including those who are left-handed, are left hemisphere dominant. The parietal lobe contains the main sensory cortex (post central gyrus), the angular gyrus (speech and reading), supramarginal gyrus (speech), the auditory and visual association cortex, and part of the visual pathways.

This patient suffered a lesion of his dominant inferior parietal lobe. Lesions here are characterised by aphasia, agraphia, acalculia, constructional apraxia, finger agnosia, and an inability to discriminate between left and right. Gerstmann's syndrome is caused by a lesion affecting the dominant parietal lobe, and features include: alexia, acalculia, finger agnosia and left–right disorientation.

Non-dominant parietal lobe lesions cause neglect of the left side of the body, anosognosia, and a lack of concern, combined with reduced motivation. Dyspraxias, which are complex cerebral motor disabilities in which the patient is able to understand a task but is unable to execute it despite adequate motor function, are also characteristic. Difficulty is especially experienced in tasks which need a sequence of actions, such as lighting a cigarette.

Lesions of the superior parietal lobe result in optic ataxia and faulty pursuit movements of the eyes. Bilateral superior parietal damage may cause Balint syndrome, which consists of optic ataxia, apraxia of eye movements, and visual disorientation.

Infarction of the main sensory cortex (post-Rolandic area) causes an inability to recognise objects placed into the hand (astereognosis), while the sensations of touch, vibration, pain and temperature are usually intact.

Answer to question 4

a) **False**
b) **False**
c) **True**
d) **False**
e) **False**

The Eaton–Lambert myopathy is most commonly associated with oat-cell (small cell) lung tumours and may precede evidence of the primary neoplasm by over a year. The main symptoms are weakness and fatigue beginning in the pelvic girdle and lower limbs, and then progressing up the body to affect the trunk and upper limbs. The tendon reflexes are reduced but increase if the muscles are voluntarily contracted repeatedly before testing. Repeated electrical nerve stimulation also enhances muscle power; and evoked muscle action potential may increase 2–6 times. The facial muscles and the bulbar muscles are usually spared. Other features may include autonomic disturbance, dry mouth, impotence, and paraesthesias. Oral guanidine hydrochloride or 3, 4 aminopyridine may potentiate muscle strength. Neostigmine helps only slightly. The mechanism is thought to be autoimmune, and neurophysiological studies suggest that there is defective ACh release from nerve terminals. Patients may benefit from a trial of prednisolone, and plasma exchange is used in some centres.

a) **False**   d) **True**
b) **True**   e) **True**
c) **False**

Pericarditis is a common cause of widespread ST elevation on the ECG, and is not an indication for streptokinase therapy. It is also important to exclude aortic dissection, oesophageal rupture, and acute abdominal emergencies.

A range of arrhythmias is associated with reperfusion, especially ventricular arrhythmias. Vagal reactions, vomiting, nausea, bradycardia, and hypotension are more common in patients with inferior infarctions.

Anti-streptokinase antibodies develop around 5 days after therapy, so streptokinase injection should not be repeated 5 days to 6 months after initial therapy. In patients with pre-existing antibodies, immune-complex-mediated pathology has been described.

In pregnancy there is an increased risk of haemorrhage and placental separation, and the drug should not be given. The ISIS-3 trial, which enrolled 46 000, showed minimal differences in 5-week mortality in patients randomised to streptokinase, t-PA (tissue plasminogen activator), or APSAC (antistreplase), and a somewhat higher incidence of cerebral bleeding in the t-PA and APSAC groups than the streptokinase group.

Answer to question 6

a) **False**   d) **True**
b) **True**   e) **False**
c) **False**

Up to 10% of pulmonary emboli have their origin outside the deep femoral system, and in up to 20% of patients with proven emboli no thrombus is found, presumably because the entire thrombus has embolised.

A recent study has demonstrated that patients with recurrent deep venous thromboses should receive long-term anticoagulation, since this leads to a 2.6% recurrence rate, as opposed to 20.7% recurrence in patients who stopped anticoagulation.

Low molecular weight heparins are used clinically by subcutaneous injection to prevent thrombosis in surgical patients, but the recommended dose is a single daily dose. Medical conditions such as homocystinuria, polycythaemia rubra vera, sickle cell (SC) disease, hyperviscosity syndrome, Behçet's disease, antiphospholipid antibodies, and paroxysmal nocturnal haemoglobinuria lead to increased risk of thrombosis. Other conditions which cause deep venous thrombosis are the thrombophilias, Factor V_{Leiden}, antithrombin III deficiency, and protein C and S deficiency. Clinical diagnosis of deep venous thrombosis is not reliable, and it is confirmed in no more than 50% of patients in whom it is suspected. Autopsy studies have also shown that most fatal pulmonary emboli are not diagnosed.

Answer to question 7

a) **False**
b) **False**
c) **True**
d) **True**
e) **False**

Gentamicin can be used in patients with renal failure, with appropriate modification of dose and dose interval. Specific recommendations relating the degree of renal impairment and dosage are provided in the British National Formulary. Monitoring of blood levels is mandatory, as in all patients receiving this drug.

1α-calcidol, which is hydroxylated, is used in patients with renal failure, since 1-hydroxylation activates vitamin D, and occurs in the normal kidney.

Erythromycin and theophylline derivatives can potentiate the nephrotoxic effects of cyclosporin. Indomethacin reduces renal blood flow and GFR (glomerular filtration rate).

In diabetic patients receiving chronic ambulatory peritoneal dialysis, insulin is usually given in the bags of dialysis fluid. This often facilitates excellent diabetic control. The insulin requirement of diabetics often becomes less when their renal function deteriorates.

Answer to question 8

a) **True**
b) **True**
c) **True**
d) **False**
e) **True**

Causes of non-infectious diarrhoea include:

Drugs — NB antibiotics, digoxin, NSAIDs, magnesium-containing antacids.

Bowel disease — diverticulitis, presentation of carcinoma of the bowel, post-vagotomy, irritable bowel syndrome, inflammatory bowel disease, small bowel malabsorption. Non-organic causes of diarrhoea, such as irritable bowel syndrome, usually do not give rise to nocturnal diarrhoea.

Endocrine — thyrotoxicosis, diabetes (often postprandial), adrenal insufficiency, carcinoid syndrome, VIPomas; Werner-Morrison syndrome or WDHA syndrome (watery diarrhoea), hypokalaemia and achlorhydria), gastrinomas (Zollinger–Ellison syndrome).

Miscellaneous — surreptitious laxative abuse; alcohol (large volumes of beer).

Hyperparathyroidism may be associated with other endocrine tumours which may present with diarrhoea, such as MEN I; or following pancreatitis secondary to hypercalcaemia. Hyperparathyroidism may also present with constipation secondary to raised serum calcium.

a) **False**
b) **False**
c) **True**
d) **True**
e) **False**

Hypertension in most patients, even in developed countries, is not well controlled, usually due to poor compliance. Sodium restriction has been shown to reduce blood pressure. However, the normal sodium intake in developed countries is about 200 mmol per day, and reduction to 100 mmol per day results in only 6 mmHg drop in blood pressure. Since 80% of salt is taken in by eating processed food, meaningful reduction of intake is very difficult. Potassium restriction is not needed to control blood pressure.

Blood pressure should be measured with a cuff which covers two-thirds of the arm; patient must not ingest caffeine for an hour before reading, and not smoke for 25 minutes. Patients over the age of 65 should be checked for postural changes. At least three readings should be taken before hypertension is diagnosed.

In a man of 40 with a systolic blood pressure of more than 195 mmHg, the presence of hypercholesterolaemia, increased left ventricular mass, smoking and impaired glucose tolerance, increases the risk of stroke from 5% to 70% in 8 years.

The combination of centripetal obesity, abnormal cholesterol, hypertension, and insulin resistance has been called the deadly quartet. Certain data have shown that a powerful predictor of mortality is left ventricular mass.

Recent data has shown that ACE inhibitors, some β blockers (carvedilol), and diuretics (thiazides) may improve left ventricular mass.

Answer to question 10

a) **False**   d) **True**
b) **True**   e) **True**
c) **True**

Enteral diets have been shown to be as effective as steroids in inducing a remission in patients with active Crohn's disease. They are not as useful in treating ulcerative colitis. Cyclosporine may be useful in patients with ulcerative colitis which is difficult to control, and in acute exacerbations of disease. Their benefit in Crohn's disease is not well documented. Azathioprine therapy may be used with or without steroids, and needs full blood count monitoring. Ileo-anal pouch procedures are generally successful in treating ulcerative colitis following a colectomy, but up to 15% develop a pouchitis, which may be difficult to treat. Pouches are not recommended for Crohn's disease. Recent experimental work has shown that anti-TNF monoclonal antibodies have improved patients with Crohn's disease.

a) **True**
b) **True**
c) **False**
d) **True**
e) **True**

The contraindications to liver biopsy include:

a) Anaemia (Hb < 10 g/dl); correct with transfusion or appropriate haematinics.
b) Abnormal clotting; correct with vitamin K, or if this fails, fresh frozen plasma. If there is any doubt then a bleeding time should be performed.
c) A platelet count below 100 × 10⁹/L, some sources say 80 × 10⁹/L; correct with platelet transfusion.
d) Hydatid cyst (infection with *Echinococcus granulosus* or *Echinococcus multilocularis*), since this may result in anaphylaxis if the cysts are punctured.
e) Haemangioma or other vascular malformation. Haemangiocarcomas however do not carry the same risk of severe bleeding and are not a contraindication to percutaneous biopsy.
f) With bile duct obstruction; there is a risk of bile peritonitis.

Relative contraindications include adhesions from previous surgery, infection around the liver, abnormally placed bowel and large amounts of ascites. These may be overcome by performing the biopsy under ultrasound control. The most common complication is pain, often referred to the shoulder. Mortality is approximately 1 in 1000.

Note: Patient cooperation is required for percutaneous liver biopsy.

Transjugular liver biopsy may be used in sedated patients who are at high risk of bleeding, and prevents biliary peritonitis in patients with bile duct obstruction.

a) **False**
b) **False**
c) **False**
d) **True**
e) **False**

Chronic granulomatous disease is inherited as an X-linked recessive disorder in two-thirds of cases, with one-third autosomal recessive. The underlying disorder is an inability to kill catalase-positive microorganisms (e.g. staphylococci and candida) which have been phagocytosed by polymorphonuclear cells due to a defect in the membrane-associated electron transport chain which impairs the post-phagocytic burst of oxidative metabolism. Catalase negative organisms (e.g. streptococci, Gram-negative rods) are killed normally, since they generate H_2O_2. The disorder manifests soon after birth with superficial skin sepsis and painful regional lymphadenopathy. Skin lesions often heal incompletely with sinus formation. Skin biopsy shows non-caseating granulomas with giant cell formation. Infections involving the respiratory tract, urinary tract and liver are common, and most patients have hepatosplenomegaly. The response to antibiotics is often slow and incomplete; surgical drainage is often necessary. Despite the use of prophylactic flucloxacillin and co-trimoxazole, survival to mid-teens is unusual and most die by 5 years of age.

Affected neutrophils are unable to reduce nitroblue tetrazolium to a blue formazan dye and this can be used as a screening test.

Answer to question 13

a) **False**
b) **False**
c) **True**
d) **False**
e) **False**

Pityriasis rosea is a dermatosis of unknown aetiology which typically affects young adults. The dermatosis is characterised by the appearance of a herald patch 2–5 cm in diameter which appears on the trunk and is followed up to 2 weeks later by a generalised eruption of discrete yellow-pink lesions over the upper torso. The lesions typically follow the lines of the ribs and on close examination a collarette of fine scales is usually apparent. Patients are usually asymptomatic apart from mild pruritus. The rash usually disappears without treatment over a 4–6 week period; ultraviolet light treatment may speed its resolution.

Answer to question 14

a) **False**
b) **False**
c) **False**
d) **False**
e) **False**

Raynaud's disease or primary Raynaud's phenomenon by definition is idiopathic. Raynaud's phenomenon describes the paroxysmal constriction of digital vessels on exposure to cold with the characteristic colour change from white to blue to red, and affects approximately 1 in 20 adults.

Causes of Raynaud's phenomenon include:
Collagen vascular diseases, e.g. SLE, MCTD, scleroderma; cervical rib, cervical spondylosis; Buerger's disease; increased plasma viscosity, e.g. Waldenstrom's macroglobulinaemia, cryoglobulinaemia; syringomyelia; drugs, e.g. ergot, β-blockers; vibrating tools, e.g. pneumatic drills. The triphasic white, blue and then red colour response is not common, and biphasic response is sufficient to make a presumptive diagnosis (white and blue). The presence of nail fold capillary changes (scleroderma, or dermatomyositis), or anti-nuclear antibodies suggests underlying disease.

Answer to question 15

a) **False**
b) **True**
c) **True**
d) **True**
e) **False**

Non-alcoholic steatohepatitis is not uncommon, and is found in up to 9% of liver biopsies. AST and ALT may be raised. Recognised causes are: diabetes, obesity, hypertrygliceridaemia, weight loss, jejunoileal bypass, amiodarone, steroids, tamoxifen, Weber Christian disease and lipodystrophy.

Although usually benign, 1 in 6 may progress to cirrhosis. Ursodeoxycholic acid may help some patients.

a) **True**
b) **False**
c) **False**
d) **False**
e) **True**

Cryptosporidia are protozoa, with acid-fast cell walls, and are resistant to chlorine treatment, as well as conventional filtering of water preparation facilities. Outbreaks can occur, usually affecting young children, but healthy adults can be involved. Diarrhoea is typical, but nausea can also be found. After a week's incubation period, the disease lasts from 1 to 3 weeks. There is no therapy which works, and when the disease occurs in an immunocompromised patient, cure is usually impossible. Recently benefit has been reported with spiramycin therapy in these patients.

Giardia lamblia causes diarrhoea and malabsorption, but not bloody diarrhoea. Cyclospora is usually a disease of HIV patients, but can be found in travellers from central Asia. *E. coli,* and specifically strain 0157, causes enterohaemorrhagic diarrhoea, and can be followed by haemolytic uraemic syndrome (renal failure, microangiopathic haemolytic anaemia, and thrombocytopenia).

Answer to question 17

a) **True**
b) **True**
c) **False**
d) **True**
e) **False**

Complications following gastrectomy include:
a) Dumping syndrome occurs in up to 40% of patients. Soon after hypertonic food enters the small bowel the patient develops nausea, abdominal discomfort and feels faint. The passage of food with a high osmotic content into the duodenum leads to a fall in plasma volume which results in postural hypotension and light-headedness. The discomfort is related to the large duodenal fluid volume. Patients should not eat high osmolarity foods such as ice cream, and not drink with meals.
b) Postgastrectomy hypoglycaemia. Meals containing large amounts of glucose pass quickly into the duodenum and are rapidly absorbed, causing a surge of insulin. 2–3 hours later the insulin 'overswing' causes hypoglycaemia.
c) Bile regurgitation.
d) Weight loss and malnutrition occur if severe symptoms lead to an inadequate diet. Rarely, steatorrhoea occurs following colonisation of a blind loop or because of decreased biliary or pancreatic flow. Too rapid a transit of food through the small bowel and poor mixing may contribute.

e) Malabsorption is rare unless there is latent enteropathy, but gastrectomy may unmask coeliac disease.
f) Iron deficiency anaemia is common following partial gastrectomy and is related to poor diet and impaired absorption of iron (after certain operations the upper duodenum, the most important site of iron absorption, is bypassed).
g) B_{12} deficiency is more common than folate deficiency. There is a lack of intrinsic factor following gastric resection and gastric mucosal atrophy caused by bile reflux. Megaloblastic anaemia occurs in 7% of patients after partial gastrectomy.
h) Osteoporosis and osteomalacia. The normal ageing of bones is advanced 10–20 years in patients with a gastrectomy. Overt osteomalacia is rare, although minor degrees of vitamin D deficiency are well recognised.
i) Gastrectomy may predispose to gallstones.
j) Ulcers may recur in the site of the anastomosis and may be difficult to diagnose.
k) Gastrectomy may predispose to carcinoma in the gastric remnant.

Patients with ileostomies have an increased incidence of renal stones, but this is not the case after gastric surgery.

Answer to question 18

a) **False**
b) **True**
c) **True**
d) **True**
e) **True**

Mycoplasma pneumoniae is the commonest cause of primary atypical pneumonia. Respiratory symptoms vary from severe pneumonia to a mild flu-like illness. Malaise and headache may precede respiratory symptoms by several days. The chest X-ray may be abnormal before the development of clinical signs. One-fifth of patients have a bilateral shadowing; usually there is evidence of a unilateral lower lobe pneumonia. Pleurisy and pleural effusions are not common. The course of the disease is often protracted and relapses occur.

Extra-pulmonary sequelae generally occur within 3 weeks in 2–10% of cases, and include:
Skin: erythema multiforme, Stevens–Johnson syndrome.

CNS: Guillain–Barré syndrome, meningitis, encephalitis, optic neuritis, transverse myelitis, cerebellar ataxia and cranial nerve palsies. A third of patients are left with a permanent deficit after developing neurological disease.

Gastrointestinal: anorexia, nausea, transient diarrhoea, hepatitis and pancreatitis.

Haematological: cold agglutinins (50%); haemolytic anaemia associated with cold agglutinins (anti-I antibodies); thrombocytopenia; DIC (very rare).

Cardiac: pericarditis and myocarditis.

Renal: acute glomerulonephritis.

Rheumatological: arthralgia, arthritis and myalgia.

Up to 20% of patients have tympanic membrane involvement, and bullous myringitis is less often seen.

Other: tubo-ovarian abscesses.

Early treatment with clarythromycin, erythromycin or tetracyclin reduces the risk of extra-pulmonary problems.
Mycoplasmas lack cell walls and are therefore resistant to penicillins.
Diagnosis depends on isolation of the organism from the respiratory tract or extra-pulmonary site and/or serological demonstration of rising antibody titres.

Answer to question 19

a) **True**
b) **False**
c) **True**
d) **False**
e) **True**

The following are X-linked recessive conditions:
Glucose-6-phosphate dehydrogenase deficiency, ichthyosis, ocular albinism, Fabry's disease, haemophilia A (VIII), haemophilia B (IX), Becker's muscular dystrophy, Duchenne muscular dystrophy, Hunter's syndrome, Lesch–Nyhan syndrome (hypoxanthine-guanine phosphoribosyl transferase deficiency), nephrogenic diabetes insipidus, Wiskott–Aldrich syndrome, complete testicular feminisation.

X-linked dominant:
Vitamin D-resistant rickets.

The following conditions show an autosomal recessive mode of inheritance:
Albinism, ataxia telangiectasia, congenital adrenal hyperplasia, Crigler–Najjar syndrome type I, cystic fibrosis, deafness (some forms), Dubin–Johnson syndrome, Fanconi's anaemia, Friedreich's ataxia, galactosaemia, Gaucher's disease, glycogen storage diseases, haemochromatosis, homocystinuria, Hurler's syndrome, limb girdle muscular dystrophy (Erb), Niemann–Pick disease, Pendred's syndrome, phenylketonuria, sickle-cell disease, Tay–Sachs disease, thalassaemias, Wilson's disease.

a) **True**
b) **True**
c) **False**
d) **False**
e) **False**

Thrombocytopenia is defined as a platelet count of less than 150×10^9 platelets/ml. Petechial bleeds usually occur at platelet levels of less than 20×10^9 ml, and at these levels post-surgical bleeding is a real threat. The factor stimulating platelet growth via the bone marrow has been identified, and clinically used in malignancy-associated thrombocytopenia. Thrombotic thrombocytopenia is not associated with DIC, although some conditions which may mimic it, such as vasculitis, malignant hypertension, may be complicated by DIC. TTP is diagnosed by the following diagnostic pentad:
1. Thrombocytopenia
2. Microangiopathic haemolytic anaemia
3. Fever
4. Transient neurological and mental disturbances
5. Renal involvement.

Plasmapheresis is the treatment of choice, and has reduced mortality dramatically. Some authors advocate the use of intravenous steroids.
Hundreds of drugs cause thrombocytopenia, but heparin, gold, quinidine, quinine and sulphonamides are commonly implicated. Idiopathic thrombocytopenic purpura is caused by IgG anti-platelet antibodies.

Answer to question 21

a) **True**
b) **False**
c) **False**
d) **False**
e) **False**

Chronic primary insomnia is diagnosed in patients who have more than one month of difficulty in initiation or maintenance of sleep, or complain of non-restorative sleep, affecting social or occupational function.
Drugs are often implicated in insomnia, and include β blockers or agonists, thyroxine, phenytoin, methylphenidate, alcohol and caffeine. The new imidazopyridine substance zolpidem has favourable effects on sleep architecture, and may have advantages over benzodiazepines especially as regards habituation. This compound also works through GABA pathways. Melatonin has been shown to have positive effects on jet-lag sufferers, as well as elderly patients. Antidepressants, especially serotonin uptake inhibitors, are useful in patients with sleep disturbance and depression.

a) **True**
b) **True**
c) **True**
d) **False**
e) **True**

Behçet's syndrome is of unknown aetiology and characterised by the triad of oral ulceration, genital ulceration and iritis. The male to female ratio is approximately 2:1 and the onset of symptoms typically occurs between 20 and 40 years. A third of cases have a family history. The disease is more frequent in people who originate from lands which lie along the old silk route from China to Turkey.

Clinical features:
Arthritis occurs in two-thirds and is generally a polyarthritis affecting knees, ankles and less often wrists, elbows and the small joints of the hands. In 10% only one joint is affected. Synovitis may become chronic or be episodic. The other clinical manifestations are episodic and vary in severity with each relapse. Both anterior and posterior uveitis occur; posterior uveitis may be apparent only if specifically sought during slit lamp examination. Skin disease includes erythema nodosum (65%), skin sepsis, and ulceration following trauma or venepuncture. Mouth ulcers occur more commonly than genital ulcers. Venous thromboses occur in a quarter of patients. Gastrointestinal features occur in more than 50% and include nausea, colicky abdominal pain, diarrhoea which may contain blood, and anorexia.

Neurological manifestations may be fatal and occur in approximately 10% of sufferers. CNS features include headache, confusion, coma, psychosis, sterile meningitis, cranial nerve palsies, fits, cerebellar or spinal syndromes and papilloedema. Examination of the CSF shows a raised protein, normal glucose, and only small numbers of polymorphonuclear and mononuclear cells.

There are no laboratory tests specific for Behçet's syndrome. Cutaneous pathergy is characteristic, and is often seen when small sterile pustules develop at venepuncture sites. Evidence of an acute phase response is seen, raised ESR, CRP and immunoglobulins, but no autoantibodies (either organ-specific or non-organ-specific) are detected in high titre. A neutrophil leucocytosis is typical and examination of synovial fluid may show evidence of inflammation. Treatment includes analgesics and NSAIDs for joint symptoms and local steroid and atropine for uveitis. Systemic steroids and immunosuppression with drugs such as cyclosporin and cyclophosphamide are used but benefit remains unproven.

Answer to question 23

a) **False**   d) **False**
b) **False**   e) **False**
c) **True**

Aplastic anaemia is a rare but very serious condition, occurring in 2 per million people per year, with an average age of 25. Drugs such as benzene and chloramphenicol are often associated, but more often than not no cause is found. There appears to be an immune reaction to the stem cell in bone marrow (CD34 antigen positive), and interferon levels in bone marrow have been shown to be abnormal. Bone marrow transplant is a rational form of therapy, but no more than 1 in 4 patients will be able to find a compatible donor. Immunosuppression has recently been shown to be effective at reversing aplasia in some patients.

Recognised causes of aplastic anaemia are:

Congenital:
Fanconi's anaemia

Acquired:
a) Radiation
b) Drugs, e.g. chloramphenicol, gold, cyclophosphamide, phenylbutazone
c) Toxins e.g. benzene
d) Infections, e.g. hepatitis A, parvovirus
e) Connective tissue disease, e.g. SLE.

Fanconi's anaemia is inherited as an autosomal recessive trait. Pancytopenia develops at approximately 5 years of age. Associated clinical features include hyperpigmentation; short stature; hypoplasia of the radius, thumb and carpus; microstomy; microcephaly; kidney malformations; mental retardation; and hypogonadism. The disorder is characterised by multiple chromosomal breaks and aberrations. Successful bone marrow transplantation is curative.

Answer to question 24

a) **False**   d) **False**
b) **True**   e) **False**
c) **False**

Randomisation will not necessarily give the same number of subjects in each treatment group. Various methods such as block, or restricted randomisation, can be used to ensure equal numbers. One of the main reasons for randomising patients in this sort of trial is so that the two groups have similar prognostic features: b) is therefore true. The other main reason for randomisation is to ensure that the investigator does not know in advance which treatment the patients will be likely to receive, and, for example, decide inappropriately to use placebo or control drugs in a patient in whom he or she thought the outlook was poor. The stem d) and e) are false; this is a double blinded study.

a) **True**
b) **False**
c) **True**
d) **True**
e) **True**

Terfenadine is a widely used histamine H1 antagonist, which is less sedative than older generation drugs such as chlorpheniramine. The drug is metabolized in a manner similar to cyclosporin, by the hepatic cytochrome system. This metabolism is inhibited by the co-administration of grapefruit juice, resulting in elevated drug levels. The drug causes a prolongation rather than a diminution in the QT interval, though this may be of no clinical significance. Drugs such as macrolide antibiotics (e.g. erythromycin, azithromycin) and the imidazoles are enzyme inhibitors, and may impair the metabolism of the drug.

Answer to question 26

a) **False**   d) **True**
b) **False**   e) **True**
c) **True**

The t-distribution (Student's t-test) may be used to analyse the means of small samples and requires the observations to be normally distributed. Two groups of patients are selected by random method; the number in each group is often different.

The null hypothesis is assumed at the outset, i.e. that there will not be a significant difference in the transit time between the two groups.

For an unpaired t-test there will be n-2 degrees of freedom where n is the total number of patients in both groups. Note: if a paired t-test had been used to compare the two laxatives each member of the sample group would receive both drugs and thus act as their own control. The number of degrees of freedom for a paired t-test would be n-1. Having obtained a p value of < 0.05 for a given value of t, we are able to say that the null hypothesis is unlikely to be true, i.e. there is likely to be a significant difference between the two samples.

Conventionally a value of p < 0.05 is taken to be statistically significant, i.e. there is less than 1:20 chance that there is no significant difference between two groups, thus allowing the null hypothesis to be rejected.

For a value of p > 0.05 there is greater than 1:20 chance that there is no significant difference between the two groups, so the null hypothesis holds.

A value of p < 0.005 suggests that there is a highly significant difference between the two groups.

The t-tests are parametric tests; they require data that is normally distributed. If data is not normally distributed, non-parametric statistical tests may be used. Examples include Wilcoxon's rank sum tests and the Mann–Whitney U-test.

a) **True**
b) **False**
c) **True**
d) **False**
e) **False**

Causes of a greatly (> 10 × normal) raised serum alpha-fetoprotein:
a) Malignancy: germ-cell tumours of the testis, primary hepatomas and some ovarian tumours.
b) Pregnancy: normal pregnancies, multiple pregnancy, threatened abortion, intra-uterine death and fetal abnormalities (anencephaly and open spina bifida cystica).
c) Rarely adenocarcinomas of the stomach, breast, lung and pancreas or secondary malignant deposits in the liver may produce a raised serum AFP but not to such high levels. A number of other conditions may be associated with moderate rises in serum alpha-fetoprotein including severe emphysema, cirrhosis of the liver, chronic active hepatitis and ataxia telangiectasia.

Answer to question 28

a) **True**
b) **True**
c) **True**
d) **False**
e) **True**

The cutaneous markers of underlying malignancy are many and varied and include:
Acanthosis nigricans, acquired hypertrichosis lanuginosa, acquired ichthyosis, bullous and non-bullous pyoderma gangrenosum, dermatomyositis, erythema gyratum repens, *Herpes zoster*, leukaemia, necrolytic migratory erythema (glucagonoma rash), nodular panniculitis, pallor, pemphigoid, pruritus, pigmentation, Paget's disease of nipple (intraductal carcinoma), recurrent facial flushing — carcinoid, superficial thrombophlebitis (Trousseau's syndrome, adenocarcinomas such as pancreatic carcinoma).

Acanthosis nigricans: brown/black warty plaques occurring in the axillae, groins and neck. This may be familial, but can also occur in diabetes and acromegaly. Onset in adult life may be associated with an underlying adenocarcinoma of gastrointestinal tract.

Erythema gyratum repens is characterised by figurate bands of erythema with associated scaling.

Granuloma annulare is characterised by an annular arrangement of firm papules, often on the back of the hand. There is an association with diabetes mellitus and with recent attacks of tonsillitis and measles, though the majority of cases are idiopathic. Histologically there are palisaded granulomas present. The natural history is usually one of spontaneous resolution; intralesional injections of steroids or topical liquid nitrogen will often hasten resolution.

a) **False**
b) **False**
c) **False**
d) **True**
e) **True**

HIV-infected T cells only survive for 2.2 days. An infected person makes 10.3×10^9 viral particles per day, even in the latent phase. This is considerably more than was initially believed, and explains the apparently high mutation rate of the virus. This has given added impetus to the 'hit hard and early' school of therapeutic thought. The presence of HIV RNA of more than 10^5 copies per ml appears to be a better predictor of outcome than low CD4 counts. Protease inhibitors and nucleoside analogues have been shown to reduce RNA 100-fold to 1000-fold. Mothers with less than 20 000 RNA particles per ml are less likely to transmit the virus.

Needle stick injury has a risk of 0.3%. Zidovudine and lamovudine combination therapy for 1 month is the therapy of choice after needle stick. This reduces infection approximately 5-fold.

Answer to question 30

a) **True**
b) **False**
c) **True**
d) **True**
e) **True**

Statin drugs, which are HMG CoA (hydroxy methyl coenzyme A) inhibitors, reduce LDL cholesterol in a non-linear fashion. The Scandinavian Simvastatin Survival Study (SSSS) trial with 4444 patients suffering from prior infarction or angina showed a reduction of LDL of 25% with statin therapy, and a significant reduction in mortality. The National Cholesterol Education Program (NCEP) guidelines suggest that patients with demonstrated coronary artery disease must have LDL cholesterol lowered to less than 2.6 mmol/L, those with 2 risk factors lowered to 3.36, and 1 risk factor to less than 4.14. Risk factors include a family history, diabetes mellitus, hypertension, and smoking. These guidelines have been criticised by some for being too strict.

Niacin leads to flushing, and bile acid sequestrants taste awful.

a) **True**   d) **False**
b) **False**   e) **False**
c) **False**

The object of a study of this sort is to assess the risk of an individual developing disease as a result of therapy. However, such a study will not be able to demonstrate that an association is in any way causal. The requirement is for controls who would have had the same opportunity for receiving treatment as the index group. These specific controls are patients who do not have brain tumours.

Stem e) is clearly false, as any study of this sort is subject to interpretive bias.

Answer to question 32

a) **True**   d) **True**
b) **True**   e) **True**
c) **False**

Ankylosing spondylitis (AS) affects males more commonly than females. The age of onset is between 15 and 30 years. Almost all patients have the HLA class I antigen B27. The illness is characterised by:
a) Recurrent enthesopathy: inflammation of the points of insertion of capsule, ligament or tendon into bone which leads first to erosions at the site of the enthesis and then calcification. When this process affects the spinal ligaments, erosion of the upper anterior corner of a vertebral body is called a Romanus lesion. Calcification of the longitudinal spinal ligaments produces first syndesmophytes and then as the whole ligament becomes calcified the radiological appearance is referred to as a 'bamboo spine'. This process may occur at any enthesis, e.g. plantar spurs, around the symphysis pubis, and the ischial tuberosities. Fractures of the spine or atlanto-axial subluxation may be fatal.
b) An oligoarthritis affecting the sacroiliac joints in almost all patients, the shoulders and hips in 40%, peripheral joints in 25% and small joints of the hand rarely.
c) Anterior iritis occurs in a quarter and conjunctivitis in a fifth of patients.
d) Reiter's disease may precede AS. However mild prostatitis is observed in up to 80% of males.
e) Cardiovascular problems: aortic incompetence 1%, conduction defects 8%.
f) Apical pulmonary fibrosis, similar to that observed in TB, is thought to be more frequent in patients with AS. Severe restriction of chest wall movement (< 5 cm) is the most common respiratory problem.
g) The cauda equina syndrome may complicate spinal disease — sphincter disturbance, sensory loss in the perineum and reduced or absent ankle jerks.
h) Amyloidosis.

The Schöber test is useful clinically, and measures flexion of the spine. Radiology of spine and sacroiliac joints confirms the diagnosis. Laboratory features may include evidence of an acute phase response but no specific autoantibodies or rheumatoid factors are detected. Treatment is a combination of physiotherapy, NSAIDs and joint replacement if necessary. Radiotherapy to the spine will relieve back pain and stiffness dramatically, but carries a risk of leukaemia and cutaneous malignancy and is now rarely used.

Answer to question 33

a) **False**
b) **True**
c) **False**
d) **True**
e) **True**

The following conditions cause a raised plasma volume (red cell mass may be normal and there may therefore be an apparent anaemia):
Second and third trimester of pregnancy, cirrhosis, nephritis resulting in fluid overload, congestive cardiac failure, splenomegaly.

Relative polycythaemia (pseudopolycythaemia or Gaisbock syndrome) is caused by a low plasma volume with a normal red cell mass. The haemoglobin and packed cell volume are raised.

Causes of relative polycythaemia include:
Stress, dehydration (e.g. with diuretic therapy), Addison's disease, prolonged bed rest, peripheral circulatory failure.

Chronic mild elevation of the haemoglobin and PCV appear to increase the risk of cerebrovascular and cardiovascular disease.

True polycythaemia is the presence of a high red cell mass (volume) which may be associated with a normal, high or low plasma volume. Estimation of the haemoglobin is insufficient to assess the severity of true polycythaemias: the red cell mass must be measured directly, usually by an isotopic labelling technique.

True polycythaemia may be primary, i.e. polycythaemia rubra vera, a myeloproliferative disease, or secondary. Causes of secondary polycythaemia include:
a) Hypoxia: altitude, chronic lung disease, hypoventilation (including Pickwickian syndrome), cyanotic congenital heart disease
b) Renal disease: tumours, cysts, post-transplantation
c) Tumours: hepatoma, cerebellar haemangioma, uterine fibromata, phaeochromocytoma.

a) **False**
b) **True**
c) **False**
d) **True**
e) **False**

The seventh cranial nerve leaves the pons in the cerebellopontine angle and with the eighth nerve enters the internal auditory canal, from which it enters the facial canal in the petrous temporal bone in close relationship to the middle ear. The greater superficial petrosal nerve leaves at the facial ganglion (geniculate ganglion) and carries secretomotor fibres to the lacrimal gland. In the middle ear the facial nerve supplies motor fibres to the stapedius muscle. The facial nerve then leaves the petrous bone via the stylomastoid foramen. Before doing so it gives off a branch, the chorda tympani, which carries taste from the anterior two-thirds of the tongue and is secretomotor to the submandibular and sublingual glands. A branch supplies the skin of the external auditory meatus. On exiting the stylomastoid foramen the nerve first supplies the stylohyoid and posterior belly of the digastric muscle before entering the parotid gland and dividing to supply the facial muscles and platysma.

Lower motor neurone lesions of the seventh nerve result in complete paralysis of all the muscles on that side of the face. In upper motor neurone lesions of the seventh nerve there is no involvement of the muscles above the palpebral fissure since the part of the facial nucleus supplying this part of the face is bilaterally innervated from the cerebral hemispheres. .

Bell's palsy denotes a lower motor neurone weakness of the seventh nerve of unknown aetiology; it is usually unilateral but may be bilateral. The onset of paralysis is usually rapid and is often preceded by an aching pain in the region of the mastoid bone. If the paralysis is partial the lower face tends to be more severely affected than the upper face. Symptoms include dysarthria, difficulty eating, with food collecting in the cheek, inability to close the eye which can result in conjunctival damage and ectropion, loss of taste and intolerance of high-pitched or loud sounds due to paralysis of the stapedius muscle.

In the majority of cases the paralysis is due to a conduction block in the facial canal with segmental demyelination, and the prognosis for full recovery within a few weeks is excellent. In 15% of cases axonal degeneration occurs, paralysis is severe and recovery slow and often incomplete as axonal regeneration has to occur.

Aberrant parasympathetic reinnervation may lead to 'crocodile tears', gustatory lacrimation, and synkinesis is frequent — blinking being accompanied by contraction of the angle of the mouth. There is some evidence that high dose corticosteroids given early are beneficial, and action to prevent corneal damage should be taken.

The Ramsay Hunt syndrome (geniculate herpes zoster): Herpes zoster leads to painful vesicles on the fauces and external auditory meatus; paralysis of the seventh nerve may be accompanied by vertigo, deafness and tinnitus if the eighth nerve is also involved.

Causes of ptosis include:
Third nerve lesion, Horner's syndrome, myasthenia gravis, dystrophia myotonica, Kearns Sayer syndrome, tabes dorsalis, congenital ptosis, hysteria.

Answer to question 35

a) **True**
b) **False**
c) **True**
d) **False**
e) **False**

Although cost increases towards the end of life, costs become less as patients become very old. Beyond 77 the costs will become less, probably because medical practitioners apply rationing.

NSAIDs impair renal function, cause gastric ulcers, and cause confusion in the elderly. The hospitalisation of elderly patients on NSAIDs is increased by up to 4 times.

Up to 50% of elderly residents of nursing homes have asymptomatic bacteriuria, which has not been shown to result in increased mortality or morbidity. Treatment is thus not recommended.

All NSAIDs inhibit cyclooxygenase enzymes (COX), and reduce production of prostaglandins. There are two isoforms: the COX 1 isoform is constitutively expressed and responsible for producing prostaglandins which protect the stomach mucosa. COX 2 is inducible, and is found in areas of inflammation. COX 2-specific drugs are potentially less toxic to the stomach. Pharmaceutical companies are trying to produce COX 2-specific drugs such as meloxicam.

Answer to question 36

a) **True**   d) **False**
b) **False**   e) **True**
c) **False**

Type II diabetics with no record of heart disease have a 30% incidence of single artery disease. Type II diabetes is an independent risk factor for coronary artery disease. Women are more significantly affected by diabetes when heart disease is considered. The risk of reinfarction is increased in diabetics and approaches 60%. A diabetic cardiomyopathy is seen, which is independent of ischaemia and is adversely affected by concomitant hypertension.

Insulin increases blood pressure, by increasing distal tubular sodium absorption, increasing the production of aldosterone, and increasing angiotensin sensitivity. Hypertension, diabetes and hyperlipidaemia conspire to cause atherosclerosis.

a) **False**
b) **False**
c) **False**
d) **True**
e) **True**

Coeliac disease is caused by a sensitivity to gliadin, a protein in wheat, barley, oats and rye. Diagnosis is made by biopsy of duodenal or jejunal mucosa, or by demonstrating the presence of antigliadin, or anti-endomysial IgA antibodies. The IgA antibodies are also found against reticulin which is found in the submucosal layer of the jejunum. These antibodies have a high specificity and sensitivity for the disease. Rectal gluten challenge has also been described as a possible way of making the diagnosis. The DR2 and DQ2 HLA molecules are often found in patients.

T cells in the lamina propria of the gut recognise peptic fragments bound to the antigen groove of the class II MHC molecule. The immune response may unmask hidden or cryptic antibodies, resulting in damage to the villi and production of IgA antibodies. The IgA antibodies may contribute to mucosal damage.

Therapy is gluten avoidance, which results in reversal of villous atrophy.

Answer to question 38

a) **True**   d) **True**
b) **False**   e) **True**
c) **False**

Strongyloides stercoralis is a hookworm endemic in the tropics. The worm may undergo a succession of generations in the same host, so the severity of the infection increases without reinfection needing to take place. Problems may arise 30 years or more after the initial infection. Veterans of campaigns in South-East Asia, and immigrants, are the main reservoirs. The worms penetrate the skin and migrate to the lungs where they enter the alveoli, mature in the bronchi and finally are swallowed. The worms complete their life cycle in the upper small intestine; with heavy infections malabsorption can occur, as well as abdominal pain and intermittent diarrhoea.

Systemic strongyloides occurs in immunocompromised hosts (e.g. patients on prednisolone, on other immunosuppressive drugs, diabetics, patients with lymphomas, transplant patients).

Fulminant disease causes marked diarrhoea and pneumonia. It is often accompanied by Gram-negative septicaemia thought to be caused by microbes carried into the circulation by the worms. Disseminated intravascular coagulation is common with or without septicaemia. The pneumonia may be complicated by alveolar haemorrhages.

Strongyloides may be treated with thiabendazole or mebendazole.

a) **False**
b) **False**
c) **True**
d) **True**
e) **False**

Constrictive pericarditis is characterised clinically by the effects of 'right ventricular outflow obstruction' leading to progressive elevation of the JVP and marked salt and water retention. The prominent y-descent of the JVP is the result of rapid right ventricular filling, from a relatively underfilled atrium. Other features are Kussmaul's sign (paradoxical rise in the JVP on inspiration), an impalpable apex beat, and soft heart sounds apart from a prominent 'pericardial knock', the result of rapid ventricular filling during early diastole. Symptoms and signs of low-output cardiac failure may also be present (tachycardia, low BP and low pulse pressure). Prolonged elevation of the venous pressure may lead to a protein-losing enteropathy or jaundice and hepatomegaly. The main causes of constrictive pericarditis are idiopathic, intrapericardial haemorrhage, tuberculosis, uraemia, and connective tissue diseases. Calcification on CXR suggests old haemorrhage or TB. It may be difficult to distinguish between constrictive pericarditis and a restrictive cardiomyopathy. The two may coexist. Clinical differences between the two conditions are listed below:

	Restrictive cardiomyopathy	Constrictive pericarditis
Apex beat	Well-defined	Ill-defined
Heart size	May be increased	Normal
Orthopnoea	++	−/+
Acute heart failure	Common	Rare
ECG: bundle branch block	Common	Rare
ECG: Q-waves	Common	Rare
Pulmonary artery systolic pressure often	> 50 mmHg	<50 mmHg

Further investigations include echocardiography (bright echoes show areas of fibrosis), cardiac catheter studies and myocardial biopsy. Restrictive cardiomyopathy is often associated with right ventricular hypertrophy. Sometimes operation may be necessary to exclude constrictive pericarditis in difficult cases.

a) **False**
b) **True**
c) **True**
d) **True**
e) **True**

The main bactericidal (bacteria-destroying) antibiotics are the penicillins, cephalosporins, aminoglycosides, co-trimoxazole and isoniazid.

The main bacteriostatic antibiotics are the sulphonamides, trimethoprim, erythromycin, chloramphenicol, the tetracyclines, linocomycin and clindamycin.

Bactericidal drugs should be used when phagocytic cells are not able to reach the site easily (e.g. infective endocarditis) or if the patient is neutropenic.

The penicillins active against *Pseudomonas aeruginosa* are (a) carbenicillin and the related compounds carfecillin and ticarcillin; (b) the ureidopenicillins — mezlocillin, azlocillin and pipericillin. Both of these groups are also active against a wide range of Gram-negative infections; however, they contain the β-lactam ring and therefore 90% of *Staphylococcus aureus* are resistant. Ceftazidime is a third generation cephalosporin which is active against *Pseudomonas aeruginosa*, as are the aminoglycosides.

Metronidazole acts by.
1) Inhibiting a reductase enzyme and blocking energy production from carbohydrates in anaerobes.
2) Being reduced to an active derivative which binds to DNA and inhibits nucleic acid synthesis.

It is active against anaerobic bacteria; protozoa, e.g. amoebic dysentery and abscesses; and the Guinea worm. It is also useful in patients with Crohn's disease with anal involvement. The principal side-effects are a metallic taste, gastrointestinal disturbances, drowsiness, an antabuse-like reaction with alcohol, and a peripheral neuropathy which may develop after prolonged exposure to the drug.

a) **False**
b) **True**
c) **False**
d) **True**
e) **True**

The aetiology of motor neurone disease (MND) is unknown and the incidence is 1.5 per 100 000. Up to 10% of cases are inherited, usually in an autosomal dominant manner. Some patients with inherited MND have mutations of the copper/zinc superoxide dysmutase gene (SOD 1 gene). This gene is found on the long arm of chromosome 21.

Glutamate is an excitatory neurotransmitter, and binds to the N-methyl D aspartate receptor (NMDA). Sodium and calcium influx follow binding. The presence of too much glutamate results in an overflow of calcium in the cell, resulting in damage and death to neuronal tissue. Glutamate is an example of excitotoxicity, and has been implicated in the damage caused by ischaemia, as well as chronic neurodegenerative diseases. Riluzole is a glutamate antagonist and has been shown to slow the progression of MND.

Free radical damage has also been proposed as a mechanism underlying damage to neurones. Agents such as N-acetylcysteine, which block free radicals, may be useful in the treatment of these patients. Neuronal growth factors (neurotropic agents) might be involved in the pathogenesis of MND, and ciliary neurotropic factor, a product of Schwann cells, has shown some useful effects in experimental systems. Clinical trials of these agents are under way.

The survival of patients with MND is poor, and most patients die within 5 years of diagnosis. Female sex, old age, and bulbar presentation are associated with an even worse prognosis. In the light of this, new therapeutic strategies are urgently required.

Answer to question 42

a) **False**   d) **True**
b) **True**   e) **False**
c) **False**

20–30% of patients with AIDS eventually develop cytomegalovirus (CMV)-related disease. Oral ganciclovir has been shown to be effective in preventing CMV retinitis, and is usually started when the CD4 count falls to below 50.

Lamivudine and zidovudine combined therapy has been shown to increase CD4 counts and HIV RNA levels, is well tolerated and results in reduced resistance to zidovudine.

Herpes simplex virus infection of the anus usually involves the pectinate line, and vesicles are seldom seen. The usual presentation is pain, and large areas of denuded mucosa. Parenteral acyclovir is helpful, and in refractory cases foscarnet and ganciclovir combination regimens are effective. Other causes for anal ulcers are CMV, papillomavirus, mycobacteria, and fungi. Many are idiopathic. AIDS patients sometimes develop fleshy skin tags which resemble anal Crohn's disease.

Pancreatitis is not described as a result of HIV infection, but CMV, *Mycobacterium avium intracellulare*, fungi and medications may affect the pancreas in HIV-infected patients.

Gastrointestinal haemorrhage is not common in AIDS patients, and the aetiology does not differ from uninfected patients. Cases of arterial bleed following Kaposi's sarcoma in the stomach have been described.

Answer to question 43

a) **False**   d) **False**
b) **False**   e) **False**
c) **True**

Variceal bleeding is usually found when portal pressure is more than 12 mmHg. The acute options are sclerotherapy, banding, vasopressin infusion, Sengstaken–Blakemore tube, or surgical intervention. Sclerotherapy must not be performed in patients who have not yet had haematemesis. There is no place for prophylactic sclerotherapy. Recent data has shown that nadolol and isosorbide nitrate therapy resulted in lower mortality than sclerotherapy. This therapy can lower the portal pressure by 25%.

Stools can be positive for faecal blood for up to 12 days after an acute bleed. Gastric bleed is not always followed by melaena, since a very brisk bleed can result in red blood being passed per rectum.

Above the age of 60, lower gastrointestinal bleeding is usually caused by diverticulosis, ischaemic bowel disease, angiodysplasia, and carcinoma. In young patients, polyps, inflammatory bowel disease and infections are more common causes.

86

Answer to question 44

a) **True**
b) **False**
c) **True**
d) **True**
e) **False**

Causes of gynaecomastia:
Physiological causes — neonates, puberty, senescence.

Increased oestrogen levels — adrenal hyperplasia, choriocarcinoma of the testes, interstitial cell carcinoma of the testes, ectopic secretion from other tumours, liver failure.

Diminished testosterone levels — Klinefelter's syndrome, testicular atrophy, anorchidism, mumps.

Drugs — amphetamines, phenothiazines, methyldopa, spironolactone, digitalis, cimetidine, metoclopramide, reserpine, stilboestrol and exogenous oestrogens.

Up to 50% of adolescent boys develop gynaecomastia which does not warrant therapy.

Answer to question 45

a) **True**
b) **True**
c) **False**
d) **True**
e) **False**

A third heart sound is heard in early diastole, 0.12–0.16 seconds after the second heart sounds. It is a low-pitched sound best heard with a lightly applied bell. By pushing the bell down on the chest this sound disappears. The sound is caused by rapid filling of the ventricle and sudden deceleration of the inflow — rather like a slack sail being suddenly filled by wind. Pathological causes include any process which decreases ventricular compliance or increases ventricular inflow — ventricular failure, cardiomyopathy, constrictive pericarditis, mitral or tricuspid regurgitation. Other causes include conditions producing a raised cardiac output — pregnancy anaemia, fever, thyrotoxicosis, etc. A third heart sound may be regarded as physiological in fit adults up to the age of 40, particularly those with slow resting pulse rates and large stroke volumes.

A third heart sound is louder if the patient is supine or has exercised. A left ventricular third sound is loudest at the apex and on expiration. A right ventricular third sound is loudest at the sternum and on inspiration.

Answer to question 46

a) **True**
b) **False**
c) **False**
d) **True**
e) **True**

Electromechanical dissociation is profound myocardial pump failure despite normal or near-normal electrical excitation. It usually occurs secondary to drugs or mechanical problems — cardiac tamponade, pulmonary embolism, tension pneumothorax, intracardiac thrombus, or tumour, myocardial rupture and hypovolaemia. Primary electromechanical dissociation is a failure of excitation contraction coupling and may occur after acute myocardial infarction, particularly inferior infarcts, or after prolonged ventricular fibrillation.

Anoxia, intracellular acidosis, hyperkalaemia, and hypocalcaemia are all thought to contribute.

Management:
a) Cardiopulmonary resuscitation with consideration of specific therapy for hypovolaemia, pneumothorax or cardiac tamponade if appropriate.
b) Pressor agents such as adrenaline and isoprenaline are given first followed by calcium chloride. Calcium chloride improves excitation-contraction coupling if there is hyperkalaemia, hypocalcaemia or the patient has received calcium antagonists.

Answer to question 47

a) **True**
b) **True**
c) **False**
d) **True**
e) **True**

Distinguishing between a ventricular (VT) and supraventricular (SVT) tachycardia is important since the management and prognosis are very different. Verapamil given to a patient with haemodynamically sustained VT is potentially fatal. There are two basic mechanisms which cause a broad complex supraventricular tachycardia:
a) Aberrant conduction — delay in the AV node leading to a right or left bundle branch block, or intraventricular conduction delay (often associated with drugs, myocardial disease or electrolyte problems).
b) Accessory pathway conduction, e.g. Wolff–Parkinson–White syndrome (WPW); these are often associated with atrial tachycardias — atrial fibrillation or atrial flutter. This is important to recognise since digoxin, verapamil, or lignocaine will increase the ventricular response and lead to haemodynamic deterioration. The presence of a delta wave during sinus rhythm suggests WPW.

Ventricular tachycardias generally arise in the myocardium, so conduction is slow and therefore the QRS complex is very wide. VT is often associated with a history of myocardial disease such as ischaemia, cardiomyopathy or heart failure and age of 35 or more. If the patient is in extremis then cardioversion is the treatment of choice. The following features on a 12 lead ECG suggest VT:

a) Regular rhythm.
b) A QRS wider than 140 ms.
c) Left axis deviation especially if there is a right bundle branch pattern. Any change in the axis or bundle branch block pattern from the sinus rhythm ECG suggests VT.
d) Evidence of AV dissociation — independent P waves (which should be regular), fusion or capture beats.
e) Pathological Q waves or evidence of ischaemia in a previous sinus rhythm ECG.
f) RBBB — pattern in V1 and RSR' with the R' > R suggests an SVT; R, Q or RS waves in V1 suggest VT.
g) LBBB — pattern is difficult to interpret; generally negative deflections (concordance) across the V leads suggest VT.

Answer to question 48

a) **True**
b) **False**
c) **False**
d) **False**
e) **True**

Nominal variables are those which are discontinuous or non-quantitative in populations, such as racial grouping or eye colour. Histograms typically show the distribution of a quantity.

The mean of a sample is not necessarily greater than the median, particularly if the data are positively skewed. The mean is not influenced by the sample size. Variables such as range, standard deviation and interquartile range are all measures of the spread of a distribution.

a) **True**
b) **False**
c) **True**
d) **True**
e) **False**

This question is best answered by drawing up a two by two table as shown.

	Control	Lupus	Total
Anti-C1q antibodies > 65 (positive)	31	22	53
Anti-C1q antibodies < 65 (negative)	40	7	47
Total	71	29	100

It is then easy to calculate the different variables. The sensitivity will be the proportion of lupus patients who are antibody positive — i.e. 22/29. The specificity of the test will be 40/71, not 22/71. The predictive value of a test of this sort will depend on the prevalence of the disease and may therefore be quite different if a different patient population were studied. From the 2 × 2 table positive predictive value will be 22/53. Therefore o) io faloc as specificity is independent of prevalence.

Answer to question 50

a) **True**
b) **True**
c) **True**
d) **True**
e) **False**

A number of drugs are commonly reported as being associated with drug-induced liver function test (LFT) abnormalities. The majority of cases occur within 3 months of starting therapy, apart from isoniazid which may occur much later. In general, if the abnormal liver function tests are caused by the drug they should have resolved by 3–4 weeks after stopping therapy. If the abnormal LFTs persist, underlying liver disease is more likely and a biopsy should be obtained. It should be noted, however, that the cholestasis with chlorpromazine and chlorpropamide may persist for several months.
    Drugs causing perturbations of liver function:

Hepatitis-like reactions:
Halothane and methoxyflurane; MAOI of the hydrazine type — phenelzine, iproniazid, isocarboxazid (up to 20% of patients develop abnormal LFTs), methyldopa (also haemolysis), isoniazid.

Cholestasis with a hepatitic component:
Phenothiazines (especially chlorpromazine); tricylic antidepressants —
imipramine, amitriptyline, etc., benzodiazepines; some NSAIDs —
phenylbutazone, indomethacin; anti-TB drugs: PAS: rifampicin,
pyrazinamide; antibiotics — erythromycin (estolate), ampicillin,
sulphonamides, nitrofurantion, fusidic acid; chlorpropamide,
tolbutamide; oestrogens (pure cholestasis), and C17 alkyl testosterone
derivatives including methyltestosterone and norethandrolone.
Tetracycline causes direct hepatotoxicity and a fatty liver.
Methotrexate causes liver fibrosis and cirrhosis often without
biochemical hepatitis. This is usually found after about 5 g in total
have been administered, and biopsy is recommended after long-term
methotrexate therapy.
Paracetamol is associated with a dose-dependent hepatic necrosis.

Answer to question 51

a) **True**
b) **True**
c) **False**
d) **True**
e) **True**

Some agents which are known to cause tumours:
a) Aromatic hydrocarbons — soot, coal, creosote, mineral oils (skin,
   scrotum, and cervix in workers' wives).
b) Aromatic amines — β-naphthylamine, magenta dye, phenacetin
   (bladder and renal pelvis).
c) Alkylating agents — melphalan, busulphan, cyclophosphamide and
   immunosuppressants e.g. azathioprine (lymphomas and
   leukaemias).
d) Other organic agents — vinyl chloride (angiosarcoma of the liver),
   acetonitrile; tobacco products and betal nuts; hardwood sawdust
   (nasopharynx); benzene (leukaemia).
e) Minerals and inorganic metals — asbestos, arsenic, nickel,
   chromates, uranium and natural isotopes (lung).
f) Radiation.
g) Unopposed oestrogenic stimuli — endometrium.
h) Infection — Epstein–Barr virus (Burkitt's lymphoma,
   nasopharyngeal carcinoma); schistosomiasis (bladder).
i) UV light — skin cancers (melanomas, squamous cell carcinoma).

a) **False**
b) **True**
c) **True**
d) **True**
e) **False**

The four main myeloproliferative disorders are polycythaemia rubra vera (PRV), chronic myeloid leukaemia (CML), essential thrombocytosis and myelofibrosis; all of these conditions may be associated with leukaemic transformation.

PRV typically presents with pruritus; moderate splenomegaly is typical. Hb is greater than 17.5 g/L, PCV > 0.55 and RBC count > 8 × 10⁹/L. Nucleated red blood cells (RBC) may be seen in the blood film. Features of other diseases in the group are common, e.g. raised platelets or WBC, and often basophilia. The erythropoietin levels are low or normal. The ESR is low because of the great increase in circulating RBC; however the plasma viscosity is typically raised. LAP (leukocyte alkaline phosphatase) is increased and may be used to distinguish PRV from CML.

PRV is associated with:
a) Increased bone marrow turnover and therefore also hyperuricaemia and gout.
b) Increased viscosity — which encourages thrombosis, especially in the peripheral circulation, and may worsen heart failure.
c) Abnormal platelet function causing haemorrhage.
d) Patients dying as a result of the cardiovascular complications, leukaemic transformation (risk increased by treatment with radiation or chlorambucil), and progression to myelofibrosis.
e) Chromosomal abnormalities are common; the Philadelphia chromosome is occasionally seen during a blast transformation.

The main aims in management are to keep the PCV within a safe range, using venesection or myelosuppression or both. Folate supplements and drugs to control the urate level may be necessary. In younger patients myelosuppression is avoided unless the platelet count is very high because of the increased risk of leukaemic transformation. Generally either busulphan or hydroxyurea are used and in older patients 32P is still sometimes administered, although this has been shown to be inferior to regular venesection.

a) **True**
b) **True**
c) **True**
d) **True**
e) **False**

This man has the syndrome of inappropriate ADH secretion (SIADH), characterised by simultaneously low plasma osmolality and relatively high urine osmolality. The clinical symptoms include weakness, confusion, depression, incoordination, nausea and vomiting. Generally if the onset is slow the patient complains of vague symptoms only. There is a risk of fits if the serum sodium falls below 110 mmol/L. The high levels of ADH or ADH-like molecules secreted by tumours result in decreased free water excretion by the renal tubules. The consequent hypervolaemia leads to dilution of solutes, and increased renal plasma flow suppresses renin and aldosterone, resulting in secondary sodium loss.

Common causes include:
a) Malignant disease — especially small cell (oat cell) lung tumours, leukaemia and lymphomas, and cerebral metastases.
b) CNS disease — following meningitis, encephalitis, strokes, head injury and the Guillain–Barré syndrome.
c) Pulmonary disease — chronic lung suppuration, tuberculosis, following pneumonia and pulmonary fibrosis.
d) Post-ventilation.
e) Drugs — chlorpropamide, carbamazepine, tricyclic antidepressants, oxytocin, and cytotoxic agents (cyclophosphamide, vincristine).

Treatment depends on the rate of onset. If the onset of hyponatraemia has been rapid (several days) or is severe (Na < 120 mmol/L) the effect on the CNS is more marked and if left uncorrected the risk of permanent neurological deficit is high. In this situation urgent reduction of cerebral oedema by increasing plasma osmolality is needed. A slow infusion of hypertonic saline (3–5% saline) using a CVP line and a loop diuretic is the treatment of choice. Until the Na^+ concentration reaches 125 mmol/L the rate of increase in plasma Na should not exceed 0.7 mmol/L/hour and 12 mmol/L/day.

If the patient has minor symptoms, fluid restriction (< 500 ml/24 hours) and correction of any underlying cause may be all that is required. If this fails then demeclocycline, which opposes the action of ADH, may be used.

If hyponatraemia is corrected too rapidly there is a risk of permanent neurological damage, such as central pontine myelinolysis. Recent data has shown that correction should not exceed 10 mmol per 24 hours. The first symptom is usually dysarthria. Some associations are alcoholism and orthotopic transplantation, but previously normal patients may suffer this potentially disastrous condition. Autopsy series have shown an incidence of up to 1/300.

a) **True**
b) **True**
c) **False**
d) **True**
e) **True**

Superior vena cava obstruction — differential diagnosis:
a) Malignancy (90%): bronchial carcinoma, lymphoma, adenocarcinoma of the breast, metastatic seminoma, Kaposi's sarcoma.
b) Others: benign mediastinal tumour, thyroid goitre, aortic aneurysm, SVC thrombosis, pericardial constriction, idiopathic sclerosing mediastinitis, a rare complication of parenteral feeding.

It is important to obtain histology before treatment, since the tumour may be responsive to chemotherapy.

Symptoms include headache, nausea, respiratory symptoms and episodes of syncope. The clinical signs in order of frequency are: thoracic vein and neck vein distension, oedema of the face, tachypnoea, plethora of the face, cyanosis, oedema of the upper extremities, paralysed vocal cord, Horner's syndrome, or oedema of the eyelids.

Treatment is almost always radiotherapy; chemotherapy is also used in oat-cell carcinoma or lymphomas. Failure to respond to treatment implies secondary SVC thrombosis, which should be confirmed by Doppler studies or venography.

Answer to question 55

a) **False**
b) **False**
c) **False**
d) **False**
e) **False**

Absolute contraindications to thrombolytic therapy include:
Active gastrointestinal bleeding, aortic dissection, head injury, neurosurgery or a CVA in the last 2 months, intracranial aneurysm or neoplasm and pregnancy (except if the mother's life is threatened).

Relative contraindications include:
Traumatic cardiopulmonary resuscitation, major surgery in the last 10 days, past history of gastrointestinal bleeding, recent obstetric delivery, prior arterial puncture, prior organ biopsy, serious trauma, proliferative diabetic retinopathy, severe arterial hypertension (systolic > 200 mmHg; diastolic > 110 mmHg).

If a patient has a relative contraindication the clinician has to balance the risk of a bleed against the risk of the myocardial infarction. The younger and fitter the patient, the more the balance favours thrombolysis.

a) **False**   d) **True**
b) **False**   e) **False**
c) **False**

Surgery for carotid artery stenosis has been recommended for symptomatic patients with a stenosis of more than 75%. A recent trial has shown that if a surgeon has a complication rate of less than 3%, then operation for asymptomatic patients with 60% or more stenosis might have survival benefit.

Thrombolytic therapy is used in some centres in the management of selected acute stroke patients. Prior trauma and surgery need to be excluded, blood pressure must be normal, and haemorrhagic stroke must be excluded radiologically. A low dose must be given and patients monitored.

Monotherapy is the optimal way of treating epilepsy. Newer medications are available, but for partial seizure carbamazepine is first choice, followed by phenytoin. For tonic–clonic seizure sodium valproic acid and carbamazepine are the drugs of choice.

Valproate may also be used in restless legs syndrome, which is a common cause of chronic insomnia and is found in up to 17% of the general population. Benzodiazepines and levodopa may also be used.

Interferon β has a limited use in multiple sclerosis. Young, mobile patients with relapsing remitting disease may find benefit from this drug. Interferon β is not recommended for severe or progressive disease. One randomised, double blind clinical trial has assessed the use of interferon β in patients with relapsing remitting multiple sclerosis. Although the methodology of this trial has been criticised, reduction of relapse frequency was documented in patients receiving the higher dosage of drug. Magnetic resonance imaging also supported the clinical impression, demonstrating fewer lesions in the patients receiving high dose therapy.

Answer to question 57

a) **False**   d) **True**
b) **False**   e) **True**
c) **True**

Protein calorie malnutrition is common in ill patients, and can be found in between 25 and 50% of hospitalised patients, medical and surgical. Nitrogen to total calorie ratio is normally 1:350, but in ill patients this ratio can be reduced to 1:150.

Drugs may be implicated in nutritional defects. Cholestyramine results in reduced absorption of fat-soluble vitamins. Metformin may damage mucosa and lead to reduced vitamin B_{12} absorption. Isoniazid competes with vitamin B_6 and tryptophan, phenytoin causes folate reduction by an unknown mechanism. Methotrexate also reduces folate.

a) **False**
b) **True**
c) **True**
d) **True**
e) **False**

Chronic diarrhoea is diarrhoea which is present for more than 3 weeks. Diarrhoea is defined as the passage of more than 200 grams of faeces per day. This definition does not hold in rural areas of developing countries, where stool mass is normally more than this. Another definition of diarrhoea is the passage of liquid stools, which take the shape of the container into which they are passed. Irritable bowel syndrome patients may pass more than 5 stools per day, but these are pellet-like, and do not exceed 200 grams.

Collecting stool is very difficult for both the patients and clinicians, but is an important first step in the examination of a patient with diarrhoea. Faecal fat is normally less than 5–7 g per 24 hours, but patients must be kept on their normal diets. Many laboratories will not measure faecal electrolytes to determine the anion gap of stool.

Laxative abuse is a difficult diagnosis to make, and repeated urine examinations must be requested. The sodium hydroxide bedside test will demonstrate phenolphthalein, which is often found in over the counter laxatives. Magnesium-containing laxatives, lactulose, and bisacodyl can all be found in the urine. Some other drug-associated causes of chronic diarrhoea include: antibiotics, antiarrhythmics (e.g. quinidine), β blockers, sulphasalazine, and artificial sweeteners. Artificial sweeteners are not digested, and may result in bacterial fermentation and increased flatus.

Bacterial overgrowth is found in post-operative blind loops, diabetic patients, diverticulae of small bowel, and scleroderma. Hydrogen breath testing relies on bacteria deconjugating radio-labelled hydrogen in the small bowel, and the hydrogen appears in the breath.

a) **False**
b) **True**
c) **False**
d) **True**
e) **False**

Chronic autoimmune thyroiditis is divided into goitrous thyroiditis (Hashimoto's), atrophic, Graves' disease (goitre, hyperthyroidism, ophthalmopathy), and silent thyroiditis (painless lymphocytic infiltrate, hypo-, or hyperthyroid). After pregnancy silent thyroiditis is called post-partum thyroiditis. Atrophic thyroiditis does not appear to be the end stage of long-standing Hashimoto's thyroiditis, since biopsies taken up to 20 years after Hashimoto's was diagnosed histologically have shown no progression to an atrophic histology.

CD4 T cells infiltrate the thyroid in Graves' disease, and the T cell receptors of the infiltrating cells have been shown to be oligoclonal. Three types of antibodies are common in Graves' disease, anti-thyroglobulin, anti-microsomal (thyroid peroxidase), and against the thyrotrophin (TSH) receptor. High titres (> 1/64 000) of microsomal antibodies are found in Graves' disease. Low titres (> 1/100) are found in 10% of women in the UK. As many as 20% of atrophic, and 10% of Hashimoto's thyroiditis have anti-thyrotrophin receptor antibodies.

Autoimmune thyroiditis is associated with Down's syndrome (20%), Alzheimer's disease, MEN II (79%), POEMS syndrome, Turner's (50%), and Addison's disease (20%). High iodine intake increases the population incidence of autoimmune thyroiditis. Thyroid lymphoma is a rare, but recognised, consequence of autoimmune thyroiditis.

Answer to question 60

a) **False**
b) **True**
c) **True**
d) **False**
e) **False**

Glucagonomas usually arise from the glucagon-producing α cells of the pancreatic islets. Patients present with necrolytic migratory erythema — a bullous rash. Other features include glossitis, stomatitis, weight loss, diarrhoea, thromboembolic disease, neuropsychiatric disease, a normochromic normocytic anaemia and impaired glucose tolerance. The plasma glucagon is raised. Angiography is used to locate the neoplasm and to guide resection. Unfortunately the majority of patients present late with liver metastases and therefore receive palliative therapy.

a) **True**
b) **True**
c) **True**
d) **True**
e) **False**

Drugs which cause pulmonary fibrosis include:
Cytotoxic drugs — bleomycin, busulphan, cyclophosphamide, methotrexate, BCNU, chlorambucil; and others — amiodarone, high-dose oxygen, nitrofurantoin, hexamethonium.

Answer to question 62

a) **True**
b) **False**
c) **True**
d) **True**
e) **False**

Causes of nail pitting include:
Psoriasis, lichen planus, eczema, alopecia areata, trauma.

Causes of blue nails include:
Subungual haematoma, melanoma, pseudomonas infection, hepato-lenticular disease.

Causes of white nails include:
Renal failure, hypoalbuminuria, fungal infection, Hodgkin's lymphoma, sickle-cell disease, malaria, leprosy, arsenic/cytotoxic drugs, Darier's disease.

Darier's disease is an autosomal dominant disease characterised by white longitudinally ridged nails, widespread crusted skin papules and low fertility.

Causes of onycholysis include:
Psoriasis, trauma, eczema, thyrotoxicosis, tinea unguium.

Koilonychia is classically associated with iron deficiency anaemia. **Beau's lines** are transverse grooves caused by a previous systemic illness. **Pterygium** is fusion of nail fold to matrix and causes include: ischaemia, lichen planus.

Yellow nail syndrome is characterised by slow-growing yellow, shiny, curved nails, pleural effusions and an increased incidence of pulmonary infections. There is an underlying abnormality of lymphatic drainage.

Nail patella syndrome (autosomal dominant inheritance) is characterised by hypoplastic nails of the thumb and great toe, small or absent patellae, and radial abnormalities. Up to half have proteinuria, and 25% develop kidney failure.

a) **True**
b) **True**
c) **False**
d) **True**
e) **True**

Hyperprolactinaemia in men causes hypogonadism, infertility, loss of libido, impotence, and galactorrhoea (1/3); FSH and LH are generally normal. In women it causes galactorrhoea and amenorrhoea.
Increased secretion is caused by stress, sleep (peak secretion is around 4 a.m.), orgasm, nipple stimulation, by drugs which antagonize dopamine — neuroleptics, reserpine and metoclopramide, and by myxoedema (increased TRH which stimulates prolactin). Morphine and endorphins also increase secretion. Dopamine and dopamine-antagonists (bromocriptine, L-dopa, apomorphine) decrease secretion.
Examination of the sella for a prolactinoma is mandatory if no clear cause is found, with assessment of pituitary function and visual field assessment, where bitemporal hemianopia should be sought. Treatment is with bromocriptine, pituitary surgery or radiation therapy.

Answer to question 64

a) **True**
b) **True**
c) **True**
d) **True**
e) **True**

Several hard ticks (Ixodidae) and soft ticks (Agasidae) are involved in transmitting a variety of infections to humans:
a) Tick-borne typhus, an illness caused by *Rickettsia conori* (*Fièvre boutonneuse*) which is distributed throughout the Mediterranean, India and Africa. Tick typhus is one of the spotted fever group of Rickettsial diseases which include Rocky Mountain spotted fever and Q fever. Rickettsiae are obligate intracellular parasites. The organisms invade endothelial cells throughout the body causing vasculitis and thrombotic occlusion with subsequent necrosis. All the rickettsial illnesses follow a similar pattern, although the severity varies. The illness is characterised by fever, headache, photophobia, malaise, a haemorrhagic or maculopapular rash which begins peripherally, lymphadenopathy, hepatosplenomegaly and central nervous system involvement. Cardiovascular failure, liver failure and renal failure may complicate Rocky Mountain spotted fever. Q fever is caused by *Coxiella burnetii*, which is usually spread by aerosols from hides, but may be spread by ticks. Specific serological tests are available for each organism. Chloramphenicol or tetracycline are the antibiotics of choice.
b) Tick-borne encephalitis (central Europe and Far East varieties) — caused by a variety of flaviviruses. Louping ill is specific to the UK.

c) Lyme disease.
d) Tick-borne relapsing fever (endemic) — soft ticks carry several Borrelia species which cause relapsing fever.
e) Congo/Crimean viral haemorrhagic fever caused by a bunyavirus and endemic in Eastern Europe and parts of the Mediterranean. Clinical features include conjunctivitis, hepatitis and jaundice, photophobia, petechial rash, and mucosal bleeding. Although disordered haemostasis is a feature of this illness, non-haemorrhagic disease is the rule.
f) Various hard ticks have a neurotoxin in their saliva which may produce a lower motor neurone paralysis similar to polio, which reverses when the tick is found and removed.

Answer to question 65

a) False   d) False
b) True   e) False
c) False

Blood should be taken into a plain tube and taken to the laboratory at 37°C, where it is allowed to clot at this temperature, prior to separation of serum, which is then left for 4–5 days at 4°C.

Types I and II cryoglobulinaemia are often associated with lymphoproliferative diseases. In type II disease monoclonal rheumatoid factors are found, usually of the IgM isotype. Low levels of C4 are typically found. C3 levels are usually normal. Mesangiocapillary nephritis is the commonest type of GN seen in cryoglobulinaemia patients, especially those with essential mixed cryoglobulinaemia. Many patients with mixed essential cryoglobulinaemia have been shown to be hepatitic C positive.

Classification of cryoglobulins

Type	Composition	Associations
Type I Monoclonal immunoglobulin	IgM IgG IgA BJP	Myeloma Waldenstrom's CLL
Type II Mixed cryoglobulin (monoclonal RF)	IgM-IgG IgA-IgG	RA, Sjögren's Mixed essential cryoglobulinaemia (often hepatitis C related) Lympho-proliferative disease
Type III Mixed cryoglobulin (polyclonal RF)	IgM-IgG IgM-IgG-IgA	SLE, RA, EBV infection CMV, HBSAg-associated vasculitis, infective endocarditis, kala-azar, leprosy PBC Post-streptococcal nephritis

a) **False**
b) **False**
c) **False**
d) **False**
e) **True**

Thromboembolic disease in pregnancy is not common, with an incidence of approximately 1:1000, but this is 5 times more common than in non-pregnant patients. The pregnant uterus affects venous flow in the legs and pelvis, while coagulation factors II, VII, and X are raised in the second trimester. Protein S is reduced, but protein C is normal. Resistance to activated protein C due to a mutation on factor V (factor V_{Leiden}), is the commonest inherited thrombophilia, and may present as thrombosis during pregnancy. The mutation is an arginine substitution of position 506 of the factor V gene. It is found in 2–7% of the normal population. PCR analyses have proven useful in diagnosis, since warfarin or other drugs do not affect the result.

Previous reports have emphasised the importance of post-partum thrombosis, but it appears that by far the most thromboses occur intra-partum in the last trimester.

Non-invasive tests such as duplex Doppler or impedance plethysmography have a role in diagnosis, since they are sensitive and specific. If diagnosis of pulmonary embolism is required a V/Q scan is indicated. Although radiological examination in pregnancy is not lightly undertaken, the combination of V/Q scanning, chest X-ray and angiogram has been shown to result in less than 0.5 Rads of irradiation to the fetus. At least 5 Rads are needed to damage the fetus.

Previously, warfarin was used in the second trimester, but current recommended therapy is heparin intravenously for 5–10 days at start of therapy, followed by subcutaneous injection 12-hourly. The APTT must be 1.5 normal when taken 6 hours after injection. Post-partum warfarinisation should continue for at least 6 weeks.

Answer to question 67

a) **False**
b) **False**
c) **True**
d) **True**
e) **False**

The aetiology of obesity is complicated, and includes dietary, behavioural and neurohumoral abnormalities. A recently described substance called leptin appears to contribute to regulation of body fat stores. Exercise, diet and behavioural therapy result in a sustained weight loss (more than a year) in less than 10% of patients.

Obesity is, after smoking, the most important preventable cause of death in the developed world. A body mass index (mass in kg/height in m^2) of 29 to 32 is associated with an increase of mortality of 60%. Even a small weight loss has been found to reduce mortality from diabetes and hypertension.

Drugs such as dexfenfluramine assist in weight loss in most people, with 64% of patients losing more than 5% of their weight and 20% losing more than 10%. The risk for pulmonary hypertension is very low, in the order of 28 per million patient years. Recent analysis has concluded that the risk of obesity reduction outweighs the risk of this rare complication.

Answer to question 68

a) **False**
b) **True**
c) **False**
d) **False**
e) **False**

Autologous transfusion is sometimes performed in patients undergoing elective surgery, but normally blood is used from unrelated donors. This is the most common type of 'allogeneic transplant', and can give rise to graft versus host disease, since live leukocytes are transferred. If this happens in patients with immunosuppression, e.g. renal transplant recipients on immunosuppressive drugs, or patients with inherited immune deficiency (Wiskott–Aldrich syndrome), fatal graft versus host disease may occur.

Febrile non-haemolytic reactions are relatively common (1/200), while haemolytic (1/10 000), and anaphylactic (1/100 000) are much less common, but more dangerous.

Platelet transfusion leads to increased platelet levels for a limited time, but they are quickly used up in conditions such as DIC.

Testing has made reactions to ABO groups rare, but anti-K or anti-Duffy, or Kidd, are now more often seen.

a) **True**
b) **True**
c) **False**
d) **True**
e) **True**

Basophilic stippling indicates defective haemoglobin synthesis (e.g. lead poisoning, thalassaemias, B_{12} deficiency).

Howell–Jolly bodies and Cabot's rings are nuclear remnants typically seen after splenectomy or in hyposplenism, e.g. associated with coeliac disease. They are also seen in megaloblastic anaemia and are occasionally associated with leukaemia.

Heinz bodies are precipitated haemoglobin or globin subunits and are associated with abnormal haemoglobins, e.g. haemoglobin S, haemoglobin C, haemoglobin D, or inability to resist oxidant stress in conditions such as G6PD deficiencies.

Siderocytes are red blood cells which contain iron granules and are often seen after splenectomy.

Target cells are cells which have an additional central stained area; the presence of these cells indicates failure of haemoglobin synthesis, the presence of abnormal haemoglobins (e.g. haemoglobin S, haemoglobin C) or liver disease, splenectomy, or abetalipoproteinaemia.

Spherocytes are RBC which have lost their central pallor and occur in haemolytic diseases, either congenital or acquired, in which case the antiglobulin test (Coombs' test) is positive.

a) **False**
b) **False**
c) **False**
d) **False**
e) **False**

HLA or MHC antigens are encoded by genes on chromosome 6. A, B and C are Class I antigens; D (DP, DR, DQ, DRW) are Class II antigens.

HLA disease associations

Disease	Antigen	Relative risk
Idiopathic haemochromatosis	A3	8
Behçet's disease	B5	6
Ankylosing spondylitis	B27	87
Reiter's disease	B27	37
Subacute thyroiditis	B35	14
Narcolepsy	DR2	50
Goodpasture's disease	DR2	16
Multiple sclerosis	DR2	4
Dermatitis herpetiformis	DR3	15
Coeliac disease	DR3	11
Idiopathic membranous nephropathy	DR3	12
Sjögren's syndrome	DR3	10
SLE	DR3	6
Addison's disease (idiopathic)	DR3	6
Graves' disease	DR3	4
IDDM	DR3	3
Myasthenia gravis	DR3	2
IDDM	DR4	6
Rheumatoid arthritis	DR4	4
Pernicious anaemia	DR5	5

The HLA A1, B8 and DR3 antigens are found together more often than would be expected by chance (linkage disequilibrium). This haplotype is often found in patients with organ specific or non-organ specific autoimmune diseases.

a) **False**   d) **True**
b) **False**   e) **True**
c) **False**

CD8 and CD4 cells recognise peptide antigens in the MHC class I and class II groove respectively. The following molecules on T cells and target cells are important in cell–cell interaction, as well as cell activation:

T cell	Target cell
CD8	MHC class I
CD4	MHC class II
CD2	LFA-3
CD28	B-7
LFA1	ICAM-1
VLA4	VCAM-1

Natural killer cells are not MHC-restricted. Perforin is a 70 kD glycoprotein produced by CD8 cells and causes cell necrosis or apoptosis. Apoptosis is programmed cell death, and is characterised by DNA condensation and digestion. Apoptotic cell DNA gives an unmistakable ladder pattern when run on a gel.

A newly described receptor on target cells, the Fas/APO-1 receptor, is 43 kD in size, and results in apoptosis of cells when its ligand binds to it. A tumour necrosis factor-like substance binds to it, and this method of killing accounts for 30% of CD8 killing, and most of CD4-associated killing.

CD8 cells kill virally-infected cells, and control infection by intracellular bacteria.

Answer to question 72

a) **False**   d) **False**
b) **False**   e) **True**
c) **True**

Significant benign prostatic hyperplasia is found in a quarter of men between 60 and 70 years old. The hyperplastic tissue is either smooth muscle or epithelial, and the ratio between these two substances varies considerably. There is no correlation between size and degree of obstruction, and some small prostates can result in obstruction.

Terazosin is an alpha-1 antagonist, inhibits smooth muscle contraction in the prostate, and has been shown to increase flow rate in patients with prostate hyperplasia. Finasteride is a 5 alpha reductase inhibitor, and results in reduced production of dihydrotestosterone intracellularly. Some series have shown either of these two medical treatment regimens to be successful in relieving obstruction to urinary flow. Some data have shown terazosin to be more effective than finasteride. Combination regimens are not useful.

a) **True**
b) **True**
c) **True**
d) **True**
e) **False**

H. pylori is implicated in the development of gastric cancer. It has been suggested that early infection, as found in developing countries, predisposes to multifocal gastric atrophy. This could eventually lead to gastric cancer. In developed countries where infection occurs later, duodenal ulcer occurs in up to 20% of the population. There is a negative association between *H. pylori*-associated duodenal ulcer and gastric cancer. Proton pump inhibitors have been implicated in multifocal gastric atrophy in patients where they have been used without prior eradication of *H. pylori*. These data are, however, controversial.

H. pylori has not been associated with Barrett's oesophagus.

Answer to question 74

a) **False**
b) **False**
c) **False**
d) **True**
e) **True**

Cocaine abuse may be associated with the abuse of other drugs, but cocaine is expensive and widely abused by individuals from higher social classes, particularly in the USA. The development of crack cocaine, which is smoked, has resulted in the spread of this drug into the inner cities of the United States. Dependence is primarily psychological, and while depression or other psychological disturbances may occur on withdrawal, physical withdrawal symptoms of the type observed in opiate abusers are not usually seen. Cocaine inhibits noradrenaline uptake by the peripheral nerves. Peripheral vasoconstriction is observed, with pupillary dilatation, agitation and a typical euphoric state of rapid onset. Absorption from the GI tract is poor, as the drug is broken down in the stomach. Nasal insufflation is the usual mode of abuse, and perforation of the nasal septum may be seen as a complication.

Recent studies have emphasised the role of cocaine in myocardial infarction, hypertension, and strokes, often haemorrhagic, in otherwise healthy young people.

a) **True**
b) **True**
c) **False**
d) **False**
e) **False**

The CD antigens which define lymphocyte subsets are clinically important. CD4 describes the T helper cell lineage, which is depleted in patients with HIV. The CD8 cells are cytotoxic and kill cells infected with viruses. The CD4 cells recognise antigen in the form of peptide fragments bound in the groove of the class II MHC molecules, while CD8 cells kill cells with peptides derived from viruses in the class I MHC groove. The CD2 antigen is found on T cells, and was first recognised by sheep cell rosetting. CD3 antigens are found on B and T cells, and the antigen complex is involved in T cell activation.

Answer to question 76

a) **True**
b) **True**
c) **False**
d) **False**
e) **False**

Tetracycline and warfarin are both teratogenic. Tetracycline also causes depression of bone growth with staining of teeth and hypoplasia of the enamel, and must not be prescribed in growing children. In patients needing anticoagulation in pregnancy, e.g. protein C or S-deficient patients, warfarin may be used in the second trimester, and heparinisation commenced at 34 weeks. This is to prevent intrapartum haemorrhage. Heparin should be used initially and warfarin can be used from the second trimester until the 34th week, when heparinisation is recommended.

Sulphonylureas are associated with fetal abnormalities and may cause neonatal hypoglycaemia.

Prednisolone is metabolised in the way described, as is hydrocortisone; dexamethasone is not, and is not generally recommended for use in pregnancy.

Detailed guidance regarding the use of drugs in pregnancy is provided in the British National Formulary. In general, drugs given in the first trimester may cause fetal malformations, and in the second and third trimester may affect growth and functional development.

a) **False**
b) **True**
c) **True**
d) **False**
e) **False**

The clinical features of Epstein–Barr infection present after an incubation period of approximately 1 month. In the developed world most infections occur in the late teens, and intimate contact such as kissing is thought to be responsible. Lymphadenopathy, pharyngitis and splenomegaly (50–75%) are common. CMV infection gives rise to a similar syndrome, and antibody tests are needed for differentiation. Both EBV and CMV are causes of viral hepatitis, which is self-limiting. Neurologic impairment is seen in 1% of patients, and may include Bell's palsy or other cranial nerve paralyses, transverse myelitis, and even Guillain–Barré syndrome.

Treatment with steroids might be useful in patients with large tonsils. The administration of ampicillin for the presumed streptococcal pharyngitis leads to a generalised maculopapular rash in the majority of patients with acute EBV infection.

Answer to question 78

a) **False**
b) **True**
c) **False**
d) **False**
e) **True**

DNA oligonucleotide hybridisation to fragments of digested DNA run on a gel is called a Southern blot, and is named after its discoverer. Protein substances blotted onto paper constitute a Western blot, and a Northern blot represents RNA. The technique of digesting DNA with enzymes which cut DNA at specific nucleotide sites, and then running the digest on a gel, and binding short segments of DNA to these gels, is known as restriction fragment/length polymorphism (RFLP). Since there are about 50 000 functional genes in the body, and many of these differ at sites of mutation, the RFLP will be unique to a certain individual. In theory identical twins will have identical RFLPs. PCR is a method of amplifying DNA fragments using primers of DNA. The DNA in question is split by heating, then doubles again with a thermo-stable DNA polymerase, followed by heating resulting in a very large number of doublings of specific DNA flanked by specific primers. This enormously amplified amount of DNA can then be sought by adding specific oligonucleotides to the final amplified product. It is very sensitive and can amplify minute amounts of DNA, which makes it very sensitive, but sometimes not specific.

a) **True**
b) **True**
c) **False**
d) **False**
e) **False**

Mycobacterium avium intracellulare (MAI) is the third most common infection of AIDS patients in the developed world (22% of patients). Pneumocystis is the most common (58%), while Kaposi's the second (28%). MAI is less commonly found in African patients with AIDS, where *M. tuberculosis* is more often found.

AIDS patients with a low CD4 count (< 50) should be offered prophylaxis against MAI. Clarithromycin and azithromycin have been proven to reduce infection by approximately 60%, and increase survival of treated patients. The chief side-effects are nausea and diarrhoea, which cause drug discontinuation in 10% of patients. Those who develop MAI on the drug (29–58%) often demonstrate resistance to these drugs.

Once infection with MAI has been diagnosed, multi-drug regimens must be used. Clarithromycin, ethambutol and rifabutin is the most successful regimen, but ciprofloxacin and rifampicin are also useful.

Answer to questions 80 and 81

80	**81**
a) **False**	a) **True**
b) **False**	b) **True**
c) **True**	c) **True**
d) **False**	d) **False**
e) **True**	e) **False**

Creutzfeldt–Jacob disease (CJD) is one of the prion diseases; transmission is by an agent which does not contain DNA or RNA, and is relatively heat-resistant. The prion protein is an abnormal variant of a normal cellular glycoprotein, PrP^c. The abnormal isoform is PrP^{sc}, and this appears to form a template resulting in overgrowth of the abnormal isoform. Other prion diseases are kuru and Gerstmann–Streussler–Scheinker disease. These diseases are rare in humans, affecting no more than 1 per million per year. The sheep disease scrapie is common, was described 200 years ago, and is similar to bovine spongiform encephalopathy.

In 1990 150 000 cattle were infected with bovine spongiform encephalopathy, and 14 young patients (< 45 years) in the UK have subsequently contracted CJD. The epidemiologic evidence thus favours BSE as a possible cause of this unexpected cluster. Cattle older than 30 months have been killed in an attempt to eradicate BSE, amid considerable political debate.

The prion diseases all have a long incubation period, and presentation is usually after the age of 45, which makes the current outbreak of CJD atypical. CJD is usually acquired or sporadic, but 15% is inherited in an autosomal dominant fashion. Clinically, cerebellar ataxia and myoclonus are seen, followed by progressive dementia and death.

In patients with possible CJD, a CT scan should be performed to rule out other causes of dementia. The CSF is normal microscopically and biochemically, but a new immunoassay has identified a protein (14–3–3), which is a marker for CJD. The EEG shows pseudoperiodic, sharp wave EEG activity. Histologically spongiform encephalopathy is seen in affected brains of humans and animals. Astrocyte proliferation is present, and 5% have amyloid plaques.

The normal prion protein is variable at the 129 amino acid position. 38% of the general population is homozygous for methionine at this position, 51% are heterozygous, and 11% are homozygous for valine at this position. Heterozygotes seem to be protected against this disease, and the latest British cluster has all involved cases homozygous for methionine. Thus only 38% of the population appear to be at risk for this specific type of disease.

Answer to question 82

a) **False**
b) **False**
c) **True**
d) **False**
e) **True**

Gallstones are the most common cause of acute pancreatitis. The common bile duct/pancreatic duct hypothesis of Opie postulates that stones in the common bile duct result in obstruction of bile duct and pancreatic duct. Other causes of acute pancreatitis are: alcohol, trauma, hypertrigliceridaemia, hypercalcaemia due to hyperparathyroidism, mumps, trauma, drugs such as steroids, the contraceptive pill, thiazides, azathioprine, hypothermia, and rare diseases such as Ascaris invasion of the pancreatic duct.

Gallstones do not cause chronic pancreatitis. It has also been shown that oxidant damage may be the underlying cause of chronic pancreatitis, and therapy with antioxidants has been helpful. Antibiotics are not routinely indicated.

A recent paper has shown that patients with pancreatitis and non-progressive jaundice should not undergo emergency ERCP with stone removal. This contradicts other authors who believe that immediate ERCP is indicated.

a) **True**
b) **True**
c) **False** ·
d) **False**
e) **True**

Pneumonia is the most common cause of infective death in the USA, despite newer and more powerful broad spectrum antibiotics. Old patients and hospitalized patients often have Gram-negative pneumonias, and this is associated with a higher mortality. Staphylococcal pneumonias also have an ominous prognosis.

Several recent publications have addressed the signs of danger in patients with pneumonia, and most of them mentioned the absence of pleuritic pain as being a predictor of death. Others are hypotension, tachypnoea, old age, high or low white cells, high urea, concomitant disease, neoplasia, confusion, vomiting and digoxin use. In spite of the danger of this disease, about 85% of pneumonia patients are treated at home.

Answer to question 84

a) **False**
b) **False**
c) **False**
d) **False**
e) **True**

Deficiency of *classical* pathway components — C1q, C3 and C4 — predisposes to SLE. These components are involved in the normal mechanisms of immune complex clearance. *Terminal* pathway defects are associated with Neisserial infections, particularly meningococcal meningitis.

Immune complexes activate complement levels via the classical pathway.

In SLE, antibodies to C1q are often found, making assays based on C1q-binding very difficult to interpret.

Complement levels usually rise in normal pregnancy.

A low C3 and CH50 correlate strongly with a very poor outcome in patients with multi-organ failure.

Answer to question 85

a) **False**
b) **True**
c) **True**
d) **False**
e) **False**

CR1 is also found on leukocytes, in both the tissues and circulation. Its main role is in immune complex handling. Patients with SLE may have low numbers of CR1: this is an acquired defect.

CR2 is important in lymphocyte interactions with other cells; EBV is a major ligand.

CR3 and CR4 belong to a family of receptors which also includes LFA 1 (a lymphocyte receptor). Deficiency mainly results in pyogenic infections, as neutrophils are unable to bind to organisms coated with C3.

Answer to question 86

a) **False**
b) **False**
c) **True**
d) **True**
e) **False**

A low iron in association with a low TIBC in a patient with rheumatoid arthritis suggests a diagnosis of anaemia of chronic disease. The ferritin is typically raised and a bone marrow will show increased iron in the reticuloendothelial cells. The table below summarises the laboratory features which distinguish iron deficiency from anaemia related to chronic disease. The mechanism which causes the anaemia of chronic disorders is unknown. However, there is evidence of a block in reticuloendothelial release of iron; a reduction in RBC lifespan, and diminished erythropoietin production. The RBCs are normally normochromic or slightly hypochromic and only rarely are they microcytic.

Anaemia of chronic disease vs iron deficiency

	Iron deficiency	Anaemia of chronic disease
Plasma Fe mmol/L	low < 7	low < 15
TIBC mmol/L	high > 75	low < 55
Transferrin saturation	low < 15	low 10–25
Ferritin mg/L	low < 10	generally high > 200
RE iron stores	nil	increased

a) **False**
b) **False**
c) **True**
d) **False**
e) **False**

CAH (congenital adrenal hyperplasia) is autosomal recessive, as are virtually all inherited enzyme deficiencies. The exception to this rule are the porphyrias, which are usually dominant. 21-hydroxylase deficiency is most common, causing accumulation of androgenic steroids, and salt loss. ACTH levels are elevated due to an interruption of pituitary feedback, and plasma and urinary 17-oxosteroid levels are increased. The rarer 11-β-hydroxylase deficiency causes virilisation, salt retention and hypertension — not salt loss.

Answer to question 88

a) **True**
b) **False**
c) **False**
d) **False**
e) **True**

Multiple sclerosis is a disease affecting approximately one million people worldwide, and is a disease of great clinical, social and economic significance. Multiple sclerosis is caused by altered immunity to myelin. TH1 cells seem to be involved. A cellular immune response is initiated against myelin. The initiating stimulus and the exact peptide specificities in human disease are not known. The animal model of experimental allergic encephalomyelitis has been helpful in showing that inoculation of myelin basic protein results in a T cell response against specific peptide/MHC complexes. Once immune activation takes place, various cytokines are involved, and nitric oxide and oxygen radicals contribute to damage of myelin sheaths.

Immune modulation aims at inhibiting T cell function (azathioprine, cyclophosphamide, methotrexate), reducing T cell traffic to the lesions (blocking adhesion molecules), inhibiting T cell peptide interactions (peptide, TCR peptide, IL-10), altering the TH1 to TH2 ratio (IL-10, anti-TNF a, interferon β). The above therapies are theoretically appealing, but it is difficult to show sustained benefit in those already tried, especially if functional status is taken as an end point. Interferon β has been shown to reduce relapse frequency by 30%, but if functional status is used as an end point, this has proven to be less impressive than it sounds. This therapy might be of use in relapsing disease, but not primary progressive disease.

Newer imaging techniques, such as gadolinium enhanced MR scanning, are promising in defining areas of activity. These techniques may be able to predict clinical relapse, and monitor the effects of therapy.

Answer to question 89

a) **True**
b) **False**
c) **False**
d) **True**
e) **True**

Short-acting calcium antagonists have been shown, in some series, to increase cardiac mortality when compared to diuretics or angina β blockers. There are some reports which have not shown this association. Diltiazem and nifedipine have been associated with the highest risk, and some data have demonstrated a 4-fold greater mortality in patients treated with these drugs. Although the short acting dihydropyridines appear to be dangerous, long acting calcium blockers seem to be safe in hypertension therapy.

Patients with angina should be treated with β blockers. Verapamil appears to be the safest calcium blocker in this situation, and is preferable to β blockers in patients with asthma.

Gastrointestinal haemorrhage may be associated with calcium antagonist use. Headache, oedema, and rash are other side-effects.

Answer to question 90

a) **False**
b) **False**
c) **False**
d) **False**
c) **False**

Idiopathic thrombocytopenic purpura is diagnosed if patients have low platelet levels, with no other haematological abnormality, and no other diseases which could be responsible for the thrombocytopenia. Examples of diseases which must be excluded are HIV, connective tissue disease (SLE), lymphoproliferative diseases, congenital or alloimmune platelet destruction. In patients over the age of 65 years a bone marrow examination may be useful, since myeloproliferative diseases are commoner in this age group.

The incidence is 13 per 100 000, and while the acute syndrome in children often recovers spontaneously, this is found in less than 5% of adults. One in 20 patients eventually die of bleeding complications, usually intracerebral haemorrhage.

Admission is recommended for patients with counts of less than 20 000, if they are symptomatic. Above 20 000 admission is not required, unless they are bleeding, while a count of 50 000 or more usually does not require therapy. Acute therapy is intravenous gamma globulin or steroid therapy. Splenectomy is only considered if the count is still under 30 000 after 6 weeks of medical therapy. Haemophilus b, pneumococcus, and meningitis vaccination should be given at least 2 weeks before elective splenectomy. A count of less than 10 000 is not an absolute contraindication to surgery.

a) **False**
b) **True**
c) **False**
d) **False**
e) **False**

Anti-mitochondrial antibody is more than 90% specific, and 95% sensitive, for primary biliary cirrhosis. Neonatal lupus, of which heart block may be a feature, can occur in the infants of mothers with antibodies to Ro (SSA) and is related to transplacental transfer, since it is an IgG antibody which can cross the placenta. While anti-Ro antibodies occur in approximately 20% of women with systemic lupus only 1:20 of their babies will develop heart block so the antibody is unlikely to be pathogenic.

There is no evidence that Wegener's granulomatosis, or microscopic polyarteritis, are caused by anti-neutrophil cytoplasmic antibodies: they are directed against myeloperoxidase and anti-proteinase III, and are 95% specific and sensitive for this condition.

Some 25% of patients with SLE do not have elevated anti-DNA antibodies at any time.

Antinuclear and anticytoplasmic antibodies — disease associations:

Group 1 DNA and histones:
Anti-dsDNA — specific SLE;
Anti-single-stranded DNA — non-specific;
Antihistone — drug-induced SLE.

Group 2 Extractable nuclear antigens:
Sm — high specificity for SLE;
Ro/SSA — Sjögren's and SLE;
La/SSB — Sjögren's, SLE, not found in RA.

RNP — MCTD 95–100%, SLE 35%;
Jo1 — myositis and lung fibrosis;
Sc170 — systemic sclerosis.

Using HEP 2 cells, anti-centromere antibody can be detected in 80% of patients with limited systemic sclerosis (the CREST syndrome).

Answer to question 92

a) **False**
b) **False**
c) **True**
d) **False**
e) **False**

Hyperpyrexia, tinnitus, and hypokalaemia are features of aspirin overdose.

Abnormalities in liver function tests and liver failure may develop up to 2–5 days after ingestion of the drug. A normal prothrombin time at 24 hours does not preclude the later development of severe hepatotoxicity. Levels of the drug should be monitored sequentially after admission, and it should not be forgotten that patients may also have ingested other drugs (e.g. alcohol, aspirin, benzodiazepines, barbiturates, opiates).

Hepatic metabolism of paracetamol is partly oxidative, and involves conjugation with glutathione. N-acetylcysteine or methionine are used in the treatment of severe overdose, and are optimally given in the first 12 hours, but have benefit if given within 24 hours or perhaps longer after ingestion of paracetamol. Treatment is initiated if paracetamol levels are > 200 mg/L at 4 hours, or 30 mg/L at 15 hours. These threshold levels are reduced by 50% in patients on anticonvulsants, or those with a high alcohol intake. In the event of hepatic failure, referral to a specialist unit is required. Aggressive supportive therapy is indicated, and in some cases hepatic transplantation may be necessary.

Answer to question 93

a) **False**
b) **True**
c) **True**
d) **True**
e) **False**

There is no specific antidote for tricyclic poisoning. Supportive therapy may be required for respiratory depression, or dysrhythmias. A prolonged QT interval should be sought.

The sedative effects of opiates can be rapidly reversed with naloxone, and flumazenil reverses the central sedative effects of benzodiazepines.

Antibodies to digoxin are used in some centres with good results.

There is no specific antidote to overdose with non-steroidal anti-inflammatory drugs. Gastric emptying, and treatment with proton pump inhibitors, H2-blockers or antiemetics may be required.

a) **True**
b) **True**
c) **True**
d) **False**
e) **False**

Detailed guidance regarding prescription of drugs during breast feeding is provided in the British National Formulary. Milk concentrations of some drugs (e.g. iodides) may be greater than those in maternal plasma.
   The following drugs are among those present in potentially harmful amounts in milk:
amiodarone, aspirin, barbiturates, benzodiazepines, carbimazole, chloramphenicol, colchicine, dapsone, ergotamine, ethosuxamide, ganciclovir, indomethacin, isoniazid, metronidazole, steroids (in high dose), sulphonamides, tetracyclines, theophylline, tricyclic antidepressants, warfarin.
   Generally caution is required when prescribing in the lactating female. Absence of a drug from the list of those positively contraindicated does not imply proven safety.

Answer to question 95

a) **True**
b) **True**
c) **True**
d) **True**
e) **True**

Co-trimoxazole (trimethoprim, sulphamethoxazole) is the treatment of choice for *Pneumocystis carinii*, but unfortunately does sometimes lead to skin reactions and bone marrow suppression in patients, especially HIV positive patients. Benzyl penicillin and gentamicin are synergistic in the treatment of streptococcal endocarditis. Resistance to penicillins is seldom found. Staphylococcal endocarditis is treated with combination therapy with flucloxacillin and gentamicin. Rifampicin and vancomycin are also effective anti-staphylococcal agents.
   Intravenous ganciclovir is the treatment of choice for severe CMV infections.

a) **True**
b) **False**
c) **True**
d) **True**
e) **False**

Ketoconazole reduces the metabolism of cyclosporine, and has even been used in developing countries as a method of reducing the dose of this expensive drug in transplant patients. The newer triazole drugs are less toxic than amphotericin, and are being increasingly used in patients with neutropenia and HIV. The problem is the development of resistant *C. albicans* and *kruzei* strains.

Systemic candidiasis (e.g. in the immunosuppressed host) should be treated with amphotericin ± flucytosine, or fluconazole.

Histoplasmosis and other systemic fungal infections should be treated with intravenous amphotericin or ketoconazole.

Answer to question 97

a) **False**
b) **False**
c) **True**
d) **True**
e) **True**

Amiodarone is used in patients with arrhythmia, but has side-effects including hypo- or hyperthyroidism, liver disease, lung disease, myopathy, neuropathy, corneal microdeposits, optic neuritis, rashes, and thrombocytopenia. The half life is 28 days.

Pulmonary complications are associated with a dose of 400 mg per day for 2 months or longer, age older than 70, concomitant lung disease, or a large total cumulative dose. Lung toxicity is unfortunately unpredictable, and is sometimes seen in patients without any of these factors.

Amiodarone lung damage is caused by T cell cytotoxicity, and patients complain of cough, dyspnoea and weight loss. The diagnosis may be difficult in patients with concomitant heart disease, since symptoms are similar to those of cardiac failure. X-ray examination may show a ground glass pattern; the lung function tests are usually obstructive but may be restrictive. Bronchoalveolar lavage demonstrates T cell infiltration, and lamellar inclusion bodies are characteristic.

Treatment is withdrawal of amiodarone therapy. This might be problematic in patients with ventricular tachycardias, and electrocoagulation of arrhythmogenic foci might be indicated in these patients. A minority of patients present with a bronchiolitis obliterans, which is responsive to steroid therapy.

a) **False**
b) **True**
c) **False**
d) **False**
e) **False**

In patients with left ventricular failure, symptoms are not directly related to degree of ventricular dysfunction. Diastolic dysfunction is defined as an increased end diastolic pressure in a normal sized heart. Systolic dysfunction is defined as a reduced ejection fraction, with an increased left ventricular volume. An ejection fraction of less than 45% is sufficient to make the diagnosis of failure.

Treatment aims at improving the quality of life, or reducing left ventricular dysfunction, and reducing mortality. Salt reduction to less than 3 g per day is not impossible. Although exercise is usually recommended, beneficial effects in patients with heart failure have been difficult to prove.

Vasodilators such as hydralazine, isosorbide dinitrate, or ACE inhibitors may be used singly or in combination. If isosorbide dinitrate is used, a nocturnal interval of 10 hours must be instituted to prevent tolerance. ACE inhibitors must be started at low doses (e.g. captopril at 12.5 mg per day), and built up to optimal dosage. Low sodium may be indicative of high renin activity, and is not a contraindication to therapy with ACE inhibitors.

Answer to question 99

a) **False**
b) **False**
c) **True**
d) **False**
e) **False**

Recommended prophylaxis for patients with prosthetic heart valves undergoing dental procedures is oral amoxycillin 3 g, 1 hour before treatment (or erythromycin, in allergic subjects). Gentamicin is added in patients i) with a previous history of endocarditis, and ii) undergoing bowel or genitourinary surgery. One dose of parenteral amoxycillin may be given in patients with prosthetic valves undergoing dental surgery under general anaesthetic, and should be followed by a further oral dose 6 hours later.

Malarial prophylaxis should be commenced a minimum of 1 week before travel to an endemic area, and should be continued for at least 4 weeks after return. Specialist advice should be sought regarding the appropriate chemoprophylaxis for the patient's planned itinerary.

Penicillin is the drug of choice (penicillin V-250 mg/day) for long-term prophylaxis post-splenectomy. The dangers of overwhelming infection with pneumococci must be considered in asplenic patients. Tetracycline is contraindicated in children.

a) **False**
b) **False**
c) **False**
d) **True**
e) **True**

Benign malaria is usually caused by *Plasmodium vivax*, and less commonly *P. malariae* and *P. ovale*.

Chloroquine is adequate treatment for *P. malariae*, but primaquine should be given following choloroquine in *P. vivax* and *P. ovale* infection to destroy liver parasites and prevent clinical relapse.

Quinine is the drug of choice for chloroquine-resistant strains, followed by oral fansidar (pyrimethamine and sulphadoxine). Chloroquine and proguanil are safe in pregnancy. Cimetidine is a hepatic enzyme inhibitor. Quinine is metabolised in the liver. Other common enzyme inhibitors are clofibrate, isoniazid, chloramphenicol, fluconazole, diltiazem, omeprazole, and ciprofloxacin.

Mefloquine is used as chemoprophylactic agent in areas where chloroquine resistance occurs. Side-effects are gastrointestinal disturbance, neuropsychiatric disturbance, which can be severe, liver impairment, bone marrow suppression, and teratogenicity. It must never be given with halofantrine, since this can result in arrhythmias, and is not suitable in children under 15 kg.

Halofantrine is not a prophylactic drug, but may be useful in treating falciparum malaria. There is new hope for successful vaccination with a circumsporozoite antigen preparation, which appears to confer some resistance to infection with falciparum malaria. Malaria causes 500 million infections per year and 2.4 million deaths, mostly in developing countries.

The cellular receptor for *P. falciparum* has been shown to be the ICAM-1 receptor. Both sickle-cell disease and thalassaemia have been shown to protect against falciparum malaria, and in certain areas up to 80% of the population has a variant of α thalassaemia.

a) **False**
b) **True**
c) **True**
d) **True**
e) **False**

Stevens–Johnson syndrome represents the severe systemic form of erythema multiforme. Clinical features include: fever, exudative conjunctivitis, corneal scarring, entropion, pneumonia and renal failure.

Erythema multiforme is characterised by crops of target lesions which classically have a purple or pallid centre surrounded by red rings but the nature of the lesions may vary from macules to blisters — hence the name erythema multiforme. The mucous membranes are commonly involved.

Recognised causes of erythema multiforme include:
Infections — e.g. herpes, mycoplasma streptococci
Drugs — sulphonamides, barbiturates, sulphonylureas, salicylates
Systemic lupus erythematosus
Carcinomas/lymphomas.

Pemphigoid is a disease of the elderly characterised by large tense blisters which heal without scarring; mucosal involvement is rare. A possible association between pemphigoid and internal malignancy has been postulated. Histologically there is evidence of a sub-epidermal split and IgG and complement may be seen at the epidermal basement membrane. Pemphigoid carries a more benign prognosis than pemphigus. Patients should be treated with oral prednisolone to control blistering.

Dermatitis herpetiformis is characterised by an itchy vesicular rash which affects the extensor surfaces. Histologically the blisters are subepidermal and IgA deposits may be seen along the epidermal basement membrane. Most cases are associated with gluten sensitivity and improve on a gluten-free diet. Dapsone has also been used with success but side-effects include haemolysis, megaloblastic anaemia, methaemoglobinaemia, neutropenia and gastrointestinal upset.

Herpes gestationis is a rare bullous disease of pregnancy mediated by an IgG autoantibody which can cross the placenta and affect the fetus. It usually manifests in the second or third trimester of the second or third pregnancy and is only rarely seen in the first pregnancy. Clinically subepidermal bullae occur on the hands, umbilicus, and around the mouth. Lesions settle soon after delivery but tend to recur with increasing severity in successive pregnancies. Exacerbations may also occur premenstrually and with the oral contraceptive pill. On skin immunofluorescence C3 and IgG may be seen along the epidermal basement membrane.

Erythema marginatum is one of the major Duckett–Jones criteria for the diagnosis of rheumatic fever.

Answer to question 102

a) **False**   d) **False**
b) **False**   e) **False**
c) **True**

'Maternity blues' follow 50% of normal deliveries and peak at 5 days post partum. Clinical features include depression, weeping and forgetfulness. Recovery is spontaneous and no treatment is indicated. Postnatal depression beginning after delivery and lasting for at least 6 months probably occurs in 5–10% of women; psychotherapy and antidepressant drugs may be necessary but the prognosis is generally good.

Puerperal psychosis occurs with an incidence of 1:1000 deliveries. It typically starts within 10 days of delivery in women who were normal before delivery, and many have no previous psychiatric history. The clinical spectrum is broad and clinical features may be of a schizophrenic illness with marked delusions, mania, hypomania or a depressive illness. Typically there is marked behavioural disturbance. Admission to hospital is often required, neuroleptic drugs are effective and electroconvulsive therapy may be beneficial, especially for marked depressive psychosis. Recovery is usually complete, though the risk of recurrence in subsequent pregnancies is of the order of 20%. Puerperal psychosis is not a contraindication to further pregnancies and is not an indication for therapeutic abortion.

Answer to question 103

a) **False**   d) **True**
b) **True**   e) **False**
c) **True**

Postural hypotension is common in old age; nearly a fifth of patients over the age of 65 have a fall in systolic BP of 20 mmHg or more and a fall in diastolic pressure of 10 mmHg or more. This patient thus qualifies for the diagnosis of orthostatic hypotension, which is defined as a systolic drop of 20 to 30, and a diastolic drop of 10 to 15. Hypotension in combination with defective cerebral autoregulation leads to inadequate cerebral perfusion and a variety of symptoms including confusion, dizziness, etc., or occasionally focal symptoms.

The principal causes of postural hypotension in the elderly:
Hypovolaemia due to salt and water depletion

Autonomic nervous system dysfunction, including diabetes mellitus and parkinsonism; rare neurological disorders such as Shy–Drager syndrome, and olivopontocerebellar degeneration

Drugs — diuretics, anti-hypertensives, phenothiazines, anti-depressants, L-dopa, vasodilators (including alcohol), narcotic analgesics, verapamil, disopyramide

Prolonged recumbency
Cardiac disease — recent MI.

a) **True**
b) **False**
c) **True**
d) **False**
e) **False**

The sensitivity of a test indicates how accurately a positive test correlates with having the disease. A sensitivity of 95% therefore means that 5% of patients with the disease will test negative. The interpretation of data of this sort is highly dependent on the criteria which are used for the definitive diagnosis of the disease (gold standard). In a situation where a tissue diagnosis can be made accurately, statistical analyses of this type are very reliable. This is not always the case in diseases such as scleroderma, the example given, because the diagnostic label is based on a clinical phenotype, which may be variable.

The specificity of a test tells you how accurately a negative result predicts absence of disease. The positive predictive value indicates the false positive rate of a test. A positive predictive value of 83% does imply that 17% of antibody positive subjects will not have the disease. The predictive value of the test is affected by the prevalence of the disease, but sensitivity is independent of prevalence. d) and e) are therefore false.

Answer to question 105

a) **True**
b) **True**
c) **False**
d) **True**
e) **False**

During acute seroconversion there is a high level of viral replication in the blood, with a marked plasma viraemia. This makes patients more infectious, in many cases, than later in the course of the disease. This viraemia is terminated by the development of a cytotoxic CD8 positive response. Anti-HIV antibodies may be detected in the blood of more than 90% of patients within 2–3 weeks of the onset of symptoms of acute seroconversion. Severe symptoms, and a prolonged illness at the time of seroconversion, are generally associated with a worse outlook for patients. Generalised lymphopenia is frequently observed and HIV infection should always be considered in a patient with an unexplained lymphopenia.

a) **False**
b) **False**
c) **False**
d) **False**
e) **False**

In idiopathic thrombocytopenia, purpura typically develop insidiously in a young or middle-aged female without any obvious cause. Platelet destruction is mediated by an IgG antibody to platelets. Sometimes the antigen on the platelets can be identified, and glycoprotein IIbIIIa has been implicated. When autoimmune haemolytic anaemia and ITP coexist, Evans' syndrome is said to be present. Patients present with purpura, bruising, recurrent nose bleeds or with a gastrointestinal bleed. Splenomegaly is unusual and suggests a leukaemia, lymphoma or portal hypertension. Fundal haemorrhages are unusual unless the patient is anaemic. Only rarely is there an associated autoimmune haemolytic anaemia; otherwise the other blood elements are normal. Bone marrow examination shows increased numbers of megakaryocytes because of increased platelet turnover.

The differential diagnosis includes:
a) Thrombocytopenia secondary to SLE, lymphoma, drug-induced autoimmune thrombocytopenia and hypersplenism. Platelet-associated IgG (PAIgG) is seen in all of the autoimmune thrombocytopenias.
b) Conditions which infiltrate or damage the bone marrow.
c) Conditions such as disseminated intravascular coagulation, thrombotic thrombocytopenic purpura, infections, and haemangiomas which cause thrombocytopenia by increased consumption.
d) Patients with platelet counts above $50 \times 10^9/l$ who have no symptoms do not need therapy. Below $50 \times 10^9/L$, treatment is with corticosteroids — the majority respond (> 80%). Splenectomy is reserved for those who remain thrombocytopenic on corticosteroids. Intravenous gammaglobulin infusions have been used successfully in acute cases of idiopathic thrombocytopenia.
e) Vitamin B_{12} or folate deficiency.

a) **True**
b) **False**
c) **True**
d) **True**
e) **True**

Hodgkin's disease is characterised by the presence of Reed–Sternberg cells (RS), malignant cells probably of histiocyte origin. The effectiveness of the host response and the histological classification, together with the extent of the disease, determine the prognosis.

There are four main histological groups:
1. Lymphocyte predominant — few RS cells.
2. Nodular sclerosis — collagen bands encircle abnormal tissue and there are fewer lymphocytes.
3. Mixed cellularity — RS cells are more numerous.
4. Lymphocyte depleted.

The prognosis worsens from 1 to 4; 1 and 2 have a better prognosis than 3 and 4. Nodular sclerosing has a high rate of relapse.

The clinical staging is also divided into four groups (Ann Arbor staging):
Stage I — a single lymph node or organ is involved.
Stage II — two groups of nodes or organs on the same side of the diaphragm.
Stage III — disease above and below the diaphragm or involvement of the spleen and a lymph node group. Involvement of the spleen often heralds haematogenous spread.
Stage IV — involvement of the bone marrow, liver and other extranodal sites.

The presence of weight loss, fever (Pel–Ebstein) or night sweats are included in the Ann Arbor classification of Hodgkin's and suggest a worse prognosis — B symptoms. Other important symptoms of lymphomas include pruritus and alcohol intolerance (specific to Hodgkin's). Patients generally present with painless lymphadenopathy. Splenomegaly occurs but is rarely massive; liver enlargement also occurs in late disease. Bone pain is common and may be associated with a raised alkaline phosphatase or calcium. Eosinophilia is common and lymphopenia occurs in late disease. Autoimmune haemolytic anaemia is a rare complication of Hodgkin's and occurs late, often with splenomegaly.

a) **True**
b) **True**
c) **False**
d) **False**
e) **True**

Medical causes of functional hyposplenism include:
Sickle-cell disease, coeliac disease, ulcerative colitis, tropical sprue, Fanconi anaemia.

Hyposplenism is associated with Howell–Jolly bodies, Cabot rings, schizocytes, target cells and acanthocytes in the peripheral blood.

Answer to question 109

a) **True**
b) **False**
c) **False**
d) **True**
e) **True**

Creatine kinase (CK) is found principally in heart, skeletal and smooth muscle and also in the brain. Different isoforms of the enzyme are found; the CK-MB fraction is found in heart muscle, and less than 2% of CK of skeletal muscle is the MB form. Diaphragm, tongue, and small intestine have a higher MB fraction. An MB level of more than 4% thus suggests a myocardial origin in patients in whom a myocardial infarction is suspected. Cardioversion, PTCA, myocarditis, and even severe tachycardia may be the cause of raised CK-MB.

The levels of CK are raised in the newborn and in the first few days of parturition. Some methods of analysis overestimate the CK value if the blood is haemolysed.

The main causes of a raised CK are:
Myocardial infarction
Rhabdomyolysis (breakdown of skeletal muscle), following surgery, after circulatory failure or cardiac arrest, following cramps or moderate exercise
Muscular dystrophies
Inflammatory muscle disease
Alcoholism (probably related to myopathy)
Following head injury and cerebrovascular accidents
Malignant hyperpyrexia
Following acute psychotic episodes
Hypothyroidism.

a) **False**   d) **False**
b) **False**   e) **True**
c) **False**

Haemoglobins with high oxygen affinities have oxygen dissociation curves shifted to the left (i.e. at low partial pressures the Hb molecules release less oxygen). Physiological mechanisms which cause a right shift (decreased affinity) in the haemoglobin dissociation curve include:
a) A rise in the P, CO_2 (Bohr effect).
b) A fall in the pH, i.e. acidaemia.
c) A rise in temperature.
d) A rise in the intra-RBC 2, 3 DPG.

Fetal haemoglobin (HbF) which is unable to bind 2, 3 DPG has a higher affinity than adult HbA, allowing transfer of oxygen from the mother to the fetus across the placenta. A number of rare haemoglobin variants which are associated with polycythaemia shift the curve to the left. In cases of alpha-thalassaemia excess of γ chains in the fetus and β-chains in the adult leads to the formation of Hb Bart's (γ4) and HbH (β4) both of which are high-affinity haemoglobins. Haemoglobin S has a lower affinity for oxygen than HBA. Low-affinity Hb variants are associated with cyanosis (e.g. Hb Kansas).

Answer to question 111

a) **False**   d) **True**
b) **True**   e) **True**
c) **True**

Sarcoidosis is a systemic disease of unknown aetiology. The disease is characterised by non-caseating granulomas found in the organs affected. The disease resolves or progresses to hyaline fibrosis. The organs most frequently affected are the lymph nodes, especially hilar and peripheral LN, lungs, skin, eyes, liver, spleen, small bones of the hands and feet and the salivary glands.

Clinical features:
a) Erythema nodosum is the commonest skin manifestation; skin sarcoids, infiltration of scars and lupus pernio are less common.
b) Fever and arthropathy are common presenting features. The knees and ankles are the commonest joints affected. Sarcoid infiltration of bone affects the phalanges, metacarpals and metatarsals. There is no periosteal reaction.
c) Bilateral hilar lymphadenopathy, lung infiltration and fibrosis are the major respiratory features. Clubbing is rarely associated with sarcoid lung fibrosis, unlike cryptogenic fibrosing alveolitis. Sarcoids may cause localised bronchial narrowing.
d) Uveitis occurs in approximately 20% of cases; other ocular complications include keratoconjunctivitis sicca, and calcium deposition in the cornea.

e) Active sarcoid is associated with a low lymphocyte count, and reduced CD4 to CD8 ratios in peripheral blood. Patients may be relatively anergic to injected antigens. Delayed hypersensitivity is depressed in patients with active disease. In contrast to this, lung tissues have an increased CD4 to CD8 ratio. Rarely, thrombocytopenia and purpura are seen.

f) Neurological involvement: cranial nerve palsies (especially VII), mononeuritis multiplex, symmetrical polyneuropathy, transverse myelitis, involvement of the meninges, obstructive hydrocephalus, sarcoids which form space-occupying lesions, involvement of the hypothalamus and pituitary gland.

g) Gastrointestinal tract symptomatic problems are rare. Liver granulomas are common.

h) Heart: rarely cor pulmonale complicates the lung disease. Granulomas may cause a cardiomyopathy, papillary muscle dysfunction, mitral regurgitation, bundle branch blocks and other rhythm disturbances.

i) Hypercalcaemia — probably by increased conversion of inactive vitamin D to the active form within the granulomas.

j) Serum angiotensin-converting enzyme levels are raised in 75% of cases. Calcium levels in blood may also be raised.

k) Renal — interstitial nephritis, proteinuria, nephrocalcinosis, renal calculi.

Answer to question 112

a) **False**   d) **True**
b) **True**   e) **True**
c) **True**

Obstructive sleep apnoea is characterised by reduced pharyngeal muscular tone during sleep which allows episodes of apnoea to occur. This may occur only during rapid eye movement (REM) sleep or, as the disease becomes more severe, in both REM and slow wave sleep (SWS). The main symptoms are hypersomnolence, heavy snoring and restless sleep. Other symptoms include poor concentration, morning headaches, nocturnal enuresis and impotence. Recurrent apnoea may lead to resetting of the resting PaO_2 and $PaCO_2$ levels, so that mild alveolar hypoventilation occurs during the day. At least five episodes of apnoea per hour, each lasting at least 10 seconds, is considered sufficient to make the diagnosis, although in the elderly there is considerable overlap with normal patterns of sleep not associated with symptoms.

Pure sleep apnoea (central apnoea) occurs in the absence of mechanical obstruction and is related to deficient central drive. Patients with chronic obstructive airways disease, cystic fibrosis, kyphoscoliosis, asthma, and patients with brain stem damage, may all develop central sleep apnoea.

The classical Pickwickian patient is obese, has evidence of mild obstructive airways disease and has reduced central drive (reduced sensitivity to $PaCO_2$).

A number of factors exacerbate the condition:
a) Pharynx: anything which may reduce the lumen — obesity, acromegaly, small jaw, glycogen storage disease, superior vena cava obstruction, enlarged tonsils, myxoedema
b) Upper-airway problems — allergic rhinitis, broken nose, enlarged adenoids
c) Drugs which depress respiration — alcohol, sedatives, strong analgesics.

Investigations should include examination of the upper airways and sleep studies. Features suggesting sleep apnoea are episodes of hypoxia and cyclical changes in the RR interval as recorded with a 24-hour ECG. Characteristic snore-silence-snore patterns may be observed, as well as paradoxical movements of the chest wall and struggling movements during periods of apnoea.

Treatment is weight reduction, stopping smoking, and using nasal cannulae with compressed air at night to increase ventilation and reduce the number of apnoeic episodes. Long-term complications of this syndrome include hypertension, cyanosis, cor pulmonale and polycythaemia. An increased incidence of road traffic accidents also contributes to morbidity and mortality, due to daily hypersomnolence.

Other causes of sleep disorders are periodic limb movement disorder, restless legs syndrome, narcolepsy, recurrent hypersomnia, and central alveolar hypoventilation syndrome.

a) **False**
b) **False**
c) **False**
d) **True**
e) **True**

Differential diagnosis of Crohn's disease and ulcerative colitis:

	Crohn's	Ulcerative colitis
Clinical features:		
Bloody diarrhoea	less common	frequent
Abdominal mass	common	rare
Perianal disease	common	less common
Malabsorption	frequent	never
Aphthous ulcers	frequent	rare
X-ray features:		
Rectal disease	less common	invariable
Distribution	discontinuous	continuous
Mucosa	cobblestone	ulceration fine
	deep fissures	double contour
Strictures	common	rare
Histology:		
Fistulae	common	rare
Distribution	transmural	mucosal
Cells	lymphocytes and	neutrophils and eosinophils
	macrophages	and plasma cells
Glands	preserved	destruction, crypt abscesses
Granulomas — if present, diagnostic of Crohn's	present	none

Despite these well-documented differences, there are patients (approximately 10%) where differentiation between diseases is not possible in spite of adequate biopsies. Malabsorption in Crohn's may involve B_{12} (ileal involvement, folate, and in extensive small bowel involvement, vitamins D and K). Gallstones and oxalate renal stones are recognised complications. Clubbing of the nails is commoner in Crohn's than in patients with ulcerative colitis. Systemic manifestations such as pyoderma gangrenosa, erythema nodosum, uveitis, liver disease, arthritis and sacroiliitis are similar in the two diseases. Amyloid rarely occurs in Crohn's and almost never in ulcerative colitis. Primary sclerosing cholangitis occurs more commonly in ulcerative colitis.

a) **True**
b) **False**
c) **True**
d) **False**
e) **False**

Cystic fibrosis is inherited in an autosomal recessive fashion and occurs in approximately 1/2000 Caucasian births. The incidence in Blacks is approximately 1/20 000. The gene is present in around 5% of Caucasian people. The defect results in abnormal exocrine function. The CF gene was found using DNA hybridisation techniques, and is called the cystic fibrosis transmembrane conductance regulator. It is found on the long arm of chromosome 7, and produces a protein of 1480 amino acids. The most common mutation responsible for the disease has been identified, and causes a loss of the phenylalanine amino acid on position 508. Up to 200 different mutations have been described, and 85% of patients have one of these mutations. The characterisation of the defective gene has led to speculation about possible gene therapy.

Clinical problems:
a) Repeated lower respiratory tract infections because the mucus is viscid and blocks bronchioles. Bronchiectasis, lung abscess, lung fibrosis and restriction, pneumothorax and clubbing are commonly seen. Eventually cor pulmonale supervenes and is the cause of death unless heart/lung transplantation is available. Allergic bronchopulmonary aspergillosis is common. The lungs often become colonised by *Staphylococcus pyogenes* and *Pseudomonas aeruginosa*. In the past many physicians recommended continuous antibiotic therapy; however, antibiotic resistance became a problem so that acute treatment of respiratory infections with broad spectrum antibiotics is now favoured. Pseudomonas can be treated with ciprofloxacin 500 mg 12-hourly, or amikacin (50 mg/kg) 8-hourly, or gentamicin (10 mg/kg) 8-hourly.
b) Infants may present with meconium ileus. Older children may present with intussusception or intestinal obstruction. Pancreatic malabsorption is common (80%). Blockage of small bile ducts leads to pericholangitis and portal hypertension.
c) There is a high sodium concentration in the sweat, which may lead to sodium depletion and collapse in hot weather.
d) Males are sterile.
e) About 50% are insulin-dependent diabetics.

Answer to question 115

a) **True** d) **False**
b) **True** e) **False**
c) **True**

Methaemoglobin is characterised by iron in the oxidised ferric (Fe^{3+}) state; this results in a conformational change so that the haemoglobin binds oxygen with a higher affinity than normal (causing a left shift in the oxygen dissociation curve) allowing less oxygen to be released in the tissues.

Causes of methaemoglobinaemia include:
Genetic — defect in NADH metabolism (autosomal recessive, heterozygotes 1100) or in haemoglobin structure (haemoglobin M, several other variants).

Acquired — generally related to chemicals or drugs which cause oxidisation of haemoglobin: aniline dyes, chlorates, chromates, dapsone, nitrates, nitrites, phenacetin, primaquine, sulphasalazine, sulphonamides, quinones.

The degree of cyanosis produced by 5 g/dl of deoxyhaemoglobin is similar to that produced by 1.5 g/dl of methaemoglobin.

Chronic methaemoglobinaemia is only rarely associated with an increase in the haemoglobin concentration or rise in red cell numbers.

Methaemoglobinaemia may be associated with acute haemolysis when oxidative damage is severe. Acute methaemoglobinaemia, if severe, will cause vascular collapse, DIC, renal failure, coma and death; treatment is with an infusion of methylene blue 1–2 mg/kg.

Answer to question 116

a) **False** d) **False**
b) **False** e) **True**
c) **False**

Infection with tetanus does not induce a sufficient antibody response against the tetanus toxoid. After recovery from acute tetanus, patients should be vaccinated with tetanus toxoid. Typhoid vaccine is recommended for travellers in certain developing countries, but has not been shown to be particularly effective. BCG vaccine is always given intradermally. All other vaccines with the exception of polio are given subcutaneously or by deep intramuscular injection.

Normal human immunoglobulin offers protection against infection with hepatitis A virus and was the preferred prophylaxis for travellers to highly endemic areas. This has now been replaced by Hepatitis A vaccines. Hepatitis A is transmitted by the faecal–oral route, and has an incubation period of 15–40 days. The clinical hepatitis is usually milder than hepatitis B infection and chronic carriage does not occur; however, occasionally a fulminant hepatitic picture may occur and lead to death.

a) **False**
b) **True**
c) **True**
d) **False**
e) **False**

Physiological murmurs are often heard in teenagers. They are normally systolic, soft, spread in the direction of the pulmonary truncus, and change with position. Diastolic murmurs are always significant. A murmur accompanied by a thrill is at least grade 4/6 and likely to be significant.

Continuous murmurs suggest an A-V fistula, a patent ductus arteriosus or a venous hum. A venous hum is most often heard in children and is caused by flow through the jugular veins. A venous hum may be abolished by compressing the veins above the stethoscope or by a change in posture. The murmur associated with patent ductus has an accentuation at the end of systole and beginning of diastole.

Other rarer causes of continuous murmurs include:
Mixed aortic valve disease (a gap between the systolic and diastolic components should be heard), VSD and aortic regurgitation, coarctation of the aorta, aortopulmonary window, ruptured sinus of Valsalva.

Murmurs heard only in the neck in young patients are likely to be physiological and in the elderly due to carotid stenosis.

Soft ejection systolic murmurs are common in pregnancy, in anaemia, and after vigorous exercise, and typically disappear when the cardiac output returns to normal. With the ready availability of ultrasound, any doubtful murmur should result in ultrasound of the heart to exclude pathology.

Answer to question 118

a) **True**
b) **True**
c) **True**
d) **True**
e) **False**

The differential diagnosis of hirsutism with raised testosterone and secondary amenorrhoea includes:
Polycystic ovary syndrome; ovarian tumours (arrhenoblastoma, hilar-cell tumour, Krukenberg tumour, luteoma of pregnancy); adrenal problems (adrenal adenoma, congenital adrenal hyperplasia, adrenal carcinoma); drugs (androgens).

In testicular feminisation the patient is genotypically male, but is resistant to the effects of testosterone and develops into a phenotypic female. The amenorrhoea is primary and the testosterone level is high.

a) **True**
b) **False**
c) **True**
d) **False**
e) **False**

Standard heparin preparations are usually described as unfractionated, and consist of multiple polysaccaride chains, with a molecular weight which varies between 3000 and 30 000. They generally have a short duration of action and initiate anticoagulation quickly. Low molecular weight heparins are purified from standard heparin preparations, and have a molecular weight of between 4000 and 6000.

Heparins are polyanionic molecules, which bind to endogenously produced antithrombin III (AT III), thus enhancing AT III activity. Standard heparin preparations accelerate inactivation of both thrombin and factor Xa, whereas low molecular weight preparations specifically bind to Xa. Low molecular weight preparations also bind to Xa on platelet surfaces.

The low molecular weight preparations have a longer half life, and can be given on a once or twice daily basis by subcutaneous injection. Dosage is determined by weight only, and clotting profile need not be monitored. Numerous preparations are available such as calciparin, tinsaparin, and anoxiparin, and are at least as safe and effective as the standard intravenous preparations.

Low molecular weight heparins have a role in the management of the antiphospholipid syndrome, particularly in pregnancy, and the drug may be self-administered. They are fairly frequently used to reduce the perioperative risk of venous thrombosis following major surgery, particularly after orthopaedic procedures. It is not generally noooooary to monitor therapy with PT or APTT, as low molecular weight heparins have a predictable dose response relationship.

a) **True**
b) **True**
c) **False**
d) **False**
e) **True**

Acute inflammation is associated primarily with infiltration by polymorphic nuclear cells, with disruption of the endothelium and increased vascular permeability. A local exudate formation will occur. There are 4 characteristic phases: rubor, calor, tumor, dolor. Complement activation is an important feature of acute inflammation, and complement breakdown products, particularly C5A, are chemotactic. The upregulation of endothelial cell adhesion molecules, and adhesive chemotactic factors, results in the egress of neutrophils from the circulation into the interstitium. In gout there is a typical neutrophil infiltrate, stimulated by uric acid crystals. On the other hand, in chronic inflammation there is typically a mononuclear cell infiltrate, and monocytes, giant cells and lymphocytes are found. IL-6 and TNF are proinflammatory cytokines, and there is increasing evidence that anti-TNF antibodies may be anti-inflammatory. Type IV hypersensitivity results in a inflammatory lesion, and is cell-mediated.

Answer to question 121

a) **False**
b) **True**
c) **True**
d) **False**
e) **False**

Splitting of the first sound is rare. Sternal depression or other causes of slight asynchrony in ventricular contraction may produce splitting of S1. A right bundle branch block has the same effect. Stenosis of the mitral valve causes delayed closure and splitting of S1.

The aortic sound A2 (high pressure) precedes the pulmonary sound and this splitting of S2 can be heard normally. During inspiration the split is maximal (increased blood from the R atrium flowing into the R ventricle, therefore P2 is delayed), and minimal during expiration. A right bundle branch block, right ventricular failure or an ASD delays the P2 so there is wide, more prominent splitting.

Early closure of the A2 (reduced outflow) as a result of a VSD or mitral regurgitation also causes wide splitting of the S2.

A left bundle branch block delays the A2 and may reverse the order causing paradoxical splitting (widest in expiration not inspiration). Paradoxical splitting may also be caused by severe aortic stenosis, left ventricular failure and severe left-outflow obstruction (e.g. HOCM).

Fixed splitting (no alteration during respiration) of the second sound occurs with an ASD.

a) **True**
b) **False**
c) **False**
d) **True**
e) **True**

Motor neurone disease is a degenerative disease of unknown aetiology that affects the motor neurones of the spinal cord, the cranial nerve nuclei and the motor cortex. Males are affected more commonly than females, the overall UK incidence is 1/100 000, and most cases present between the ages of 40 and 70 years. A familial form with autosomal dominant inheritance has been described.

Classically there are three modes of presentation:

a) Progressive muscular atrophy — the patient presents with lower motor neurone-type weakness of the hands with muscle wasting, weakness and fasciculation. This is then followed by lower motor neurone weakness of the arm and the leg. Tendon reflexes are lost early; there are no sensory signs.

b) Progressive bulbar palsy — lower motor neurone weakness of the tongue and pharynx presents with dysarthria, dysphagia, choking and nasal regurgitation. The seventh cranial nerve nucleus may be affected but the third is only rarely involved.

c) Amyotrophic lateral sclerosis — a combination of upper motor neurone weakness affecting the legs and lower motor neurone weakness affecting the arms.

Any combination of the above three groups can occur. A mixed upper and lower motor neurone lesion affecting the lower limb would result in absent knee jerks with extensor plantars. The upper limbs usually exhibit lower motor weakness and the lower limbs upper motor weakness. Pseudobulbar palsy with a brisk jaw jerk and emotional lability is uncommon. Abdominal reflexes tend to be preserved and sphincters are not affected. Motor neurone disease tends to be relentlessly progressive, with death usually occurring within 2–4 years of presentation, though the progressive muscular atrophy type has a slightly better prognosis.

Electromyography and muscle biopsy confirm neurogenic atrophy, the serum creatinine phosphokinase is raised in over 40% of cases and 20% have a high CSF protein in the absence of a pleocytosis.

Causes of absent reflexes and extensor plantars include:
Friedreich's ataxia, motor neurone disease, taboparesis, B_{12} deficiency (subacute combined degeneration of the cord), conus medullaris, diabetes mellitus.

Conditions which should be excluded when considering the diagnosis are: motor neuropathies caused by lead, porphyria, nitrofurantion, dapsone, hexosaminase deficiency, CIDP (chronic inflammatory demyelinating polyneuropathy), diabetic polyneuropathy, cervical spondylosis, syringomyelia, post-polio syndromes, and myopathies.

a) **False**
b) **False**
c) **False**
d) **False**
e) **False**

Extrinsic allergic alveolitis is a hypersensitivity pneumonitis to organic dusts. The antigens include avian droppings, mouldy hay (*micropolyspora faeni*), mouldy sugar cane (bagassosis), fungus spores in humidifiers, and many more. Three clinical syndromes occur: acute, after heavy exposure, with severe dyspnoea, fever, tachycardia, malaise; subclinical; and chronic, with progressive lung fibrosis. The patient complains of breathlessness, a dry cough, arthralgia and myalgia. Examination reveals basal crackles. Wheeze is not a feature; there is no airway obstruction. After repeated attacks lung fibrosis occurs which if allowed to progress will lead to cor pulmonale. Recovery requires identification of the antigen at home or work. Precipitating antibodies are found in a substantial number of workers, e.g. 30% of grain handlers, but the majority do not develop hypersensitivity pneumonitis. The demonstration of precipitins is therefore not specific, and since all workers with this syndrome do not have precipitating antibodies, it is not sensitive either. Bronchoalveolar lavage may show increased immunoglobulins in the lavage liquid, with a predominance of CD8, cytotoxic cells. Pulmonary function shows a pure restrictive defect.

Chest X-ray in chronic cases shows predominantly upper lobe fibrosis without hilar enlargement, and a lung biopsy, a lymphocyte infiltrate with granuloma formation. The disease is predominantly a type IV hypersensitivity reaction. Peripheral eosinophilia is rare. Steroids are helpful in severe cases or when the antigen is not identified.

Face masks are useless; an exclusion hood with positive pressure may be used if avoidance of the antigen is not possible.

a) **True**
b) **True**
c) **False**
d) **True**
e) **True**

ALL (acute lymphoblastic leukaemia) has a biphasic incidence with one peak in 3–4-year-olds and a second peak after the age of 40; it may be divided into three broad groups on the basis of the characteristics of the blast cell:
a) Common ALL — no T- or B-cell-specific surface markers, identified by 'Greaves' antisera (75%)
b) B-ALL — immunoglobulin on the cell surface (5%)
c) T-ALL — T-cell surface markers (20%).

The prognosis is best for the non-T non-B group and worst in the B-ALL group. T-ALL occurs more often in males, and in older children it typically presents with a thymic mass.

Patients may present with infection, bleeding or bruising (low platelets), malaise, weight loss, anaemia and joint or bone pain (radiolucent areas or osteoporosis may be apparent on X-ray). Minute haemorrhages are often seen in the fundi. The total WBC is high and the majority of cells are abnormal lymphoblasts. Other laboratory abnormalities may include: abnormal liver function tests (infiltration), a high urate, raised fetal haemoglobin, raised serum copper and raised serum iron. The diagnosis is made on bone marrow biopsy.

Induction and consolidation therapies often include: vincristine, prednisolone, L-asparginase, cytosine arabinoside and adriamycin. Intrathecal methotrexate is given during consolidation. Cranial irradiation is given when remission is achieved. Up to 90% of adults achieve remission, and in 40% this is permanent.

Relapse is highest in:
a) Children under 2 and over 10 years of age
b) Boys rather than girls (testicular disease and higher T-ALL)
c) Patients with high peripheral lymphocyte counts
d) Patients with extramedullary disease
e) The chromosomal translocations: t(9;22), and t(4;11)
f) Patients older than 35 years.

Allogeneic bone marrow transplantation may be useful in those patients who relapse, but graft versus host disease and unavailability of donors limits this therapy.

a) **True**
b) **False**
c) **True**
d) **False**
e) **True**

Acute myeloblastic leukaemia may occur at any age and carries a worse prognosis than ALL (acute lymphoblastic leukaemia). These diseases are clonal disorders of maturation of haematological precursors. Auer rods in the myeloblasts are pathognomonic of AML. Skin infiltration and gum hypertrophy are features of acute monocytic leukaemia. Promyelocytic leukaemia is associated with DIC, and fatal cerebral haemorrhage may occur early in the course of the illness.

AML is classified into seven groups:
M0 — undifferentiated blast cells
M1 — poorly differentiated myeloblastic
M2 — myeloblastic with differentiation
M3 — promyelocytic (hypergranular — associated with DIC)
M4 — myelomonocytic (AMML)
M5 — monocytic
M6 — erythroleukaemia: presents with fever, splenomegaly and bizarre erythroblasts in the peripheral blood. Later the disease progresses to a myeloblastic stage.

M1 and M2 make up 40% of cases. M2–M5 stain with Sudan black. Trisomy 8 is a common AML chromosomal abnormality.

Daunorubicin and cytosine arabinoside are used to induce remission, and 20% cure rates are usual. Bone marrow transplant, which is limited to younger patients (< 55 years) with an HLA matched sibling or twin, produces a 50% cure rate.

a) **False**
b) **True**
c) **False**
d) **True**
e) **True**

CML (chronic myeloid leukaemia) is characterised by proliferation of stem cells with excess granulopoiesis and sometimes excess platelet production. Haemopoiesis is ineffective and there is typically a mild anaemia. There is a leucoerythroblastic peripheral blood film appearance and reticulocytosis. The WBC count is very high but with few blasts. The age of presentation is most often between 40 and 45 years. In the elderly the course is more benign.

Clinical presentations may be from symptoms of splenomegaly (which may be massive), symptoms of hypermetabolism (loss of weight, night sweats, loss of appetite, raised urate), venous or arterial thrombosis, or incidental blood count.

The neutrophil alkaline phosphatase is reduced and B_{12} binding protein is increased. The Philadelphia chromosome is found in 95% of patients, and represents the translocation of the c-abl oncogene on chromosome 9 to the bcr (breakpoint cluster region) on chromosome 22, which is a tyrosine phosphokinase (210 kD). The majority of patients develop AML-blast crisis (80%), and 20% develop an ALL-blast crisis. Blast crises may be heralded (accelerated phase) by increasing anaemia, a high blast count, rapid enlargement of the spleen, lymph nodes or skin infiltration. Treatment is the same as for ALL or AML depending on the blast type.

Generally treatment is aimed at keeping the granulocyte mass controlled with courses of busulphan or hydroxyurea. Splenic radiation or splenectomy may be useful. Bone marrow transplantation should be considered in patients under the age of 50, and results in cure of 60% of chronic phase patients, and 40% of acute phase patients.

Causes of massive splenomegaly are as follows.

Massive splenomegaly: causes	
Infective	Malaria (tropical splenomegaly syndrome)
	Kala-azar
Malignant	Lymphomas (non-Hodgkin's, Hodgkin's, CLL)
	Hairy cell leukaemia
	CML
Haematologic	Myelodysplastic syndromes (polycythaemia rubra vera,
	myelofibrosis)
	Thalassaemia major
Infiltrative	Gaucher's disease
	Amyloidosis
Others	Felty's syndrome
	Sarcoidosis

a) **False**
b) **False**
c) **False**
d) **False**
e) **False**

Three viruses result in chronic liver disease, B, C, and D (in combination with B), while A and E produce acute liver disease. Chronic viral hepatitis has become the most common reason for liver transplant in some centres. Hepatitis G and GB have also been described, but the clinical importance of hepatitis G is not clear.

Hepatitis B is responsible for 10% of chronic liver disease in the USA. Interferon α is used to treat patients with abnormal aminotransferases, histologically demonstrable liver disease, demonstrable HBV DNA, and antigen e in serum. If e disappears, remission is usually sustained. Hybridisation tests can diagnose as few as 10^5 genomes per ml. Interferon α, given for 4 months, results in long-term remission in up to 40% of patients. Side-effects of interferon α are flu-like symptoms, myalgia, headache, bone marrow suppression, and worsening jaundice. Therapy should be stopped if jaundice worsens.

Hepatitis C is the commonest cause of cirrhosis in the developed world after alcohol. Interferon α is also given to patients with hepatitis C virus infection. Normal aminotransferases may be seen in the presence of histologically demonstrated hepatitis, and minimal, or fluctuating, changes of aminotransferase levels are typical of hepatitis C. Approximately 20% of hepatitis C infections develop cirrhosis. Interferon α therapy is given at a lower dose for 6–12 months (3 million units, 3 times a week), and results in sustained response in 25%. If PCR is positive for RNA after 3 months, response is unlikely. Good prognostic signs are age less than 45, less than 5 years of disease, low iron in liver, low RNA, and genotypes 2 or 3. Genotype 1 has a poor prognosis. Recently, combination therapy with ribavirin and α interferon has shown promise.

Although hepatitis D is the least common of the chronic viral liver infections, it results in the highest rate of cirrhosis (> 25%). The delta agent needs prior hepatitis B to replicate.

a) **True**
b) **True**
c) **True**
d) **True**
e) **False**

Macrocytosis generally indicates a dyserythropoiesis or premature release of red blood cells from the bone marrow. Causes of macrocytosis and macrocytic anaemia may be divided into causes associated with megaloblastic changes and those associated with normoblastic changes on bone marrow histology.

Megaloblastic anaemias arise because of inhibition of DNA synthesis in the bone marrow. B_{12} or folate deficiency are the most common causes; other causes include drugs which inhibit purine or pyrimidine synthesis (5-fluorouracil, hydroxyurea, cytosine arabinoside) and a number of rare congenital disorders of B_{12} and folate metabolism or DNA synthesis, (e.g. Lesch–Nyhan syndrome, orotic aciduria).

Causes of B_{12} deficiency:
Nutritional — vegans (rare)
Malabsorption — Addisonian pernicious anaemia, lack or abnormality of intrinsic factor, partial or complete gastrectomy, stagnant loop syndrome (jejunal diverticulosis, ileocolic fistula, blind loop), ileal resection or Crohn's disease, chronic tropical sprue, fish tapeworm (*Diphyllobothrium latum*), transcobalamin II deficiency.

Causes of folate deficiency:
Nutritional — common, especially in the poor and elderly
Malabsorption   coeliac diseases and tropical sprue
Pregnancy and lactation
Increased cell turnover — haemolysis (sickle-cell disease, thalassaemias), dyserythropoiesis (myeloproliferative diseases, leukaemia), malignancy, chronic inflammatory diseases (SLE, rheumatoid arthritis), psoriasis, acute or chronic infections (e.g. TB, malaria).

Patients who have had extensive gastric or small bowel surgery are at increased risk of developing folate deficiency. Patients with liver disease, congestive cardiac failure, and who are on dialysis have a high loss of folate in the urine or dialysate. The antiepileptic drugs phenytoin, primidone and phenobarbitone are also associated with folate deficiency.

Macrocytosis with a normoblastic bone marrow may be due to a high reticulocyte count, e.g. in haemolytic conditions or after severe haemorrhage, aplastic anaemia, red cell aplasia, liver disease, alcoholism, hypothyroidism, acquired sideroblastic anaemia, myelodysplastic syndromes, myeloid leukaemias, cytotoxic drug therapy (e.g. with azathioprine), chronic respiratory failure, myelomatosis, and in cases of a leucoerythroblastic anaemia.

a) **True**
b) **True**
c) **False**
d) **True**
e) **True**

Fulminant hepatic failure is a multisystem disorder which also affects the lungs, cardiovascular system and kidneys. Patients have a high risk of infection.

Liver failure may occur before the patient is clinically jaundiced; the early indicators include:
a) A rise in the prothrombin time of more than 20 seconds in 24 hours
b) Development of a metabolic acidosis
c) The onset of renal impairment
d) The patient becomes encephalopathic (marked by confusion, irrational behaviour, euphoria). Important signs include fetor, flapping tremor, slurred speech and constructional apraxia (writing, copying a diagram).

Patients should have vascular access established and a dextrose infusion set up (to prevent hypoglycaemia). The patient should be managed in an environment where intubation and rapid ventilation is easily accessible. Patients are best nursed at 45° to minimise the effects of a raised venous pressure on intracranial pressure.

Dietary protein is withdrawn and oral lactulose and neomycin commenced. Parenteral vitamin K is given along with high dose vitamins (thiamine).

In established hepatic failure the following problems may occur:
a) Coagulation problems — a mixture of DIC (raised fibropeptide-A and fibrin fragments), reduced hepatic coagulation proteins, and a low platelet count because of DIC and bone marrow suppression.
b) CVS hypotension and tachycardia. Vasodilatation, A-V shunting and a high cardiac output, and depression of the myocardium contribute to cardiac failure.
c) Respiratory failure patients may develop the adult respiratory distress syndrome. A Swan–Ganz catheter may be necessary to distinguish between cardiac and non-cardiac pulmonary oedema.
d) Renal failure — this is best managed by haemofiltration and intermittent haemodialysis.
e) Encephalopathy — may be the result of cerebral oedema, hypoglycaemia, electrolyte abnormality or drug accumulation. Mannitol (20%) should be infused if the patient develops cerebral oedema. Some authors recommend an intracerebral pressure transducer; and mechanical hyperventilation to lower the PCO_2 is beneficial.
f) Infections — staphylococci and gut organisms are the commonest pathogens. Broad spectrum antibiotics are used. Fungal infection should be suspected if the patient fails to respond or the cultures are negative, and amphotericin commenced immediately (i.e. before the fungal cultures return).

If a patient fails to recover using supportive measures he or she should be considered for a liver transplant.

Note: It is important to establish body thiamine stores before commencing a dextrose infusion. Glucose should not be given to patients with alcoholic liver disease in the absence of thiamine.

Answer to question 130

a) **False**
b) **True**
c) **False**
d) **True**
e) **True**

Irritable bowel syndrome can be divided into three groups:
a) Pain predominant, bowel habit change not prominent
b) Bowel habit change, alternating diarrhoea and constipation, the most common
c) Diarrhoea predominant, the rarest of the three.

The most useful point in differentiating organic from non-organic diarrhoea is the absence of nocturnal diarrhoea (nocturnal diarrhoea suggests organic aetiology, until proven otherwise). Typically irritable bowel syndrome patients complain of morning diarrhoea. Other symptoms are: chronic relapsing abdominal pain (often colicky) with disturbance of defecation — either constipation (faeces are often likened to rabbit pellets) or apparent diarrhoea. The majority of patients are young at the onset of symptoms (< 40 years). Typically 'diarrhoea' is actually frequency of stool rather than watery material. Patients also complain of abdominal distension. Two further symptoms are the passage of small amounts of mucus and a sensation of incomplete evacuation. Various criteria have been devised to aid diagnosis (Drossman, Manning), but do not supplant a good history and examination.

A full clinical history and investigation is appropriate. Full blood count and sedimentation rate must be normal. In patients over the age of 40, endoscopic or radiological examination should be performed to rule out malignancy.

Patients have a long history of symptoms, with relapses often associated with stress, or symptoms of mild anxiety and depression. The mechanism involves disturbances of gut motility. Increased rectal sensation to balloon insufflation is sometimes found during sigmoidoscopy.

Management involves reassurance, and explanation of the origin of the symptoms. Bran or high fibre diet tends to worsen symptoms, but stool-bulking agents may be useful. Antispasmodics are useful (e.g. buscopan, mebeverine).

a) **False**
b) **True**
c) **False**
d) **True**
e) **True**

Androgen-dependent hirsutism is the development of terminal (as opposed to fine vellous) hair, in a male pattern. Male areas of terminal hair growth are the face, shoulder and back, chest, and limbs. Sternal hair is seen in less than 3% of females, and shoulder and back hair should not be seen in women.

The main causes of hirsutism are:
Adrenal — congenital adrenal hyperplasia: 21 hydroxylase, 11β hydroxylase deficiency
Pituitary — Cushing's disease, acromegaly
Ovarian — tumours: gonadal stroma, germ cell tumours; polycystic ovarian syndrome
Drugs — phenytoin, diazoxide, minoxidil, corticosteroids, anabolic steroids
Idiopathic
Porphyrias
Anorexia nervosa
Familial and racial
Menopause.

Note:
Polycystic ovarian syndrome typically presents in early adulthood with irregular periods or secondary amenorrhoea, obesity, hirsutism and occasionally virilism. Characteristically there is a low FSH, high LH, high oestradiol and high androgen levels.

Ultrasound shows enlarged ovaries with a high ratio of stromal to follicular tissue. The underlying defect is not established, but there appears to be defective ovarian production of oestradiol with overproduction of precursor molecules which are converted into androgens in extraglandular tissue. A variant of this disease includes insulin resistance and acanthosis nigricans. This disease is caused by high insulin levels stimulating somatomedin C secretion, leading to ovarian production of androgens.

Suppression of the pituitary ovarian axis is achieved by birth control pills, or gonadotrophin releasing hormone, which restores periods and reduces hirsutism. Fertility management should be left to special centres, since these patients are susceptible to ovarian hyperstimulation after clomiphene treatment. In vitro techniques have been successfully used in these patients.

a) **True**
b) **True**
c) **False**
d) **True**
e) **True**

Osteoporosis is defined as a disorder characterised by a reduced volume of trabecular bone per unit volume of bone; the bone that is present is of normal composition. Osteoporosis is the commonest metabolic bone disorder. With advancing age a degree of osteoporosis is invariable. Vertebral collapse with loss of height is common and osteoporosis is a major cause of fractures (wrist, spine and hip) especially in the elderly and postmenopausal women. Spine radiographs may show unequal collapse with variable wedging, and herniation of the intervertebral discs through the end plates may lead to the appearance of Schmorl's nodes. In the femur a decrease in cortical bone thickness with loss of trabecular bone may be apparent. Typically the serum calcium, phosphate and alkaline phosphate levels are normal. Bone biopsy is helpful in complicated cases as, for example, when there is coexisting osteomalacia.

The mechanism of postmenopausal osteoporosis remains uncertain.

Preventing significant osteoporosis from developing is the key to management. Hormone replacement therapy with oestrogen/progesterone combinations should be considered for high-risk groups, e.g. thin Caucasian or Oriental women, early menopause, post-oophorectomy. Calcium dietary supplements and exercise may help. Fluoride has been used with varying success in the treatment of established osteoporosis in combination with calcium and oestrogens. Biphosphonates, such as alendronate, pamidronate and etidronate, which inhibit osteoclasts both directly and indirectly (by stimulating osteoblasts), are clinically useful in treating osteoporosis. A reduction of bone absorption is achieved, and 1% increase in bone density has been recorded after 2 years of therapy, with a demonstrable reduction of fracture rate.

Causes of osteoporosis include:
Senile osteoporosis, postmenopausal, immobolisation, hypogonadism (e.g. Turner's syndrome), Cushing's syndrome, thyrotoxicosis, hypopituitarism, rheumatoid arthritis, osteogenesis imperfecta, homocystinuria, heparin, alcohol, cigarette smoking, scurvy, pregnancy-associated osteoporosis, idiopathic juvenile osteoporosis.

a) **True**
b) **True**
c) **True**
d) **False**
e) **True**

Osteomalacia/rickets arises from vitamin D deficiency, and is characterised by an excess of unmineralised bone or osteoid. There are two forms of vitamin D, cholecalciferol D_3 and ergocalciferol D_2. The former is manufactured in the skin by the action of ultraviolet light on precursor molecules and is also obtained from dietary fish oils and dairy produce. The latter is obtained from plants after ultraviolet irradiation and is used to fortify margarine.

Vitamins D_3 and D_2 are 25-hydroxylated in the liver; measurement of the 25-hydroxylated derivative provides an index of body levels. Further hydroxylation occurs in the kidney, either to the active 1,25 $(OH)_2$ Vit D or the less active 1,24 $(OH)_2$ Vit D. 1 alpha-hydroxylation is stimulated by low plasma calcium and phosphate levels, PTH, oestrogens, prolactin and somatomedins. 1,25 $(OH)_2$ Vit D increases calcium and phosphate absorption from the gut and increases bone resorption.

Clinical features of osteomalacia
Biochemically, in the initial stages a low plasma calcium may be the only abnormality. This leads to secondary hyperparathyroidism which tends to correct the calcium (levels still low to normal) whilst lowering the phosphate. The alkaline phosphatase is high and urine calcium low. In cases of osteomalacia secondary to renal failure, phosphate levels are high. Radiologically Looser zones occur in the scapulae, long bones, ribs and pelvis; the vertebral bodies become bioconcave, to produce the typical codfish spine. In rickets the growth plate is typically widened and the metaphysis becomes cupped and ragged. The radiological changes of hyperparathyroidism (subperiosteal erosions) may be superimposed.

Bone pain and tenderness are common symptoms, proximal muscle weakness occurs and can be associated with a waddling gait. Deformity is common in rickets, with frontal bossing, bowing of the femur and tibia and enlargement of the costochondral junctions (rickety rosary). Hypocalcaemic symptoms with tetany, carpopedal spasm, stridor and fits can occur.

Simple dietary osteomalacia will respond to oral vitamin D. In renal failure 1-hydroxylated derivatives must be given.

Causes of osteomalacia include:

Lack of vitamin D (common in elderly and Asian communities) — poor diet, low exposure to sunlight. In Edmonton, Canada, for instance, no skin conversion is possible between October and March.

Malabsorption of vitamin D — coeliac disease, postgastrectomy, small intestine surgery, biliary disease, e.g. biliary cirrhosis.

Renal disease — chronic renal failure, vitamin-D-resistant rickets, causes of renal tubular acidosis (both proximal and distal), e.g. cystinosis, galactosaemia, both causes of PRTA.

Miscellaneous — phenytoin-induced osteomalacia, sclerosing haemangiomas can lead to hypophosphataemic rickets, vitamin-D-dependent rickets type 1, partial deficiency of 1α-hydroxylase enzyme, and type 2, end organ resistance to 1,25 $(OH)_2$ Vit D.

Answer to question 134

a) **False**
b) **False**
c) **True**
d) **False**
e) **True**

Paget's disease has an overall prevalence in the United Kingdom of 3%. Primarily it is a disease of the elderly with an incidence of 10% in those older than 85 years; it is commoner in men than women. Whilst a common disease in Anglo-Saxons and American Blacks, it is rarely seen in Chinese, Africans and Indians. The aetiology remains a mystery. There is evidence to support a slow viral infection; inclusion bodies have been identified in the nuclei of osteoclasts, and Paget's disease is believed to be primarily a disorder of osteoclasts. Initially, increased osteoclastic bone resorption is matched by increased osteoblastic activity, resulting in greatly increased bone turnover, but the bone formed is soft and disorganised. Later in the disease osteoblastic activity overrides bone resorption, leading to brittle, hard bone.

The disease usually affects the axial skeleton and weight-bearing bones. The majority of patients (> 90%) are asymptomatic. Clinical features include pain, often deep and aching in nature, warmth of an affected limb, skeletal deformity (e.g. bossed forehead, bowed leg, pathological fractures), neurological involvement with deafness, spinal cord compression, high output cardiac failure secondary to increased vascularity of pagetic bone and, rarely, an increased risk of osteosarcoma (< 1%; femur is the commonest site). Serum calcium and phosphate levels are usually normal, though calcium can rise with immobilisation. Serum alkaline phosphatase and urine hydroxyproline excretion are elevated and reflect disease activity. X-rays show enlarged deformed bones with an altered trabecular pattern. There is usually a mixed lytic/sclerotic picture.

Specific treatment with calcitonin is warranted for the following situations: pain resistance to analgesics and non-steroidal anti-inflammatory agents, neurological complications, Pagetic fractures and prior to orthopaedic surgery. Calcitonin needs to be given subcutaneously or intranasally. Side-effects include facial flushing and nausea. Alternatives to calcitonin include biphosphonates (pyrophosphate analogues) such as pamidronate.

Causes of frontal bossing include:
Paget's disease, acromegaly, achondroplasia, rickets, thalassaemia/sickle-cell disease, Gorlin's syndrome, congential hydrocephalus.

Causes of bowing of the tibia include:
Paget's disease, syphilis, rickets, Albright's disease/polyostotic fibrous dysplasia.

Answer to question 135

a) **True**
b) **True**
c) **False**
d) **True**
e) **False**

There have been many advances in the understanding of gastric (MALT) lymphoma. Between 90 and 98% of these lymphomas are associated with *H. pylori* infection, and there is increasing evidence that many patients who have this malignancy respond to eradication of the organism, although this is only true of low grade disease. There is evidence for T cell proliferation occurring specifically in response to the infection, and an abnormal B cell clone may be detected by gene rearrangement studies.

Typical abnormalities may also occur, and it is common to detect a paraprotein in the circulation. Immunocytochemical studies demonstrate that the T cells in the tumour are restricted in these cases.

Patients with low grade disease are rarely treated surgically, and those patients who do not respond, or in whom *H. pylori* eradication regimens are not considered sufficient therapy, receive standard chemotherapy regimens for non-Hodgkin's lymphoma. The prognosis is good.

a) **True**
b) **False**
c) **True**
d) **True**
e) **True**

Paraproteinaemia is common in elderly patients and in the absence of other features suggestive of myeloma, frequently requires no specific therapy. Paraproteins are not infrequently also found in younger patients, and may have no apparent immediate consequences for the patient. The situation is often described as 'MGUS' — monoclonal gammopathy of undetermined significance. In younger patients, evidence of immunosuppression (diminished levels of other immunoglobulins), bony lesions, or cytological bone marrow abnormalities (e.g. an excess of plasma cells, or abnormal plasma cell morphology) should be sought.

The clinical consequences of paraproteinaemia depend on the physicochemical properties, or immunological effects, mediated by the paraprotein concerned. Some paraproteins are cryoprecipitable, resulting in the syndrome of type I cryoglobulinaemia, and other paraproteins have rheumatoid factor activity, resulting in a formation of cryoglobulin consisting of IgM directed against IgG — this is type II cryoglobulinaemia. Some paraproteins can specifically activate complement by binding to $C1_q$ of the classical pathway, or to factor H, one of the control proteins of the alternative pathway.

a) **True**
b) **False**
c) **False**
d) **False**
e) **True**

Homocystinuria is an autosomal recessive disorder resulting in deficiency of the enzyme cystathionine synthase, resulting in accumulation of homocystine, increased amounts of urinary homocystine and deficiency of cystine and cystathione.

Homocystine in the urine gives a positive result with the cyanide nitroprusside test. Clinical features include excessive height, long extremities with span greater than height, scoliosis, depressed sternum, high arched palate, joint and ligamentous laxity, tendency to recurrent herniae, downward dislocation of the lens, myopia, cataracts, low IQ (may be normal), epilepsy, recurrent arterial and venous thrombosis, fair hair, malar flush and osteoporosis. Valvular and aortic root problems do not occur.

The clinical features of the dominantly inherited Marfan's syndrome include skeletal abnormalities and ligamentous laxity similar to homocystinuria, upward dislocation of the lens, normal IQ, aortic incompetence, aortic root dilation, and mitral valve prolapse. Osteoporosis and recurrent thromboses are not clinical features of Marfan's syndrome.

Treatments for homocystinuria include dietary restriction of methionine, cystine supplements and oral pyridoxine.

Answer to question 138

a) **True**
b) **True**
c) **False**
d) **True**
e) **True**

Hartnup disease is an autosomal recessively inherited disorder affecting 1/16 000, characterised by increased renal clearance and decreased intestinal absorption of the neutral amino acids including tryptophan. Some patients are asymptomatic. Tryptophan deficiency may produce a pellagra-like picture due to nicotinamide deficiency. Clinical features include a degree of mental retardation, psychiatric illness, cerebellar signs, convulsions, dermatitis affecting sun-exposed areas, and diarrhoea. Treatment involves dietary supplementation with oral nicotinamide.

Cystinosis is a lysosomal storage disorder, characterised by an accumulation of cystine in the cells of the reticuloendothelial system. There are three distinct types of cystinosis which vary in their severity; all are autosomal recessively inherited. In the infantile form, symptoms develop at 6 months. Clinical features include: failure to thrive, nephrogenic diabetes insipidus, rickets, glycosuria, generalised aminoaciduria, hyperphosphaturia, acidosis, hypokalaemia and proteinuria (all features of the Fanconi syndrome), corneal opacities, conjunctival cystine crystals and depigmentation of the retina. Progressive renal failure ensues, with early death. Cystine crystals may be demonstrated in the bone marrow, leukocytes or conjunctiva and prenatal diagnosis is now possible. In the juvenile form presentation is later, from 2 to 17 years, and the Fanconi syndrome less severe; cystine is deposited in the bone marrow and eye. In the adult form, patients tend to be asymptomatic; the eyes and kidneys are unaffected. When symptomatic, treatment is supportive and is aimed at correcting the metabolic abnormalities. Renal transplantation for end stage renal failure may be appropriate as the transplanted kidney does not develop overt disease.

Cystinuria results from the autosomal recessively inherited deficiency of the carrier protein for the dibasic amino acids cystine, ornithine, arginine and lysine (COAL). The carrier protein deficiency is apparent in the renal tubule and small intestine. Urinary stones are the sole manifestation of cystinuria. The stones are radio-opaque. Treatment involves high fluid intake, and penicillamine has been used with success. The drug reacts in vivo with cystine to form a penicillamine-cystine complex which has greater solubility. Although increasing urine pH is associated with increasing cystine solubility, the increased risk of bacterial infection and phosphate stone formation outweigh the potential benefits.

a) **False**
b) **False**
c) **False**
d) **True**
e) **True**

Leishmaniasis is caused by parasites of the genus Leishmania. At least 12 species cause disease in man. Reservoirs of infection include: man, rodents (e.g. gerbils) and foxes. Sandflies transmit the disease to man.

Visceral leishmaniasis or kala-azar due to *Leishmania donovani* occurs in Asia, Africa and South America. For every case of classical visceral leishmaniasis there are 30 subclinical cases. Patients with visceral leishmaniasis rarely have a primary skin infection. The incubation period varies from 2 to 8 months; males are affected more commonly than females. Established cases are characterised by a lack of cell-mediated immunity and a negative leishmanian skin test (in contrast to cases of cutaneous and mucocutaneous leishmaniasis). Parasites multiply freely in the bone marrow and reticuloendothelial system.

Clinical features include: fever (spikes twice a day), weight loss, malaise, diarrhoea, splenomegaly (may be massive), hepatomegaly, lymphadenopathy and general hyperpigmentation which is characteristic. Occasionally patients are jaundiced and suffer epistaxis and retinal haemorrhages. Progressive emaciation is usual, predisposing to secondary infection. Untreated, mortality rates approach 80%.

Hypergammaglobulinaemia (both IgG and IgM) is common, high titre of immune complexes may be detected but immune-complex-mediated disease is rare. Plasma albumin is often low due to malabsorption. Anaemia (combination of splenic pooling/decreased survival), neutropenia and thrombocytopenia are common.

The diagnosis may be confirmed by isolating the organism from spleen, bone marrow, liver, lymph node, and buffy coat. Serology may be helpful.

Pentavalent antimonials, e.g. sodium stibogluconate (i.m. or i.v.) are the drugs of choice, and a dose of 20 mg/kg is given daily for up to 20 days. Recognised side-effects of treatment include: muscle pains, nausea, anorexia, prolongation of QT interval, secondary T wave changes and arrhythmias. Other drugs such as pentamidine isothionate, or even liposomal amphotericin have been used in resistant patients.

Prevention rests with controlling the reservoir hosts and vectors. In Israel, live *Leishmania major* is inoculated to induce a controlled immunising infection.

Note: cutaneous leishmaniasis is endemic in Africa, South America and the Middle East. Following a sandfly bite usually on the face or arms, ulcerative nodules 1–4 cm in diameter form, which discharge and crust. Natural progression leads to healing with the formation of unsightly scarring.

a) **False**
b) **False**
c) **False**
d) **False**
e) **True**

Mycobacterium leprae is an acid- and to a lesser extent alcohol-fast intracellular rod. Man is essentially the only natural reservoir of the disease, and lepromatous leprosy patients are the main source of infection. Organisms are disseminated in nasal droplets and enter susceptible hosts via the nasal mucosa. The incubation period is wide and may be years. Individual susceptibility varies greatly and the spectrum of disease reflects the interaction between the host and the bacillary load.

Five varieties of leprosy are identified in the disease spectrum:
i) tuberculoid leprosy, ii) borderline tuberculoid leprosy, iii) borderline leprosy, iv) borderline lepromatous leprosy and v) lepromatous leprosy.

Tuberculoid leprosy is characterised by a high degree of cell-mediated immunity. Infection is confined to the skin and nerves. Typically one to three cutaneous lesions develop. Lesions tend to be large and annular with a raised outer edge and a hypopigmented centre, though hypopigmented macules may occur. Lesions are hypoanaesthetic and anhydrotic. Thickened peripheral nerves are typical of the tuberculoid part of the spectrum. Histologically on skin biopsy non-caseating granulomata are present; bacilli are only rarely seen. Caseating granulomata may however be seen in affected nerves. The lepromin skin test, a guide to cell-mediated immunity, is strongly positive in tuberculoid leprosy. CD4 T cells are found in biopsy specimens.

Lepromatous leprosy is characterised by a high bacillus load (demonstrated by Wade's slit-skin smear test) and a low level of cell-mediated immunity, resulting in a negative lepromin test.

Clinical features include generalised infiltration of the skin, resulting in thickening and coarsening of facial features — leonine facies, loss of eyebrows and eyelashs, iritis, destruction of the nasal cartilage, lymphadenopathy, testicular atrophy, gynaecomastia and a glove-and-stocking sensory neuropathy. Painless burns are common and Charcot joints may result. Circulating IgG levels are high and there is a decrease in the absolute number of circulating T cells with a reduction in CD4$^+$ to CD8$^+$ ratio.

More than 50% of lepromatous patients treated with chemotherapy will experience an episode of erythema nodosum leprosum which manifests as a crop of painful papules, which develop acutely, often over the extensor surface of the limbs. These gradually subside. The rash may be accompanied by fever, painful neuritis, lymphadenopathy, iritis and orchitis. Histologically, lesions resemble the Arthus reaction with vasculitis and a polymorphonuclear infiltrate.

Chemotherapeutic agents used in the treatment of leprosy include dapsone, rifampicin, clofazimine, prothionamide, ethionamide, and thalidomide. The latter is used in non-pregnant women for the treatment of erythema nodosum leprae.

a) **False**
b) **True**
c) **False**
d) **True**
e) **True**

Sickle-cell anaemia affects patients of African, Afro-Caribbean, Middle Eastern, Indian, and Mediterranean descent. The affected genes code for the β chain of adult haemoglobin.
The abnormality is a mutation on the sixth position of the β chain (glu-val substitution). This mutation confers protection against severe falciparum malaria, thus positively selecting heterozygotes. Heterozygotes (haemoglobin AS) are virtually normal and have few problems. In homozygous sickle-cell anaemia (haemoglobin SS), problems may occur from 6 months when the levels of fetal HbF decline to the adult level. Patients heterozygous for HbS and HbC (SC-disease), patients with HbS and β-thalassaemia trait (Sb-thalassaemia) have a slightly milder disease but may still develop life-threatening crises. Sickling is caused by polymerisation of deoxygenated HbS molecules in erythrocytes and may be precipitated by dehydration, acidosis, fever or hypoxia. The sickled cells increase the blood viscosity and block capillaries.
Chronic haemolysis results in anaemia (Hb 8 g/dl, 10–30% reticulocytes). Folate supplements are usually given. Haemoglobin S releases oxygen more easily so patients tolerate low haemoglobin levels well (right shift of oxygen dissociation curve).
Painful crises are the result of vascular occlusion and bone marrow infarction; juxta-articular areas of long bones, ribs, pelvis and back are the most common sites. Such bone infarcts can become infected and patients are at increased risk of osteomyelitis due to Gram-negative rods. Anaemic crises result from bone marrow aplasia which may be triggered by viral infection (e.g. parvovirus). Other causes of anaemic crises include visceral sequestration of RBC (spleen or liver), haemolysis and folate deficiency.
Splenic dysfunction develops early in infancy, and the spleen is reduced to a fibrous nubbin in homozygous patients following repeated splenic infarcts. Patients are at increased risk of pneumococcal and meningococcal infection. Pneumococcal vaccine and prophylaxis using phenoxymethylpenicillin afford some protection.
Infection may also trigger a severe chest syndrome (chest pain, fever, leucocytosis, thrombocytopenia) which is the commonest cause of death in all age-groups. Strokes occur in about 6% of patients and are an indication for immediate transfusion. Other complications include proliferative retinopathy, aseptic necrosis of the hip, gallstones, renal failure, enuresis and nocturia because of isosthenuria (inability to concentrate), priapism and leg ulcers.
Antenatal diagnosis is possible from chorionic villus samples or amniocentesis. Screening of children at risk should occur at birth using a cord sample.

a) **False**
b) **False**
c) **True**
d) **False**
e) **False**

A single pulmonary nodule in a patient with seropositive rheumatoid arthritis is four times more likely to be a malignant than a benign rheumatoid nodule. The lesion should therefore be biopsied.

Solitary pulmonary nodules — differential diagnosis:
a) Primary neoplasia — rare in patients under the age of 35 who are non smokers.
b) Secondary neoplasia — most commonly from breast, kidney, testes, or ovary. In patients under 35 years lymphoma or germ-cell tumours must always be considered.
c) Granulomatous disease — tuberculosis (old cavities may give rise to aspergillomas which may appear as solid masses on X-ray).
d) Sarcoidosis.
e) Vasculitis — Wegener's granulomatosis, Churg–Strauss syndrome, polyarteritis nodosa.
f) Pneumonia.
g) Infarction
h) Others — Benign adenoma, hamartoma, bronchogenic cyst, A-V malformation, hydatid cyst.

In a young non smoker a single pulmonary nodule should be thoroughly investigated at discovery to determine its nature.

Calcification is common in healed granulomas and haematomas; occasionally primary neoplasms may show areas of calcification, and malignancy may complicate long-standing granulomatous lesions.

The only lesions which may be conservatively managed are small (< 35 mm) lesions in young (< 35 years) non-smokers, or unequivocally radiologically benign lesions (popcorn hamartoma, bull's eye lesion, concentric calcification). An Echinococcus cyst should not be aspirated, due to anaphylaxis danger.

a) **True**
b) **True**
c) **True**
d) **True**
e) **True**

Pre-eclampsia is usually found after the 20th week of pregnancy, and 7 days before giving birth. Old or young primigravidae are most often affected. The diagnosis can be made if blood pressure in the second or third trimester increases by 30/15 mmHg compared to booking values or if the blood pressure exceeds 140/90 mmHg. A diastolic pressure of greater than 75 and 85, in the second and third trimesters respectively, should alert the clinician. Vasospasm, secondary to reduced PGI_2 has been postulated as an aetiologic mechanism, and low dose aspirin may prevent pre-eclampsia. Proteinuria > 300 mg a day is usual and the patients are oedematous. Epigastric pain, migraines and visual disturbances are also common. An elevated serum uric acid level is an early finding in pre-eclampsia. An elevated blood pressure in the first trimester indicates chronic hypertension. Pre-eclampsia may be complicated by placental ischaemia, fetal growth failure, disseminated intravascular coagulation and eclampsia.

Signs of severity are: blood pressure elevated above 160/110; heavy proteinuria; low urine output (< 400 ml/day); thrombocytopenia, or abnormal coagulation; elevated liver enzymes; CNS signs; pulmonary oedema. Eclampsia is commonest at low altitudes and may also complicate chronic hypertension. Patients show cerebral irritability and hyperreflexia; complications include cerebral haemorrhage, aspiration pneumonia, renal failure (may be prerenal due to low plasma volume, acute tubular necrosis or renal cortical necrosis) and liver failure.

Note: phaeochromocytomas may present in pregnancy and urine VMAs should be performed.

a) **True**
b) **True**
c) **True**
d) **False**
e) **False**

Glucose-6-phosphate dehydogenase deficiency is a sex-linked disorder affecting heterozygous males and homozygous females. Female heterozygotes have two populations of cells and are generally unaffected. The main populations affected are West African, Mediterranean, Middle Eastern and South-East Asian. A large number of isoenzymes have been described; clinically the two important groups are the African type (10–20%) and the Mediterranean type (0–7%). Low levels of G6PD result in reduced glutathione, which is essential for protecting the red cell from oxidation. Irreversible oxidation of haemoglobin and precipitation of globin chains leads to Heinz body formation. Cells containing Heinz bodies lyse readily in both intra-and extravascular compartments.

Four clinical syndromes are described in G6PD-deficient patients:
a) Drug-sensitive haemolytic anaemia
b) Favism
c) Neonatal jaundice
d) Congenital non-spherocytic haemolytic anaemia.

Drugs implicated include primaquine, chloroquine, dapsone, sulphonamides, nitrofurantoins, some analgesics (aspirin and phenacetin), water-soluble analogues of vitamin K and, in the Mediterranean form only, chloramphenicol and quinine.

Neonatal jaundice may occur in all forms and may be severe. Exchange transfusions may be required. Congenital non-spherocytic haemolytic anaemia is rare and characterised by mild continuous haemolysis which may be made worse by drug ingestion or infection. Favism is characterised by acute intravascular haemolysis in the Mediterranean type, 6–24 hours after eating fava beans or within minutes of inhaling pollen in the spring. Spontaneous recovery is normal although the haemolysis may be severe.

Laboratory investigations show features of haemolysis. Diagnosis is confirmed by a dye test — brilliant cresyl blue is discoloured if sufficient NADPH, and therefore G6PD, is present. Enzyme assays, genetic analysis and family studies are required. Patients should receive folate supplements.

a) **False**
b) **False**
c) **False**
d) **True**
e) **False**

Wilson's disease (hepatolenticular degeneration) is an autosomal recessive disorder, with an incidence of 1/200 000, characterised by increased copper deposition in the tissues. The gene is found on chromosome 13. First degree relatives of patients should be screened, since treatment with penicillamine will prevent complications. Serum caeruloplasmin, a copper-carrying glycoprotein, is low in 95% of patients. Copper is underexcreted in bile, resulting in build-up, primarily in liver cells. Serum copper levels are normal or low and urine copper levels are high.

Clinical features include: hepatic insufficiency and cirrhosis; neurological involvement with chorea, tremor, rigidity, dysarthria and dementia; corneal Kayser–Fleischer rings (seen by slit lamp); cataracts; proximal renal tubular acidosis, haemolysis, and impaired bone healing. Untreated, the disease is fatal. Penicillamine is used as a chelating agent.

Causes of chorea include:
Sydenham's chorea
Huntington's chorea
Benign hereditary chorea
Drugs, e.g. phenothiazines, phenytoin, alcohol
Stroke
Tumour
Thyrotoxicosis
Polycythaemia rubra vera
Systemic lupus erythematosus
Primary antiphospholipid antibody syndrome
Hypernatraemia
Hypoparathyroidism.

a) **False**
b) **True**
c) **True**
d) **True**
e) **True**

Causes of generalised pruritus include:
Obstructive jaundice, particularly primary biliary cirrhosis
Chronic renal failure
Haematological disorders, e.g. iron deficiency anaemia, mastocytosis, myeloproliferative disorders; polycythaemia rubra vera, particularly after a hot bath
Carcinoma and lymphoma
Endocrine disorders, e.g. myxoedema, hyperthyroidism, hypoparathyroidism, carcinoid
Drugs, e.g. cocaine, morphine
Allergies
Parasites, e.g. threadworms, roundworm, trichiniasis, onchocerciasis
Neurological disorders, e.g. tabes dorsalis
Psychogenic disorders
Dermatological disorders, e.g. scabies, eczema, urticaria, lichen planus, lichen simplex, dermatitis herpetiformis, milaria rubra, nodular prurigo, lichen sclerosus et atrophicus, and systemic mastocytosis.

Note:
a) Nodular prurigo — characterised by 1–2 cm warty nodules which are intensely itchy. Histologically there is lichenification, and local proliferation of nerve fibres. These lesions may represent a local response to scratching.
b) Lichen sclerosus et atrophicus — characterised by atrophic areas around vulva which arise in response to scratching.
c) Diabetes mellitus rarely causes generalised pruritus.

a) **False**
b) **True**
c) **False**
d) **False**
e) **False**

Warfarin inhibits post-ribosomal modification of vitamin-K-dependent clotting factors (II, VII, IX, X). Therapy is monitored by comparing the patient's prothrombin time with a laboratory standard.

In a patient with a prosthetic heart valve, overdose of the drug should be treated acutely with fresh frozen plasma, as vitamin K therapy will preclude effective anticoagulation for some time.

A number of drugs which act either as hepatic enzyme inhibitors or inducers may influence the metabolism of the drug, and thus its anticoagulant potency. Drugs such as rifampicin, carbamazepine, phenobarbitone, or primidone are all enzyme inducers, and reduce the efficacy of the drug. Cimetidine, allopurinol, clofibrate and a number of antibiotics, such as chloramphenicol, erythromycin, metronidazole, sulphonamides, and nalidixic acid enhance drug efficacy by enzyme inhibition or other mechanisms. Aspirin and non-steroidal anti-inflammatory drugs increase the risk of bleeding by their effect on platelets.

Answer to question 148

a) **True**
b) **True**
c) **False**
d) **True**
e) **True**

Turner's syndrome has an incidence of 0.3/1000 live births. The usual karyotype is 45,X0 (Barr body negative), but 30% of patients show mosaicism. Clinical features include: short stature, webbed neck, low hairline, cubitus valgus, shield chest, short metacarpals, lymphoedema, delayed sexual maturity, congenital heart disease (usually coarctation of the aorta, also ASD, VSD and AS), horseshoe kidney, ovarian dysgenesis with infertility, and an increased risk of osteoporosis. Turner's patients are susceptible to X-linked disorders and there is a higher incidence of autoimmune disease. It is one of the most common causes of primary amenorrhoea.

Noonan's syndrome affects males and females. Females have a Turner's phenotype but a normal chromosomal constitution and normal ovarian function. Pulmonary stenosis is the commonest cardiac abnormality complicating Noonan's syndrome, but HOCM has also been described.

a) **True**
b) **False**
c) **True**
d) **False**
e) **False**

Chronic lymphocytic leukaemia typically presents in the 55–75-year age-group. Patients have a very high lymphocyte count, and smear or basket cells are seen in the peripheral film. Patients may present with malaise, fever and anaemia. Many patients have no symptoms, and diagnosis is made by routine blood examination. Other features include lymph node enlargement, hepatosplenomegaly, acquired haemolytic anaemia and skin infiltration (local or a generalised eczematous rash, '*l' homme rouge*'). Haemolytic anaemia is associated with a raised unconjugated bilirubin, a positive direct Coombs' test and the presence of warm antibodies (IgG). Hypogammaglobulinaemia is the rule and patients have an increased risk of infections of all types. Respiratory infections and viral infections appear to be the most frequent

Chronic lymphatic leukaemia does not transform into an acute leukaemia. Staging is as follows: stage 0 = lymphocytosis only; Stage I = lymphocytosis and lymphadenopathy; Stage II = lymphocytosis and hepato/splenomegaly; Stage III = lymphocytosis and anaemia; Stage IV – lymphocytosis and anaemia and thrombocytopenia. Survival is stage dependent, with 10 years or more survival at stage 1 and 2–3 years at stage IV.

Asymptomatic patients with no evidence of bone marrow failure often require no treatment. Prednisolone is indicated to treat autoimmune haemolytic anaemia and in patients with bone marrow failure.

Alkylating agents, e.g. chlorambucil, may be used to decrease a high circulating lymphocyte count. Radiotherapy is used to treat enlarged lymph nodes causing compressive symptoms.

a) **True**
b) **True**
c) **True**
d) **True**
e) **False**

Listeria monocytogenes is a Gram-positive coccus that is widely distributed throughout the animal kingdom and is regularly found in water, earth and sewage. Man is infected by eating contaminated food. The bacillus can multiply at 4°C. Cold meats, particularly chicken, pasteurised milk, soft cheeses and coleslaw are common sources of infection. Being an intracellular parasite, a T-cell-mediated immune response is required to eliminate infection. Those at increased risk of disease include the immunocompromised, neonates, the elderly and pregnant women. Asymptomatic carriage is common, and 1% of healthy people and almost 5% of abattoir workers excrete Listeria in faeces. When symptomatic, symptoms resemble influenza; in addition, enlargement of the salivary glands and a purulent conjunctivitis are common features. Listeria has also been associated with arthritis, osteomyelitis, infective endocarditis, pneumonitis, peritonitis, urethritis, cutaneous maculopapular lesions and local abscess formation.

Meningoencephalitis primarily occurs in the newborn and immunosuppressed. The onset is often insidious with low-grade fever, followed by focal neurological signs, drowsiness and eventually coma. CSF shows a normal or low glucose, high protein and a pleocytosis (lymphocytes or polymorphonuclear cells may predominate).

Primary infection in pregnancy is often complicated by loin pain, and following delivery there is often a recurrence of symptoms with or without fever that is attributed to reinfection from the infected placenta. Persistent listeria infection is a cause of recurrent abortions.

Neonates may be infected either by transplacental haematogenous spread or following inhalation of infected amniotic fluid at delivery. Early onset infection often results in fetal death. The remainder show a high incidence of prematurity complicated by respiratory distress, meningoencephalitis and subsequent hydrocephalus.

Diagnosis is confirmed by isolating organisms from affected sites (e.g. blood, throat, conjunctiva, CSF, etc.). Serological tests are unreliable. Haemophilus, pneumococci and diphtheroids may be mistaken for Listeria.

Ampicillin is the treatment of choice, and gentamicin may be added for serious disease. Erythromycin is effective in penicillin-sensitive patients. The prognosis for listeriosis in adults without meningoencephalitis is excellent.

Answer to question 151

a) **True**
b) **True**
c) **True**
d) **False**
e) **False**

The transfer factor (TLCO) or diffusing factor (DLCO) is a measure of the lungs' ability to transfer carbon monoxide from the alveoli to the blood and is therefore a measure of gas transfer. The KCO (transfer coefficient) is the same measurement corrected for lung volume. Gas transfer is influenced by ventilation perfusion matching, the alveolar capillary membrane, the area of membrane at which transfer can take place (number of functioning alveolar units), the pulmonary capillary blood flow, the haemoglobin concentration, and the rate at which CO reacts with the haemoglobin.

The TLCO and KCO are reduced in:
a) Conditions which affect the lung parenchyma — infiltrative conditions, fibrosing alveolitis, sarcoidosis, pneumonitis associated with connective tissue diseases.
b) Decreased lung capillaries — pulmonary emboli, pulmonary hypertension, emphysema.
c) Ventilation pertusion mismatch or shunts — pulmonary oedema, pneumonia, A-V malformations, cirrhosis.
d) Anaemia.

The KCO is normal in asthma but the TLCO is increased.

Both the KCO and TLCO are elevated in:
a) Conditions which cause pulmonary haemorrhage, e.g. anti-GBM disease (Goodpasture's syndrome).
b) Polycythaemia (increased haemoglobin).

If there is simply loss of lung volume then the TLCO is reduced but KCO preserved. In cases of patchy parenchymal damage in which the rest of the lung is intact (e.g. mild alveolitis associated with scleroderma or SLE), the TLCO is reduced but the KCO is preserved, i.e. there has been loss of 'complete functional units'.

a) **False**
b) **True**
c) **False**
d) **True**
e) **False**

Haemolytic anaemias may be due to inherited abnormalities affecting red cell structure or metabolism, or may be acquired. Causes include:

Genetic:
a) Membrane disorders — hereditary spherocytosis, hereditary elliptocytosis, stomatocytosis.
b) Metabolic defects — pyruvate kinase deficiency (glycolysis), G6PD deficiency (oxidation-reduction).
c) Abnormal haemoglobins — thalassaemias, sickle-cell disease (see above), HbC, D, and E.

Acquired:
a) Immune — isoimmune (Rh, ABO incompatibility), autoimmune (idiopathic, drug-induced, associated with malignancy, other auto-immune disease or infections).
b) Traumatic red cell destruction — microangiopathy, valve prosthesis, burns, exercise.
c) Membrane defects — paroxysmal haemoglobinuria, liver disease.
d) Others — malaria, infections, chemicals, drugs, venoms, hypersplenism, dyserythropoiesis.

Haemolysis is also divided into intra- and extravascular. Traumatic, ABO incompatibility, G6PD, cold haemolytic disease, are examples of intravascular haemolysis, while spherocytosis and splenomegaly are examples of extravascular haemolysis.

Note: target cells are a feature of some congenital haemolytic anaemia. Bone pain is a feature of sickle-cell disease.

a) **True**
b) **False**
c) **False**
d) **False**
e) **False**

Pneumocystis carinii exists in three distinct morphological forms, as cysts, sporozoites and trophozoites. Asymptomatic infection in healthy individuals is common, but the organism produces an extensive pneumonitis in immunocompromised hosts, which is unusual in that it does not disseminate outside the lungs. Tachypnoea is the commonest clinical sign, cough is usually non-productive and fever may be absent in 50% of adults. The chest X-ray classically shows bilateral diffuse alveolar shadowing which spreads out from the hila; the apices tend to be spared. Up to 10% of patients may have a normal X-ray, despite clinical infection. Blood gases usually show a marked degree of hypoxia with a respiratory alkalosis. The white blood count is not contributory to the diagnosis. LDH rises in patients, and a rising LDH level during treatment is a poor prognostic sign.

Identification of the organism is essential for a definite diagnosis either by saline nebulisation or fibreoptic bronchoscopy. Saline nebulisation produces a sensitivity of almost 80%, while bronchoalveolar lavage has a sensitivity of up to 97%. Serological tests are of no value in the diagnosis of infections in adults.

Treatment:
Co-trimoxazole (trimethoprim and sulphamethoxazole) is the agent of choice, though there is a high incidence of side-effects (40–80%) which include fever, rashes, neutropenia, and hepatic dysfunction, especially in patients with the acquired immune deficiency syndrome. Intravenous or intramuscular pentamidine is reserved for those intolerant of co-trimoxazole. A number of serious side-effects have been associated with its use, including nephrotoxicity, hepatotoxicity, haematological abnormalities, hypoglycaemia, hypocalcaemia, hypotension and rashes.

Untreated, the disease is universally fatal in the immunocompromised. With treatment, 75% survive, though recurrence is common. Patients with HIV infection and a CD4 count below 200 should receive prophylactic co-trimoxazole, and since the risk of reinfection in AIDS patients approaches 60% per year, prophylaxis should be offered to all HIV-infected patients who have been infected.

a) **False**
b) **False**
c) **False**
d) **False**
e) **True**

The sciatic nerve divides into the common peroneal and posterior tibial nerves. The common peroneal nerve (L4, L5, S1, S2) passes through the popliteal fossa, winds around the neck of the fibula and divides into deep and superficial branches. The superficial nerve supplies sensation to the second, third and fourth toe interspaces, the dorsum of the foot and lateral part of the lower leg and is motor to the peroneal longus and brevis muscles. The deep branch supplies sensation to the first interspace, and innervates extensor hallucis longus (nerve root L5), tibialis anterior, extensor digitorum longus and brevis, and peroneus tertius. Common peroneal nerve palsy thus results in weakness of ankle eversion, ankle dorsiflexion and toe extension, and loss of sensation in the territory indicated above.

Answer to question 155

a) **True**
b) **False**
c) **False**
d) **True**
e) **True**

Diabetic neuropathy may take several forms:
a) A peripheral sensory neuropathy. Affects large fibres conveying joint position and vibration sense and small fibres conveying pain and temperature. Results in the typical symmetrical glove-and-stocking neuropathy. Legs are affected more severely, with early loss of ankle reflexes, dorsal column involvement and loss of pin prick and temperature. Some patients suffer from dysaesthesiae which can vary from mild tingling symptoms to excruciating discomfort.
b) A proximal motor neuropathy. Usually occurs in non-insulin-dependent diabetics over the age of 50. There is often a rapid onset of asymmetrical weakness of hip and knee and the patient may complain of intense pain in the thigh. Muscle power is normally regained, though recovery may be incomplete. The extraocular muscles may also be affected due to involvement of cranial nerves III and VI. Fibres subserving pupil constriction are carried superficially so are affected early in compressive lesions but tend to be spared in diabetes and vascular lesions.

Answer 155 continued

c) Mononeuropathy. Can result from pressure — diabetics are predisposed to carpal tunnel syndrome, lateral popliteal nerve palsies, etc. Peripheral nerves may also be affected by local vascular events. Involvement of several peripheral nerves simultaneously can result in a mononeuritis multiplex picture.

d) Autonomic neuropathy. Clinical features include postural hypotension, impotence, diarrhoea (nocturnal/postprandial), gustatory sweating, urinary retention and abnormal pupillary reflexes.

Common causes of mononeuritis multiplex include: diabetes mellitus, sarcoidosis, rheumatoid arthritis, polyarteritis nodosa (Churg-Strauss syndrome), malignancy, leprosy, and AIDS. Lyme disease is also a well recognised but rare cause of mononeuritis multiplex.

Answer to question 156

a) **False**
b) **False**
c) **False**
d) **True**
e) **False**

The five common filariid species which affect man are *Wuchereria bancrofti, Brugia malayi, Brugia timori, Onchocerca volvulus* and *Loa loa*. Fertilised females in the human host produce large numbers of microfilariae which are ingested by insect vectors, in which they mature to the larval stage. These are transmitted to man by the same vector and mature into the adult form.

Wuchereria bancrofti, Brugia malayi and *Brugia timori* are characterised by worm colonisation of the lymphatics. They predominantly occur in Asia but are also prevalent in Africa and South America. Mosquitoes are the insect vectors (Culex, Anopheline and Aedes). Acute infections are characterised by fever and painful lymphadenitis. Chronically, lymphadenopathy, lymphoedema and the typical elephantiasis picture occur. Bancroftian filariasis commonly involves the male genitalia. Hydrocele formation is common and elephantiasis usually takes the form of unilateral involvement of the whole of a lower limb. Brugian filariasis never involves the genitals and elephantiasis is restricted to the arm below the elbow or the leg below the knee. Tropical pulmonary eosinophilia with cough, shortness of breath, eosinophilia, high IgE levels and flitting chest X-ray shadows can occur with all types.

Diagnosis is confirmed by isolating microfilariae from the blood at times of peak periodicity (corresponds to vector biting time).

Diethylcarbamazine is the drug of choice.

Onchocerciasis (river blindness): *Onchocerca volvulus* infection is transmitted by Simulium vectors or blackflies, which inhabit fast-flowing waters of Africa and South America. Adult worms live in fibrous nodules which may be palpable subcutaneously or lie in deeper tissue planes. Involvement of the skin chronically leads to lichenification, hyperpigmentation, ulceration and elephantiasis. Heavy microfilarial infections or head nodules are usually associated with eye involvement; punctate keratitis, sclerosing keratitis, uveitis, retinitis and optic neuritis can occur. Blindness rates in some African villages approach 15%.

Diagnosis may be confirmed by detecting microfilariae in skin snips or in the eye. A Mazzoti (diethylcarbamezepine) provocation test may help.

Treatment: Diethylcarbamazine or suramin.

Loiasis: *Loa loa* infection is transmitted by the redfly or Chrysops fly and is predominantly confined to Africa. Intermittent painful oedematous 'Calabar' swellings are typical and adult worms may be seen crossing the conjunctiva where they cause redness, discomfort and swelling (such worms should be removed surgically). Diagnosis is primarily clinical with the combination of Calabar swellings and eosinophilia.

Treatment: Diethylcarbamazine. Prophylaxis: Intermittent diethylcarbamazine.

Answer to question 157

a) **True**
b) **False**
c) **False**
d) **True**
e) **False**

In the UK, in neonates *Escherichia coli*, group B streptococcus and *Listeria monocytogenes* are the commonest organisms causing bacterial meningitis. In pre-school children, *Haemophilus influenzae* is the commonest cause followed by *Neisseria meningitidis* and *Streptococcus pneumoniae*, whilst in adults, *Neisseria meningitidis* and *Streptococcus pneumoniae* predominate.

The classical symptoms and signs of meningitis include fever, headache (> 90%), meningism (85%), and photophobia. To these may be added confusion, altered conscious level, convulsions and focal neurological signs. Kernig's and Brudzinski's signs are both no more than 50% sensitive.

The overall prognosis for pneumococcal meningitis is poor, with mortality rates in industrialised countries in excess of 20%. Cranial nerve palsies, especially third and sixth palsies, not uncommonly complicate pneumococcal meningitis. Petechial haemorrhages occur in pneumococcal meningitis in approximately 10% of cases.

Haemophilus meningitis primarily due to encapsulated type B strains usually occurs in children between the ages of 3 months and 4 years, and petechial rashes may also occur. The overall mortality is approximately 5% but residual sequelae are not uncommon in up to 20% of cases. The Hib vaccine is an effective preventative measure.

The cerebrospinal fluid in cases of bacterial meningitis classically shows an elevated cell count of the order 1000–2000/mm³, predominantly polymorphonuclear cells, an elevated protein level of 1–1.5 g/L, and a low glucose level. Opening pressure of more than 20 cm is almost always found in bacterial meningitis.

Beta lactamase-producing strains of *H. influenzae*, as well as chloramphenicol resistance, are increasing, and more than 50% of Spanish isolates are resistant to chloramphenicol. Third generation cephalosporins are recommended for *H. influenzae* meningitis (cefotaxime, or ceftriaxone).

Benzylpenicillin is the treatment of choice for *Neisseria meningitidis* and *Streptococcus pneumoniae*, but resistance has been reported in certain areas. Third generation cephalosporins are an alternative. Group B streptococci and *Listeria monocytogenes* infections are treated with ampicillin, but ampicillin and gentamycin are synergistic and can be used against these organisms. Cefotaxime is effective against *E. coli*.

When the diagnosis of bacterial meningitis is suspected, blood cultures should be drawn and a third generation cephalosporin (ceftriaxone) given immediately.

In aseptic meningitis (viral meningitis) the typical CSF findings are of a normal glucose, elevated protein and a lymphocytosis 5–200 mm³ (though initially polymorphonuclear cells may predominate).

In tuberculous meningitis the CSF shows a low glucose, high protein with a pleocytosis 5–500 mm³, initially of polymorphonuclear cells and then lymphocytes. PCR may be useful in diagnosing chronic tuberculous meningitis. In cryptococcal meningitis the CSF shows a low glucose, high protein, with a lymphocyte pleocytosis.

158: a) **False**   **159:** a) **True**
   b) **True**   b) **True**
   c) **True**   c) **True**
   d) **False**   d) **False**
   e) **True**   e) **True**

The normal CSF has a pressure of approximately 12 cm of water (range 5–20 cm), a protein content of 0.2–0.4 g/L, a glucose level of 2.5–4 mmol/L (the CSF glucose is normally 66% of the blood glucose and should always be interpreted in conjunction with the latter), and a cell count of 1–3 mononuclear cells per mm³.

Causes of a high CSF protein include:
Meningitis, encephalitis, multiple sclerosis, syphilis, Guillain–Barré, intracranial tumour — especially acoustic neuroma, compression of spinal cord (Froin's syndrome), diabetes, hypothyroidism, postcerebral infarction, subarachnoid hemorrhage.

Causes of high CSF immunoglobulins/oligoclonal bands:
Multiple sclerosis, neurosyphilis, sarcoidosis, systemic lupus erythematosus, subacute sclerosing panencephalitis.

Causes of low CSF glucose include:
Bacterial meningitis, tuberculous meningitis, fungal meningitis, amoebic meningitis, cysticercosis, sarcoidosis, vasculitis, post-subarachnoid haemorrhage, mumps meningitis (25%), herpes encephalitis (10–20%).
   Normally viral infections do not lower CSF glucose.
   With acute syphilitic meningitis the CSF glucose is usually normal.

a) **False**
b) **False**
c) **True**
d) **True**
e) **True**

Benign intracranial hypertension (pseudotumor cerebri) is the syndrome of elevated cerebrospinal fluid pressure in the absence of ventricular dilation or intracerebral mass. In 4% of cases it may be associated with an empty pituitary sella.

Benign intracranial hypertension is predominantly a disease of obese young and middle-aged women. The aetiology is unknown though it is associated with: a) pregnancy; b) drugs (e.g. tetracyclines, oral contraceptive pill, vitamin A toxicity, nalidixic acid, nitrofurantoin, lithium and corticosteroids); c) head injury. Clinical features include headache, the commonest symptom, with varying severity, nausea, vomiting, blurred vision, visual obscurations, papilloedema (may be unilateral), diplopia (sixth nerve palsy — false localising sign), field defects (e.g. enlargement of the blind spot, central scotoma) and blindness. Depressed consciousness and impaired intellect are not features of the syndrome. The diagnosis is confirmed at lumbar puncture after excluding enlarged ventricles or a mass at CT scanning (in 5% of cases CT may show an empty sella — a recognised association). The CSF composition is usually normal, but protein content may be low. Pattern reversal visual evoked responses may be abnormal. Dural sinus thrombosis should always be excluded by MRI or venous phase of a digital subtraction angiogram, as the clinical picture may mimic benign intracranial hypertension.

Treatment in general aims at reduction of intracranial pressure to preserve vision and relieve symptoms. Initially therapeutic lumbar punctures may be performed. Thiazide diuretics and carbonic acid anhydrase inhibitors are effective, as are high-dose corticosteroids. Surgical shunting of cerebrospinal fluid may be needed if visual loss is progressive and the response to steroids is slow.

Most cases undergo clinical remission either spontaneously over approximately 2 years, or in response to treatment, though CSF pressure may remain high. Permanent visual loss occurs in up to 50%, and this may be severe in 10% of patients.

a) **True**
b) **True**
c) **False**
d) **True**
e) **True**

Antiglomerular basement membrane antibody disease is characterised by the linear deposition of autoantibodies along the glomerular basement membrane, resulting in glomerulonephritis.

Goodpasture's syndrome is the combination of glomerulonephritis and lung haemorrhage, and occurs when autoantibodies which cross-react with the alveolar basement membrane are present.

Goodpasture's syndrome typically occurs in young men; however, antiglomerular basement membrane antibody disease presenting solely with glomerulonephritis shows a peak in elderly women.

Susceptibility seems to be conferred by possession of the HLA antigen DR2. Lung haemorrhage occurs exclusively in smokers and infections of any sort can precipitate lung haemorrhage, as may fluid overload.

The term 'rapidly progressive glomerulonephritis' describes the tendency for rapid acute deterioration of renal function, which occurs, and is typical of antiglomerular basement membrane disease. Renal biopsy shows a diffuse crescentic pattern, and proliferation of cells around the glomerulus and within Bowman's capsule. Immunofluorescence reveals linear IgG and complement along the glomerular and tubular basement membranes.

Immunosuppressive treatment and plasma exchange is effective in treating lung haemorrhage and saving renal function in non-dialysis-dependent cases of glomerulonephritis. The prognosis for regaining renal function in patients who require renal dialysis is poor. For patients rendered dialysis-dependent, renal transplantation can be successfully undertaken 6 months after the disappearance of the pathogenetic autoantibodies.

a) **True**
b) **False**
c) **True**
d) **False**
e) **True**

The polymerase chain reaction is a powerful diagnostic technique, which utilises in vitro enzymatic amplification of DNA. The most commonly used enzyme is TAQ polymerase. It is possible to amplify DNA from a single cell, and the technique is widely used in antenatal diagnosis of genetic disorders, diagnosis of infections, and forensic medicine. The technique requires a knowledge of the flanking regions of the DNA template to be amplified, as specific oligonucleotide primers need to be designed.

The PCR can be used to diagnose herpes infection of the CNS, using cerebrospinal fluid samples, but at present this technique is only performed in a small number of reference laboratories. The technique is available for the diagnosis of mycobacterial infection, but the specificity and sensitivity of the currently available methods remain to be proven. This method is at present not used routinely for the diagnosis of mycobacterial infections.

The most commonly used PCR methods produce a final product consisting of double stranded DNA.

Answer to question 163

a) **False**
b) **True**
c) **True**
d) **True**
e) **True**

Diffuse systemic sclerosis is characterised by widespread thickening of the skin extending above the elbows and knees and onto the trunk. Severe interstitial lung disease, gastrointestinal complications, and renal impairment with or without hypertension, are well recognised. In all patients in whom the diagnosis is suspected, a full evaluation of pulmonary function is indicated, including respiratory function testing, plain radiograph, and ideally fine cut CT scanning. Interstitial lung disease is generally considered to be an indication for aggressive anti-inflammatory and immunosuppressive therapy.

High dose oral steroids may precipitate scleroderma renal crisis. The hypertension in these patients may be difficult to treat, and a hypertensive crisis with a rapid deterioration in renal function sometimes occurs. ACE inhibitors are the treatment of choice, and are used in some centres to treat patients without significant systolic hypertension or renal impairment. The early use of ACE inhibitors has been shown to decrease significantly the mortality of scleroderma renal disease.

A variety of autoantibodies have been described in patients with systemic sclerosis and other forms of scleroderma. Antibodies to scleroderma 70 (SCL 70) are directed against topoisomerase I, and are found in roughly 40% of patients. There is increasing interest in anti-endothelial cell antibodies, and there is some evidence that they activate endothelium and induce expression of adhesion molecules implicated in the inflammatory process. They are also found in Kawasaki's disease, and in some patients with SLE, though whether they have any immunopathogenetic role in these conditions is not clear at present.

Answer to question 164

a) **True**
b) **False**
c) **False**
d) **True**
e) **False**

Xanthinuria is a very rare metabolic disorder, characterised by the deficiency of xanthine oxidase, resulting in high levels of xanthine and very low levels of its metabolite, uric acid. Urate retention is a hallmark of pre-eclampsia. An increased MCV may be due to alcohol abuse or a myelo- or lymphoproliferative disorder, all of which are associated with hyperuricaemia and hyperuricuria.

Recognised causes of hyperuricaemia include:
Increased synthesis of uric acid:
Primary gout (25%) — increased synthesis of purines adenine and guanine

Lesch–Nyhan disease — X-linked hypoxanthine guanine phosphoribosyl transferase deficiency — associated with self-mutilation and low IQ
Myeloproliferative disorders/psoriasis
Diet high in purines
Glucose 6 phosphatase deficiency (glycogen storage disease type I).

Decreased uric acid excretion:
Primary gout (70%)
Hyperparathyroidism
Lead nephropathy (renal tubule damage)
Down's syndrome
Exercise
Starvation
Alcohol
Toxaemia of pregnancy
Hyperlipidaemia
Drugs — low-dose salicylates, diuretics, ethambutol, pyrazinamide, allopurinol.

Uricosuric agents are: probenecid, high-dose aspirin, sulphinpyrazone, azapropazone.

a) **False**
b) **True**
c) **False**
d) **True**
e) **True**

Clostridium perfringens (*Clostridium welchii*), an anaerobic, spore-forming Gram-positive bacillus, is a common component of the normal faecal flora. An exotoxin producing *Clostridium perfringens* is responsible for gas gangrene. Gas gangrene is usually seen complicating traumatic injuries, operations subject to faecal contamination or operations on ischaemic limbs, but may be seen as a primary infection of the perineum and scrotum. Other clostridial species implicated include *Clostridium novyi* and *septicum*. The incubation period varies from a few hours to 4 days.

Symptoms and signs develop rapidly and include: pain (an early symptom), marked tachycardia, mild fever, discolouration of overlying skin accompanied by a vesicular eruption, and characteristic crepitus (a late sign). The diagnosis is a clinical one. X-rays may show small amounts of gas in the muscle. Surgical excision of all damaged muscle is indicated. Intravenous penicillin, hyperbaric oxygen therapy and antitoxin may also help.

Approximately 33% of cases of food poisoning in the UK are due to a heat-resistant enterotoxin producing *Clostridium perfringens* type A. Clostridium food poisoning usually occurs on rewarming contaminated poultry or meat and produces symptoms of abdominal pain and diarrhoea 12 hours later. Fever and vomiting are usually absent. *Clostridium perfringens* may also cause necrotising enterocolitis — characterised by extensive necrosis of the intestinal mucosa.

Clostridium difficile, an exotoxin-producing, spore-forming, anaerobic Gram-positive bacillus, is responsible for pseudomembranous colitis, an exudative infection of the colon due to overgrowth of toxin-producing clostridia, and is seen in patients following antibiotic therapy (ampicillin, cephalosporins and clindamycin) and as a complication of colonic obstruction or uraemia. Almost all antibiotics can predispose to this disease. The clinical illness may vary from mild to severe diarrhoea with marked debilitation and a toxic megacolon. Fever and mild peritonism are common, and are often accompanied by a neutrophilic leukocytosis.

Two types of toxin have been isolated, A and B. Toxin B is 1000 times more toxic than A, and appears to be the main mediator of pseudomembranous colitis. The colonoscopic appearance is one of raised yellowish plaques, up to 1 cm in diameter. These may coalesce, and in severe disease the epithelium may slough. Distinction from inflammatory bowel disease may be difficult, and sometimes in mild disease the colon is macroscopically normal. Diagnosis depends on demonstrating *C. difficile* toxin in stools.

Treatment consists of stopping the offending antibiotic therapy, and administering antibiotics which are active against *C. difficile*. Oral vancomycin and oral metronidazole are effective treatments, with 95% success rates, but relapse is high (up to 55% for vancomycin).

a) **True**
b) **True**
c) **True**
d) **True**
e) **False**

Pulmonary emboli most commonly originate from thrombosis in the deep saphenous or pelvic veins. Risk factors include surgery, hereditary thrombophilia, heart failure, obesity, bed rest, post partum, intravenous drug abuse, pelvic masses and the pill.

Symptoms include pleurisy, haemoptysis, syncope, breathlessness and confusion. Patients may be pyrexial and have evidence of a pleural rub, small pleural effusion or right heart failure (raised JVP, tachycardia, and a low BP).

The chest X-ray may 1) be normal, 2) show areas of oligaemia with decreased pulmonary markings, 3) show the classical wedge-shaped area of atelectasis with a small pleural effusion and a raised hemidiaphragm, and 4) may show the 'pear shaped' appearance of the pulmonary artery due to embolic occlusion. ECG changes include atrial fibrillation, and the S1,Q3,T3 pattern (an S wave in lead I, Q wave in lead III and an inverted T wave in lead III), right ventricular strain (T inversion in leads VI–4), and a right bundle branch block. The arterial PO_2 falls with large emboli and is associated with hypocapnia due to hyperventilation. Angiography is the definitive investigation; otherwise a combined ventilation and perfusion isotope scan will detect areas of underperfusion. V/Q scans have a false positive rate, however. V/Q scans are graded according to high, low or intermediate risk, and further treatment may be tailored accordingly. Perfusion scans on their own have a high sensitivity but low specificity. A normal perfusion scan rules out a large embolus.

Small emboli are treated with intravenous heparin followed by oral warfarin, keeping the INR above 2. Treatment is stopped after 6 months unless the emboli are recurrent, when treatment for life may be needed. Massive emboli, which compromise the cardiovascular system or raise the pulmonary arterial pressure (above 40 mmHg), should be treated by embolectomy or thrombolysis with streptokinase or t-PA. Mortality usually occurs in the first two hours following massive pulmonary embolism.

Answer to question 167

a) **True**
b) **True**
c) **True**
d) **True**
e) **False**

Avascular necrosis is caused by a variety of conditions which cause aseptic bone infarction, usually by interfering with the local blood supply, e.g. arteritis, trauma or pressure to the vessel, thrombosis or embolism.

Causes of avascular necrosis include:
a) Trauma — e.g. fractured neck of femur.
b) Idiopathic avascular necrosis — affects the hips or knees of middle-aged men or women (4:1) or, rarely, other non-weight-bearing joints. Perthe's disease affects the hips of children below the age of 16 years. Theimann's disease (autosomal dominant), avascular necrosis of the epiphyses of small joints of the hands or feet in childhood or early adolescence.
c) High doses of corticosteroids or Cushing's syndrome.
d) Pregnancy.
e) Systemic illness, e.g. SLE, haemoglobin S and SC, alcoholism, chronic liver disease, pancreatitis, hyperlipidaemia, obesity, Gaucher's disease, dysbarism (Caisson's disease — decompression syndrome), radiation, diabetes mellitus, polycythaemia rubra vera, infectious endocarditis.

Answer to question 168

a) **False**
b) **True**
c) **True**
d) **False**
e) **False**

Phaeochromocytomas are catecholamine-secreting tumours which account for 0.5–1% of hypertensive patients. Noradrenaline is the predominant catecholamine secreted but adrenaline and dopamine are also secreted in varying amounts. A high proportion of adrenaline is said to favour an adrenal source. 90% arise from the adrenal medulla. The commonest extra-adrenal site is the organ of Zuckerkandl (located adjacent to the bifurcation of the aorta) but tumours can arise anywhere in relation to chromaffin-derived sympathetic ganglia. 10% of tumours occur bilaterally, 10% are malignant and approximately 10% are associated with other syndromes, e.g. Sipple's syndrome (MEN type II), neurofibromatosis and the von Hippel–Lindau syndrome.

Hypertensive patients with severe anxiety attacks, young patients with weight loss or seizures, tachycardias, hypertensive crises, especially during surgery or parturition, hyperdynamic beta-adrenergic states, and hot flushes should be examined for phaeochromocytoma. Hypertension is sustained in 50% and intermittent in 50% of cases. Usually both systolic and diastolic pressures are elevated. If adrenaline is the predominant catecholamine there may be disparity, with an elevated systolic and a depressed diastolic pressure. The predominant clinical features associated with paroxysms of hypertension, which coincide with outpourings of catecholamines and last for approximately 15–45 minutes, include: headache, pallor, cyanotic facial flushing, sweating, palpitations, anxiety, nausea, vomiting, abdominal pain and glycosuria. Precipitating factors of these paroxysms are many and varied, and are often related to tumour site. They include: exercise, stress, change in posture, swallowing, abdominal pressure and micturition. Many patients have a measurable degree of postural hypotension which is attributed to blunting of the normal sympathetic reflexes involved in blood pressure control due to chronic catecholamine overload. A paradoxical rise in blood pressure may also be seen after beta-blockade.

The diagnosis is confirmed by demonstrating increased excretion of catecholamine metabolites, e.g. vanillylmandelic acid, metadrenaline, and normetadrenaline on 24-hour urine collection. Alternatively, plasma concentrations of adrenaline and noradrenaline may be measured directly. As these tumours secrete intermittently, a normal result does not rule out a phaeochromocytoma. A pentolinium suppression test may be employed; pentolinium is a ganglion-blocker which inhibits the release of catecholamines from sympathetic nerves and the normal adrenal medulla. In normal subjects, plasma adrenaline and noradrenaline levels fall after pentolinium, but adrenaline levels fail to fall in patients with a phaeochromocytoma. CT scanning or an[131] I MIBG scan may be used to localise the tumour. Nuclear MRI shows T2 weighted images of adrenal tumours which appear brighter than surrounding tissue.

Surgical excision is curative in 75% of cases. Prior to surgery the patient should first be alpha-blocked with phenoxybenzamine to normalise blood pressure and prevent hypertensive surges. Phenoxybenzamine is a non-competitive alpha antagonist, and the dosage is increased daily to about 80 mg per day prior to surgery. The patient should then be beta-blocked with propranolol to prevent cardiac arrhythmias. The effect of introducing beta-blockers prior to alpha-blockade results in peripheral vasoconstriction and an elevated blood pressure.

During surgery, care must be taken not to manipulate the tumour. After surgery, blood pressure may fall dramatically and good monitoring is necessary.

a) **True**
b) **True**
c) **False**
d) **True**
e) **True**

Syringomyelia is characterised by an asymmetrical fluid-filled cavity lying close to the central canal of the cervical cord. When the cavity extends into the medulla it is known as syringobulbia. In the majority of cases it is associated with a mild Arnold–Chiari malformation and it has been suggested that the blockage of CSF flow caused by the malformation raises CSF pressure in the central canal, leading to rupture into the substance of the cord. Other associated skeletal malformations include kyphoscoliosis, Klippel–Feil syndrome (fused cervical vertebrae) and spina bifida.

The cavity usually starts at the C7–T1 region. Clinical features, which are often asymmetrical, are usually present by early adult life and include: loss of pain and temperature sensation causing painless burns to the arms, due to the spinothalamic fibres crossing over at spinal level. Wasting and weakness of the small muscles of the hand, loss of reflexes, a Horner's syndrome, loss of abdominal reflexes and lower limb pyramidal signs are also seen. The symptoms and sings tend to be slowly progressive. Exacerbations may be precipitated by bouts of sneezing and coughing which raise intracranial pressure. Charcot's joints are a late complication. Syringobulbia affects the 12th, 11th, and 10th cranial nuclei, often asymetrically. Nystagmus is common and sensory loss affecting the face occurs in a 'balaclava'-type distribution, i.e. affecting the peripheries but sparing the nose and mouth. The diagnosis can be made by myelography, CT scanning or nuclear magnetic resonance imaging. Surgical decompression often leads to clinical improvement and may prevent further deterioration.

The differential diagnosis of wasting of the small hand muscles includes:
Cord T1 lesions affecting anterior horn cells: motor neurone disease, syringomyelia, cord compression extrinsic/intrinsic, meningovascular syphilis, poliomyelitis.
Root lesions: cervical spondylosis, neurofibroma.
Lesions of the brachial plexus: cervical rib, Pancoast's tumour, Klumpke paralysis.
Peripheral nerve lesions: Charcot–Marie–Tooth disease, Friedreich's ataxia, and all causes of median and ulnar nerve lesions.
Miscellaneous: diffuse atrophy, rheumatoid arthritis.

a) **True**
b) **True**
c) **False**
d) **False**
e) **True**

Guillain–Barré and poliomyelitis are associated with a flaccid paresis.

Recognised causes of a spastic paraparesis include:
Multiple sclerosis, cord compression, cerebral palsy, motor neurone disease, Friedreich's ataxia, syringomyelia, anterior spinal artery thrombosis, sagittal sinus thrombosis, subacute combined degeneration of the cord, parasagittal meningioma, general paralysis of the insane, hereditary spastic paraplegia.

Friedreich's ataxia is a hereditary spinocerebellar disease which is inherited as an autosomal recessive trait (in some families autosomal dominant trait). The disease usually manifests between the ages of 5 and 15 years and there is no sex difference.

Degenerative changes are prominent in a) the larger dorsal root ganglion cells with subsequent loss of the larger myelinated fibres in the peripheral nerves, b) degeneration of the dorsal columns, c) the corticospinal and spinocerebellar pathways, d) cerebellum and e) the optic nerves.

An ataxic gait is often the initial presenting feature, with upper limb involvement following. Cerebellar signs include intention tremor, nystagmus and dysarthria. Titubation, i.e. a regular tremor of the head, may be present. Position and vibration sense are absent, the muscles are weak, tone is decreased, reflexes are diminished or absent, and the plantar responses are extensor. There may be evidence of wasting of the small hand muscles due to loss of anterior horn cells. 33% of patients develop optic atrophy. Other features include skeletal deformities, especially pes cavus and kyphoscoliosis, sensorineural deafness (10%), diabetes mellitus (10%), cardiomyopathy, decreased IQ, and retinitis pigmentosa.

The disease progresses slowly, death usually occurring in the fourth to fifth decades.

Hereditary spastic paraplegia: autosomal dominant or autosomal recessive forms are recognised. The recessive type has an earlier onset (10 years of age) and is more severe. Spasticity is the predominant problem, muscle power being relatively preserved, and the legs are affected more than the arms. The abdominal reflexes are often preserved and intact sphincteric function is characteristic. Sensory loss occurs late and is usually confined to the dorsal columns.

a) **True**
b) **True**
c) **False**
d) **True**
e) **True**

Cataracts occur in response to a wide range of physical, chemical or mechanical insults to the eye.

Causes of cataracts include:
Congenital: galactosaemia; dystrophia myotonica; hepatolenticular degeneration; Down's syndrome; Refsum's disease; Laurence Moon-Biedl syndrome; rubella; cretinism.

Acquired: old age; secondary to ocular disease, e.g. chronic uveitis, retinal detachment, myopia; diabetes mellitus; hypoparathyroidism; ionising, infra-red and microwave radiation; drugs, e.g. chronic use of corticosteroids and phenothiazines.

Answer to question 172

a) **False**
b) **False**
c) **False**
d) **False**
e) **True**

Malignancy is the commonest cause of hypercalcaemia in hospitalised patients. Overall hypercalcaemia occurs in approximately 5% of malignancies and is commonest with breast and lung lesions. Prostatic carcinoma commonly metastasises to bone, but the lesions are osteosclerotic and hypercalcaemia is rare. In the majority of cases hypercalcaemia occurs in the setting of disseminated disease; only rarely is it the presenting feature of malignancy.

Symptoms of hypercalcaemia associated with malignancy include nausea, vomiting, thirst, polyuria, impaired renal function, constipation, abdominal pain and muscular weakness. Such patients often have a hypochloraemic metabolic alkalosis which contrasts with the hyperchloraemic metabolic acidosis of primary hyperparathyroidism.

The pathogenesis of malignancy-associated hypercalcaemia is incompletely understood, but theories include a) the production of a PTH analogue (128 amino acid, parathyroid-hormone related peptide) or the release of cytokines (interleukin 1, 6, and tumour necrosis factor) by bone secondaries which then act locally leading to bone resorption.

Symptoms of hypercalcaemia may be improved by simply rehydrating the patient. Once this has been achieved frusemide may be used to increase urinary calcium excretion. Thiazides are contraindicated, since they can cause hypercalcaemia, and increased PTH per se. Corticosteroids, mithramycin and calcitonin have been used to try to correct the hypercalcaemia of malignancy but with little effect. Recently the intravenous biphosphonates, e.g. pamidronate, have been used with more success. Oral phosphate has been advocated in those with a normal serum phosphate and normal renal function. These are temporary measures and long-term treatment involves treating the underlying cause.

Note: corticosteroids are often effective in multiple myeloma.

The differential diagnosis of hypercalcaemia includes:
a) Malignancy
b) Hyperparathyroidism — primary or tertiary
c) Sarcoidosis
d) Multiple myeloma
e) Vitamin D intoxication
f) Immobilised cases of Paget's
g) Thyrotoxicosis
h) Recovery of acute tubular necrosis
i) Infantile hypothyroidism
j) Adrenal failure
k) Milk alkali syndrome
l) Phaeochromocytoma
m) Thiazide diuretics (increase renal tubular calcium reabsorption)
n) Artefactual causes, e.g. venous stasis.

a) **False**
b) **False**
c) **True**
d) **False**
e) **True**

Lyme disease is caused by the spirochaete *Borrelia burgdorferi* and is transmitted by ixodes ticks (*Ixodes dammini* in the USA, *Ixodes ricinus* in Europe) whose natural hosts include horses, deer and fieldmice. The disease is prevalent throughout the temperate regions of the world and is commoner in the spring and summer. The natural history may be divided into early and late stages.

Stage 1: Erythema chronicum migrans — 70% of cases (33% remember the initial tick bite). Regional lymphadenopathy and fever may also occur.

Stage 2: Dissemination phase. Features include: fever, malaise, cutaneous annular lesions, diffuse erythema, arthralgia, myalgia, meningitis, radicular pain, cranial nerve palsies (seventh lesions are common), mononeuritis multiplex, lymphadenopathy, atrioventricular block (prolonged PR interval is common), pancarditis, conjunctivitis, mild hepatitis and microscopic haematuria.

Stage 3: Late untreated stage. Features include: the rashes acrodermatitis chronica atrophicans and lymphadenitis benigna cutis, a large joint arthritis with synovial hypertrophy (rheumatoid factor is typically negative, the ESR is elevated) and enthesopathy, chronic encephalomyelitis, spastic paraparesis, cerebellar signs and dementia.

The diagnosis is confirmed serologically. Tetracyclines are the drug of choice in adults. Ampicillin, third generation cephalosporins and erythromycin may also be used. Avoidance of tick bites is sound advice in endemic areas, such as the east coast of the USA.

In Lyme disease the VDRL and TPHA tests should be negative. Normal PR interval 0.12–0.2 seconds.

Causes of prolonged PR interval include: coronary artery disease, digitalis effect, acute rheumatic fever, Lyme disease, atrial septal defect, cardiomyopathy.

Causes of short PR interval include: dissociated beat, Wolff–Parkinson–White syndrome, Lown–Ganong–Levine syndrome, HOCM, Duchenne muscular dystrophy.

a) **False**
b) **False**
c) **True**
d) **True**
e) **True**

The inhalation of volatile organic chemicals is not a new problem; glues, petrols, cleaning fluids, etc, have been inhaled for their stimulant effect for years. Today, adolescent boys are the commonest offenders, though all age-groups indulge. Benzene is the principal aromatic hydrocarbon constituent of glue, and toxic side-effects include: a) an aplastic anaemia, b) hepatitis, c) renal damage which can manifest as proteinuria, haematuria, calculi and distal renal tubular acidosis, d) neurological damage — cerebellar degeneration, optic atrophy, peripheral neuropathy, encephalopathy — and e) rhabdomyolysis.

Rhabdomyolysis with myoglobinuria is a well-recognised cause of acute renal failure and may occur in the absence of the classical signs of muscle pain and tenderness.

Other causes of rhabdomyolysis include:
Muscle injury — trauma, burns, polymyositis, ischaemia, severe exercise, convulsions
Infections — viruses (coxsackie, glandular fever, influenza), staphylococci, sepsis
Drugs and toxins — alcohol, heroin abuse, snake venom, carbon monoxide poisoning
Metabolic — hypokalaemia
Congenital disorders — McArdle's syndrome.

Features which suggest a diagnosis of rhabdomyolysis include: raised muscle enzymes (CPK, AST, LDH), hyperphosphataemia, hyperkalaemia (often marked), hypocalcaemia, hyperuricaemia, serum creatinine elevated out of proportion to serum urea, myoglobinuria.

a) **False**
b) **False**
c) **True**
d) **False**
e) **False**

Graph of lung volumes

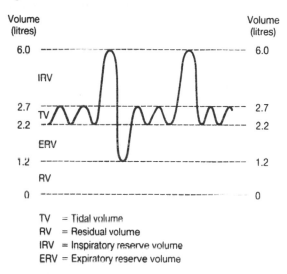

TV = Tidal volume
RV = Residual volume
IRV = Inspiratory reserve volume
ERV = Expiratory reserve volume

The TIDAL VOLUME (approximately 500 ml) is the volume of air breathed in and out of the lungs during normal respiration.
The INSPIRATORY RESERVE VOLUME (2–3 L) is the maximum volume of air which can be inspired after a normal tidal breath.
EXPIRATORY RESERVE VOLUME (750–1000 ml) is the maximum volume of air which can be expired after a normal tidal expiration.
The VITAL CAPACITY (4.8 L male, 3.2 L female) is the maximum · volume of air which can be expelled after a maximal inspiration.
The vital capacity is related to surface area and increases in the erect position due to a decrease in the volume of pulmonary venous blood.
The RESIDUAL VOLUME (1.2 L) is the volume of air remaining in the lungs at the end of a maximal expiration.
The FORCED EXPIRATORY VOLUME is the volume of air that can be expelled in 1 second starting from a maximal inspiration and should be 70–80% of the FORCED VITAL CAPACITY.
Typically: In obstructive airways disease the ratio of FEV_1/FVC is reduced.
In restrictive airways disease the FEV_1/FVC ratio remains normal or is even increased as the decrease in FVC is greater than the decrease in FEV_1.

a) **False**
b) **True**
c) **False**
d) **True**
e) **False**

Antiphospholipid antibodies are immunoglobulins of the IgG and IgM class which are directed against negatively charged phospholipid molecules. They were first described in systemic lupus erythematosus but have since been described in a wide range of autoimmune and non-autoimmune diseases (e.g. TB, leprosy) and can occur in isolation — the antiphospholipid syndrome. High titres of the antibody are particularly associated with thrombosis (venous and arterial), recurrent abortions and thrombocytopenia. A wide range of neurological diseases have been linked to the presence of antiphospholipid antibodies, including recurrent migraines, chorea and transient ischaemic attacks. Other associations include livedo reticularis, endocardial lesions and pulmonary hypertension.

The presence of antiphospholipid antibodies may be suggested by:
a) A positive VDRL.
b) The presence of a lupus anticoagulant as indicated by a prolonged PTTK time which cannot be corrected by the addition of normal plasma.

Antiphospholipid antibodies per se are detected by radioimmunoassay or ELISA using phosphatadyl serine and phosphatadyl choline as anionic phospholipids.

Note: a negative VDRL or the absence of a lupus anticoagulant does not exclude the presence of antiphospholipid antibodies.

Answer to question 177

a) **False**
b) **True**
c) **True**
d) **False**
e) **False**

HIV-associated neurological disease is very common in patients with AIDS, affecting around 40–60%. It is the commonest cause of dementia in young American males. HIV dementia is the commonest manifestation of HIV-associated neurological disease in adults, while in children encephalopathy occurs more frequently. The adult disease can also result in unsteady gait and tremor. Apathy and cognitive defects, motor abnormalities and loss of libido are seen.

Viral structural proteins are found in cells of the monocyte lineage such as microglia and multinucleated giant cells. Efficient productive HIV infection is not found in astrocytes or neurones, which are of neuroectodermal origin.

HIV 1 leukoencephalopathy is the other major neuropathological manifestation of infection. This results in white matter pallor, a reactive astrocytosis, but little in the way of inflammatory infiltrate. Multinucleated giant cells may be found. A vacuolar myelopathy has also been described in the disease. A number of components of HIV 1 are potentially neurotoxic, such as the GP 120 protein. Prostaglandins and a range of cytokines are elevated in HIV brain disease.

Answer to question 178

a) **True**
b) **False**
c) **True**
d) **True**
e) **True**

Atherosclerotic plaques primarily develop in the intimal layer of blood vessels. They result from interactions between the endothelial cells, inflammatory cells, and monocytes which have migrated into the intima from the blood stream, and smooth muscle cells. There is in vitro evidence that LDL can directly activate endothelium, without regulation of adhesion molecules, precipitating the egress of mononuclear cells into the vessel walls. Smooth muscle cell proliferation is an important feature of atherogenesis, and a range of inflammatory mediators including TPA and metaloproteinases have been implicated. There is increasing interest in immune mechanisms of atherogenesis. Accelerated atheroma formation in the coronary vessels typically occurs after heart transplantation. This process is somewhat retarded in patients who have donor organs which are well matched for HLA molecules.

a) **False**
b) **True**
c) **True**
d) **False**
e) **False**

Ventricular thrombus is found in 10–40% of patients after anterior infarction. Six months of anticoagulation is recommended by some authors in patients with large anterior infarctions, dyskinetic segments, visible large thrombus (by ultrasound), or congestive heart failure.

Troponin C and I bind calcium ions to myosin in the heart muscle, and are released during infarction. Recent studies, as well as the GUSTO study, have demonstrated that increased levels are a powerful predictor of mortality.

Both papillary muscle rupture and ventricular rupture are usually fatal. These are not uncommon, and cause 5% and 10% of deaths due to myocardial infarction.

Right ventricular infarction often is associated with inferior myocardial infarction, and is diagnosed by ST elevation of as little as 0.5 mm in V3R and V4R leads (right side of chest). Mortality is approximately 5-fold higher in inferior and right ventricular infarction when compared to right ventricular infarction alone. Atrial pressure rises to 10 mmHg, and Kussmaul's sign may be positive. Pre-load reduction must be avoided, and pulmonary artery wedge pressure must be kept in the region of 20 mmHg.

Answer to question 180

a) **False**
b) **True**
c) **False**
d) **False**
e) **False**

Neisseria meningitidis is a Gram-negative diplococcus. Capsular polysaccharides allow differentiation into eight main serogroups. Groups B and C are responsible for most cases of meningococcal meningitis in the UK.

The meningococcus, spread by nasal droplets, can produce a variety of clinical pictures which include:
a) Asymptomatic nasopharyngeal carriage — the commonest consequence.
b) Acute meningococcaemia with widespread petechial haemorrhages and shock due to circulating endotoxin. Disseminated intravascular coagulation and widespread haemorrhage can occur, the so-called Waterhouse–Friderichsen syndrome (characterised by bilateral adrenal haemorrhage. **Note:** circulating cortisol levels are high).

c) Meningococcal meningitis when endemic usually affects children under 5 years. During epidemics the incidence in older children and adults rises. Clinical symptoms include: fever, malaise, headache, photophobia, nausea, vomiting and myalgias (particularly pronounced in adults). Signs of meningeal irritation are common and petechiae visible on the skin, conjunctiva and mucosal membranes occur in up to 50%. Focal neurological signs — most commonly third and sixth cranial nerve palsies — do occur, but less commonly than in pneumococcal meningitis.

d) Chronic meningococcaemia — a low-grade vasculitic illness with fever, arthritis, rashes and splenomegaly.

e) Specific organ involvement, pericarditis, pneumonia, pleurisy, arthritis, eye involvement (conjunctivitis, endophthalmitis), proctitis, urethritis and hepatitis can all occur.

Diagnosis depends on a high degree of clinical awareness and may be confirmed by a) blood cultures, b) CSF examination which typically shows high protein, low glucose with a polymorphonuclear pleocytosis (in partially-treated cases lymphocytes may predominate); meningococci may be Gram-stained or cultured from the CSF in up to 80% of cases, and tests are available to detect meningococcal antigen, c) nasal swabs. Meningococcal serology (IgM) may also be useful.

Treatment: Intravenous benzylpenicillin is the treatment of choice, but third generation cephalosporins are an alternative. Acute meningococcaemia requires intensive care for cardiorespiratory support. Chemoprophylaxis in the form of rifampicin or ciprofloxacin should be given to close contacts for at least 3 days. There is now increasing resistance to sulphonamides.

Vaccines are available against serogroups A, C, Y and W135, but not yet against the poorly immunogenic group B. Meningococci can cause rapid death in previously healthy young people.

Answer to question 181

a) **True**
b) **True**
c) **False**
d) **False**
e) **False**

The sympathetic nervous system arises from cells in the lateral column of grey matter in the spinal cord from T1 to L2. These cells synapse with fibres from the hypothalamus. Myelinated white rami communicantes leave these cells and synapse in the ganglia of the sympathetic chain which runs from the base of the skull to the coccyx; postganglionic fibres then join the anterior nerve roots.

The parasympathetic nervous system arises from the nuclei of cranial nerves III, VII, IX and X and the grey matter of the 2nd, 3rd and 4th sacral segments. The long preganglionic fibres synapse in peripheral ganglia.

Stimulation of the sympathetic nervous system leads to a) pupil dilation, b) bronchodilation, c) peripheral vasoconstriction, d) a positive inotropic and chronotropic response, e) inhibition of gut peristalsis and an increase in gut sphincter tone, f) inhibition of micturition by a negative effect on the bladder musculature and increased sphincter tone, g) stimulation of sweating and hair erection, h) liver glycogenolysis and i) adrenal stimulation leading to high circulating adrenaline and noradrenaline levels.

Stimulation of the parasympathetic nervous system leads to a) pupil constriction, b) bradycardia, c) increase in gut peristalsis with increased secretions and relaxation of gut sphincters and d) stimulation of bladder detrusor muscle with inhibition of the internal sphincter.

Acetylcholine is the neurotransmitter at:
a) All parasympathetic and sympathetic ganglia where it acts at nicotinic receptors
b) The skeletal neuromuscular junction — nicotinic receptors
c) The adrenal medulla — nicotinic receptors
d) Parasympathetic nerve effector junction — muscarinic receptors
e) Anomalous sympathetic nerve effector cell junction (mediates sweating) — muscarinic receptors.

Acetylcholinesterase hydrolyses acetylcholine at the synaptic cleft and terminates its actions. Pseudocholinesterase is present in the plasma and gut where it hydrolyses acetylcholine. Noradrenaline is released at the postganglionic sympathetic nerve ending and mediates its effects through alpha and beta receptors.

The actions of noradrenaline and adrenaline are terminated in two ways:
a) Primarily by re-uptake into the sympathetic nerve endings where the majority is stored in vesicles ready for re-release, the remainder being metabolised by intraneural monoamine oxidase.
b) The rest is metabolised extraneuronally by catechol-O-methyltransferase to normetanephrine and metanephrine.

a) **True**
b) **True**
c) **True**
d) **False**
e) **True**

Symptoms and signs of autonomic neuropathy include: postural hypotension, loss of sweating, gustatory sweating (eating can provoke severe sweating and facial flushing), impotence, urinary retention, alteration in bowel habit (diabetics are predisposed to gastric paresis and postprandial diarrhoea) and loss of eye accommodation.

Causes of autonomic neuropathy include: diabetes; pure progressive autonomic neuropathy; autonomic neuropathy with Parkinson's disease; Shy–Drager syndrome — multiple system atrophy with disturbance of brain stem function and basal ganglia; amyloid; alcoholism/vitamin deficiencies; paraneoplastic syndrome; Guillain–Barré syndrome/viral infections; Chagas' disease (South American trypanosomiasis); drugs, e.g. ganglion-blocking drugs; congenital, e.g. familial dysautonomia. Other causes are: Fabry's disease, HIV, phaeochromocytomas, hyperaldosteronism, Menke's syndrome and many more.

Tests for the presence of autonomic neuropathy include: Heart rate variation: The normal heart rate varies with respiration (sinus arrhythmia). This is dependent on an intact parasympathetic system. The patient takes 6 deep breaths per minute and the maximum and minimum RR intervals are calculated and expressed as the difference in beats per minute. A normal subject shows a variation of > 15 beats/minute. A variation of less than 10 beats/minute is typical of autonomic neuropathy.

Blood pressure:
The presence of a postural drop in blood pressure and an inappropriately low blood pressure response to sustained hand grip are indicators of damage to the sympathetic nervous system.

Valsalva manoeuvre:
The physiology of the Valsalva manoeuvre needs to be understood. The patient blows into a mouthpiece connected to a sphygmomanometer and holds the column of mercury at 40 mmHg for 15–20 seconds (the manoeuvre should not be performed in patients with proliferative retinopathy, aortic stenosis, and epilepsy). There are four phases:
Phase 1 — normally there is a transitory rise in blood pressure as the increased intrathoracic pressure is transmitted to the great vessels, with an increase in heart rate.
Phase 2 — the blood pressure then rapidly decreases due to a decrease in venous return; blood pressure goes down, cardiac output is reduced. Baroreceptor responses and reflex tachycardia return blood pressure to normal.
Phase 3 — expiration against pressure stops, the pressure around the great vessels and aorta is relieved, blood pressure then drops.

Phase 4 — blood pressure overshoots, due to increased venous return and continued vasoconstriction. Bradycardia is then recorded, and the blood pressure returns to normal.

The Valsalva ratio is the ratio of the longest RR interval (during the bradycardia) to the shortest RR interval (during the tachycardia). Normal Valsalva ratio is 1.2; an abnormal ratio indicative of autonomic dysfunction is < 1.1.

Pupillary responses:
a) 1:1000 adrenaline has no effect on the normal pupil but induces dilation in the presence of postaganglionic sympathetic denervation.
b) 5% cocaine causes dilation of the normal pupil but has no effect in the presence of sympathetic denervation.
c) 5% methacholine has no effect on the normal pupil but induces constriction in the presence of parasympathetic denervation.

Isometric hand grip:
Pressure increases by 15 mmHg, after 3 minutes of squeeze; cold water response after 60 seconds of hand immersion at 4° also gives blood pressure rise of 15 mmHg.

Sweating:
Absent or impaired sweating in response to raising core body temperature.

Answer to question 183

a) **True**
b) **False**
c) **True**
d) **True**
e) **False**

As the name implies, familial Mediterranean fever (recurrent polyserositis) has a familial background in the majority of cases and is probably transmitted by an autosomal recessive gene. Familial Mediterranean fever is predominantly seen in Arab and Jewish people (both in Israel and the USA), Armenians and Turks.

The disease usually manifests before the end of the second decade. Abdominal pain due to peritonitis is the commonest presenting symptom and may be associated with pyrexia, tachycardia, vomiting, and constipation. Other clinical features include: pleurisy (50%), large joint arthritis (50%), rash, cutaneous vasculitis, myalgia, episcleritis, headaches, pericarditis and splenomegaly.

Attacks are characteristically self-limiting and subside after 24–48 hours. The diagnosis is essentially a clinical one. Investigations are non-specific and may show a polymorphonuclear leucocytosis, an elevated ESR, CRP, serum fibrinogen and serum immunoglobulin level during an acute attack.

The use of intravenous metaraminole (a sympathomimetic agent) as a diagnostic test is said to be both a sensitive and specific test for familial Mediterranean fever. The development of amyloidosis in later life, particularly renal amyloid and its associated nephrotic syndrome, is associated with a poor prognosis. The incidence of amyloid in various series ranges from 0 to 27% of patients but is highest in Sephardic Jews in Israel.

Oral colchicine is of value during an acute attack and, taken regularly, decreases the frequency of acute attacks, though its value in preventing amyloid deposition remains unclear. Abdominal surgery should be avoided, but sometimes is performed for presumed appendicitis.

Answer to question 184

a) False
b) True
c) True
d) False
e) True

Amyloidosis results from the accumulation of protein fibrils and may be localised to specific organs (brain, skin, joints and heart) or disseminated throughout the body.

Systemic amyloidosis may be subdivided according to the predominant protein which is deposited along with amyloid P protein in the tissues.

AL amyloid

Associated with B-lymphocyte dyscrasias, e.g. myeloma, Waldenstrom's macroglobulinaemia, lymphomas and benign monoclonal gammopathy. The amyloid AL fibrils are derived from monoclonal light chains and are primarily deposited in mesenchymal tissues. Clinical features include:

a) Nerves — peripheral and autonomic neuropathy, carpal tunnel syndrome
b) Tongue — macroglossia
c) Heart — restrictive cardiomyopathy. Increased sensitivity to digoxin: digoxin administration may result in fatal arrhythmias
d) Joints — large joint arthropathy
e) Skin — papules, nodules, non-thrombocytopenic purpura
f) Spleen — hyposplenism
g) Kidneys — proteinuria/nephrotic syndrome
h) Gut — motility disorder, malabsorption, haemorrhage
i) Acquired depletion of clotting factors 10 and 9
j) Adrenal — hypoadrenalism.

AA amyloid
Associated with chronic inflammatory conditions (e.g. rheumatoid arthritis, Crohn's disease), chronic infective conditions (e.g. bronchiectasis, osteomyelitis, tuberculosis, leprosy) and certain chronic malignancies (Hodgkin's disease, hypernephroma).
   AA amyloid is characterised by fibrils of AA protein deposited primarily in parenchymal tissue. Clinical features include:
a) Kidney — the primary organ affected, leading to proteinuria/nephrotic syndrome/end stage renal failure (cause of death in approximately 50% of cases)
b) Hepatosplenomegaly
d) Adrenal — hypoadrenalism
e) Gut involvements as with AL amyloid
f) Small, clinically insignificant cardiac deposition.

Hereditary syndromes associated with disseminated amyloid deposition:
e.g. Autosomal dominant type 1 familial amyloid polyneuropathy, familial Mediterranean fever.
   Familial amyloid polyneuropathy is caused by mutations of the transthyretin gene, and several Portuguese, Spanish, Japanese and German kindreds have been described. Finnish and type III disease are caused by mutations to gelsolin and apoprotein genes respectively.
   Senile systemic amyloidosis: with advancing age, amyloid deposition increases primarily in the heart and vessel walls.
   The diagnosis of amyloidosis is made histologically. Staining of affected tissue with Congo red and viewing under polarised light gives the typical apple-green birefringence. Rectal biopsy is positive in approximately 90% of cases of systemic amyloidosis. Immunohistochemistry allows distinction between AA and AL amyloidosis. Radiolabelled serum amyloid P (SAP) is a new technique which allows imaging of tissue amyloid deposition.
   Treatment of amyloidosis is primarily the treatment of the underlying disease, i.e. removing the precursor AL or AA fibrils in an attempt to prevent further amyloid deposition.

   Note: long-term haemodialysis may result in amyloid deposition in the joints and carpal tunnel, with beta 2 microglobulin the primary constituent.

Answer to question 185

a) **False**
b) **True**
c) **False**
d) **False**
e) **False**

Alport's disease (hereditary nephritis) usually presents in childhood. The exact mode of inheritance is uncertain and varies from pedigree to pedigree; males are affected more commonly and more severely than females.

The primary defect is thought to lie in the glomerular basement membrane. Electron microscopy shows a typical split lamellated appearance of the basement membrane and, interestingly, glomeruli do not react with antiglomerular basement membrane antibodies.

Haematuria is the commonest presenting feature and is later followed by proteinuria. High tone sensorineural deafness occurs in approximately one-third of patients. Other associated features include ocular abnormalities (lenticonus, spherophakia, retinitis pigmentosa and perimacular lesions), and megathrombocytopenia. Serum complement levels are normal. Progressive renal failure occurs before the age of 25 years in males; affected females rarely develop renal failure. The disease does not usually recur in transplants.

Answer to question 186

a) **False**
b) **False**
c) **True**
d) **False**
e) **True**

Anderson–Fabry disease is inherited in an X-linked recessive manner. There is deficient activity of the enzyme alpha galactosidase A, leading to the accumulation of glycosphingolipids in endothelial, perithelial and smooth muscle cells of blood vessels. The disease usually presents in childhood or adolescence with burning pain or paraesthesiae in the extremities. Angiokeratoma corporis diffusum is the classical rash with reddish-black telangiectasia typically clustering in the bathing-trunk area and hence often overlooked. The diagnosis is often not made until the development of renal failure or when cerebrovascular complications occur. End stage renal failure frequently occurs by the fifth decade; the accumulation of glycosphingolipid in blood vessel walls leads to myocardial ischaemia and strokes. Other recognised complications include valvular heart disease, corneal and lens opacities, pulmonary infiltrates, avascular necrosis and lymphoedema.

Most female carriers remain asymptomatic but can be detected by demonstrating reduced levels of the enzyme in leukocytes and by slit lamp examination of the cornea, which demonstrates corneal verticulata.

There is no specific treatment. Renal transplantation is appropriate for renal failure; low-dose aspirin may help prevent vascular complications. Genetic counselling is important and prenatal diagnosis is now available using amniocytes or chorionic villus biopsies.

Note: hexosaminidase A deficiency is the enzyme deficiency underlying Tay–Sachs disease.

Answer to question 187

a) **False**
b) **True**
c) **True**
d) **True**
e) **False**

Diabetic nephropathy occurs in between 40 and 45% of patients with type 1 insulin-dependent diabetes after 20–25 years. The natural history can be divided into two stages, the pre-clinical and the clinical stage.

In the pre-clinical stage the renal size is increased and the glomerular flow rate elevated by 30–40%. A phase of microalbuminuria precedes the development of clinical proteinuria (microalbuminuria is present when there is an elevation above the normal albumin excretion rate but below the 350 ug/L level, at which point albustix becomes positive). The presence of microalbuminuria is used to help predict which patients with type 1 diabetes will develop nephropathy. The pre-clinical stage may last 10 years or more before progressing to the clinical stage, manifest by proteinuria, hypertension, a falling glomerular filtration rate and a deterioration in renal function, until end stage renal failure is reached. The development of the nephrotic syndrome is a particularly poor prognostic sign. Rigid diabetic control has been shown to be valuable. Normalisation of blood pressure, a low dietary protein and the use of angiotensin-converting enzyme inhibitors may all slow disease progression.

Histology commonly shows a diffuse intercapillary glomerulosclerosis, and less commonly a nodular pattern as described by Kimmelstiel and Wilson. Linear IgG staining along capillary walls in immunofluorescence is typical.

Renal transplantation is the treatment of choice for end stage renal failure: 5-year patient and graft survival rates of 79% and 68% have been achieved using live, related donors. Overall transplantation results are worse in diabetics compared to other patients with chronic renal failure, especially in the elderly diabetic with vascular disease.

If dialysis is required, chronic ambulatory peritoneal dialysis (CAPD) has significant advantages over haemodialysis, namely:
a) Continuous ultrafiltration facilitates better fluid balance and control of blood pressure
b) The addition of insulin to the dialysis fluid allows better overall control of blood glucose
c) Avoids need for vascular access
d) A better prognosis for vision on CAPD compared with haemodialysis — 45% of diabetics on haemodialysis show a deterioration in vision.

There is little difference in the incidence of peritonitis between diabetic and non-diabetic patients.

Other renal complications of diabetes include:
a) Papillary necrosis
b) Pyelonephritis
c) Bladder dysfunction with secondary obstructive uropathy.

Note: diabetics with impaired renal function are particularly sensitive to intravenous contrast medium, which can precipitate acute renal failure.

Answer to question 188

a) **True**   d) **True**
b) **False**   e) **False**
c) **True**

Serum creatinine is filtered at the glomerulus but some is also actively secreted by the renal tubules. In contrast, urea which is filtered at the glomerulus undergoes a degree of reabsorption by the tubules. This reabsorption is particularly pronounced at low flow rates.

Causes of an elevated plasma urea include:
Low glomerular filtration rate (GFR), gastrointestinal bleed, dehydration/ urine flow rates less than 2 ml/min, drugs — particularly steroids and tetracyclines, catabolic states, high protein diet.

Causes of an elevated plasma creatinine include:
Low GFR, large muscle bulk, acute rhabdomyolysis, high meat diet, drugs — e.g. trimethoprim and cimetidine.

Causes of a low plasma urea include:
Liver disease, anabolic states, starvation or low protein diet, pregnancy, increased antidiuretic hormone.

Causes of a low plasma creatinine include:
Small muscle mass, pregnancy, increased antidiuretic hormone.

Common causes of an inappropriately elevated urea compared to creatinine: gastrointestinal bleed, dehydration.

Plasma urea and creatinine start to rise sharply when the glomerular filtration rate falls below 30 ml/min, and the deterioration in renal function can be followed with a plot of reciprocal creatinine concentration against time.

a) **False**
b) **True**
c) **True**
d) **True**
e) **True**

Between 80 and 90% of the total body sodium is located in the extravascular compartment where it influences the volume of extracellular fluid.

Causes of hypernatraemia include:
a) Pure water deficiency — e.g. diabetes insipidus
b) Hypotonic fluid loss — e.g. urine losses, sweating, vomiting, diarrhoea
c) Salt gain — e.g. mineralocorticoid excess, intravenous hypertonic saline
d) Hypotonic fluid loss (the majority of cases).

Causes of hyponatraemia include:
a) Pure water retention — e.g. inappropriate antidiuretic hormone
b) Combined retention of sodium and water with an excess of water — e.g. nephrotic syndrome, cirrhosis, congestive heart failure. (**Note:** in these disease states total body sodium is increased)
c) Salt loss — e.g. diuretic therapy, Addison's disease, salt-losing nephropathy.

Causes of pseudohyponatraemia include: hyperlipidaemia, hyperproteinaemia.

The concentration of sodium is measured in terms of plasma volume. If the percentage of water in a volume of plasma is decreased, for example in the presence of high concentrations of lipid or protein, then the amount of sodium in that volume of plasma will be decreased, even though the sodium concentration in plasma water may be normal. In such cases of pseudohyponatraemia the calculated osmolality will be less than the measured osmolality.

The osmolality is a measure of the total number of particles present in solution, expressed as mosmol/kg, which may be roughly calculated as follows:

Calculated osmolality = $2 \times$ (Na mmol/L + K mmol/L) + Urea mmol/L + glucose mmol/L. Normal range 285–290 mosmol/kg.

The osmolal gap is the difference between measured and calculated osmolalities and is usually less than 10 mosmol/kg. Large plasma concentrations of alcohol, ethylene glycol or methanol may also result in a large osmolal gap.

Central pontine myelinolysis is associated with rapid correction of hyponatraemia. Clinical features include a rapidly progressive quadriplegia (may be flaccid or spastic), associated with bulbar involvement. Eye movements and conscious level are usually normal. Complete recovery may occur, though overall the mortality is high. Correction of hyponatraemia should be slow, not more than 1 mmol/hour, and even slower in patients with underlying alcoholism.

a) **False**
b) **False**
c) **True**
d) **False**
e) **False**

The polio virus is a picorna enterovirus. Three serotypes (types 1, 2 and 3) exist, type 1 being responsible for the majority of outbreaks of paralytic polio, whilst type 2 is the strongest immunogen giving the highest rate of seroconversion after vaccination. The faecal–oral route is the primary mode of transmission and the virus is stable in food, water and milk. On entering the gastrointestinal tract, the virus multiplies in epithelial cells, Peyer's patches and the tonsils. Following this initial multiplication stage, spread occurs to regional and draining lymph nodes, where further viral replicating occurs. The virus then enters the blood stream and produces a mild febrile illness. Dissemination of the virus to reticuloendothelial cells follows, where further multiplication occurs, leading to a persistent viraemia 90–95% of individuals infected with the virus are asymptomatic as the virus is contained in regional lymph nodes; 4–8% experience a mild flu-type illness with fever, sore throat, myalgias and gastrointestinal upset, corresponding to the initial viraemic phase; 1–2% develop a major aseptic meningitis and a small percentage may develop classical paralytic polio, pain and stiffness preceding paralysis. The virus affects the anterior horn cells of the spinal cord (legs are affected more than arms, often asymmetrically), cranial nuclei of the brain stem (bulbar polio) and cells of the motor cortex. Paralysis is less common in children than adults. Tonsillectomy increases the incidence of bulbar polio.

The virus may be cultured from stools up to 5 weeks after onset of the illness. Serologically, the diagnosis can be confirmed by a 4-fold rise in antibody titre between acute and convalescent sera. CSF shows a high protein, normal glucose and a pleocytosis, initially polymorphs followed by lymphocytes.

Management of an acute attack is supportive; ventilation may be required (paralysis of respiratory muscles is usually irreversible).

Live oral polio vaccine (Sabin vaccine) is routinely used in the UK. It contains live attenuated strains of types 1, 2 and 3. The virus multiplies in the gut and stimulates local production of IgA in addition to serum antibodies. Excretion of the virus leads to secondary spread and increases herd immunity.

a) **False**
b) **True**
c) **True**
d) **False**
e) **True**

T lymphocytes are primarily implicated in defence against viral infections, and in chronic inflammation. They have an important role, in addition, in helping B cells to produce immunoglobulins. They express the CD3 antigen on the cell surface, and this is closely associated with T cell receptor antigens. T helper cells are primarily CD4 positive, while cytotoxic cells are CD8 positive, and there is considerable variation in the CD4/CD8 ratio in the normal population. T cells can produce IL-1, but the main cytokine is interferon gamma. Lymphocytes are primarily involved in type IV hypersensitivity reactions, and are not implicated in immune complex-mediated or allergic reactions.

Answer to question 192

a) **False**
b) **True**
c) **False**
d) **True**
e) **True**

Wernicke's encephalopathy results from the deficiency of thiamine (vitamin B_1), and consists of a triad of acute confusion, ataxia, and opthalmoplegia. Chronic alcoholism with malnutrition is the commonest cause in the UK. Other recognised causes include carcinoma of the stomach, malabsorption, hyperemesis gravidarum and haemodialysis. The classical signs are mental confusion, ophthalmoplegia with nystagmus, cerebellar ataxia and a peripheral distal symmetrical sensory neuropathy (rarely, motor neuropathies can occur). Korsakoff's psychosis, which is also attributed to a deficiency of thiamine, can accompany, follow or occur in isolation from Wernicke's encephalopathy; classically, the patient is alert with severe short-term memory loss and hence a tendency to confabulate.
    The diagnosis is made clinically and is a medical emergency. Treatment consists of immediate intravenous thiamine. No alcoholic should receive intravenous glucose with thiamine administered at the same time.

Note: a carbohydrate load can worsen or precipitate the syndrome. Thiamine deficiency can later be confirmed by finding a depressed red cell transketolase and an elevation in blood pyruvate. With prompt treatment, the signs of Wernicke's encephalopathy are completely reversible, unlike the memory loss of Korsakoff's psychosis which is usually irreversible.

Pathologically, the distribution of the lesions in both conditions is the same. Acutely, small haemorrhages may be seen in the region of the periacqueductal region of the mid-brain, thalamus, hypothalamus and mamillary bodies.

Thiamine deficiency may affect the heart — the so-called 'wet beri-beri' syndrome consists of biventricular heart failure and peripheral vasodilation (prevalent in Asia in those living on diets containing large proportions of polished rice).

Answer to question 193

a) **True**
b) **True**
c) **True**
d) **True**
e) **False**

Hepatocellular carcinoma develops in approximately 15% of patients with alcoholic cirrhosis. In France and Australia there is a strong correlation between alcoholic cirrhosis and diffuse mesangial IgA glomerulonephritis. There is a J-shaped relationship between alcohol consumption and ischaemic heart disease. Moderate alcohol intake has a protective effect which may be related to higher HDL levels, but chronic alcohol abuse is an independent risk factor for cardiac ischaemia. Alcoholics do not have an increased incidence of lymphomas. In reported series of avascular necrosis of the femoral neck, up to 40% of the cases had a significant alcohol intake.

Recognised associations of excess alcohol consumption include:
a) Alimentary system: reflux oesophagitis, Mallory–Weiss tear, oesophageal carcinoma and oropharyngeal carcinoma, haemorrhagic gastritis, malabsorption and nutritional deficiencies, acute pancreatitis, chronic pancreatitis, alcoholic liver disease, fatty liver (steatosis), alcoholic hepatitis, cirrhosis, haemosiderosis, hepatocellular carcinoma
b) Endocrine and metabolic abnormalities: pseudo-Cushing's syndrome, pseudothyrotoxicosis, hypoglycaemia, hyperglycaemia, hypogonadism, hypertriglyceridaemia, hyperuricaemia, porphyria cutanea tarda
c) Haematological: macrocytosis, megaloblastosis, iron deficiency anaemia, sideroblastic anaemia, haemolysis, thrombocytopenia, prolongation of PT and PTTK times
d) Bones: aseptic necrosis, osteoporosis
e) Muscles: acute painful myopathy, chronic myopathy

f) Cardiovascular: cardiomyopathy, hypertension, myocardial ischaemia
g) Psychiatric problems: alcohol dependence; withdrawal syndromes
   — e.g. delirium tremens, epilepsy; hallucinosis, morbid jealousy,
   affective illness, anxiety, phobias
h) Neurological: Wernicke's encephalopathy, Korsakoff's psychosis,
   cerebellar degeneration, peripheral neuropathy, tobacco/alcohol
   amblyopia, central pontine myelinolysis, hepatic encephalopathy,
   alcoholic dementia, trauma.

Miscellaneous:
a) Mesangial IgA glomerulonephritis
b) Increased risk of injuries while intoxicated
c) Increased risk of infections — TB, streptococcal pneumonia and
   meningitis
d) Fetal alcohol syndrome — low birth weight, microcephaly,
   clindodactyly, camptodactyly, ASD/VSD, low IQ, increased
   perinatal mortality.

Answer to question 194

a) **True**   d) **True**
b) **True**   e) **True**
c) **False**

Recognised causes of secondary hyperlipidaemia are listed below.

Secondary hyperlipidaemia	Triglyceride	Cholesterol
Nephrotic syndrome	+	+
Diabetes mellitus	+	+/–
Hypothyroidism		+
Obstructive jaundice		+
Hypergammaglobulinaemia	+	+
Renal failure	+	
Acute pancreatitis	+	
Alcohol	+	
Pregnancy	+	+
Oral contraceptive pill	+	
Thiazides	+	
Acute porphyria		+

Moderate nephrotic syndrome is associated with
hypercholesterolaemia, whilst severe hypoalbuminaemic states can
lead to elevated triglyceride and cholesterol levels.
Normal fasting blood cholesterol levels: 4.0–6.7 mmol/L.
Normal fasting blood triglyceride levels, male: 0.7–2.1 mmol/L.
Normal fasting blood triglyceride levels, female: 0.6–1.2 mmol/L.

a) **False**
b) **True**
c) **False**
d) **True**
e) **True**

Lipids are carried in the plasma in combination with apoproteins. The major lipoproteins are:
a) Chylomicrons — composed primarily of triglycerides. Dietary fat absorbed from the gut is initially transported in the form of chylomicrons
b) Very low density lipoproteins (VLDL) — composed primarily of triglycerides; transport endogenous triglycerides from the liver to adipose tissue
c) Intermediate density lipoproteins (IDL) — an intermediate stage between VLDL and LDL
d) Low density lipoproteins (LDL) — composed primarily of cholesterol, LDL is the end product after triglycerides have been removed from VLDL
e) High density lipoproteins (HDL) — have a high content of apoprotein A and are rich in phospholipids; they carry cholesterol from peripheral sites to the liver. HDL normally comprises approximately one-fifth of blood cholesterol levels. High levels are associated with a reduced risk of ischaemic heart disease.

Lipoprotein electrophoresis produces four bands: alpha (HDL), beta (LDL), pre-beta (VLDL) and chylomicrons.
The Fredrickson/WHO classification of hyperlipidaemias is summarised below:
TYPE I: Hyperchylomicronaemia. Autosomal recessive inheritance. Deficiency of either the extrahepatic enzyme lipoprotein lipase or apoprotein C II; leads to very high circulating levels of chylomicrons. Presents in childhood; features include eruptive xanthomatosis, lipaemia retinalis, acute pancreatitis and hepatosplenomegaly. No excess risk of ischaemic heart disease.
TYPE IIa: Hypercholesterolaemia — high LDL levels. Deficiency in LDL receptors. Autosomal dominant inheritance. Early onset ischaemic heart disease is the commonest mode of presentation in heterozygotes and the average age-span for untreated homozygotes is 20 years. Other features in heterozygotes include tendon xanthomas (Achilles, extensor tendons of hands), xanthelasmas, corneal arcus and a polyarthritis. In addition, homozygotes have cutaneous xanthomas and may develop supravalvular aortic stenosis.
TYPE IIb: Mixed hyperlipidaemia — increased LDL and VLDL levels. Autosomal dominant inheritance. Clinical features include corneal arcus, xanthelasma, increased risk of ischaemic heart disease.
TYPE III: Remnant hyperlipoproteinaemia — increased levels of IDL and some increase in VLDL (abnormality in apoprotein E). Clinical features include linear xanthomas in the palmar creases, cutaneous xanthomas, generalised atherosclerosis (propensity for the lower limbs), pancreatitis, glucose intolerance, gout and, rarely, hepatosplenomegaly.

TYPE IV: Familial hypertriglyceridaemia — primarily increased levels of VLDL, though cholesterol and chylomicron levels may also be raised. Impaired glucose intolerance and obesity are commonly associated. Clinical features include eruptive cutaneous xanthomas (usually on extensor surfaces), acute pancreatitis and severe abdominal pain, lipaemia retinalis, hepatosplenomegaly and, more rarely, peripheral neuropathy and dementia. There is probably an increased risk of atherosclerosis.
TYPE V: A combination of types I and IV — increased chylomicrons and VLDL.

Answer to question 196

a) **True**   d) **False**
b) **True**   e) **True**
c) **False**

Cerebrospinal fluid is formed by a combination of secretion and filtration in the choroid plexus of the cerebral ventricles. It circulates through the ventricles and the subarachnoid space before being reabsorbed by the arachnoid villi of the dural venous sinuses. The ventricular system consists of two lateral ventricles which communicate via the interventricular foramina of Munro with the third ventricle. The third ventricle communicates with the fourth ventricle via the cerebral aqueduct of Sylvius and the fourth communicates with the subarachnoid space via the foramen of Magendie and the foramina of Luschka.

Hydrocephalic states are characterised by dilation of the cerebral ventricles due to an excess of cerebrospinal fluid under increased pressure, and should be distinguished from conditions which lead to atrophy of cerebral tissue with a compensatory increase in cerebrospinal fluid under normal pressure.

Hydrocephalic states may be divided into two groups:
a) Non-communicating hydrocephalus — the obstruction is in the ventricular system or at the exit foramina leading to the subarachnoid space. Causes include: aqueduct stenosis often associated with spina bifida; Arnold–Chiari malformation: herniation of the cerebellar tonsils or other parts of the hind brain into the foramen magnum with obstruction to outflow of cerebrospinal fluid, often associated with syringomyelia and spina bifida; Dandy Walker syndrome: atresia of foramen of Magendie, hypoplasia of cerebellar vermis and dilation of the fourth ventricle; tumours in the third or fourth ventricle.
b) Communicating hydrocephalus — free flow of CSF occurs between the ventricles and subarachnoid space. Causes include: intraventricular haemorrhage in pre-term infants; congenitally acquired toxoplasmosis; tuberculous meningitis and rarely, increased CSF production (choroid plexus papilloma).

The term 'normal pressure hydrocephalus' is used to describe a group of patients with a communicating hydrocephalus who are thought to have defective absorption of cerebrospinal fluid. The ventricles are large on CT scanning but the pressure as measured at lumbar puncture is normal (the underlying pathology of this syndrome is not understood). Classically, there is a history of progressive dementia with memory loss, unsteady gait, incontinence of urine and bilateral pyramidal signs with extensor plantars. Shunting the cerebrospinal fluid is often associated with improvement of symptoms and arrests further decline. Moebius syndrome is the syndrome of congenital bilateral seventh nerve palsy, often associated with sixth nerve palsy and rarely with other cranial nerve palsies.

Answer to question 197

a) **False**
b) **False**
c) **True**
d) **True**
e) **False**

There is an increased perinatal mortality rate in babies born to diabetic mothers. There is also an increased incidence of premature labour, pre-eclampsia, polyhydramnios, macrosomia, hyaline membrane disease and congenital abnormalities (e.g. caudal regression syndrome, characterised by sacral agenesis and bony abnormalities of the lower limbs). Many of these complications are related to poor blood glucose control; post-mortem studies on neonates from diabetic mothers show pancreatic islet cell hyperplasia. Blood glucose should be normalised where possible and should always be kept to less than 7.5 mmol/L (preprandial levels < 5.5 mmol/L, postprandial levels < 7.5 mmol/L). This necessitates regular monitoring of blood glucose, dietary control, 150–250 g of carbohydrate per day and a twice to three times daily insulin regimen (combinations of a short- and a medium-acting insulin). Oral hypoglycaemic agents should not be used.

a) **True**
b) **True**
c) **True**
d) **True**
e) **False**

A grief reaction is a normal consequence of bereavement and needs to be worked through. Sedatives and antidepressants should not be routinely used in uncomplicated grief reactions.

The following are recognised features of normal grief: a sense of numbness, anger (often directed against the medical profession or God), guilt, disbelief, an urge to cry out, anxiety, agitation, pining, an awareness of the presence of the deceased or a tendency to search for the lost person, and the adoption of attitudes and mannerisms of the deceased. Somatic symptoms are also common and include diarrhoea, loss of appetite, weight loss, sighing respiration, palpitations and insomnia. With the resolution of acute grief, a feeling of apathy may predominate and may last for months. The anniversary of the death and special occasions can induce a resurgence of acute grief.

Delayed grief is said to occur if more than 2 weeks elapse before grieving begins. Elderly widowers show a 40% increase in mortality compared to their married counterparts in the 6 months following a bereavement (most deaths are attributed to cardiovascular disease). Pathological depression with suicidal tendency can manifest as an abnormal grief reaction and suicidal rates tend to peak on anniversary dates.

Answer to question 199

a) **True**
b) **True**
c) **True**
d) **True**
e) **True**

Methylenedioxymethylamphetamine (Ecstasy) is a phenylethylamine compound, which has similarities with amphetamines and mescaline. It was first made by Merck in Germany in 1914. Tablets are 90 to 100 mg, but there are many drugs which are similar in appearance and effect, such as MDA (methylenedioxyamphetamine), MDEA, and even LSD mixed with adrenaline. Recognised side-effects of Ecstasy are: fulminant hyperthermia, which may be fatal and needs intensive care admission. Convulsions and rhabdomyolysis have also been described. Psychosis and depression are also seen. An inappropriate ADH secretion is also described, as is DIC. Interaction with lithium and phenalzine give a serotonin-like syndrome with muscle contraction, tremulousness, tachycardia and hypertension. Liver damage may be severe, and in some cases transplantation is life-saving.

a) **False**
b) **True**
c) **False**
d) **True**
e) **True**

Acute post-streptococcal glomerulonephritis was the commonest type of glomerulonephritis presenting with acute renal failure, but its incidence in the developed world has markedly declined. Diffuse proliferative glomerulonephritis associated with systemic lupus erythematosus, Henoch–Schönlein purpura and the vasculitides (Wegener's, and microscopic polyarteritis) now account for the majority of cases of rapidly progressive glomerulonephritis.

An acute nephritic illness with hypertension, haematuria, oliguria and oedema is the commonest presentation of a post-streptococcal GN (usually β-haemolytic streptococci); the nephrotic syndrome is rare. Histology shows proliferation of endothelial and mesangial cells and neutrophil accumulations; in severe cases crescents can occur. Subepithelial immune deposits (C3, IgG, IgA, IgM) are typical. Generally the prognosis is good, with over 90% recovering from the initial nephritic illness, though a small percentage may later develop chronic renal failure.

In mesangial IgA disease (Berger's disease), IgA and C3 are deposited in the mesangium in association with proliferation of the mesangial cells in a diffuse or focal manner; rarely, crescents are present. Asymptomatic haematuria or proteinuria are the commonest presenting features, and macroscopic haematuria may be provoked by viral infections. Rarely, the presentation may be with a nephritic or nephrotic illness. In general, the natural history is very good, though approximately 10% will progress to chronic renal failure.

Diffuse proliferative glomerulonephritis with crescents (which fill Bowman's space) may complicate any form of primary diffuse or focal GN or occur in association with diseases such as SLE, HSP, anti-GBM, and the vasculitides. The usual mode of presentation is with oliguric acute renal failure. Hypertension is not common. Urine is positive for blood and protein and usually has red cells and granular casts. Overall, the prognosis for renal function recovery is related to the severity and extent of the crescent formation. Immunosuppressive drugs, including pulse therapy with cyclophosphamide, and plasma exchange have been shown to improve the short-term prognosis, though in the long term, progressive glomerulosclerosis tends to lead to end stage renal failure. Patients initially rendered anuric by their diseases have a particularly poor prognosis.

On urine phase contrast microscopy, if greater than 70% of the red blood cells are dysmorphic then glomerular bleeding should be suspected. Normal urine contains small numbers of dysmorphic red blood cells, suggesting that they enter at the glomerulus level. Red cell casts are highly suggestive of glomerulonephritis but can also occur in accelerated hypertension, haemolytic uraemic syndrome and interstitial nephritis.

A renal biopsy should be performed in all suspected cases of glomerulonephritis, the only exception being children with the nephrotic syndrome and minimal urine sediment, who have a 90% chance of minimal change disease. They should be biopsied only if they fail to respond to steroids.

Answer to question 201

a) **False**
b) **False**
c) **True**
d) **True**
e) **False**

Two types of membranoproliferative (mesangiocapillary) glomerulonephritis are recognised. Both show diffuse thickening of capillary walls. (**Note:** similar histological changes may be seen in the glomerulonephritis associated with SLE.)
   The usual presentation of MPGN is a nephritic or nephrotic syndrome and, less commonly, microscopic or macroscopic haematuria. The disease is rare in children less than 5 years of age.
   Type 1, with subendothelial immune deposits (IgG, IgM, IgA, C3 and C4) is associated with thickening of the capillary walls due to mesangial interposition. Hypocomplementaemia is common (70%) and reflects activation of the classical pathway with low C3 and C4.
   Type 2, or dense deposit disease, is characterised by an intramembranous deposit of electron-dense material within the basement membrane. C3 is found along capillary loops but, unlike type 1, no immunoglobulins are found. Hypocomplementaemia is also common (70%). An autoantibody, the C3 nephritic factor, is found in 70% and this stabilises C3b Bb (alternate convertase enzyme), allowing uncontrolled activation of the alternate pathway resulting in low C3, low factor B and properidin levels, but normal levels of C4. There is an association between dense deposit disease and partial lipodystrophy.
   The natural history of membranoproliferative glomerulonephritis is a gradual deterioration to end stage over a 10-year period. Type 2 deteriorates more quickly than type 1. The presence of crescents and the development of the nephrotic syndrome are poor prognostic signs.

Answer to question 202

a) **True**
b) **True**
c) **True**
d) **True**
e) **False**

Recognised causes of optic atrophy include:
Congenital:
Leber's optic atrophy, Friedreich's ataxia, retinitis pigmentosa.
Acquired:
Trauma/pressure — surgery, Paget's disease, aneurysm, tumour, glaucoma, chronic papilloedema, exophthalmos.
Infections — choroidorenitis, e.g. toxoplasmosis, syphilis.
Ischaemia — giant cell arteritis, elderly hypertensive diabetic patients severe anaemia.
Demyelination — multiple sclerosis.
Toxic — lead, ethambutol, methylalcohol, tobacco.
Metabolic — vitamin B_{12} deficiency, tropical ataxic neuropathy.

Answer to question 203

a) **True**
b) **False**
c) **True**
d) **True**
e) **True**

Causes of tunnel vision (concentric diminution in visual fields) include:
retinitis pigmentosa, choroidoretinitis, papilloedema, glaucoma, optic atrophy due to tabes dorsalis, migraine, bilateral lesions of the anterior calcarine sulcus, hysteria.

Retinitis pigmentosa may be inherited as a distinct entity (autosomal recessive, autosomal dominant and X-linked), or can be associated with several syndromes, including Refsum's disease, abetalipoproteinaemia, Friedreich's ataxia and Lawrence–Moon–Biedl syndrome, and Kearns–Sayer syndrome.

Abetalipoproteinaemia is an autosomal recessive disorder characterised by defective synthesis of apoprotein B, which results in an inability to absorb and transport triglycerides. Clinical features include: failure to thrive, steatorrhoea, ataxia, nystagmus, retinitis pigmentosa and acanthocytes in the peripheral blood.

Refsum's disease is an autosomal recessive disease which arises from an inability to metabolise phytanic acid. Clinical features include: cataracts, retinitis pigmentosa, optic atrophy, deafness, cerebellar signs, peripheral neuropathy, cardiomyopathy and ichthyosis.

Optic papillitis is associated with a large central scotoma.

a) **True**
b) **False**
c) **False**
d) **True**
e) **False**

Reiter's syndrome (first described in 1916) is a reactive seronegative spondyloarthritis which affects males more commonly than females. 70–90% of patients are HLA B27 positive. Peak age of onset 20–35 years. Reiter's syndrome may be triggered by:
a) Genitourinary tract infection (mycoplasma and chlamydia have both been implicated)
b) Dysentery (*Shigella flexneri* and *dysenteriae*, Salmonella, *Yersinia enterocolitica* and Campylobacter have all been implicated).

The classical triad of acute Reiter's syndrome includes arthritis, conjunctivitis and urethritis. The arthritis typically affects the large and small joints of the lower limbs in an asymmetrical fashion. Achilles tendonitis, plantar fasciitis and sausage toes are commonly found. The conjunctivitis is usually bilateral and mild. The urethritis is also usually mild.

Other features include:
a) Mild systemic disturbance
b) Keratoderma blenorrhagica — yellow, waxy papules on the palms and soles
c) Circinate balanitis — vesicles on the coronal margin of prepuce — painless
d) Buccal ulcers — painless.

The initial disease is usually self-limiting, but up to 60% develop chronic disease with an asymmetrical sacroiliitis and an upper and lower limb arthritis.

Other features of the chronic stage include: chronic uveitis, aortic regurgitation, conduction defects, pericarditis, pulmonary infiltrates, peripheral neuropathy. Treatment is symptomatic with NSAIDs.

205: a) True	206: a) True	207: a) False
b) False	b) False	b) True
c) False	c) True	c) False
d) True	d) False	d) False
e) False	e) False	e) True

The porphyrias are a family of diseases which result from enzyme deficiencies in the haem biosynthetic pathway. They may be divided into the acute and non-acute porphyrias. All porphyrias show photosensitivity with the exception of acute intermittent porphyria.

Acute porphyrias:
a) Acute intermittent porphyria	Autosomal dominant
b) Variegate porphyria	Autosomal dominant
c) Hereditary coproporphyria	Autosomal dominant

Non-acute porphyrias:
a) Cutaneous hepatic porphyrias	Autosomal dominant

Erythropoietic porphyrias
a) Congenital porphyria	Autosomal recessive
b) Erythropoietic protoporphyria	Autosomal dominant

Simplified stages of haem synthesis:

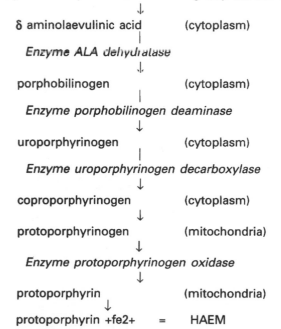

Glycine + succinyl Co enzyme A (mitochondria)

Enzyme ALA synthase (Rate limiting step increased in all porphyrias)

δ aminolaevulinic acid   (cytoplasm)

Enzyme ALA dehydralase

porphobilinogen   (cytoplasm)

Enzyme porphobilinogen deaminase

uroporphyrinogen   (cytoplasm)

Enzyme uroporphyrinogen decarboxylase

coproporphyrinogen   (cytoplasm)

protoporphyrinogen   (mitochondria)

Enzyme protoporphyrinogen oxidase

protoporphyrin   (mitochondria)

protoporphyrin +fe2+   =   HAEM

Note: Enzyme ALA = delta amino laevulinic acid synthase

All porphyrias are characterised by increased aminolaevulinic acid synthase, so leading to over-production of porphyrins and their precursors. In non-acute porphyrias, enzyme porphobilinogen deaminase activity is also increased, so excess porphobilinogen and delta aminolaevulinic acid are converted to porphyrins. In acute porphyrias, level of porphobilinogen deaminase is reduced or normal; hence aminolaevulinic levels are increased, which may be responsible for the neurological abnormalities recorded.

Acute intermittent porphyria:
The majority with the genetic trait remain silent. Females are affected more commonly than males. The disease normally presents in the late 20s and is uncommon in childhood.

Clinical features include:
a) Gastrointestinal (95%): abdominal pain, vomiting, constipation, occasionally diarrhoea
b) Peripheral neuropathy (66%): primarily a symmetrical motor neuropathy affecting the upper limbs more than the lower limbs. Sensory symptoms may also be present. Trunk weakness and cranial nerve palsies can occur
c) Psychiatric symptoms (50%): depression, hysteria and psychotic symptoms. Grand mal epilepsy (20%)
d) Other clinical features during an acute attack include fever, sinus tachycardia, hypertension, papilloedema, left ventricular failure, proteinuria, elevated blood urea which may persist, leucocytosis, abnormal liver function tests and hyponatraemia (increased anti-diuretic hormone secretion).

Acute intermittent porphyria is characterised by raised levels of delta aminolaevulinic acid and porphobilinogen in the urine, which are further increased during an acute attack. The urine turns red/brown on standing. The diagnosis may be confirmed by detection of excess porphobilinogen in the urine, using Ehrlich's aldehyde reagent, which turns pink and is insoluble in chloroform/butanol (unlike urobilinogen, which also turns pink with Ehrlich's reagent but is soluble in chloroform/butanol).

Many drugs are known to precipitate an acute attack. The most important are sulphonamides, barbiturates, anticonvulsants (carbamazepine, phenytoin), the pill. Other precipitating factors include periods, pregnancy, infection, dieting and alcohol.

Variegate porphyria (prevalent in South Africa):
This was spread from a single affected patient in 1668. Reduced activity of protoporphyrinogen oxidase. Affects young adults.
a) Neurological and gastrointestinal features as well as a photosensitive blistering rash. The skin lesions can persist and may be the sole manifestation of the disease
b) An acute attack may be precipitated by barbiturates, sulphonamides, anticonvulsants, and the pill.

Diagnosis: faecal porphyrins are high and increased during an attack; aminolaevulinic acid and porphobilinogen levels are raised only during an acute attack. β-carotene may help the photosensitivity.

Hereditary coproporphyria:
Very rare. Clinical features: neurological, gut and skin manifestations — skin lesions do not occur in isolation.

Acute porphyrias — specific management points:
Screen asymptomatic relatives.

High carbohydrate intake suppresses hepatic ALA synthase and decreases production of porphyrins. Intravenous haematin which also suppresses ALA synthase has been used for extensive attacks with progressive neuropathy.

Diazepam may be used to terminate an epileptic attack and sodium valproate or clonazepam are probably the prophylactic anti-convulsants of choice, being the least likely to exacerbate an attack.

Non-acute porphyrias:
Porphyria cutanea tarda (cutaneous hepatic porphyria). autosomal dominant inheritance or acquired. Reduced activity of hepatic uroporphyrinogen decarboxylase.

Clinical features include skin fragility which may be the predominant feature, a photosensitive blistering rash, pruritus, bullae which heal with scar formation, hyperpigmentation and hirsutism. Hepatomegaly and abnormal liver function tests with siderosis or chronic active hepatitis on liver biopsy are common, especially when alcohol is the cause. Serum levels of iron and transferrin are often high. Diabetes mellitus commonly occurs.

Alcohol is the commonest precipitating agent. Others include oestrogens and polychlorinated hydrocarbons. Aminolaevulinic acid and porphobilinogen levels are never elevated. Increased urinary uroporphyrin levels occur during an acute attack, as fewer porphyrins are excreted in the faeces. In remission, increased faecal porphyrins and decreased urine porphyrins occur. Venesection leads to lower urine and faecal porphyrin levels.

Treatment: withdrawal of alcohol often leads to clinical remission. Venesection 500 ml/week or until Hb falls to 12 g/dl. Approximately 10 litres of blood should be removed. Low dose weekly chloroquine may also be useful in increasing urine porphyrin levels and hence decreasing plasma levels.

Erythropoietic protoporphyria:
Presentation is with photosensitivity and severe burning pain; protoporphyrins are hepatotoxic and lead to raised liver enzymes.

Diagnosis: red blood cells may fluoresce, and red blood cell and faecal protoporphyria levels are increased. Treatment with β-carotene helps to ameliorate photosensitivity.

Congenital porphyria:
Very rare. Clinical features: photosensitivity, bullae which heal with deforming scars, increased pigment hypertrichosis, dystrophic nails, brown teeth, anaemia, and splenomegaly are seen. Treatment: chloroquine.

a) **True**
b) **False**
c) **False**
d) **False**
e) **False**

In health, the body needs a balanced intake of water, carbohydrate, protein, lipid, vitamins, electrolytes and trace elements.

Bed-bound medical patients have a metabolic rate of approximately 30 kcal/kg/day in males and 25 kcal/kg/day in females, with an average daily calorie requirement of 2000–3000 kcal and a daily nitrogen requirement of 8–12 g (1 g nitrogen = 6.25 g protein). Hypercatabolic patients (trauma, postoperative, sepsis or burns) have an increased metabolic rate and nitrogen excretion rate, with an increased caloric requirement of approximately 3500 kcal/day and a nitrogen requirement of upwards of 16 g/day. Hypercatabolic patients with high circulating levels of insulin contrast with starvation states, where insulin levels are low, and ketosis is thus prominent only in the latter.

The following criteria are used to identify malnourished patients:
a) > 10% body weight loss
b) body weight < 20% of expected weight
c) Reduced triceps skin fold thickness (estimate of fat reserves), reduced mid-arm circumference (estimate of muscle protein reserves)
d) Low levels of visceral proteins (albumin, transferrin, etc.)
e) Impaired immune function (lymphopenia < 1.2×10^9/L, negative candida skin tests).

When hyperalimentation and nutritional support are thought necessary, the options are enteral or parenteral routes.

In general, due to the expense and infectious complications of parenteral feeding the enteral route is preferred. Carbohydrate in the form of low osmolar starch hydrosylates (oligosaccharides) is the primary energy source in most enteral feeds. Lactose is not used, because:
a) Inherited lactase deficiency is not uncommon, particularly in Asians
b) Malnutrition per se depletes the mucosal levels of lactase. Failure to digest and absorb lactose leads to profuse diarrhoea. Lactose deficiency does not result in abdominal pain.

a) **False**
b) **False**
c) **True**
d) **False**
e) **True**

The annual incidence of schizophrenia in the UK is of the order of 0.1–0.2 per 1000. There is an undoubted genetic tendency to develop schizophrenia: first degree relatives have a relative risk several times greater than that of the general population, and if one monozygotic twin is affected the other has a 50% chance of being similarly affected. Some patients experience an acute schizophrenic attack from which they make a complete recovery, whilst others develop a chronic form of the disease.

Symptoms of acute schizophrenia include delusions, which tend to be persecutory or grandiose, auditory hallucinations, thought disorder, abnormal affective responses and disordered behaviour (the so-called positive symptoms).

Schneider's first-rank symptoms for the diagnosis of schizophrenia:
a) Thought insertion (experience of thoughts being put into one's mind)
b) Thought broadcasting (experience of one's thoughts being known to others)
c) Hearing one's thoughts spoken out aloud
d) Auditory hallucinations in the form of a running commentary
e) Auditory hallucinations in the form of voices discussing the patient and referring to the patient as 'he' or 'she' — third person hallucinations
f) Feelings or actions experienced as made or influenced by others, i.e. feelings of passivity
g) Primary delusions, which arise inexplicably from normal perceptions, e.g. on seeing the traffic lights change to red the patient thinks he is God.

Occasionally, somatic hallucinations, i.e. uncomfortable feelings in the chest, abdomen or genitalia are the first evidence of schizophrenia and these may be interpreted in a delusional way. Visual hallucinations may also occur but are not part of the diagnosis of schizophrenia. The main features of chronic schizophrenia include slowness, apathy, and social withdrawal (so-called negative symptoms), though any of the positive symptoms may occur.

Note: memory and conscious level are unaffected in schizophrenia.

The management of schizophrenia involves a combination of:
a) neuroleptic drugs which may be given in the form of fortnightly intramuscular depot injections of fluphenazine
b) Adequate social support. The latter is extremely important in providing a stable non-stressful environment that the patient can fit into. Discharge into the community, while useful in some cases, might not provide enough structure for these patients.

Neurological side-effects of neuroleptics (dopamine antagonists) include: Parkinson's disease, akathisia, acute dystonia, tardive dyskinesia. Clozapine is indicated in patients with severe negative symptoms, who are not treatable by other more conventional drugs such as chlorpramazine, pimozide, fluphenthixol, haloperidol, fluphenazine or thioridazine (anti-muscarinic effects). Clozapine is only given to patients who are registered with the Clozaril (Clozapine) Patient Monitoring Service, and monitoring for leukopenia must be done weekly for 18 weeks, and then fortnightly. A white cell count of less than 3000/mm^3, or neutrophil count of less than 1500/mm^3 is an indication for further monitoring. The danger of leukopenia may be less than previously reported, and this drug has had dramatic effects in selected patients.

Answer to question 210

a) **False**
b) **True**
c) **True**
d) **True**
e) **False**

Depression is a normal human experience. Depressive illness forms a clinical spectrum and is best thought of in terms of severity, be it mild, moderate or severe. Approximately 3% of men and 7% of women will suffer from a depressive illness at some time. The prevalence is higher in the lower social classes, in alcoholics and in those who attend their doctors frequently.

Symptoms of depressive illness include: depressed mood, crying, hopelessness, suicidal thoughts, self-depreciation, loss of confidence, feelings of worthlessness and guilt, loss of interest, impaired concentration and poor memory, anxiety and agitation, preoccupation with health, panic attacks and phobias, early morning waking, loss of libido, loss of appetite, weight loss, psychomotor retardation, which at its worst can lead to a stuporose state, and psychotic symptoms with delusions and hallucinations.

With mild depressive illness, excess worry is often a feature and patients may complain of difficulty falling asleep. Daily fluctuations in mood are common, but as the severity of the depression increases these fluctuations disappear. In severe depression, delusions develop out of hypochondrial ideas, leading to nihilistic delusions, e.g. the patient feels his 'insides are rotting'. Hallucinations may be auditory (e.g. the patient hearing voices telling him he is useless), or olfactory.

Treatment for depression includes psychotherapy and cognitive therapy, improving any predisposing social factors, drugs and electroconvulsive therapy.

Drugs used in depressive illness include:
Tricyclic antidepressants — e.g. amitriptyline and dothiepin which are sedating, imipramine which is non-sedating and protryptiline, which has a stimulant effect. Mechanism of action: inhibit re-uptake of monoamines from the synaptic cleft. Onset of action takes 10–14 days; insomnia and anxiety are often the first symptoms to respond. Side-effects include dry mouth, blurred vision, constipation, urinary retention, postural hypotension, drowsiness, arrhythmias.
Monoamine oxidase inhibitors — e.g. phenalzine. Mechanism of action: inhibit monoamine oxidase. Onset of action similar to tricyclic antidepressants. Interact with tyramine-containing food stuffs and pethidine. On stopping an MAO inhibitor, a 2-week gap should elapse before changing to a tricyclic antidepressant agent, and vice versa.
Newer antidepressants — e.g. mianserin (side-effect: bone marrow depression) and lofepramine.
Selective serotonin re-uptake inhibitors (SSRI) — e.g. fluoxitene (Prozac), citalopram, fluvoxamine and sertraline. These selectively inhibit the uptake of 5-hydroxytryptamine. They have less sedative and antimuscarinic effects, and do not lead to weight gain. Indeed the sometimes prominent gastrointestinal side-effects of nausea and vomiting may induce weight loss which makes them attractive for fashion-conscious patients. They are used widely in the USA. Headache, restlessness and anxiety can occur. SSRI should not be started within 2 weeks of MAOI usage.
Lithium — good for recurrent depressive illnesses complicated by hypomania.

a) **True**
b) **True**
c) **True**
d) **True**
e) **False**

Anorexia nervosa shows a marked female predominance and the incidence in girls (age 13–14 years) attending private schools approaches 1%. Anorexics have an overwhelming fear of being fat and often perceive themselves as being overweight even though they may be underweight. They tend to be obsessed with food, generally deny watching their weight, and will often prepare food for others. At mealtimes they tend to pick at food and eat little, often leave the table early and vomit in private. Exercise is often taken daily in a bid to help weight loss. The patients are thin with excess fine lanugo hair; axillary and pubic hair is absent or scanty and amenorrhoea may be present. Loss of 25% of original body weight and failure to maintain body weight above the minimum for height and age are used as diagnostic criteria for anorexia nervosa. Severe weight loss can lead to hypotension, oedema and bradycardia. Anorexics tend to be bright and hard working, though about 10% show other behaviour disorders, e.g. shoplifting, promiscuity. Management is best undertaken in specialist units where psychotherapy is given, target weight gains can be set and feeding supervised. Weight gain is often achieved in the short term, but most retain a preoccupation with body image and food.

Bulimia nervosa is likewise commoner in women than men, though it tends to occur in an older age group (17–18 years of age). Patients have the same preoccupation with body weight and many are clinically depressed. Strict calorie restriction through the day is punctuated by intermittent bouts of secret bingeing on high calorie carbohydrate foods; following a binge, vomiting is induced. In addition, patients abuse laxatives and purgatives. In some women, bingeing occurs in the premenstrual period only. Hypokalaemia is a common metabolic consequence and can lead to renal damage, arrhythmias, paraesthesia and seizures. Menstrual disturbance secondary to weight loss is common. Parotid enlargement may occur early on and chronic cases may develop clubbing. Treatment in the form of tricyclic antidepressants alone or in combination with psychotherapy is usually on an outpatient basis. The prognosis is better than for anorexia, with a 50–70% remission rate. Severe vomiting may however lead to aspiration and death.

a) **True**
b) **False**
c) **True**
d) **False**
e) **True**

Alzheimer's disease is the commonest cause of progressive pre-senile dementia. Some studies have shown an incidence of dementia of approximately 50% in patients 85 years or above. It is characterised by neurofibrillary tangles, amyloid plaques and amyloid angiopathy. The presence and density of dense β amyloid plaques predicts disease severity. The amyloid precursor protein has been placed on chromosome 21. Apoprotein E2 homozygosity has also been described as a risk factor for the disease. Degeneration of specific cholinergic neurones in the nucleus basalis has been described. There is an increased incidence in Down's syndrome, but the pathogenetic link between the chromosomal abnormality and the disease has not been firmly established. Widespread changes throughout the frontal, temporal and occipital lobes are found. Cerebellar involvement is not typically found. CSF examination is normal; diffuse slow wave activity on the EEG is typical. CT scan may show narrowed gyri, widened sulci and enlarged ventricles. Life expectancy is greatly reduced.

Answer to question 213

a) **True**
b) **True**
c) **True**
d) **True**
e) **False**

The sideroblastic anaemias are characterised by dyserythropoiesis and marked iron loading of red cell precursors; many cases are also associated with defective iron metabolism and widespread haemosiderosis.

The main causes are:
Congenital
X linked

Acquired
Idiopathic
Drugs — e.g. isoniazid, pyrizinamide, chloramphenicol, alcohol, lead
Myeloproliferative disorders
Rheumatoid arthritis and vasculitis
Malabsorption states
Secondary carcinoma.

Ring sideroblasts may be seen in a number of systemic diseases such as SLE, rheumatoid arthritis, hypothyroidism and infections. In such cases, the ring sideroblasts are unexplained and the anaemia is related to the underlying disease.

The sideroblastic anaemias are characterised by marked iron loading of the RBC precursors — ring sideroblasts. The excess iron is mostly in mitochondria which circle the nuclei. Typically, the peripheral blood film shows a dimorphic picture. Mature RBC are hypochromic since haem synthesis is defective; it is not known whether this is a primary or secondary phenomenon. The mitochondrial enzymes ALA synthetase and haem synthetase have both been implicated.

Many patients in whom the primary cause is not known run a protracted course and, because of inappropriate iron absorption from the gut, develop haemosiderosis. Venesection or chelation therapy should be given if there is evidence of iron overload. Since there is dyserythropoiesis, folate supplements are usually given. Some patients respond to pyridoxine therapy.

Answer to question 214

a) **False**   d) **True**
b) **False**   e) **True**
c) **False**

Blinding in the context of clinical trials refers to the practice of keeping one or more parties unaware of the treatment being administered. In a single-blind clinical trial, one party, usually the patient, is unaware of the treatment being administered. In a double-blind trial, both the patient and the doctor are unaware of the respective treatments and in a triple-blind trial the patient, doctor and a third party (involved in some aspect of trial organisation) are all unaware of the specific treatment administered.

A placebo is a pharmacologically inactive substance given as if it were an active agent. Many patients exhibit placebo response, in that they appear to respond to being treated with an inactive agent. Blue and green colours are popularly associated with poisons and a placebo response is more likely if the placebo is coloured red, brown or yellow.

The majority of clinical trials are conducted in a parallel fashion so that each patient is exposed to a single treatment only. In a crossover trial, each patient is exposed to both treatments, thus allowing within-patient treatment comparisons. Fewer patients are needed for crossover studies compared to parallel studies. This problem with parallel trials has been addressed by using large multi-centre trial designs. Crossover studies are best used for drugs with a short duration of onset of action, and may be used for looking for short-term relief in chronic conditions. In crossover studies, a washout period is essential to eradicate potential carry-over effects before commencing the second treatment. Recent crossover trials have claimed that digoxin is useful in heart failure patients in sinus rhythm, but a short washout period has placed some doubt on the results.

a) **False**
b) **False**
c) **False**
d) **False**
e) **True**

The HIV attachment to cells has been shown to be more complicated than simply binding of the glycoprotein 120 (gp 120), on the surface of the HIV particle, to the CD4 molecule on the human T cell surface. CCRS and SCCR4 molecules, which are recently described chemokines with a 7 membrane spanning domain, are other T cell surface molecules. The glycoprotein 41 (gp 41), on the HIV particle, binds to the chemokine molecules, after binding of gp120 to CD4. This causes viral ingestion, and replication. These two different and complementary means of HI-T cell binding offer an explanation for the poor clinical success of monoclonal anti-CD4 antibodies.

Unlike human T cell lymphotropic virus (HTLV), which is only transmitted to humans within cells, HIV can be transmitted in a cell-free form. Thus HIV viral particles can transfer infection.

There are many other causes of a low CD4 count, such as malnutrition and bone marrow infiltrative diseases (in conjunction with other cytopenias). Rare patients have been described with a very low CD4 count and no other illness.

ELISA is very sensitive, but less specific than the more expensive Western blot test, which uses proteins on nitrocellulose paper to demonstrate antibody binding to specific glycoproteins.

Reverse transcriptase inhibitors, combined to antiproteases, hold new hope for infected patients, and some remarkable results have been achieved. Patients with very low CD4 counts have recovered their cell counts to almost normal levels using combination therapy. This therapy has severe side-effects and is very expensive.

a) **False**
b) **False**
c) **True**
d) **True**
e) **True**

Toxocariasis in man is due to the nematode *Toxocara canis*. Adult worms live in the intestine of dogs and foxes and produce large numbers of eggs, which are passed in the stool and can survive in soil for months. Man becomes infected by ingesting eggs, which hatch into larvae and migrate through the liver and lungs. The larvae induce local granuloma formation and are accompanied by a peripheral eosinophilia. Infection is self-limiting as the larvae die after a period of 1 year, since man is not a natural host.

Many infections are subclinical. Visceral larva migrans is the name given to clinically-apparent disease, the main features of which are fever, asthma and hepatomegaly. Surprisingly, ocular lesions are not common in those with gross larva migrans. The diagnosis may be confirmed by finding larvae in liver granulomas at biopsy and serologically.

Ocular toxocariasis tends to present in children less than 6 years of age with local granulomas near the macula threatening vision or inducing squints. Eosinophilia is usually absent and serological tests may be negative. The diagnosis is confirmed by finding toxocara antibodies in the aqueous or vitreous humour. It has been proposed that ocular toxoplasmosis represents reactivation of an infection acquired in utero, whereas visceral toxoplasmosis is due to ingestion of a heavy egg load.

Treatment: Diethylcarbamazepine and thiabendazole have been used with varying degrees of success. Vitrectomy and photocoagulation have been used for ocular lesions.

Methods to prevent infection in man include excluding dogs from children's play areas and regular deworming of pups and adult dogs with effective antihelminths.

Answer to question 217

a) **False**   d) **True**
b) **True**   e) **True**
c) **False**

Toxoplasmosis is a zoonosis, caused by the protozoan *Toxoplasma gondii*. The cat is the primary host and excretes infectious oocytes. Man is infected on ingesting oocytes or by eating inadequately cooked meat containing cysts. In the gut, sporozoites are released which disseminate widely via the blood stream and multiply in the tissues, forming cysts. The majority of toxoplasma infections are subclinical. In the UK 50% of those over the age of 70 have toxoplasma antibodies present, whilst the prevalence in France is even higher. Clinical features of *Toxoplasma gondii* infection include fever, sore throat, non-tender lymphadenopathy (which may be localised to the cervical region or generalised), a maculopapular rash, hepatomegaly and splenomegaly. Rarely, myocarditis and encephalitis occur, the latter being much commoner in immunosuppressed patients, with a very poor prognosis. Primary infection with toxoplasmosis in pregnancy, especially in the first trimester, may result in abortion or severe congenital infection. Features of congenital toxoplasmosis include: microcephaly, convulsions, low IQ, spasticity, cerebral calcification and chorioretinitis. Chorioretinitis, although usually acquired in utero, may not present until the late teens. Patients may then present with loss of vision; examination reveals areas of focal retinitis which heal with scar formation, though there may be local recurrence. The diagnosis may be confirmed by isolation of the parasites from affected tissue, e.g. lymph node, eye and brain. The diagnosis is usually made serologically. A number of tests are available and include an indirect fluorescent antibody test, an indirect haemagglutination assay and the Sabin Feldman dye test which utilises live toxoplasma and hence is restricted in its availability. A rise in IgM confirms a recent infection, as does a rise in antibody titre between acute and convalescent sera.

The dye test and indirect fluorescent antibody test measure the same antibody, and titres reach a peak a few weeks after onset of the illness. The indirect haemagglutination assay measures a different antibody which peaks after several months. Hence a positive dye test and negative indirect haemagglutination assay indicate recent infection. Congenital infection is confirmed by a high titre of antibody persisting for 6 months.

Treatment is usually combination therapy with pyrimethamine and sulphadiazine. Pyrimethamine should not be used in pregnancy and spiramycin can be substituted.

Causes of calcification visible on plain skull X-ray include:
a) Tumours — pinealoma, craniopharyngioma, oligodendroglioma, meningioma
b) Infections — toxoplasmosis; cysticercosis; tuberculoma
c) Miscellaneous — tuberous sclerosis; Sturge–Weber syndrome, hypoparathyroidism, systemic lupus erythematosus, calcified cerebral vessels, calcified chronic subdural haemorrhage.

a) **False**   d) **False**
b) **True**   e) **False**
c) **False**

Pityriasis versicolor is due to the yeast *Pityrosporum orbiculare (Malassezia furfur)*. Infection often manifests after sunbathing, when pale small scaly patches become visible on the torso and upper face. The yeast produces a substance which interferes with melanin production; hence affected lesions are pale in comparison with tanned skin. The diagnosis may be confirmed by finding spores and hyphae on skin microscopy. Selenium sulphide shampoo lathered over head and trunk is effective if applied daily for 4 weeks, but infection recurs frequently.

Answer to question 219

a) **True**   d) **False**
b) **True**   e) **False**
c) **True**

Pulmonary eosinophilia is defined as the combination of a peripheral blood eosinophilia with an eosinophilic lung infiltrate, usually manifested by shadowing on the chest X-ray. The normal eosinophil count is $0.04-0.4 \times 10^9$/L ($40-400$/mm^3). The majority of patients with pulmonary eosinophilia have counts of the order $1000-50\ 000$/mm^3. Pulmonary eosinophilic infiltrates can be confirmed at lung biopsy or by bronchoalveolar lavage.

Recognised causes of true pulmonary eosinophilia:
1) **Fungi,** commonly *Aspergillus fumigatus* which colonises the airways. A number of distinct pictures are seen:
a) Simple asthma with eosinophilia
b) Fleeting segmental eosinophilic pneumonias
c) Mucoid impaction with associated collapse
d) Chronic airway damage with proximal segmental bronchiectasis and upper zone fibrosis
e) Invasive aspergillosis
f) Aspergilloma.
   Aspergillus may be found in the sputum, skin prick tests are positive, serum-precipitating antibodies are positive and serum IgE levels are raised. In cases of segmental pneumonia, corticosteroids are associated with rapid clearing of the chest X-ray but maintenance steroids may be necessary. The above syndrome, which is often called allergic bronchopulmonary aspergillosis, is different from infiltration of lung tissue by *A. fumigatus*, which may be seen in immunocompromised hosts. It must also be differentiated from an aspergilloma, which is a fungus ball in a previously damaged lung (e.g. tuberculosis).

2) **Drugs and toxins** — sulphonamides, tetracyclines, nitrofurantoin, non-steroidal anti-inflammatory drugs, Spanish toxic oil syndrome. Three patterns of disease are recognised:
   a) A pneumonic illness with fever and patchy alveolar infiltrates; rapid resolution on drug withdrawal is typical
   b) Pulmonary vasculitis which often requires corticosteroids
   c) A fibrosing alveolitis-type picture.
3) **Parasites,** including ascaris, strongyloides, ankylostoma, filaria and schistosomiasis. Transient pulmonary shadows correspond with parasitic migration through the lungs and are associated with very high serum IgE levels. Episodes of haemoptysis are common. Microfilaria are associated with asthma, and chronic infestation can lead to pulmonary fibrosis. Chronic schistosomiasis infection can lead to pulmonary hypertension.
4) **Vasculitis** — Churg–Strauss syndrome defined as asthma, eosinophilia and vasculitis affecting two or more organs apart from the lungs.
5) **Cryptogenic pulmonary eosinophilia** — syndrome of fever, weight loss, eosinophilia and widespread peripheral alveolar shadowing. Asthma is common. Rapid resolution in response to corticosteroids is the rule.
6) **Hyperoosinophilic syndrome** — very high eosinophil count, 50 000–100 000/mm³; it would appear to represent a myeloproliferative state. Pulmonary involvement with diffuse infiltrates on X-ray is asymptomatic; eosinophilic invasion of the heart is associated with a restrictive and obliterative cardiomyopathy, central nervous system involvement can occur and hepatosplenomegaly is common. Hydroxyurea and cyclophosphamide have been used with benefit.
7) **Diverse** — High eosinophil counts without pulmonary involvement occur in eczema, scabies, pemphigus, pemphigoid, rheumatoid arthritis, Addison's disease, and Hodgkin's disease.

a) **True**
b) **True**
c) **True**
d) **True**
e) **True**

Photosensitive drugs sensitise the skin to normally harmless doses of ultraviolet and visible radiation. Ultraviolet B (wavelength 290–320 nm) is responsible in the main for sunburn and solar-induced skin cancer, whereas the action spectrum of most photosensitive drugs is in the ultraviolet A range (wavelength 320–400 nm). The action spectrum of a drug is the range of wavelength that produces the clinical effect. Drugs may induce photosensitivity in two ways:
a) Directly by a direct toxic effect or photoallergic response
b) Indirectly, e.g. drug-induced systemic lupus erythematosus, drug-induced porphyria, drug-induced pellagra (e.g. isoniazid-induced).

As one would predict, photosensitive rashes affect primarily light-exposed skin on the face (classically there is sparing of the submental region and upper eyelids), back of the hands, nape of neck and back of legs.

Drugs which induce photosensitivity directly include:
Amiodarone; antibiotics, e.g. tetracyclines, nalidixic acid, sulphonamides; NSAIDs, e.g. benoxaprofen, piroxicam; diuretics, e.g. thiazide diuretics, frusemide; sulphonylureas, e.g. chlorpropamide; phenothiazines; quinine and quinidine; tricyclic antidepressants; retinoids; psoralens; anti-cancer drugs, e.g. fluorouracil; topical coal tar.

Drug-induced lupus erythematosus:
The commonest agents implicated are procainamide, hydralazine, phenytoin, isoniazid, chlorpromazine and minocycline.
Others rarely implicated include the contraceptive pill, griseofulvin, methyldopa, methysergide, penicillin, sulphonamides and penicillamine.
The onset of the disease appears to be related to a cumulative effect, and other recognised risk factors include: slow acetylator status and the possession of the allele HLA DR4. Clinical features of drug-induced lupus include polyarthritis, skin rashes, polyserositis, hepatomegaly, lymphadenopathy and pulmonary infiltrates. Renal and central nervous system disease is rare. The ANA may be positive with a high titre, and anti-histone antibodies are characteristic of drug-induced lupus. Remission following drug withdrawal is the rule.

a) **False**
b) **False**
c) **False**
d) **True**
e) **False**

Blood urea and uric acid levels are decreased in pregnancy due to an increase in the glomerular filtration rate. Serum alkaline phosphatase is elevated due to placental production. Serum lipids are commonly elevated, serum albumin is typically low, thyroxine-binding globulin is high (hence total serum thyroxine is a poor guide to thyroid status). Fasting blood glucose levels also tend to be low, but the response to a glucose load may be impaired. In pregnancy there is a lower renal threshold for glucose reabsorption; hence glycosuria is common.

Answer to question 222

a) **True**
b) **False**
c) **False**
d) **True**
e) **True**

Untreated gastro-oesophageal reflux disease (GORD) affects quality of life as severely as stable angina or the menopause. Medical therapy with proton pump inhibitors is more effective than H2 antagonists. PPIs result in more complete acid suppression, since they block the H^+/K^+ pump which is the final common pathway for secretion of acid in the stomach. Side-effects are minimal, apart from a reported increase in chronic active gastritis in patients with *H. pylori* infection. Up to 40% of the general population have GORD, and 10% take regular therapy for this.

Barrett's oesophagus is caused by long-standing reflux, and may lead to adenocarcinoma of the oesophagus. This malignancy is increasing alarmingly in the developed world, and PPI therapy does not reduce the risk.

Angiogram-negative chest pain is a symptom which is not uncommon, and is associated with an abnormal 24 hour oesophageal pH study in up to 65% of patients. This examination is performed by placing a pH sensitive electrode in the distal oesophagus of the patient, and recording acid reflux during 24 hours. This study is the most sensitive examination in these patients.

a) **True**   d) **False**
b) **True**   e) **True**
c) **False**

A sensitive assay is one which detects all the true positive results, so that all the negative results will be true negatives, i.e. few false negatives. A specific test is one which will detect only the positive results, so that all the positives will be true positives, i.e. few false positives. Therefore the more specific a test, the less sensitive it is.

The definitions of precision and accuracy are correct. Precision results may still be inaccurate.

The incidence of a disorder is the number of new cases diagnosed per head of the population in a given time (usually per year). The incidence of a disorder is best determined using a longitudinal study.

The prevalence of a disorder is the number of cases suffering from the disorder per head of the population at any given time. The prevalence of a particular disorder is determined by a cross-sectional study of the population.

The attack rate for a disease is the proportion of people exposed to infection who develop the disease.

Answer to question 224

a) **True**   d) **True**
b) **True**   e) **False**
c) **True**

Anxiety neurosis is a syndrome characterised by a degree of anxiety out of proportion to the stress that the patient is experiencing. It occurs in approximately 3% of women and 1% of men. Symptoms may be psychological or physical. Psychological symptoms include impaired concentration, poor memory, disturbed sleep (though not early morning waking), irritability, restlessness and a sense of fearful anticipation.

Physical symptoms are due to:
a) Autonomic overactivity — palpitations, sweating, dry mouth, diarrhoea, frequency and failure of erections
b) Hyperventilation leading to dizziness, paraesthesia and faintness
c) Increased skeletal muscle tone resulting in tension headaches and neck pain.

Some patients exhibit sudden unexplained precipitations of their symptoms, so-called 'panic attacks'. In others, attacks are provoked by well-recognised stimuli ('phobic attacks').

In general, patients with anxiety neurosis provoked by short-term stressful events recover, whilst those associated with personality disorders or prolonged problems tend to persist. Management involves reassurance, behavioural therapy, psychotherapy and drugs. Drugs used include benzodiazepines, β blockers, tricyclic antidepressants and monoamine oxidase inhibitors.

Phobic neuroses are characterised by an intense dread of a particular situation or object. Phobias are common, with an overall prevalence of 1:200. Simple phobias occur in response to objects such as snakes or spiders. Social phobias occur in response to social gatherings and meetings.

Agoraphobia describes anxiety on leaving home or entering crowded places. In addition to the usual features of anxiety, patients often feel faint and experience loss of control. Agoraphobics often complain of physical illness, and accordingly seek medical attention. Patients tend to avoid the precipitating situation. Their lives are subsequently restricted, and secondary depressive symptoms are common.

Phobias are best treated with behavioural therapy tailored to the individual's needs.

Answer to question 225

a) **True**
b) **False**
c) **True**
d) **True**
e) **True**

Complications of ulcerative colitis include:
Gastrointestinal: fever; anaemia (Fe^{++} loss); weight loss; hypoalbuminaemia and oedema; hypokalaemia; lethargy; intestinal dilatation; toxic mega-colon; perforation of the colon; fistulae (rare); carcinoma of the colon.

Hepatobiliary: carcinoma of the bile duct; chronic active hepatitis; fatty infiltration of liver, pericholangitis, primary sclerosing cholangitis; ascending cholangitis; secondary biliary cirrhosis.

Systemic: erythema nodosum; erythema multiforme, pyoderma gangrenosa; leg ulcers; urticaria; aphthous mouth ulceration; uveitis; episcleritis; arthritis (rheumatoid factor negative); sacroiliitis; ankylosing spondylitis; venous thrombosis of the legs.

Most of these complications respond to resolution of the underlying colitis, apart from sclerosing cholangitis and ankylosing spondylitis, which may proceed independently of the disease.

a) **False**
b) **False**
c) **True**
d) **False**
e) **False**

Cholera is caused by the enterotoxin-producing *Vibrio cholerae* (a Gram-negative rod) of the classical and El Tor biotypes. The incubation period varies from a few hours to 5 days. Transmission is faecal-oral and infection is contracted from contaminated water and foodstuffs such as shellfish. Cholera is endemic in the Indian subcontinent. In the UK there have been approximately 50 imported cases over the last 20 years. In endemic areas, attack rates are highest in children (1–5 years). When the disease spreads to new areas, attack rates in adults are as high as in children.

Achlorhydria renders subjects prone to cholera infections as the organisms are normally sensitive to low pH. In normal individuals a very high bacterial load must be ingested to allow *Vibrio cholerae* to colonise the small bowel and produce symptoms. The enterotoxin binds to gut epithelial cells and stimulates production of cAMP which leads to the secretion of electrolytes into the gut lumen. Absorption of sodium chloride via the neutral sodium chloride transport system is also impaired, so the net result is loss of isotonic fluid. Analysis of the watery diarrhoea in adults shows a concentration of sodium and chloride similar to plasma, a potassium concentration at least three times that of the plasma, and a bicarbonate concentration twice that of plasma, but in children the stool sodium concentration is less than that of plasma, i.e. stools are hypotonic.

Asymptomatic cases are common and mild diarrhoea is often the sole manifestation of infection with El Tor. Clinical features of the acute severe illness include watery diarrhoea, dehydration, muscle cramps, circulatory collapse and a metabolic acidosis. Patients may exhibit neurological symptoms — stupor, coma and convulsions.

Cholera is a clinical diagnosis and prompt treatment is essential. The biochemical abnormalities are rapidly corrected with appropriate rehydration. Untreated, mortality rates approach 50%. In adults, oral rehydration with a glucose electrolyte solution may be appropriate. The glucose is essential as cholera does not impair glucose-facilitated sodium absorption, but does impair the neutral sodium chloride transport.

Tetracyclines have been shown to reduce the severity of the diarrhoea and eradicate faecal vibrio excretion. The classical motile rods may be seen by dark ground microscopy of stool and may be immobilised by type-specific sera which allows serotyping. Cholera vaccine is a heat-inactivated vaccine which prevents subjects from becoming asymptomatic carriers and offers some protection against contracting infection from both biotypes for 3–6 months.

Cholera vaccine is of no value in the control or spread of infection or in the management of contacts of imported cases.

a) **True**
b) **True**
c) **False**
d) **False**
e) **True**

H. pylori was seen in gastric antral pathology samples more than 100 years ago. Clinicians at the time believed that this motile, flagellated rod-shaped organism, living deep within the mucosa of the stomach in man, was a harmless commensal. In 1983 Barry Marshall in Australia 'rediscovered' the organism, and suggested that it might be important in the genesis of duodenal ulcer. It is now known that *H. pylori* plays an important role in the causation of 90% or more duodenal ulcers, and in those gastric ulcers not related to NSAID use. Transmission of infection is probably faecal–oral, and the infectivity is very high in children in developing countries. In the developed world 30–50% of 50 year old patients will be infected. Once infected, always infected, unless eradication is performed.

Diagnosis depends on demonstrating urease activity in antral biopsies, breath tests (which are non-invasive), serology and culture.

There have been thousands of papers and abstracts concerning eradication, but a consensus is now emerging from the considerably smaller literature which has been well performed and included enough patient numbers. The optimum therapy includes a proton pump inhibitor twice daily, and one of the following antibiotics: metronidazole, clarithromycin, or amoxil (MACH study). This results in a 90% or more eradication. Unfortunately metronidazole and even clarithromycin resistance is emerging, particularly in the inner cities. All patients with duodenal ulcer and those with non-NSAID gastric ulcers need eradication.

H. pylori causes chronic atrophic gastritis, and gastric cancer may be associated with this organism, although this has not been proven. Mucosal associated lymphoma (MALT) is a rare neoplasm which is associated with *H. pylori* infection. Primary therapy for this condition is eradication of *H. pylori*. Eradication for the prevention of gastric cancer cannot yet be recommended.

a) **True**
b) **False**
c) **False**
d) **False**
e) **True**

The premotor area of the frontal lobe contains the voluntary gaze centre. Descending pathways pass in the corona radiata via the internal capsule to the pons where they decussate to the contralateral pontine gaze centre. The adjacent VI nerve is activated by this centre, as is the opposite III nerve nucleus via the medial longitudinal bundle relay pathway, so coordinating conjugate movements of the eyes. Damage to the medial longitudinal bundle results in an internuclear ophthalmoplegia, and such lesions may be unilateral or bilateral.

Two distinct types of internuclear ophthalmoplegia are recognised:
a) In the classical type, on attempted conjugate lateral gaze to one side the contralateral medial rectus fails to contract, as impulses do not reach the III nerve nucleus, yet the muscle will contract on convergence. The abducting eye often shows nystagmus. The classical internuclear ophthalmoplegia is commonly seen in multiple sclerosis.
b) In the second type, there is failure of complete abduction of the abducting eye which may well exhibit nystagmus, though adduction of the adducting eye is complete. Here, the medial longitudinal bundle appears to be intact but the relay to the VI nerve nucleus is thought to be defective.

Nystagmus arises because of a weakness in the mechanisms responsible for maintaining conjugate eye movements or due to an imbalance of the postural control of the eyes. The laterally deviated eyes tend to drift slowly back to the midline (this is the pathological component) followed by a fast compensatory lateral flick. Somewhat confusingly, nystagmus is defined as the direction of the fast flick. Nystagmus may be described as horizontal, vertical, rotary or pendular. Many authors grade nystagmus according to severity, minor degrees being apparent only on full lateral gaze to the weak side, and when severe, apparent at rest. **Note:** normal subjects will often exhibit nystagmus if the test object is held within 2 feet of the eye or if the object is moved too fast.

Congenital nystagmus is typically pendular in nature and the subject is asymptomatic. In children, nystagmus may be the presenting manifestation of cataracts, albinism or macular disease.

Lesions affecting the semicircular canals, VIII nerve or its central nuclei will result in nystagmus which will be maximal on looking towards the opposite side.

Cerebellar hemisphere disease results in nystagmus which is maximal towards the side of the lesion.

Vertical nystagmus is a feature of intrinsic brain stem disease (though horizontal nystagmus is commoner) but also occurs with high levels of anticonvulsants, e.g. phenytoin.

a) **False**
b) **False**
c) **True**
d) **False**
e) **False**

Barrett's oesophagus refers to columnar cell epithelium in the lower oesophagus and is an acquired condition as a result of gastro-oesophageal reflux. About 10% of people with reflux develop Barrett's oesophagus. The condition is premalignant and adenocarcinoma develops in about 8–10% of cases. The commonest complication is stricture formation, and may be seen in up to 40% of patients with gastro-oesophageal reflux (GORD strictures). Deep penetrating ulcers can give rise to massive bleeding. Treatment depends on the pathological changes that have developed; options range from medical treatment and oesophageal dilatation, to surgery (anti-reflux procedure and sometimes oesophagectomy). The most important aspect is the taking of biopsies every year and careful monitoring. Four biopsies must be taken every centimetre. Dysplasia is pre-malignant, and up to 30% of patients with high grade dysplasia will develop adenocarcinoma. Oesophagectomy is thus indicated.

Answer to question 230

a) **False**
b) **False**
c) **False**
d) **True**
e) **True**

Primary pulmonary hypertension (PPH) is defined as a pulmonary artery pressure of more than 25 mmHg at rest, and 30 mmHg during exercise. Left ventricular disease, lung disorders and thromboembolic diseases must be absent.

A familial form has been described with autosomal dominant inheritance, which is found in up to 6% of patients. The use of appetite suppressants for 3 months or more has also been associated with PPH. The pathogenesis appears to be related to a decrease in nitric oxide (NO), which is a vasodilator, and increased endothelin, a potent vasoconstrictor. Dyspnoea is the most common symptom, and Raynaud's is found in 10%. Hypoxia is usual, particularly after exercise.

Treatment is with nitric oxide (NO), prostacyclin (epoprostanol), adenosine, and calcium antagonists. NO, prostacyclin (epoprostanol), and adenosine need to be given intravenously. Epoprostanol therapy is very expensive. Patients who respond to calcium antagonists may have a 5-year survival of up to 95%. Anticoagulation is recommended and an INR of > 2.0 is also recommended. Atrial fibrillation is almost never seen in these patients.

Lung transplantation has been successfully performed in patients with PPH.

a) **False**
b) **True**
c) **False**
d) **True**
e) **True**

Basal cell carcinomas are the commonest skin tumour. The incidence of malignant melanoma is increasing and the incidence in Queensland, Australia, may be as high as 23: 100 000 of the population. Xeroderma pigmentosa is an autosomal recessive disease where the genes coding for the enzymes responsible for the repair of the sun-damaged DNA are mutated. Basal cell carcinomas can be treated by surgical excision or radiotherapy, but, if near cartilage, surgery is preferred as radiotherapy can induce radionecrosis of the cartilage.

Lentigo maligna (Hutchinson's melanotic freckle) can develop into an invasive melanoma, when it is known as lentigo maligna melanoma. Breslow showed that the thickness of a malignant melanoma was inversely proportional to the 5-year survival. If a stage 1 malignant melanoma is < 0.75 mm in thickness, the 10-year survival rate is 98–99%. If it is between 1.5 and 3.0 mm, the survival at 10 years is 70%.

Answer to question 232

a) **True**
b) **True**
c) **True**
d) **True**
e) **False**

Parasuicide or attempted suicide due to drug overdose is the commonest cause of acute female medical admissions, and in males is second only to acute myocardial ischaemia. In many cases of self-poisoning or self-injury, death is not the intended outcome: the motivation may be complex and not clear-cut, though often the object is to draw attention to themselves. Parasuicide is commonest in young adults (< 35 years of age) and risk factors include:
a) Low social class
b) Unstable relationships
c) Unemployment
d) Chronic medical illness, e.g. epilepsy
e) In less than 10% a serious psychiatric illness (usually depressive), though the majority will exhibit transient psychiatric illness.

Parasuicide is often preceded by heavy alcohol consumption and usually involves little premeditation.

Approximately 1% of patients who have a documented episode of parasuicide will die due to suicide within 1 year of the attempt and approximately 15% will repeat the attempt.

The following factors are associated with an increased suicide risk after an attempted suicide:
a) Male, over 45 years of age
b) Unemployed
c) Socially isolated, e.g. divorced or widowed
d) History of physical or mental illness. Patients who experience a profound sense of hopelessness regarding their future.
e) Previous suicide attempts often of a violent nature, e.g. hanging or jumping
f) Writing a suicide note.

Answer to question 233

a) **True**
b) **True**
c) **False**
d) **True**
e) **True**

This autosomal dominant disease has a prevalence of 1:20 000. The abnormal gene is on the short arm of chromosome 4 (4p 16.3), and has been shown to be due to CAG DNA triplet repeats. Spontaneous mutations are virtually unknown. Atrophy of the caudate nucleus and cerebral cortex is common. There is loss of GABA-ergic and cholinergic striatal neurones.

Presentation in adults occurs typically between 30 and 50 years, with personality changes and choreiform movements. A minority of patients present in childhood, and in this group, epilepsy and severe dementia are common. Phenothiazines may be helpful in the therapy of the movement disorder. Antenatal diagnosis is now possible, and referral for specialist genetic counselling is advised. Eventually patients suffer from dementia.

a) **True**
b) **True**
c) **False**
d) **True**
e) **False**

Hunter and Sly syndrome are mucopolysaccharidoses, with deficient alpha iduronidase and beta glucuronidase respectively. Friedreich's ataxia, Fragile X syndrome, Machado Joseph disease, Kennedy's syndrome (X-linked spinal and bulbar atrophy), and Huntington's chorea are neurological diseases which are caused by an increase in triplet repeats in the DNA. Friedreich's ataxia and Machado Joseph disease are spinocerebellar ataxias. Fragile X is associated with 4000 triplets of the CGG type, whereas normals have up to 54. Huntington's chorea has 36–121 CAG repeats, as opposed to 11–30 in normals.

The triplets may result in abnormal methylation of genes, or interfere with excision of introns, producing problems with spliceosome docking.

Answer to question 235

a) **False**
b) **True**
c) **True**
d) **False**
e) **False**

Coarctation of the aorta is usually diagnosed in children, and is commoner in males than females. Lesions may be classified according to the anatomical site. The commonest lesion is distal to the left subclavian artery and proximal to the ductus arteriosus. Associated abnormalities include: a bicuspid aortic valve, VSD, mitral regurgitation and berry aneurysms. On examination, typical findings in the adult are: hypertension, prominent carotid pulses, radio-femoral delay, left ventricular hypertrophy, an ejection systolic murmur which may be maximal over the back, an apical click from the aortic valve; and an aortic diastolic murmur may also be heard. Rib-notching due to collateral vessels is not typically observed in infants or young children under the age of 4 years. Coarctation resulting in hypertension should be treated surgically. Surgical correction, however, does not always normalise the blood pressure.

a) **False**
b) **True**
c) **False**
d) **True**
e) **False**

Asbestosis is caused by occupational exposure to fibres of asbestos (< 3 μ diameter, >10 μ length). Pleural plaque formation, asbestosis and lung cancer complicate all types of asbestos exposure. The development of mesothelioma is a well-recognised complication of asbestos exposure, and is particularly associated with crocidolite and amosite fibres. Often exposure occurred many years prior to mesothelioma developing.

Silicosis is associated with occupational exposure to crystalline Sio_2 in pottery workers, quarrymen, and related trades. Subacute exposure causes clubbing, upper lung fibrosis, and the characteristic eggshell calcification of the hilar lymph nodes. There is an increased risk of a range of mycobacterial infections, unlike in asbestosis, where the risk is not elevated.

Beryllium is used in ceramics and fluorescent tube manufacture. Chronic exposure may result in an illness, the clinical and radiological features of which may resemble those of sarcoidosis.

Coalworker's pneumoconiosis is caused by inhalation of coal dust. Two main syndromes are described: simple and progressive massive fibrosis. The former is characterised by the formation of small discrete intrapulmonary nodules, and patients are asymptomatic. When one or more nodules exceed 1 cm in diameter, 'progressive massive' fibrosis is said to be present. Calcification is not a usual radiologic feature. Fibrosis in the upper lobes is typical, and cavitation may occur. Clubbing is not a feature and there is no increased absolute risk of mycobacterial tuberculosis or lung cancer. There is a reported increased incidence of atypical mycobacterial infections. Death may result from right heart failure.

a) **False**
b) **True**
c) **True**
d) **False**
e) **False**

Mitral stenosis is associated with rheumatic heart disease, while mitral incompetence has many causes including rheumatic heart disease, ventricular dilatation, Marfan's syndrome, chorda rupture, mitral valve prolapse (the commonest cause in developed countries), methysergide (fibrosis), and myocardial infarction. Connective tissue diseases such as SLE, rheumatoid arthritis and ankylosing spondylitis also cause fibrosis and valvular leak. Mixed mitral valve disease is typical of rheumatic valvular disease.

   Patients with NYHA class I and II with mitral incompetence have an eventual 90% mortality, unless surgery is performed. An ejection fraction of 55% or lower, with a shortening fraction of 30%, is already an indication for surgery. The only patients that can be safely watched are those with a normal left ventricular size, and an ejection fraction of 60% or more. Regular echographic examination (6 months to a year) are required.

Answer to question 238

a) **True**
b) **True**
c) **False**
d) **False**
e) **False**

Coxiella burnetii is a rickettsial illness characterised by fever, headache, myalgia and atypical pneumonia. A rash is unusual, in contrast to other rickettsioses. The incubation period is 2–3 weeks. Man is infected by inhalation of infected material from cattle and sheep.

   One-third of patients develop an acute or chronic hepatitis, and liver biopsy will show a diffuse granulomatous infiltration. *C. burnetii* is a recognised cause of infective endocarditis, especially in patients with abnormal aortic valves. Antibodies to phase II antigens are elevated during the acute illness and antibodies to phase I antigen during chronic illness such as endocarditis.

   C. burnetii is sensitive to tetracyclines and chloramphenicol.

a) **False**
b) **False**
c) **True**
d) **True**
e) **True**

Haemochromatosis is an autosomal recessive disease, which affects approximately 5 per 1000 people. The gene frequency is 1/10 to 1/15. Linkage with HLA A3, B3, B14 is seen in the majority. HLA H, a class I-like gene, has been identified as a candidate gene for this disease. HLA H seems to be important in interaction of β2 microglobulin with class I molecules. A mutation of HLA H has been reported in 83% of patients.

The sex ratio is 5:1, and presentation is usually after 40 years. Clinically the triad of diabetes, hepatomegaly and skin darkening is seen in about a third of patients. Diabetes is found in 60%, and cardiac arrhythmias in 15%. Up to 50% of patients have an arthropathy, due to deposition of calcium pyrophosphate crystals with iron in the synovium. The second and third metacarpal/phalangeal joints are often radiologically involved, leading to misdiagnosis of rheumatoid arthritis.

Answer to question 240

a) **False**
b) **False**
c) **False**
d) **False**
e) **False**

Pemphigus vulgaris is an autoimmune blistering disease associated with antibodies directed against the intercellular cement of the spindle cell layer of the epidermis. The age of onset is usually between the fourth and sixth decades, with men and women affected equally; Jewish patients have an increased risk of developing the disease.

Mucous membranes are commonly involved: oral lesions are the presenting feature in 60% of patients. The blisters are widespread, rupture easily (intact blisters are rare) and heal without scarring. The blisters occur most commonly in the axillae, the groin or in pressure areas. Nikolsky's sign will be positive — mild pressure plus a mild shear force applied to areas of normal skin lead to blister formation.

Pemphigus vulgaris is associated with other autoimmune disorders including systemic lupus erythematosus, autoimmune thyroid disease, and myasthenia gravis. There is an association between pemphigus vulgaris and some neoplasias, particularly lymphomas, thymomas and carcinomas. Pemphigus vulgaris is a recognised side-effect of penicillamine.

The diagnosis is confirmed by skin biopsy. Light microscopy shows acantholysis and intra-epidermal blister formation. The diagnosis is confirmed by direct immunofluorescence, using fluorescein labelled anti-human IgG, which detects autoantibodies of the IgG class directed against antigens in the intercellular cement.

Treatment: high-dose corticosteroids are life-saving (doses >100 mg daily are used); azathioprine or other cytotoxics are added if the disease does not respond, or as steroid-sparing agents. The disease itself may remit spontaneously after several years. Prior to corticosteroid therapy, death within 2 years was invariable.

Answer to question 241

a) **False**   d) **True**
b) **False**   e) **False**
c) **False**

The spinal cord extends from the foramen magnum to the upper border of the second lumbar vertebra. Pyramidal tracts from the cerebral cortex decussate in the medulla before descending on the contralateral side and synapsing with the motor cells of the anterior horn. Pain and temperature fibres enter the posterior nerve roots and are carried in the lateral spinothalamic tracts which ascend the cord for a few segments before decussating anterior to the spinal canal. As the fibres cross the cord the lowest fibres are pushed laterally by fibres entering higher up. Fibres subserving fine touch (including 2 point discrimination) and position sense are relayed in the ipsilateral dorsal column to the medulla where decussation occurs prior to passing to the thalamus and sensory cortex.

Note: vibration sense is carried in several ill-defined pathways and not solely the dorsal columns.

Upper motor neurone signs arising from cord lesions are usually bilateral. If such lesions are present in the arms the lesion is above C5; if the abdominal reflexes are lost the lesion is above T9 and if the legs are affected the lesion is above the conus medullaris. Lower motor neurone signs due to lesions affecting the anterior horn cells help to define the level of the cord lesion.

A Brown–Séquard lesion due to hemisection of the spinal cord is associated with:
a) A lower motor neurone weakness at the level of the lesion
b) Upper motor neurone signs below the level of the lesion
c) Ipsilateral loss of vibration and position sense below the level of the lesion
d) Contralateral loss of pain and temperature (since fibres entering this tract ascend for several segments before decussating, the upper level of this sensory loss is usually below the level of the lesion itself, and similarly there may be a narrow band of analgesia just below the lesion as ipsilateral spinothalamic fibres are caught before they decussate).

Answer 241 continued

In extrinsic cord compression, symptoms and signs are
predominantly motor. The onset of sensory symptoms or the
involvement of the sphincters often herald a rapid deterioration.
Intrinsic lesions of the cord, be they tumour or syrinx, due to their
anatomical position, first affect the decussating fibres subserving pain
and temperature at the level of the lesion, resulting in pain and a
sensory deficit. As the lesion enlarges, reflexes are lost. In general,
pyramidal signs are late and dorsal columns tend not to be affected
with intrinsic lesions. The phenomenon of sacral sparing is
characteristic of advanced intrinsic lesions and anatomically can be
explained by the fact that fibres carrying sacral pain and temperature
lie most laterally in the spinothalamic tracts so are affected last by an
expanding central lesion.

A lumbar myelogram will not help in the diagnosis of a spastic
paraparesis but myelography of the cervical and thoracic cord may.

Answer to question 242

a) **False**
b) **False**
c) **True**
d) **False**
e) **False**

Nicotinamide deficiency results in pellagra. The clinical features of
pellagra are a light-sensitive dermatitis, diarrhoea, dementia and
death. Nicotinamide is obtained in the diet and may be synthesised
from dietary tryptophan. Deficiency may complicate poor diet,
isoniazid therapy, Hartnup disease or carcinoid syndrome.
Pyridoxine deficiency is rare but may accompany poor diet or occur
as a side-effect of drugs, e.g. isoniazid. Clinical features include:
peripheral neuropathy, seborrhoeic dermatitis, glossitis, lymphopenia
and anaemia.
Vitamin C deficiency in adults causes gingival hyperplasia and
bleeding (if teeth are present), perifollicular haemorrhages, bruising,
painful woody oedema of the legs, coiled hairs, poor wound healing
and myalgia. In children, irritability, weakness of the legs, bleeding
(subperiosteal haemorrhages), leucocytosis and a hypochromic
microcytic anaemia are common features.
Hypercarotenosis results from excessive carrot consumption or
defective carotene metabolism, as may occur in diabetes mellitus,
hypothyroidism and anorexia nervosa. Features include yellow-
orange staining of the palms and soles of the feet but not the sclerae.
Vitamin A deficiency usually occurs in the setting of generalised
protein energy malnutrition. Clinical features include: a) poor night
vision; b) xerosis or dryness of the conjunctiva followed by Bitôt's
spots (which are composed of keratinised epithelial cells), and finally
keratomalacia complicated by infection which leads to loss of sight;
c) growth retardation; d) increased infections; e) anaemia; and
f) perifollicular hyperkeratosis.

Acrodermatitis enteropathica is a hereditary disorder associated with malabsorption of zinc which results in growth retardation, hypogonadism, loss of taste, hair loss, apsoriasis-like rash, diarrhoea and an increased incidence of bacterial and fungal infections.

Answer to question 243

a) **False**   d) **True**
b) **True**   e) **True**
c) **False**

Carcinoid tumours may arise from any part of the primitive endoderm. Approximately 50% of all carcinoids occur in the appendix but these are usually benign and do not metastasise. The other main sites of origin are small bowel (25%), colorectal region (12%) and stomach (12%). Symptoms of the carcinoid syndrome do not develop with gut carcinoids unless liver secondaries are present. Solitary primary bronchial carcinoids may however be associated with symptoms as these tumours drain systemically.

Clinical features of the carcinoid syndrome include:
a) Flushing (predominantly head and neck), initially transient but chronically may be associated with a reddened cyanotic face associated with telangiectasia. The flushing may be accompanied by oedema and pruritus
b) Diarrhoea
c) Wheezing
d) Hypotension
e) Palpitations
f) Right-sided heart involvement, classically leading to pulmonary stenosis and tricuspid regurgitation
g) Hepatomegaly and right hypochondrial pain
h) Increased incidence of peptic ulceration
i) Secondary pellagra
j) Ectopic ACTH production.

Many of the symptoms (diarrhoea and bronchoconstriction) are attributable to the production of 5-hydroxytryptamine (serotonin) which is synthesised from dietary tryptophan. Flushing, which may be provoked by alcohol, stress and various foods, may be related to bradykinin secretion. Histamine release (predominantly from gastric carcinoids) has been implicated in the production of oedema.

The diagnosis is confirmed by measuring urinary 5-hydroxyindole acetic acid production (5- HIAA), the main metabolite of 5-hydroxytryptamine. Up to 30 mg per day may be produced. False positive results occur if the patient has a diet rich in foods such as bananas and walnuts which contain 5-hydroxytryptamine, and in certain malabsorption syndromes such as coeliac disease and bacterial overgrowth. False negatives occur in patients on phenothiazines. Liver imaging is essential to document the presence of secondaries.

For primary bronchial carcinoids without secondaries, surgery may provide a cure.
Surgical debulking or hepatic artery ligation may help chronic symptoms.

Drugs used to control symptoms include:
5-hydroxytryptamine antagonists — cyproheptadine and methysergide
Alpha-blocking agents — phenoxybenzamine
Histamine antagonists
Somatostatin
Cytotoxic agents — 5-fluorouracil, streptazotocin
Nicotinamide
Codeine phosphate
Antiprostaglandins
Somatostatin, either i.v. or subcutaneous
Octreotide, either i.v. or subcutaneous.

Answer to question 244

a) **True**
b) **False**
c) **True**
d) **False**
e) **False**

Herpes simplex encephalitis can affect any age-group and has a predilection for the temporal lobes. The predilection may be explained by spread of reactivated virus from the trigeminal ganglion through nerve fibres subserving sensation to the dura. Clinical features include symptoms of meningitis, altered consciousness, convulsions and symptoms of temporal involvement, e.g. behavioural abnormalities, olfactory and gustatory hallucinations. Visible herpetic lesions on the nasal mucosa or face are rare. Marked cerebral oedema and haemorrhage are typical. The CSF shows a lymphocytic pleocytosis, an elevated protein concentration and a normal glucose.

Early diagnosis is essential. Intravenous acyclovir is the drug of choice, and patients in the early stages should be managed in intensive care. The CSF may be normal when first examined in up to 10% of cases. NMR or CT scanning will demonstrate the affected areas, and the diagnosis may be confirmed by a brain biopsy. Serology merely confirms infection and is of limited value in acute management.

The overall mortality exceeds 50% and survivors often show permanent neurological damage.

Topical idoxuridine is used for treating cutaneous herpetic lesions.

a) **False**   d) **False**
b) **True**   e) **False**
c) **True**

Benign essential tremor is inherited as an autosomal dominant trait. It may present at any age and is characterised by a postural tremor, primarily of the arms and head, which disappears at rest. The underlying aetiology has not been established. In most cases, symptoms are not progressive and a characteristic feature is the response to small amounts of alcohol. Beta-blockers are also effective in relieving symptoms.

Answer to question 246

a) **False**   d) **True**
b) **False**   e) **False**
c) **False**

Many biological characteristics, e.g. height, confirm to a normal Gaussian or bell-shaped distribution.

Some biological variables assume a skewed distribution, e.g. serum triglyceride levels are positively skewed or skewed to the right (i.e. the tail on the right is longer than the tail on the left).

The median value is the central value of the distribution such that half the values are greater or equal to it and half are less or equal to it.

The mean is the average value, i.e. that obtained by dividing the sum of all the individual values added together by their number.

The mode of the distribution is the value which occurs most frequently.

In a normal distribution the mean, mode and median all have the same value.

The standard deviation is a summary measure of the differences of each observation from the mean. To calculate the standard deviation we first calculate the variance:

$$\text{Variance} = \frac{\text{sum } (x - \text{mean})^2}{n - 1} = \frac{\text{sum of the squares}}{\text{degrees of freedom}}.$$

Standard deviation = square root of the variance.

For a Gaussian distribution:
68% of the population lie between +/– 1SD from the mean
95% of the population lie between +/– 2SD from the mean
99.7% of the population lie between +/– 3SD from the mean.

Standard error of the mean = standard deviation/square root of n.

The standard error of the mean of one sample drawn from a larger population is an estimate of the standard deviation that would be obtained from the means of a larger number of samples drawn from that population.

Note:
x = value of observation
n = number of observations.

a) **True**
b) **True**
c) **True**
d) **True**
e) **False**

Membranous glomerulonephritis is idiopathic in 90–95% of cases. Recognised causes of membranous glomerulonephritis include:
Malignancy in up to 25% of patients over 50
Drugs and toxins, e.g. penicillamine, gold, mercury
Systemic lupus erythematosus
Infections, e.g. syphilis, hepatitis B.

The usual clinical presentation is with proteinuria which often renders the patient nephrotic. Microscopic haematuria occurs in up to 20% of patients, but macroscopic haematuria is rare. Untreated, the nephrotic syndrome spontaneously remits in 25%, though this is often temporary. Children have a better prognosis than adults. Up to 40% develop renal vein thrombosis, which necessitates anticoagulation.

Membranous nephropathy usually progresses to end stage renal failure after a mean period of 9–10 years.

Histologically, there is diffuse glomerular involvement with thickening of the glomerular basement membrane. Immune deposits (primarily IgG and C3; also IgA and IgM) may initially be seen on the outer aspect of the basement membrane, later becoming intramembranous. Trials with alternating prednisolone and chlorambucil, alternate day prednisone (2 mg/kg), interferon for hepatitis B patients, and cytotoxic therapy pulses have been tried. There is no consensus for optimal treatment. Poor prognostic signs are: protoinuria of > 10 g/day, hypertension, male sex, and renal failure.

Answer to question 248

a) **False**
b) **True**
c) **False**
d) **True**
e) **False**

Vasculitis may affect all sizes of vessels, and most of the modern classification of vasculitides discriminate between disease entities on the basis of vessel size, e.g.:
Takayasu's arteritis and giant cell arteritis — large arteries
Churg–Strauss syndrome and polyarteritis nodosa — medium arteries
Henoch–Schönlein purpura, microscopic polyangiitis — small vessels.

Vasculitis may develop in association with a number of viral infections, such as parvovirus B19, hepatitis B and C, and HIV. Not all patients with vasculitis are ANCA positive, but this test is useful in patients with Wegener's, microscopic polyangiitis, and Churg–Strauss syndrome. More than 80% of patients with active Wegener's are C-ANCA positive. P-ANCA positivity is found in 50–60% of patients with microscopic polyangiitis. P-ANCA is generally thought to be less specific and sensitive than C-ANCA. Low complement levels may occur in patients with systemic vasculitis and SLE or hypocomplementaemic urticarial vasculitis. Severe renal disease can occur in patients with vasculitis, in the absence of any skin lesions.

Answer to question 249

a) **True**   d) **True**
b) **True**   e) **True**
c) **False**

Gastric acid is produced in parietal cells. Gastrin, produced in antral G cells, histamine, amino acids and acetylcholine stimulate acid production. Low pH of the antrum inhibits gastrin, which is one of the chief stimulants of gastric secretion. Gastrin occurs in many forms, but the 17 amino acid form is most important. A circulatory 34 amino acid form is also found. Men have higher acid production than women. *H. pylori* reduces the secretion of somatostatin by D cells, thus resulting in higher acid levels.

Answer to question 250

a) **True**   d) **True**
b) **True**   e) **True**
c) **True**

Gorlin–Goltz syndrome (basal cell naevus syndrome) may be familial and is characterised by the appearance in early adult life of multiple basal cell naevi. Associated features include dental and bone cysts which may become malignant, bifid ribs and cerebellar medulloblastoma. Porokeratotic palmar and plantar pits 1–3 mm in diameter are diagnostic.

Epiloia or tuberous sclerosis is an autosomal dominant disorder characterised by multiple cutaneous angiofibromas (predominant in the nasolabial folds), low IQ and epilepsy. Other clinical features include: ash-leaf white macules on the trunk which fluoresce under Wood's light, shagreen patch, nail-fold fibromas, ocular abnormalities, rhabdomyosarcoma, and renal tumours. Plain skull X-ray may show calcified fibromas in the periventricular area.

Tylosis (palmoplantar hyperkeratosis) is an autosomal dominant disease characterised by palmoplantar thickening. There is a well-recognised association with oesophageal carcinoma.

Ataxia telangiectasia is an autosomal recessive disorder characterised by multiple facial telangiectasia, cerebellar signs, IgA and IgE deficiency, lymphopenia and an increased incidence of malignancy in both homozygotes and heterozygotes.

The Chediak–Higashi syndrome is a rare autosomal recessive disorder characterised by defective neutrophil function and a relative neutropenia. Death before 10 years of age is usual, due either to infection or underlying lymphoma. Associated features include: albinism, nystagmus, hepatosplenomegaly, and lymphadenopathy.

Answer to question 251

a) False   d) True
b) False   e) False
c) True

In trying to differentiate between prerenal and established renal failure in patients with oliguric (< 500 ml urine in 24 hours) acute renal failure, it is helpful to analyse and compare the biochemical quality of urine and plasma.

Prerenal failure is due to inadequate perfusion of the kidney, which responds by conserving water and sodium and excreting small volumes of highly concentrated urine. If renal perfusion is quickly restored then acute tubular necrosis may be avoided. In contrast, in established renal disease the kidney does not conserve sodium and excretes poor quality urine that resembles glomerular filtrate.

Prerenal failure:
Urinary sodium ≤ 10–20 mmol/L
Urinary urea > 250 mmol/L
Urine osmolality > 500 mosmol/kg
Urine:plasma urea > 20
Urine:plasma osmolality > 1.1
Urine:plasma creatinine > 20
No urinary sediment.

Established renal failure:
Urinary sodium > 20 mmol/L
Urinary urea < 150 mmol/L
Urine osmolality < 350 mosmol/kg
Urine: plasma urea < 10
Urine:plasma osmolality < 1.1
Urine:plasma creatinine < 15
Urinary sediment may be present

The above criteria cannot be rigidly applied if diuretics have been given.

a) **True**
b) **False**
c) **True**
d) **True**
e) **False**

During the first trimester, cardiac output rises by 1.5 L/min. The peripheral vascular resistance decreases, however, leading to a net fall in blood pressure. During the later weeks of pregnancy the diastolic pressure rises slowly to pre-pregnant values. Supine hypotension complicates 10% of normal pregnancies as the gravid uterus impairs venous return. Pregnancy is associated with a hyperdynamic circulation and the following are normal findings: collapsing pulse, palpable apex, pulmonary flow murmur and third heart sound. A diastolic murmur represents pathology and should be investigated.

Answer to question 253

a) **False**
b) **False**
c) **True**
d) **False**
e) **False**

Acute fatty liver is a rare complication of pregnancy. Patients are typically primigravidae and are pre-eclamptic. Clinical features include: sudden onset of abdominal pain, jaundice, headaches and vomiting. Patients are generally afebrile. Biochemical abnormalities include: a low glucose, high uric acid and relatively low bilirubin and transaminase levels. Liver biopsy shows centrilobular fat deposition and renal histology shows fatty infiltration of the renal tubules. The development of disseminated intravascular coagulation, encephalopathy and renal failure carry a poor prognosis. Overall, maternal and perinatal outcomes are generally poor though the liver damage is potentially fully reversible on delivery.

Answer to question 254

a) **True**
b) **False**
c) **True**
d) **True**
e) **True**

Primary biliary cirrhosis (PBC) is a disease of middle-aged women, 95% of patients being female. Antimitochondrial antibodies are positive in 95% of patients, but may be seen in chronic autoimmune hepatitis. IgM and antinuclear antibodies are elevated. In the beginning of the disease alkaline phosphatase and not bilirubin may be elevated. The disease may be inherited. CD8 and CD4 cells are found in the portal triads. Bile ducts express integrin molecules (ICAMI) and class II molecules. Granulomas are also seen histologically. Thyroiditis, scleroderma, and rheumatoid arthritis may be associated with PBC.

Pruritus is the most troublesome symptom, and can occur in the absence of jaundice. Osteoporosis and hypercholesterolaemia are also typical. Ursodeoxycholic acid relieves pruritus and may delay transplant. Colchicine has also been used to some effect, as well as weekly methotrexate. PBC is one of the most common indications for hepatic transplantation in the developed world.

Answer to question 255

a) **True**
b) **False**
c) **True**
d) **False**
e) **True**

Melatonin (N acetyl 5 methoxytryptamine) is secreted during darkness, from the pineal gland. Several putative functions have been ascribed to it:
a) Free radical scavenger
b) Ovarian function
c) Sleep–wake cycle
d) Prevention of ageing.

These have not been proven, but it has been shown that melatonin is useful in treating jet lag. It may also be used in restoring sleep patterns in old patients.

a) **False**
b) **True**
c) **False**
d) **False**
e) **True**

Pulmonary alveolar proteinosis is commoner in males than females. The aetiology is unknown. The lungs are filled with an amorphous PAS-positive substance. Clinical features include: fever, cough, haemoptysis, and shortage of breath. Lung function tests show a restrictive pattern.

Secondary infection is common, especially with nocardia, aspergillus, candida and cytomegalovirus. Chest X-ray shows alveolar shadowing spreading out from the hila; lymphadenopathy is not a feature. The diagnosis is confirmed by demonstrating amorphous PAS-positive material on bronchoalveolar lavage. In one-third of patients treatment is not required and spontaneous resolution occurs. Therapeutic bronchoalveolar lavage is effective in removing the amorphous substance. Corticosteroids are ineffective and contraindicated due to the increased risk of infection.

Answer to question 257

a) **False**
b) **False**
c) **True**
d) **True**
e) **False**

Intracranial aneurysms have a prevalence of 6% in the general population, but most people remain asymptomatic. A third of patients have multiple aneurysms. Patients who have suffered an aneurysmal bleed have a 2% per year chance of a re-bleed. Intracranial aneurysms are more dangerous than extracranial, since intracranial arteries do not have a tunica elastica. Smoking, hypertension and inheritance contribute to aneurysms.

Headache precedes rupture in up to a third of patients. If aneurysm is suspected the definitive diagnosis is an angiogram, which has a mortality of 0.1% in experienced hands. CT scanning is the choice examination after rupture. Magnetic resonance angiography is safer than conventional angiography, and is only limited by cost and availability. Patients with previous aneurysm surgery, with clips in place, may not undergo MR scanning.

a) **True**
b) **True**
c) **False**
d) **True**
e) **True**

The extra-articular features of rheumatoid arthritis include:
Lung involvement: pleurisy; pleural effusion — high protein, high LDH, high WBC, low glucose, low C3, positive rheumatoid factor; pleural nodules; parenchymal nodules upper lobes; interstitial fibrosis: only 2% have classical FA (fibrosing alveolitis) and 40% have low KCO; obliterative bronchiolitis; Caplan's syndrome.

Anaemia: Iron deficiency secondary to drugs, normochromic normocytic anaemia of chronic disease, marrow hypoplasia secondary to drugs, folic acid deficiency, Felty's syndrome, associated pernicious anaemia, sideroblastic anaemia, dilutional anaemia.

Neurological involvement: carpal tunnel syndrome, distal sensory neuropathy, mononeuritis multiplex, radiculopathy, cervical myelopathy, disuse atrophy.

Lymphoreticular system: lymphadenopathy 50% soft mobile non-tender; splenomegaly 5% with disease activity.

Felty's syndrome: splenomegaly, rheumatoid arthritis leukopenia, weight loss, lymphadenopathy and evidence of vasculitis.

Eye involvement: sicca syndrome 25%, episcleritis, scleritis/ scleromalacia perforans, tenosynovitis ocular muscles, drug side-effects, e.g. cataracts, retinopathy (chloroquine).

Cardiac involvement: pericarditis, pericardial effusion, cardiac nodules, valvular disease and conduction abnormalities, e.g. heart block and arrhythmias.

General features: pitting oedema; lymphoedema, nodules RF positive; cutaneous vasculitis — splinter haemorrhages, palpable purpura; osteoporosis; late complication AA amyloidosis.

a) **False**   d) **True**
b) **False**   e) **False**
c) **True**

X-ray features of rheumatoid arthritis:
Juxta-articular osteoporosis, marginal erosions, joint space narrowing, deformities, geodes (fluid-filled cysts in subchondral bone), soft tissue swelling, atlanto-axial subluxation, vertebral subluxation, carpal ankylosis, resorption of distal end of clavicles.

X-ray features of osteoarthritis:
Loss of joint space, articular sclerosis, osteophyte formation, subchondral cysts, loose bodies, subluxation of distal interphalangeal joints.

Answer to question 260

a) **True**   d) **True**
b) **True**   e) **False**
c) **False**

Carbamazepine and valproate are associated with an increased risk of fetal neural tube defects.
    Lamotrigine is used for partial and secondary generalised epilepsy. Liver functions must be carefully monitored, and liver disease is a contraindication to its use. Rash and bone marrow impairment are sometimes seen.
    Vigabantrin is useful as a second-line agent against seizures which are not controlled by other medications. Kidney failure, fatigue and dizziness are side-effects.
    Gabapentin is useful for partial seizures, as an adjunctive therapy, but can cause drowsiness.
    Benzodiazepines such as clobazam lose effectiveness when used chronically.

Answer to question 261

a) **True**   d) **True**
b) **True**   e) **True**
c) **True**

The following have clinically important first pass hepatic metabolism:
Propranolol, labetolol, oxprenolol, lignocaine, glyceryl trinitrate, isosorbide dinitrate, chlormethiazole, pethidine, pentazocine, imipramine, nortriptyline, amitriptyline, prazepam, enalapril, oestrogens, aspirin and chlorpromazine.

a) **False**
b) **True**
c) **False**
d) **False**
e) **True**

The major features of hypokalaemia in the ECG are:
A prominent U wave
Flattening of the T wave until it becomes inverted
The ST interval becomes depressed
The PR interval becomes prolonged
Rarely, complete SA block occurs
There is an increased frequency of the paroxysmal ventricular tachycardia *torsades de points*
The QRS axis rotates over a sequence of 5–30 beats and may be mistaken for ventricular fibrillation.

ECG features of hyperkalaemia include:
Peaked T waves
Wide QRS complex
Flat P waves
Prolonged PR interval
Bradycardia/asystole
Arrhythmias.

Answer to question 263

a) **True**
b) **False**
c) **True**
d) **True**
e) **False**

Prolongation of the QT interval is found in the following:
Congenital syndromes: Jervell–Lange–Nielson syndrome, Romano–Ward syndrome
Anti-arrhythmic agents: quinidine, procainamide, sotalol, amiodarone, bretylium, bepridil
Other drugs: prenylamine, tricyclic antidepressants, phenothiazines, erythromycin
Electrolyte disturbances: hypocalcaemia, hypomagnesaemia
Bradyarrhythmias: complete AV block, sick-sinus syndrome
Other medical conditions: anorexia nervosa, hypothermia, liquid protein diets, ischaemic heart disease, myxoedema, mitral valve disease, CNS disease.

Prolongation of the QT interval predisposes to ventricular tachycardias, particularly *torsades de points*.

a) **True**
b) **False**
c) **True**
d) **True**
e) **False**

The main clinical features of hypothermia are clouding of consciousness or coma, muscular rigidity, bradycardia, hypotension, oliguria or a diuresis, vomiting and a depressed cough reflex. Complications include pancreatitis, hypoglycaemia and ventricular arrhythmias.

The ECG findings include bradycardia, J waves (Osborn waves), and prolongation of the QT interval.

Treatment is supportive with slow rewarming, ventilation if necessary, replacement of fluids with CVP monitoring, i.v. antibiotics, monitoring of glucose and electrolytes. If rewarming is performed too quickly, profound hypotension may occur which can lead to myocardial infarction or stroke. Finally the underlying problem should be sought.

Causes of hypothermia include:
a) Increased heat loss, e.g. cold environment, alcohol intoxication
b) Failure of thermoregulation, e.g. stroke, drugs (barbiturates), diabetes
c) Decreased heat production, e.g. hypothyroidism, hypopituitarism.

Death in a patient with profound hypothermia should only be diagnosed on rewarming.

Answer to question 265

a) **True**
b) **True**
c) **True**
d) **True**
e) **True**

Causes of pulmonary hypertension
a) Conditions which lead to pulmonary arterial hypertension:
   1. Hyperdynamic causes, e.g. L-R shunts, hypoxia, liver failure
   2. Obstructive/obliterative causes, e.g. COAD, PRU, sickle-cell disease, multiple emboli
   3. Vasoconstrictive/vasoreactive causes, e.g. hypoxia, systemic sclerosis, primary pulmonary hypertension, rapeseed oil, aminorex, sarcoidosis.

b) Conditions which lead to pulmonary venous hypertension:
   1. Chronic left ventricular failure
   2. Mitral valve disease, cor triatriatum, myxoma
   3. Pulmonary venous occlusive disease.

a) **True**
b) **True**
c) **True**
d) **False**
e) **True**

After presentation of antigen to T cells by macrophages, IL-1 is produced. IL-1 activates the acute phase response, induces the adherence of neutrophils, lymphocytes and monocytes to endothelial cells and activates T-helper cells to produce IL-2 and γ-interferon.

IL-2 has a relatively restricted repertoire of actions; it promotes the activation and growth of T cells, increases NK cell (natural killer cell) activity, and promotes the growth and activity of B cells. T cells have been shown to be divided into Th 1 and Th 2 cells. Th 1 cells produce IL-2 and help CD8 T cells, enhancing cytotoxicity and clonal proliferation. Th 2 cells produce IL-4 and 10 and help B cells. These cells may therefore determine which pathway is activated in autoimmune disease, the antibody or the cytotoxic pathway.

Interferons stimulate cytotoxic, NK and B cells; they are involved in the recovery from virus infections. There are three main types: α, β and γ. Gamma-interferon is involved in immune regulation and will cause the expression of class II HLA molecules on cell surfaces and the production of antibody by B cells.

Tumour necrosis factor α (TNF-α) is produced by macrophages and has similar effects to IL-1. It can induce IL-1 production, activate osteoblasts causing bone resorption and activate fibroblasts and other cells to produce degradative enzymes. TNF-α is probably responsible for the cachexia seen with some tumours and inflammatory disorders.

Answer to question 267

a) **True**
b) **True**
c) **False**
d) **False**
e) **True**

Legionella pneumonia has an incubation period of approximately 7 days. Legionnaire's disease commonly presents with extrapulmonary disease, particularly gastroenteritis. Other manifestations include headache, encephalopathy, hypotension and arrhythmias, pneumonia, myalgia and rhabdomyolysis, hepatitis and renal failure. A third of patients have evidence of involvement of at least one major organ. Raised creatine kinase, liver enzyme elevation, hyponatraemia, a moderate polymorphonuclear leucocytosis and lymphopenia are common.

Splenomegaly and cold agglutinins are features of mycoplasma infection.

Erythromycin or one of the other macrolide antibiotics are used to treat patients with legionella infection.

a) **False**
b) **False**
c) **False**
d) **False**
e) **False**

Myocardial infarction (MI) is associated with several arrhythmias. Bradycardias are seen in both inferior and anterior infarction and are relatively benign. First degree atrioventricular block is found in 13% after MI, and is relatively benign. Second degree block is found in 10%, and type I (sequential prolongation of PR, followed by a dropped beat) is usually responsive to atropine. Type II block (no PR lengthening) is more serious and often requires pacing. Bundle branch block implies a large infarction.

Ventricular fibrillation is found in 18% of MI patients, and is one of the major causes of death, particularly before admission. Amiodarone has been shown to reduce mortality, but antiarrhythmics like sotalol increase mortality.

Answer to question 269

a) **False**
b) **False**
c) **True**
d) **False**
e) **False**

Pupil size is controlled by parasympathetically innervated constrictor fibres (dominant at rest), balanced by sympathetically innervated radially-arranged dilator fibres.

Parasympathetic pathway: Light stimulation of the retina is conveyed via the optic nerve and tracts to both Edinger–Westphal nuclei lying in the lateral geniculate bodies. Parasympathetic nerve fibres leave the nuclei and are carried superficially on the outside of cranial nerve III, relay in the ciliary ganglion and reach the constrictor muscles via the short ciliary nerves with subsequent pupil constriction. On convergence, the Edinger–Westphal nuclei are also stimulated, mediating the accommodation reflex.

Sympathetic pathway: The pathway may be mapped from the ipsilateral hypothalamus, which relays to the grey matter of the thoracic cord. The second neurone of the pathway leaves the cord in the T1 root and synapses in the superior cervical ganglion, from whence the third and final neurone reaches the pupil.

The **Marcus Gunn** pupil is an afferent pupillary defect. Lesions in the retina, optic nerve or tract result in a decrease in the direct light reflex from the affected side. On direct light stimulation of the normal eye there is a direct and consensual light reflex. If the source of the light is then transferred to the affected eye, the pupil will start to dilate as the pupil escapes from the consensual response.

The typical **Argyll–Robertson** pupil of meningovascular syphilis is small, irregular, with depigmentation of the iris, does not react to light but does react to accommodation and is believed to be due to a lesion in the periaqueductal area of the midbrain. Other causes of Argyll–Robertson pupils include alcohol, diabetes, brain stem encephalitis and pinealomas, though these tend to give fixed dilated pupils. Argyll–Robertson pupils do not constrict in response to atropine.

The **Holmes–Adie** pupil (often unilateral) is widely dilated and hypotonic, reacting only very slowly to bring light but more consistently to accommodation. It results from denervation of nerve cells in the ciliary ganglion. Associations include loss of reflexes and impaired sweating.

A **Horner's syndrome** arises from interruption of the sympathetic pathway anywhere along its path. The typical clinical features are a) meiosis (constricted pupil); b) ptosis; c) enophthalmos; d) nasal congestion; and e) reduced sweating (central lesions reduce sweating over the face, arm and torso of the same side; neck lesions affect sweating over the face, and lesions above the superior cervical ganglion may not affect sweating at all).

Horner's syndrome due to a lesion above the superior cervical ganglion: adrenaline 1:1000 will dilate the pupil as there will be a decrease in the monoamineoxidase concentration. Adrenaline has no effect on the normal eye or a Horner's due to a lesion below the superior cervical ganglion.

Horner's syndrome due to a lesion below the superior cervical ganglion: cocaine 4% will dilate the pupil, as cocaine works by blocking monoamineoxidase which in a central Horner's will not be depleted. Cocaine has a similar effect on normal eyes.

Intrapontine haemorrhage is characterised by bilateral pinpoint pupils, deep coma and bilateral pyramidal signs.

a) **True**
b) **True**
c) **True**
d) **False**
e) **False**

Approximately 60% of the total serum calcium, representing the non-protein bound fraction, is filtered at the glomerulus. Most of this, approximately 60%, is passively reabsorbed along with sodium and water in the proximal convoluted tubule. Smaller percentages, 25%, 10% and 5%, are reabsorbed in the loop of Henle, the distal tubule and the collecting duct, and active transport mechanisms play a progressively greater role. Approximately 2% of the filtered load is eventually excreted and this is critically regulated by distal tubular function, mainly under the control of PTH. The treatment of acidosis and correction of hypophosphataemia will also reduce calcium excretion.

Causes of hypercalciuria include:
All causes of hypercalcaemia, idiopathic hypercalciuria, acromegaly, Cushing's syndrome, renal tubular acidosis.

Answer to question 271

a) **False**
b) **False**
c) **False**
d) **True**
e) **False**

Type A lactic acidosis (Cohen–Woods classification) is characterised by hypoxia and is seen in: congestive cardiac failure, haemorrhagic shock, leukaemia.

Hypocapnia is common and hypotension the rule. Otherwise, this has all the characteristics of a high anion gap metabolic acidosis. The normal range for the anion gap $[Na^+ + K^+] - [Cl^- + HCO_3^-]$ is 10–18 mmol. The normal range for the base deficit, i.e. the amount of alkali in mmol necessary to return the pH of the blood in vitro to normal at PCO_2 of 5.6 kPa is 2 to 4.

Causes of a normal anion gap metabolic acidosis:
Renal tubular acidosis, ureterosigmoidostomy, acetazolamide therapy, severe diarrhoea, e.g. cholera, loss of HCO_3^- from a pancreatic fistula.

An increased serum chloride is responsible for normalising the anion gap.

Type B lactic acidosis without hypoxia is seen with:
Drugs and toxins, e.g. phenformin, salicylate, ethylene glycol and methanol; renal failure; hepatic failure; diabetes.

a) **False**
b) **True**
c) **False**
d) **True**
e) **True**

Urobilinogen in haemolysis, phenolphthalein in many laxatives, homogentisic acid in alkaptonuria, and porphobilinogen in acute intermittent or variegate porphyria are all causes of this phenomenon.

Answer to question 273

a) **True**
b) **False**
c) **False**
d) **True**
e) **False**

Many of the symptoms and signs of thyrotoxicosis may be mimicked by normal pregnancy. Graves' disease is the commonest cause of thyrotoxicosis in pregnancy; others include multinodular goitre, hydatidiform mole and choriocarcinoma. Untreated maternal thyrotoxicosis is associated with an increased risk of perinatal mortality and pre-eclampsia. Small amounts of thyroxine do cross the placenta but fetal thyrotoxicosis results from transplacental transfer of the maternal IgG antibody which stimulates the fetal thyrotrophin receptor. Subtotal thyroidectomy is not recommended in pregnancy, and medical treatment is advised. Carbimazole or propylthiouracil both cross the placenta and inhibit fetal thyroxine production. Mild hypothyroidism is common in many neonates but this does not seem to have any long-term deleterious effects. Occasionally, it is necessary to give the mother thyroid supplements as the dose of carbimazole required to render the thyrotoxic fetus euthyroid renders the mother hypothyroid.

The fetus may also be affected by transplacental passage of maternal IgG in cases of: myasthenia gravis, herpes gestationis, idiopathic thrombocytopenic purpura, systemic lupus erythematosus. SSA/Ro antibodies cause fetal heart block.

a) **True**   d) **False**
b) **True**   e) **False**
c) **True**

Atrial fibrillation (AF) is the most common of the sustained tachyarrhythmias. The incidence of atrial fibrillation increases with age and underlying heart disease. There are three approaches to management of this condition: a) revert to sinus rhythm; b) reduce the ventricular response to the fibrillation; and c) prevent thromboembolic complications.

In the absence of cardiac failure, calcium channel blockers and β blockers are effective. Antiarrhythmic medication is associated with some risk of ventricular arrhythmias, but may have a role in maintaining sinus rhythm in cardioverted patients.

The most unequivocal benefit derives from preventing thromboembolic complications. Patients at highest risk are those with hypertension, previous strokes or TIAs, diabetes mellitus, age above 65 years, or recent heart failure. In these patients stroke rates approach 5%–7% of patients with AF per year. Five randomised controlled clinical trials have shown unequivocal benefit for warfarin therapy with an INR of between 2 and 3. Aspirin as monotherapy has not produced measurable benefit.

Electric or drug-induced cardioversion is associated with risks of embolism, particularly if thrombus is present in the ventricle. Patients should be on warfarin with INR of 2 to 3 for 4 weeks prior to cardioversion. A recent study did not show definite benefit by using a transoesophageal echo to monitor ventricular thrombosis before proceeding with cardioversion.

Answer to question 275

a) **False**   d) **False**
b) **True**   e) **True**
c) **True**

Most cases of chondrocalcinosis are idiopathic and age-related. The knee is the commonest joint involved.

The causes of chondrocalcinosis are many; they include:
Paget's disease, ochronosis, acromegaly, haemochromatosis, Wilson's disease, hyperuricaemia, hyperparathyroidism, hypophosphatasia (low alkaline phosphatase and skeletal abnormalities), hypomagnesaemia, hypothyroidism, diabetes mellitus, hypertension, renal failure, osteoarthritis, rheumatoid arthritis.

Note: viewed with polarising light, monosodium urate crystals are negatively birefringent and calcium pyrophosphate dihydrate crystals weakly positively birefringent when the crystals are parallel to the direction of polarising light.

a) **False**   d) **True**
b) **True**   e) **True**
c) **False**

Genomic imprinting was first discovered in mice, and examples were then found in humans. The definition of genomic imprinting is the inactivation of autosomal genes of either the maternal or the paternal genome. This inactivation probably is caused by DNA methylation. The Prader–Willi syndrome is an example of genomic imprinting in humans, since it is only found if the paternal 15th chromosome, with an inactivated genetic segment, is inherited. If the same genetic segment is inactivated on the maternal chromosome, a different type of disease develops.

DNA techniques of antenatal screening do not depend on fetal gene expression, since DNA analysis examines both expressed and unexpressed genes. Chorionic villus biopsy is performed earlier than amniocentesis, and results are attained more quickly.

Restriction fragment length polymorphism looks at polymorphisms which are inherited with a mutant gene. If two RFLPs on either side of a mutant gene are inherited, the chance of inheriting the abnormal gene is much higher.

Answer to question 277

a) **False**   d) **False**
b) **False**   e) **False**
c) **False**

The normal sagittal diameter of the cervical canal is 15–20 mm. If the diameter is < 13 mm, minor spondylotic changes can lead to cord compression. There are 7 cervical vertebrae but 8 cervical nerves. The C1 nerve root emerges over the top of the first cervical vertebra.

Most movement in cervical spine, and hence most spondylosis, occurs at C5/6, C6/7, C4/5 so the roots most often affected are C6, C7 and C5.

The lumbar nerve roots emerge below their respective vertebral bodies, i.e. the L4 nerve root emerges between the 4 and 5 lumbar vertebrae. The nerve roots typically exit high into the foramen, so a prolapsed disc at L4/5 will affect the 5 lumbar nerve root. L5 and S1 root lesions account for > 95% of disc lesions.

Neurology of the legs
Hip flexion is mediated by iliopsoas — nerve roots L1,2,3, — femoral twigs and direct supply from sacral plexus.
Hip extension is mediated by the glutei — nerve roots L4/5 — gluteal nerves.
Hip abduction is mediated by the glutei and tensor fascia lata — nerve roots L4/5 — gluteal nerves.
Hip adduction is mediated by the adductor muscles — nerve roots L2,3,4 — obturator nerve.

Knee flexion is mediated by the hamstrings — nerve roots L5/S1 — sciatic nerve.

Knee extension is mediated by the quadriceps — nerve roots L3/4 — femoral nerve.

Ankle plantar flexion is mediated by the calf muscles — nerve roots S1/2 — posterior tibial nerve nerve.

Ankle dorsiflexion is mediated by tibialis anterior — nerve roots L4/5 — anterior tibial nerve.

Ankle inversion is mediated by tibialis anterior and tibialis posterior — nerve root L4.

Ankle eversion is mediated by the peroneal muscles — nerve roots L5/S1 — common peroneal nerve.

Great toe dorsiflexion is mediated by extensor hallucis longus — nerve root L5 — common peroneal nerve.

Neurology of the arms

Shoulder abduction is mediated by a) supraspinatus nerve root C5 — suprascapular nerve and b) deltoid C5 — axillary nerve.

Shoulder adduction is mediated by pectoralis major and latissimus dorsi — nerve root C6/7.

Shoulder external rotation is mediated by infraspinatus — nerve root C5 — suprascapular nerve.

Shoulder internal rotation is mediated by subscapularis and teres minor — nerve root C5 — suprascapular nerve.

Elbow flexion is mediated by biceps/brachioradialis — nerve roots C5 and C6 — musculocutaneous nerve.

Elbow extension is mediated by the triceps — nerve roots C7 and C8 — radial nerve.

Wrist extension is mediated by the long extensors — nerve roots C6 and C7 — radial nerve.

Wrist flexion is mediated by wrist flexors — nerve roots C7/8 — median and ulnar nerve.

Finger extension is mediated by finger extensors – nerve roots C8/7 — radial nerve.

Finger flexion is mediated by the finger flexors — nerve roots C8 — median and ulnar nerves.

Finger abduction is mediated by the interossei — nerve root T1 — ulnar nerve.

Thumb abduction is mediated by abductor pollicis brevis — nerve root T1 — median nerve.

Answer to question 278

a) **False**
b) **False**
c) **True**
d) **False**
e) **True**

Paget's disease is found in 3% of the general population over the age of 55. Osteosclerotic enlargement is unique to Paget's disease, since prostate carcinoma, which also results in bone sclerosis, does not lead to enlargement. Bone pain is common, and 50% of patients have joint pain due to joint damage, following poor alignments of bones. Only 1% of patients develop osteosarcoma. ALP (alkaline phosphatase) is an enzyme which reflects bone building, while hydroxyproline measures bone breakdown. Urinary hydroxyproline is a better measure of bone breakdown than serum enzyme values. Up to 15% of patients have normal enzymes, since they have localised disease.

Biphosphonates are phosphate carbon molecules, and stop metabolism of calcium phosphate, increase apoptosis of osteoclasts, promote formation of lamellar bone, reduce new bone formation. Pamidronate and alendronate are more potent than etidronate. They have been shown to relieve pain, and prevent pain and deformity. All these drugs are associated with gastrointestinal side effects such as abdominal bloating, diarrhoea, and constipation. Alendronate has been associated with oesophageal ulceration.

Answer to question 279

a) **True**
b) **True**
c) **False**
d) **False**
e) **True**

Movement of the diaphragm causes the kidney to move down in inspiration and upwards in expiration of the order 3–5 cm. Gerota's fascia is a fibro-elastic connective tissue which surrounds the kidney (a thin anterior leaf, Toldt's fascia, and a stronger posterior fascia of Zuckerkandl). At the hilum the vein lies anteriorly to the artery which is anterior to the renal pelvis.

Ureteric duplication with ectopic ureter is not easily seen on IVP.

The estimated incidence of crossed renal ectopia is 1:7000. The kidney lies below or is fused to the lower pole of the opposite kidney.

a) **True**   d) **True**
b) **True**   e) **True**
c) **False**

The first desire to defecate occurs at 18 mmHg. When this pressure reaches 55 mmHg, the contents of the rectum are expelled (unless centrally inhibited). This explains the reflex evacuation in spinal patients.

Defecation is a spinal reflex that can be voluntarily inhibited by the external but not internal sphincter. Distension of the stomach can lead to the desire to defaecate: this is the gastrocolic reflex. Anal manometry is useful in assessing the function of both internal and external anal sphincters. Urge incontinence is seen in patients with external sphincter damage, and is caused by damage to the voluntarily controlled external sphincter. Passive incontinence is defined as leak of faeces, and is caused by internal anal sphincter damage.

Answer to question 281

a) **False**   d) **True**
b) **False**   e) **True**
c) **False**

Sympathetic fibres inhibit micturition; parasympathetic fibres cause contraction of the bladder. The second, third and fourth sacral spinal segments form the spinal reflex arc. During normal filling the bladder pressure will remain low until the bladder is nearly full. The law of Laplace states that the wall tension is equal to pressure times radius/2. Thus as the volume increases the radius increases, which should lead to increased wall tension. This does not occur due to relaxation of the detrusor muscle. In the female, urine remaining in the urethra drains by gravity.

Answer to question 282

a) **True**   d) **True**
b) **False**   e) **False**
c) **True**

Digoxin has been shown in several randomised controlled clinical trials to reduce heart failure, increase exercise capacity, and improve quality of life. Some case control studies have shown an increase in heart attacks. The Digitalis Investigation Group has recently concluded a large and well designed trial, showing that hospitalisation was reduced by 8% in treated patients, but no mortality reduction was seen. A slight increase in arrhythmic deaths was found.

a) **True**
b) **False**
c) **False**
d) **False**
e) **True**

Low serum complement C3 levels occur with:
Systemic lupus erythematosus, mesangiocapillary glomerulonephritis, infective endocarditis, post-streptococcal glomerulonephritis, infected ventricular shunts.

Cryoglobulinaemia is classically associated with low levels of C4 and normal levels of C3.

Answer to question 284

a) True
b) **False**
c) **False**
d) **False**
e) **True**

Causes of a positive R wave in lead V1 include:
Wolff–Parkinson–White syndrome type A; a posterior wall myocardial infarction; right bundle branch block; dextrocardia; right ventricular dominance; normal variant, incorrect lead placement.

Causes of right bundle branch block include:
Right ventricular hypertrophy; hypertension; ischaemic heart disease; myocarditis; rheumatic heart disease; pulmonary embolism; atrial septal defect (ostium primum – left axis deviation, ostium secundum – right axis deviation).

Clinical features of Kartagener's syndrome:
Autosomal recessive, ciliary immobility, dextrocardia, situs inversus, otitis media, infertility.

a) **True**
b) **False**
c) **False**
d) **True**
e) **True**

Dominance refers to which coronary artery supplies the interventricular artery. In 90% of cases this is the right coronary artery. The sinoatrial node is supplied by the proximal branches of the right coronary artery in 60% of cases and by the left in 40%. The left ventricle is supplied by both left and right coronary arteries. The atrioventricular node is supplied by the inferior ventricular artery, a branch of the right coronary artery, in 90% of patients, and the distal branches of the left coronary artery in 10% of cases.

Arrhythmias following inferior infarctions are often related to vagal disturbance and are usually transient. Conduction disturbance and anterior infarction are usually associated with underlying septal damage.

ANATOMY:

Right coronary artery:
Arises from the anterior aortic sinus, passes between the pulmonary trunk and the right atrium and descends in the atrioventricular groove to lie on the anterior surface of the heart. It continues in the atrioventricular groove to anastomose with the left coronary artery on the posterior surface of the heart.

Branches:
a) Atrial and ventricular branches.
b) Marginal branch — runs along the lower heart border towards the apex.
c) Posterior interventricular artery — runs in the inferior ventricular groove to anastomose with the anterior interventricular artery at the apex.

Left coronary artery:
Arises from the left posterior aortic sinus, passes behind and then lateral to the pulmonary trunk. The first part of the left coronary artery is known as the left main stem.

Branches:
a) Atrial and ventricular branches.
b) Anterior interventricular artery — descends in the anterior interventricular groove and anastomoses with the posterior interventricular artery.
c) Circumflex artery — passes posteriorly to anastomose with the right coronary artery on the posterior surface of the heart.
d) Marginal artery — a branch of the circumflex which runs along the left heart border.

a) **True**
b) **True**
c) **False**
d) **False**
e) **True**

The right main bronchus makes a 25° angle to the vertical and the left a 45° angle. The apical segment of the right lower lobe is the first posterior branch of the bronchial tree, and inhaled liquids or foreign bodies are therefore more likely to lodge here. The carina lies to the left of the midline. The pulmonary ligament is not a ligament but a sleeve of pleura surrounding the lung root. It allows expansion of the structures in the lung root. The oblique fissures are indicated by a line joining the spine of the third thoracic vertebra to the sixth rib in the midclavicular line. This is approximately in line with the lie of the fifth rib.

Answer to question 287

a) **False**
b) **True**
c) **True**
d) **True**
e) **False**

Both hypo- and hyperkalaemia may be associated with periodic paralysis.

Hyperventilation may persist for some time following the correction of a systemic metabolic acidosis with intravenous bicarbonate. The mechanism depends on the easier passage of carbon dioxide across the blood – brain barrier compared to bicarbonate. Following administration of bicarbonate, peripheral chemoreceptor respiratory drive is inhibited, CO_2 rises, crosses into the CSF and leads to a decrease in CSF pH, which stimulates respiration until bicarbonate equilibration occurs. Neutrophilia commonly accompanies a metabolic acidosis per se.

Causes of hypokalaemia include:
Drugs — diuretic therapy, NSAIDs, liquorice; (carbenoxolone)
Mineralocorticoid excess — Cushing's syndrome, Conn's syndrome
Increased renal loss — diabetes mellitus, recovery phase of acute tubular necrosis, renal tubular acidosis
Gastrointestinal loss — vomiting, diarrhoea.

a) **True**
b) **True**
c) **True**
d) **True**
e) **True**

The causes of a salt-losing nephritis include:
Causes of renal papillary necrosis, polycystic kidney disease, relief of an obstructed uropathy, pyelonephritis, recovery of acute tubular necrosis, recovery of cortical necrosis.

Causes of renal papillary necrosis include:
Diabetes mellitus, tuberculosis, analgesic abuse, sickle-cell disease, dysproteinaemias.

Answer to question 289

a) **False**
b) **False**
c) **True**
d) **False**
e) **False**

Causes of a respiratory acidosis include:
Respiratory centre depression — CVA, drugs (e.g. opiates, barbiturates) Neuromuscular disease — polio, Guillain–Barré, muscular dystrophy
Thoracic and chest wall disease — COAD, acute severe asthma, pneumothorax, flail chest
Severe kyphoscoliosis, ankylosing spondylitis.

Causes of a respiratory alkalosis include:
Causes of central respiratory stimulation — anxiety, pregnancy, hypoxaemia, salicylate poisoning, hepatic encephalopathy, CNS: infection or injury
Pulmonary causes — asthma, pulmonary oedema, pulmonary embolism, mechanical ventilation.

   Note: Salicylates in large dosages in children may cause a metabolic acidosis.
   Nikethamide and doxapram are respiratory stimulants.

a) **True**   d) **True**
b) **False**   e) **True**
c) **True**

Hypothalamic lesions may affect the optic chiasma and lead to a bitemporal hemianopia. Lesions may also interfere with the dopaminergic inhibitory pathway which inhibits prolactin secretion, hence hyperprolactinaemia may occur.

Acute lesions of the lateral area of the supraoptic regions of the hypothalamus result in hyperphagia, while chronic lesions cause weight loss, apathy, and decreased activity.

Medial lesions lead to obesity, hypogonadism, hyperthermia, and sometimes rage reactions.

Causes of hypothalamic lesions include:
Tumours — e.g. craniopharyngiomas, Langerhans cell histiocytosis*, tuberculosis, sarcoidosis

Other causes are autoimmune lymphocytic hypophysitis, Sheehan syndrome, gliomas, mycoses, irradiation, haemochromatosis, and surgery.

*Langerhans cell histiocytosis is the current term for what was previously called eosinophilic granuloma, Hand–Schuller–Christian disease, Letterer–Siwe disease, and histiocytosis X. Although usually seen in children of less than 2 years, adults are also affected. Most patients survive, but 25% can die of infection or complications of treatment.

Answer to question 291

a) **False**   d) **False**
b) **False**   e) **True**
c) **True**

Adrenal adenoma or carcinoma suppresses plasma ACTH to undetectable levels. Cortisol levels in Cushing's disease (pituitary-dependent Cushing's syndrome) suppress in response to a high-dose dexamethasone test. Patients with pseudo-Cushing's syndrome (obese, alcoholic, depressed patients) will often show suppression of plasma cortisol levels in response to a low-dose dexamethasone suppression test. Conn's syndrome (primary hyperaldosteronism) is associated with retention of sodium, hypertension and a hypokalaemic metabolic alkalosis.

Secondary adrenal failure (low plasma ACTH levels) is associated with generalised hypopigmentation. Primary adrenal failure (Addison's disease) is associated with high ACTH levels and hyperpigmentation.

Transsphenoidal surgery is followed by rhinorrhoea in 10%, diabetes insipidus in some, and recurrence of disease in up to 25%.

Radiation is more successful if combined with ketoconazole therapy, which suppresses cortisol production.

a) **False**   d) **False**
b) **False**   e) **False**
c) **True**

Exercise electrocardiography is contraindicated in patients with unstable angina. Cold spots during an exercise 201-thallium scan indicate ischaemic areas. Within 4 hours of a myocardial infarction a hot spot may appear on a pyrophosphate scan. A submaximal exercise ECG is of value 10 days post infarction; a maximal test is contraindicated at this stage but may be performed 6–8 weeks after discharge.

Coronary angiography has a mortality rate of 0.05%. Angioplastic revascularisation is effective in 90% of patients, but re-stenosis occurs in up to 30%. The use of stents has markedly reduced the incidence of re-stenosis.

Patients with left main artery disease and subnormal left ventricular function have an improved survival after bypass grafting. Left main disease has a 5-year death rate of more than 50%, while triple vessel disease has an 11% 5-year mortality. Quality of life assessment may favour bypass grafting.

Answer to question 293

a) **True**   d) **True**
b) **False**   e) **True**
c) **False**

Ostium secundum defects comprise 70% of cases of atrial septal defect. The defect is in the region of the foramen ovale and allows a left to right shunt. Symptoms are uncommon in childhood and these defects are usually detected on routine examination. Clinical signs include wide fixed splitting of the second heart sound and a pulmonary flow murmur. Chest X-ray may show pulmonary plethora and the ECG shows right ventricular hypertrophy, right bundle branch block and right axis deviation. Surgical closure is recommended for significant shunts (pulmonary blood flow twice that of systemic circulation) to prevent secondary pulmonary hypertension and an Eisenmenger syndrome from developing.

Ostium primum defects represent abnormal development of the fetal septum primum and are associated with abnormalities of the mitral and tricuspid valves. Bacterial endocarditis is commoner than with secundum defects. Ostium primum defects are usually symptomatic and require surgery. The ECG shows a right bundle branch block pattern with left axis deviation.

Recognised causes of atrial fibrillation include:
Ischaemic heart disease, thyrotoxicosis, mitral valve disease, sick sinus syndrome, myocarditis, cardiomyopathy, constrictive pericarditis, atrial septal defect in adults, pulmonary embolism, carcinoma of the bronchus.

a) **True**
b) **True**
c) **True**
d) **True**
e) **True**

Other neurological signs of hypothyroidism include:
Slow relaxing reflexes, dementia, myxoedema madness, coma, cerebellar signs, peripheral neuropathy, deafness (Pendred's syndrome), Hoffman's syndrome (aching and slowness of the muscles to contract and relax, similar to myotonia).

Pendred's syndrome is a congenital form of hypothyroidism associated with nerve deafness, characterised by a failure to iodinate tyrosine. The perchlorate discharge test is diagnostic; patients are given radioactive iodine followed by potassium perchlorate and the loss of radioactive iodine from the thyroid gland is measured.

Answer to question 295

a) **False**
b) **True**
c) **True**
d) **False**
e) **True**

Dystrophia myotonica shows autosomal dominant inheritance. Males are affected more commonly than females.

Clinical features include:
Frontal balding; ptosis; cataracts; wasting and weakness of the facial and limb muscles — smooth forehead, lateral smile; reduced reflexes; myotonia — increased by cold, excitement, exercise; hypogonadism; diabetes mellitus; cardiomyopathy; low IQ; dysphagia; goitre; abnormal liver function test; slow recovery after anaesthetic is a feature.

A variant, myotonia congenita — Thomsen's disease (autosomal dominant), is characterised by myotonica, but no weakness and, paradoxically, the muscles are often hypertrophied.

a) **False**   d) **False**
b) **True**   e) **True**
c) **True**

Osteogenesis imperfecta occurs with an incidence of between 1:20 000 and 1:50 000. The underlying abnormality is in the alpha chain of type 1 collagen. Four main types are described:
Type 1 — autosomal dominant — associated with blue sclerae, otosclerosis and fragile bones
Type 2 — most are new mutations and die in utero
Type 3 — autosomal recessive — associated with normal sclerae; fractures are prominent
Type 4 — autosomal dominant — associated with normal sclerae and fragile bones.

Other clinical feature include:
Wormian bones in the skull, aortic regurgitation, ligamentous laxity, elevated alkaline and acid phosphatase, elevated 24-hour urine hydroxyproline.
    The differential diagnosis of blue sclerae includes: Marfan's syndrome, Ehlers–Danlos, pseudoxanthoma elasticum.

Answer to question 297

a) **False**   d) **False**
b) **True**   e) **True**
c) **False**

Vitamin-D-resistant rickets is inherited in an X-linked dominant manner. An affected mother will thus transmit the disease to 50% of her sons and 50% of her daughters and an affected male will transmit the disease to all his daughters but none of his sons. Males tend to have a more severe form of the disease than females. The underlying abnormality is a failure of the renal tubules to reabsorb phosphate, thus leading to hypophosphataemia. Serum alkaline phosphatase levels are often normal. Children have the deformities associated with rickets and impaired growth. In later life, calcification of the ligamentum flavum occurs and may lead to paraplegia. Treatment is with large doses of vitamin D and phosphate supplements. At birth, it is possible to diagnose the disease from the plasma phosphate level.
    With an X-linked recessive condition, a carrier female will transmit the disease to 50% of her male offspring and 50% of her daughters will be carriers. An affected male's daughters will all be carriers whilst his sons will be unaffected. Some heterozygote females may manifest clinical disease, as is the case with glucose-6-phosphate dehydrogenase deficiency. This is dependent on the percentage of normal X chromosomes which are randomly inactivated 12 days after fertilisation. According to the Mary Lyon hypothesis, if the majority of the cells have the affected X chromosome active, the disease may be clinically apparent.

Answer to question 298

a) **False**
b) **False**
c) **True**
d) **True**
e) **True**

Rifampicin is a bactericidal drug. The drug is hepatically metabolised and is a hepatic enzyme inducer. Recognised side-effects include hepatitis, thrombocytopenia, haemolytic anaemia, red urine and 'rifampicin flu' — associated with intermittent doses of rifampicin.
Isoniazid is a bactericidal agent. Side-effects are commoner in slow acetylators and include peripheral neuropathy, occasionally optic neuritis and mental symptoms (these may be prevented by the prophylactic use of pyridoxine), convulsions, mild hepatitis and marrow suppression. It may induce a lupus-like syndrome. A rise in hepatic enzymes should not lead to discontinuation if less than twice normal. Monitoring is essential.
Ethambutol is a bacteriostatic drug. The drug can cause a dose-related optic neuritis which often presents with impairment of red – green vision. Other side-effects include hyperuricaemia, peripheral neuropathy and hepatitis. Particular care is needed in patients with impaired renal function.
Pyrazinamide is a bactericidal drug. Side-effects include anorexia, nausea, vomiting, arthralgia, and hyperuricaemia.

Answer to question 299

a) **True**
b) **True**
c) **False**
d) **True**
e) **True**

Causes of a painful myopathy may be divided into:
Inflammatory causes — polymyositis
Infective causes — e.g. *Trichinella spiralis*, cysticercosis
Drug and toxic causes — e.g. alcohol, heroin
Metabolic causes — e.g. osteomalacia, hypokalaemia, McArdle's disease.

McArdle's disease is type IV glycogen storage disease (muscle phosphorylase deficiency) characterised by proximal myopathy and muscle cramps. The disease is compatible with a normal lifespan.

a) **False**
b) **True**
c) **True**
d) **True**
e) **True**

Infectious mononucleosis is caused by a herpes virus, the Epstein–Barr virus. The disease presents with a flu-like illness, a sore throat with tonsillar swelling and palatal petechial haemorrhages. Typically there is generalised lymphadenopathy and splenomegaly. Recurrent abdominal pain may be the result of mesenteric adenitis which may mimic appendicitis or be caused by splenic infarction. Other features include: thrombocytopenia, minor cardiac conduction problems, meningitis, encephalitis, polyneuritis, pneumonitis, nephritis and hepatitis.

The atypical mononuclear cells have T cell markers on their surface. B virus infects B cells but is controlled in vivo by T cells. Diagnosis is confirmed using the Paul–Bunnell test in which heterophile agglutinins for sheep RBC are detected. False positives occur in patients exposed to horse serum, other causes of infectious hepatitis, Hodgkin's disease and acute leukaemia. False negative tests also occur. Specific tests which detect virus capsid antibody are useful in these circumstances.

Index

NB: Numbers in the index refer to
questions not pages. Numbers in
italics indicate that specific mention
of the subject is made only in the
answers section.